DEPARTMENT OF HEALTH AND SOCIAL SERVICES

REGISTRAR GENERAL NORTHERN IRELAND

THE NORTHERN IRELAND CENSUS 1991

SUMMARY REPORT

Prepared pursuant to Section 4(1) of The Census Act (Northern Ireland) 1969

BELFAST: HMSO

First published 1992

ISBN 0 337 07749 5

CONTENTS

Page

Synopsis of Key Results . . . v
Programme of Census Reports . . . vii

Explanatory Notes and Definitions:
Area and Administrative Divisions . . . ix
Population . . . ix
Households . . . ix
Dwellings . . . x
Communal Establishments . . . x
Age . . . xi
Usual Address . . . xi
Term-time Address of Students and Schoolchildren . . . xi
Country of Birth . . . xi
Religion . . . xii
Long-term Illness . . . xii
Irish Language . . . xii
Economic Activity . . . xii
Academic Qualifications . . . xiii
Rooms . . . xiii
Tenure . . . xiv
Density of Occupation . . . xiv
Household Amenities . . . xiv
Cars and Vans . . . xv
Presentation Conventions . . . xv
Towns . . . xv

Tables:

1. Population 1821-1991 . . . 1
2. Population 1981 and 1991, and intercensal changes . . . 2
3. Population, dwellings, private households and area (Local Government Districts) . . . 3
4. Population, dwellings, private households and area (Wards) . . . 4
4A. Population and households (Towns) . . . 14
5. Age by single years, sex and marital status . . . 18
6. Population under 25 years by individual years and 25 years and over by quinquennial groups, sex and marital status . . . 20
7. Population by sex, marital status, area of enumeration, country of birth, and whether visitor to Northern Ireland . . . 46
8. Religion . . . 56
8A. Analysis of column headed 'Other Denominations' in Table 8 . . . 58
9. Households by tenure and rooms . . . 59
10. Private households by size, rooms, dwelling type and population . . . 66
11. Private households by size, dwelling type and density of occupation (persons per room) . . . 80
12. Households by dwelling type, number of rooms and household amenities . . . 94
13. Households by number of cars . . . 121
14. One and two person households containing persons of pensionable age by sex/condition combination . . . 125
15. Persons enumerated in each type of non-private establishment . . . 126
16. Economically active persons by sex and status . . . 132
17. Population with long-term illness by area, age and sex . . . 146
18. Population economically active aged 16-64 by occupation, religion and sex . . . 147
19. Population economically active aged 16-64 by religion and sex . . . 148
20. Term-time address of students and schoolchildren . . . 149
21. Population aged 16 years and over: Persons by age, sex and highest level of academic qualification . . . 150
22. Population aged 16 years and over: Economic activity by religion, sex and highest level of academic qualification . . . 151
23. Population aged 3 years and over by knowledge of Irish language . . . 159

Map . . . 160

H Form . . . 162

1 The Summary Report - Synopsis of Key Results

1.1 The subjects covered in this Report include area, population, households, age, sex, marital status, birthplace, religion, dwelling type, tenure, household size, occupational density, amenities, cars, economically active persons, long-term illness, term-time address of students and schoolchildren, academic qualifications, and Irish language. More detailed information on each of these subjects will follow later in the specific topic reports.

Population Present on Census Night

1.2 As enumerated at midnight on 21 April 1991 the Northern Ireland population was 1,573,282. This is an increase of 3,311 on the provisional figure of 1,569,971 stated in the Preliminary Report issued in July 1991.

Usually Resident Population (Present/Absent Base)

1.3 The number of people usually resident in Northern Ireland (i.e. excluding visitors but including those who were stated as being usually resident in Northern Ireland, whether or not they were at their usual address on Census night) was enumerated at 1,577,836.

Young and Old

1.4 Compared with the 1981 Census the figures reveal a higher proportion of elderly persons in the population, with 15.0% of persons of pensionable age (men aged 65 or over and women aged 60 or over), and 5.2% aged 75 or over. In 1981, 14.5% of the population were of pensionable age and 4.4% were 75 years or over. In 1991 26.0% of the population were aged under 16 years, compared with 27.9% in 1981.

Religion

1.5 The figures show that 7.3% of the population did not answer the voluntary question on religion. This compares with 18.5% in 1981. 3.8% of the population stated they had no religion.

Employment

1.6 In the week preceding Census day (14-20 April 1991) of the total population aged 16 and over, 72.7% of males and 45.2% of females were economically active. Of these 81.0% of males and 89.2% of females were in employment while 19.0% of males and 10.8% of females were out of employment.

Households

1.7 There were 530,369 enumerated private households, which on the basis of usually resident population contained an average of 3.0 persons per household. In 1981 there were 456,348 enumerated private households containing an average of 3.2 persons per household.

Living Alone

1.8 The number of households in which one person usually lives alone was 119,980 or 22.6% of private households with a usual address in Northern Ireland. In 1981 the comparable figures, based on the population present, were 85,238 and 18.7% respectively.

Overcrowding

1.9 In 4.8% of households there was more than one person per room compared with 10.4% in 1981.

Owner Occupiers and Tenants

1.10 62.3% of households were in owner occupied accommodation and 29.4% in accommodation rented from a local or public authority. The comparable 1981 figures are 49.4% and 39.3% respectively.

Household Amenities

1.11 2.0% of households lacked or had to share with another household the use of a fixed bath or shower. 1.6% of households lacked or had to share an inside WC. The corresponding figures for 1981 were 9.6% and 8.9% respectively.

Availability of Cars

1.12 64.5% of households had one or more cars available for use by members of the household, compared with 59.9% in 1981.

Long-term Illness

1.13 The figures reveal that 11.8% of the population recorded themselves as having a long-term illness, health problem or handicap which limited their daily activities or the work they could do.

Highest Level of Academic Qualification

1.14 65.0% of all persons aged 16 and over had no formal academic qualifications. 35.1% had some form of academic qualification and 6.5% had a qualification at degree level or higher.

Irish Language

1.15 The question on Irish was included for the first time in the Northern Ireland Census of Population. Its wording was identical to the wording of the Gaelic question in the 1991 Census for Scotland. In response to the question 4.2% of the population claimed that they could either speak, read or write Irish and 5.3% claimed ability to do all three.

2 1991 CENSUS - Programme of Census Reports

Preliminary

2.1 This report was published in July 1991 and contained provisional figures of the population and private households for each of the 26 local government districts with a brief statistical commentary.

Summary

2.2 The Summary Report contains information for Northern Ireland and for each of the 26 local government districts. The subjects covered include age distribution, sex, marital status, birthplace, religion, households, tenure, amenities, occupation density, availability of cars, communal establishments, economically active population, employment status, long-term illness, term-time address of students and schoolchildren, and Irish language.

Belfast Urban Area

2.3 The tables in this report will contain detailed information to ward level for the Belfast Urban Area as defined by the Department of the Environment for Northern Ireland Town and Country Planning Service. The subjects covered will include age distribution, sex, marital status, birthplace, religion, households, tenure, amenities, occupation density, availability of cars, communal establishments, economically active population, employment status, long-term illness, term-time address of students and schoolchildren, and Irish language.

Religion

2.4 All tables in this report will contain information at Northern Ireland level and some will give details to local government districts on the main religious denominations. The subjects covered will include population by age, sex, marital status, occupation, industry, and other characteristics.

Economic Activity

2.5 This report will contain tables giving the figures for both the economically active and economically inactive population. The employed population will be analysed by industry and occupation classifications and related to age, marital status, employment status, socio-economic groupings, area of workplace, etc. All tables will contain information at Northern Ireland level but some will give details for local government districts.

Workplace and Transport to Work

2.6 Employed population details in relation to area of workplace/residence will be contained in this report. Workplace movement by socio-economic group, occupation, industry, and means of transport to work will also be detailed to local government district level.

Housing and Household Composition

2.7 All tables in this report will contain information at Northern Ireland level but some will give details for local government districts. Tables will include information on households, tenure, occupation density, car availability, age, sex, marital status and will relate household composition to social and other economic characteristics.

Migration

2.8 Numbers and characteristics of the population who changed their usual address in the year before Census day will be contained in this report. Migrant households will be detailed by age, sex, marital status, etc. Some tables will refer to Northern Ireland and others will be detailed to local government districts.

Education

2.9 This report will contain information at Northern Ireland level of age, sex, occupation, and industry by highest level of academic qualification. Also included will be socio-economic group by religion and economic activity by marital status related to highest level of academic qualification.

Irish Language

2.10 This report will contain information on the population aged 3 years and over, recorded as having knowledge of Irish language. The tables covered will include knowledge by age, sex, religion, economic position, and highest level of academic qualification to Northern Ireland level.

3 Explanatory Notes and Definitions of terms used in the report

Area and Administrative Divisions

3.1 The figures on areas have been supplied by the Ordnance Survey for Northern Ireland and rounded to the nearest hectare. They include all islands and inland water. A hectare is equivalent to 2.471 acres. The local government districts and wards for which statistics are presented in this report are those in existence at the date of the Census.

Population

3.2 Census results are presented as cross tabulations, each counting a particular population, for example, people, households, families, or people in communal establishments. It is important to know exactly what is being counted, i.e. the population base. Information on whereabouts and usual address given for each person listed on the Census form can be used to derive the population base.

3.3 The **population present on Census night (present population)** in an area is the count of all people recorded as spending Census night in the area regardless of whether or not this was where they usually lived; that is, all persons recorded on the Census H Forms for whom the whereabouts on Census night was given as the relevant household, plus all persons recorded as being in communal establishments.

3.4 The **usually resident population** in an area is the count of those people recorded on the forms for the area as usually living 'at this address' whether or not they are present on Census night.

3.5 **Shipping:** Apart from houseboats (enumerated as private households), vessels were treated in a similar way to communal establishments with a listing form and individual return form for each person on the ship. Persons on naval vessels in Northern Ireland waters or ports on Census night were included as present in the home base port of the ship. Generally persons on other vessels were counted as present in the area in which the form was collected.

3.6 For the 1991 Census there were some minor changes made to the enumeration of shipping. Vessels on coastal trips, fishing voyages and voyages between Great Britain and Northern Ireland were not enumerated. However, foreign registered ships in Northern Ireland ports, excluded in 1981, were enumerated.

Campers, persons sleeping rough, etc.

3.7 The present population also includes persons not enumerated in private households or communal establishments, for example, persons sleeping rough and persons enumerated in caravans or other non-permanent structures which were not the usual residence.

Population covered in this Report

3.8 **Figures contained in this report refer to the usually resident population with the exception of Tables 1 and 15. Table 1 gives details of the population present in Northern Ireland, as recorded in Census from 1821 to 1991.**

3.9 In Table 15 (Communal Establishments) the figures relate to the persons present in these establishments on Census night.

Households

3.10 A household is either one person living alone or a group of people (who may or may not be related) living at the same address with common housekeeping. Persons staying temporarily with the household are included. A group of people is treated as a household if there is any regular arrangement to share at least one meal a day. Two people who share one room, although each may have separate catering arrangements, are treated as one household. A household must have exclusive use of at least one room.

3.11 **Absent households** are those households where all residents of the household were recorded as absent from their usual address on Census night and at which no other person was present.

Dwellings

3.12 Dwellings are defined as 'structurally separate accommodation' and are classified into permanent and non-permanent accommodation.

3.13 Permanent accommodation includes:

- a whole house or bungalow, whether detached, semi-detached or terraced;

- the whole of a purpose built flat or maisonette including any situated in a commercial building (for example in an office building or hotel or over a shop) or in a block of flats;

- part of a converted or shared house, bungalow or flat with a separate or shared entrance into the building. This includes a one roomed flatlet, one room or a bedsit not self-contained, a self-contained flat or accommodation with two or more rooms, or two or more rooms not self-contained.

3.14 Non-permanent accommodation includes:

- caravans or mobile structures and such non-permanent structures as huts, shacks, tents, etc., are treated as dwellings only if they were some person's usual residence on Census night. If such structures were vacant on Census night they were excluded.

3.15 **A vacant dwelling** is one which was fit or ready for habitation but was awaiting occupancy - this type of dwelling would invariably be unfurnished. Derelict or uninhabitable dwellings are excluded.

Shared dwellings

3.16 A shared dwelling is a dwelling sharing an entrance into the building and comprising two or more household spaces that are not self-contained.

3.17 **Other dwellings** include student or holiday accommodation or second residences in which all the persons present on Census night have a more permanent address elsewhere.

Communal Establishments

3.18 People were enumerated in a variety of communal establishments (non-private establishments) such as hotels, boarding schools, hospitals, prisons, religious communities, etc. The population enumerated in communal establishments plus persons sleeping rough and campers is referred to as the population in non-private households. It includes all those present in the establishment on Census night and all who arrived on Monday 22 April 1991 and who had not been included on a Census form as present elsewhere. Non-resident staff/personnel on duty in the premises on Census night are not included.

3.19 Separate buildings in the grounds of an establishment for the accommodation of private households, such as a doctor's house or caretaker's cottage in the grounds of a hospital, are classed as private residences and not as part of the communal establishment. People occupying flats or suites of rooms within the main building of an establishment are treated as part of the main establishment and included on the L form. Service families or civilians living in married quarters of the Armed Services are treated as private households whether the quarters were located within or outside the boundaries of the service establishment.

3.20 Annexes to communal establishments are treated as part of the main establishment if located in the same enumeration district or if meals were taken at the main establishment even though the annexe was in a different enumeration district.

Establishment classification

3.21 The categories are as follows:

1. Hotels, etc.
2. NHS hospitals and statutory homes (psychiatric).
3. NHS hospitals and statutory homes (others).
4. Non-NHS hospitals and statutory homes (psychiatric).
5. Non-NHS hospitals and statutory homes (others).

6. Homes for the old and disabled.
7. Children's homes.
8. Educational establishments.
9. Places of detention.
10. Defence establishments including naval vessels and service hospitals.
11. Civilian ships, boats and barges.
12. Hostels and lodging houses.
13. Other miscellaneous establishments.
14. Campers and persons sleeping rough.

Residence classification

3.22 Persons enumerated in groups 1 to 9 and 12 to 14 above are given one of the 3 following residence classification codes:

(i) Managers and staff.
(ii) Boarders, patients and inmates.
(iii) Others.

3.23 All persons present in groups 10 and 11 are classed under category (ii). Boarders include hotel guests, persons in lodgings and military personnel in communal establishments including naval vessels.

Age

3.24 Age is the completed years of age at Census date, as derived from the date of birth question.

Pensionable age

3.25 Pensionable age is the minimum age at which a person may receive a National Insurance Retirement Pension - 60 for women and 65 for men.

Usual Address

3.26 In most cases the answer to the usual address question is straightforward. However, students and schoolchildren away from home during term-time were to regard their home address as their usual address. Boarders were to decide whether they considered as their usual address, the address of the relevant household. Household heads, living away from home for part of the week, were to regard their home address as their usual address.

3.27 Persons who failed to answer the relevant questions appear as part of the usually resident population in the area in which they were enumerated and are included as part of a usually resident private household.

Term-Time Address of Students and Schoolchildren

3.28 Term-time address is the address at which a student or schoolchild is resident during term-time. It permits the compilation of the term-time population for an area by omitting resident students or schoolchildren with a term-time address outside the area and including any students or schoolchildren resident outside the area but living in the area in term-time.

Visitors to Northern Ireland

3.29 Visitors to Northern Ireland are those present at the relevant household address on Census night whose usual address is outside Northern Ireland.

Country of Birth

3.30 Persons born in Northern Ireland, England, Scotland, Wales or the Republic of Ireland were asked to tick the appropriate box. Persons born in another country were asked to tick the 'Elsewhere' box and write the present name of the country.

Religion

3.31 It was not obligatory to answer the question on religion. The question was worded as follows:

> Please state the Religion, Religious Denomination or Body to which the person belongs. The term 'Protestant' should not be used alone and the denomination should be given as precisely as possible.
> If none write NONE.

3.32 The classification of religions includes a separate heading for each religion. Religions which differ only or mainly in denominational terminology are generally grouped together and the figures for the group as a whole are shown under the name by which the group is officially or commonly known. Thus the heading Presbyterian includes United Presbyterian, Trinitarian and Church of Scotland. Church of Ireland is regarded as embracing both Anglican and Episcopalian except for persons so described whose usual address was in England: in such cases the Church of England classification was applied.

3.33 Also included was a heading for persons who stated they had no religion.

Long-Term Illness

3.34 Long-term illness covers any long-term illness, health problem or handicap which limits a person's daily activities or the work he/she can do.

Irish Language

3.35 The question on Irish language asked whether persons aged 3 years or over could either speak, read or write Irish. It also contained a category for those with no knowledge of Irish.

Economic Activity

3.36 The economic activity tables describe some of the economic characteristics of the population. The characteristics include both those obtained directly from census questions, for example, economic position, and occupation, and others derived from combining answers to census questions on occupation and industry, for example, employment status. Persons on a Government employment or training scheme are regarded as economically active in employment. However, while information about the particular scheme was not collected in the Census, persons on these schemes are included as a separate group in tables which give details on economic position and occupation.

3.37 Only specified groups were required to answer some of the economic activity questions and this is reflected in the population to which tables refer. Thus:

(a) Tables relating to economic position include only persons aged 16 years and over.

(b) Tables relating to occupation cover the economically active.

(c) Tables relating to employment status cover persons in employment.

Economic position

3.38 The classification by economic position is as follows:

Economically active

In employment means having a job during the week ended 20 April 1991. Temporary, part-time or casual employment is included. Persons absent from their employment due to holiday, strikes, lock-outs, short-time working or temporary stoppages are regarded as in employment. Persons off work sick are regarded as in employment if their jobs are waiting for them on return.

Out of employment means seeking work or prevented by temporary sickness from seeking work or waiting to take up a job already accepted.

Economically inactive

Looking after the home means having full-time responsibility for looking after the home.

Long-term sick/disabled means being unable to work because of long-term sickness or disability.

Retired means wholly retired from employment and no longer seeking paid work.

Students are persons in full-time attendance at an educational establishment irrespective of whether or not they may have part-time or seasonal employment.

Others are persons economically inactive and include persons in unpaid work in a family business including a shop or farm, or looking after the house or family, or in voluntary work, or never in employment and not seeking work, and those of independent means.

Employment status

3.39 The classification of employment status is as follows:

Self-employed

1. With employees.
2. Without employees.

Employees

1. Managers.
   (a) extra large establishments.
   (b) large establishments.
   (c) small establishments.

2. Foremen and supervisors.
   (a) manual.
   (b) non-manual.

3. Professional employees.

4. Other employees.

3.40 Information on occupation is used to distinguish the various types of employees and information on name and business of employer to distinguish the size of the establishment. **Extra large establishments** are those classified as having 500 or more employees. **Large establishments** are those having between 25 and 499 employees. **Small establishments** are those with fewer than 25 employees.

Academic Qualifications

3.41 Academic qualifications have been classified into 7 levels as follows:

1. Degree level or higher.
2. BTEC (Higher), BEC (Higher), TEC (Higher), HNC, HND.
3. GCE 'A' Level, Advanced Senior Certificate.
4. BTEC (National), TEC (National), BEC (National), ONC, OND.
5. GCSE, GCE 'O' Level (including CSE grade 1), Senior Certificate, BTEC (General), BEC (General).
6. CSE (other than grade 1).
7. No formal qualifications as above.

Rooms

3.42 Private households were asked to count the number of rooms in their accommodation, but not to count the following:

Kitchens less than 2 metres (6 feet 6 inches) wide, bathrooms or toilets.

3.43 In unshared dwellings the head of the household provided information. In shared dwellings the enumerator was instructed to enquire of each household in the dwelling if any room was shared by another household. If any room was shared by 2 or more households the enumerator was further instructed to identify separate households where appropriate.

3.44 In the tables classifying households by rooms occupied, any room shared by 2 or more households is allocated to one household to avoid the use of fractions and to ensure that the total number of rooms in the dwelling is not altered.

Tenure

3.45 Heads of households were required to indicate under the following headings how they occupied their accommodation.

As an owner occupier:

1. Through mortgage or loan.
2. Owning the property outright.

By renting, rent free or by lease:

3. From a public authority (e.g. NI Housing Executive).
4. From a housing association or charitable trust.
5. Unfurnished from a private landlord, company or other organisation.
6. Furnished from a private landlord, company or other organisation.

In some other way

If the Census form indicated more than one form of tenure but gave no further information the tenure was assigned to this category where no tenure was stated on the Census form, the accommodation was similarly assigned.

3.46 A shared dwelling was classified according to the tenure stated by the main household.

Density of Occupation

3.47 The density of occupation of a private household is the ratio of the number of persons in a private household with usual residents to the number of rooms occupied by the private household. The following ratios of density are used:

Over 1.5 persons per room.
Over one and up to 1.5 persons per room.
Over 0.75 and up to one person per room.
0.5 and over and up to 0.75 persons per room.
Less than 0.5 persons per room.

Household Amenities

3.48 The amenities on which information was collected in respect of each private household are listed below. In the case of fixed bath or shower and flush toilets the householder was required to indicate whether individual amenities were used only by the household, shared with another household or were not available.

(a) A fixed bath or shower permanently connected to a water supply and waste pipe.
(b) A flush toilet (WC) with entrance **inside** the building.

3.49 Additional information on amenities was collected in respect of each private household. Householders were required to indicate whether the household had use of the following amenities:

Central heating

Central heating includes night storage heaters, warm air or under-floor heating, whether actually used or not. It is categorised as follows:

1. All living rooms and bedrooms centrally heated.
2. Some (not all) living rooms and bedrooms centrally heated.
3. No living rooms or bedrooms centrally heated.

Water supply

1. Public supply piped into house.
2. Public supply at a standpipe.
3. Other.

Domestic sewage disposal

1. Public sewer.
2. Septic tank/cesspit for use only by the household.
3. Septic tank/cesspit for use also by another household.
4. Dry closet/chemical toilet.

Cars and Vans

3.50 The number of cars and vans normally available for use by the household include any car or van provided by employers but exclude vans used solely for the carriage of goods.

Presentation Conventions

3.51 A dash (-) indicates that the entry is zero. A blank indicates that a particular combination of line and column is impossible. In the presentation of rates, a rate shown as 0 indicates that the actual rate is less than one half of a unit but is not zero.

H Form

3.52 For reference purposes the H form used for private households in the 1991 Census is produced at the end of this report.

Towns

3.53 The towns listed in Table 4A of this report are urban areas with no legally defined boundaries and with a recorded population of 1,000 or more. In 1971 towns were defined in terms of local government administrative areas but with local government reorganisation on 1 October 1973 towns with legally defined boundaries disappeared. In the 1991 Census (as in the 1981 Census) information for towns has been obtained by relating urban areas to specific Irish Grid squares.

Table 1 Population 1821 - 1991

Date of Census	Population			Intercensal variation				Females per 1,000 males
	Persons	Males	Females	Persons	Males	Females	Per cent (persons)	
1821	1,380,451	665,212	715,239					1,075
1831	1,574,004	762,396	811,608	+ 193,553	+ 97,184	+ 96,369	+ 14.0	1,065
1841, June 6-7	1,648,945	799,711	849,234	+ 74,941	+ 37,315	+ 37,626	+ 4.8	1,062
1851, March 30-31	1,442,517	697,887	744,630	- 206,428	- 101,824	- 104,604	- 12.5	1,067
1861, April 7-8	1,396,453	667,935	728,518	- 46,064	- 29,952	- 16,112	- 3.2	1,091
1871, April 2-3	1,359,190	647,285	711,905	- 37,263	- 20,650	- 16,613	- 2.7	1,100
1881, April 3-4	1,304,816	620,839	683,977	- 54,374	- 26,446	- 27,928	- 4.0	1,102
1891, April 5-6	1,236,056	590,352	645,704	- 68,760	- 30,487	- 38,273	- 5.3	1,094
1901, March 31 - April 1	1,236,952	589,955	646,997	+ 896	- 397	+ 1,293	+ 0.1	1,097
1911, April 2-3	1,250,531	602,539	647,992	+ 13,579	+ 12,584	+ 995	+ 1.1	1,075
1926, April 18-19	1,256,561	608,088	648,473	+ 6,030	+ 5,549	+ 481	+ 0.5	1,066
1937, February 28 - March 1	1,279,745	623,154	656,591	+ 23,184	+ 15,066	+ 8,118	+ 1.8	1,054
1951, April 8-9	1,370,921	667,819	703,102	+ 91,176	+ 44,665	+ 46,511	+ 7.1	1,053
1961, April 23-24	1,425,042	694,224	730,818	+ 54,121	+ 26,405	+ 27,716	+ 3.9	1,053
1966, October 9-10	1,484,775	723,884	760,891	+ 59,733	+ 29,660	+ 30,073	+ 4.2	1,051
1971, April 25-26	1,536,065	754,676	781,389	+ 51,290	+ 30,792	+ 20,498	+ 3.5	1,035
* 1981, April 5-6	1,532,619	749,623	782,996	- 3,446	- 5,053	+ 1,607	- 0.2	1,045
1991, April 21-22	1,573,282	765,822	807,460	+ 40,663	+ 16,199	+ 24,464	+ 2.7	1,054

This table is on a population present base
* 1981 figures, as revised, take account of non-response

Table 2 Population 1981 and 1991, and intercensal changes

Local Government Districts		1981 *	1991	Intercensal variation: By excess of births over deaths — Persons	Per cent	By net migration — Persons	Per cent	Total changes — Persons	Per cent
NORTHERN IRELAND	**(PERSONS)**	**1,532,196**	**1,577,836**	**+ 115,060**	**+ 7.5**	**- 69,420**	**- 4.5**	**+ 45,640**	**+ 3.0**
	(MALES)	**749,480**	**769,071**	**+ 60,528**	**+ 8.1**	**- 40,937**	**- 5.5**	**+ 19,591**	**+ 2.6**
	(FEMALES)	**782,716**	**808,765**	**+ 54,532**	**+ 7.0**	**- 28,483**	**- 3.6**	**+ 26,049**	**+ 3.3**
Antrim	(Persons)	45,016	44,516	+ 4,792	+ 10.6	- 5,292	- 11.8	- 500	- 1.1
Ards	(Persons)	57,792	64,764	+ 3,341	+ 5.8	+ 3,631	+ 6.3	+ 6,972	+ 12.1
Armagh	(Persons)	49,223	51,817	+ 3,604	+ 7.3	- 1,010	- 2.1	+ 2,594	+ 5.3
Ballymena	(Persons)	54,814	56,641	+ 3,570	+ 6.5	- 1,743	- 3.2	+ 1,827	+ 3.3
Ballymoney	(Persons)	22,946	24,198	+ 1,689	+ 7.4	- 437	- 1.9	+ 1,252	+ 5.5
Banbridge	(Persons)	30,110	33,482	+ 1,559	+ 5.2	+ 1,813	+ 6.0	+ 3,372	+ 11.2
Belfast	(Persons)	314,270	279,237	+ 12,292	+ 3.9	- 47,325	- 15.1	- 35,033	- 11.1
Carrickfergus	(Persons)	28,625	32,750	+ 1,995	+ 7.0	+ 2,130	+ 7.4	+ 4,125	+ 14.4
Castlereagh	(Persons)	60,785	60,799	+ 298	+ 0.5	- 284	- 0.5	+ 14	+ 0.02
Coleraine	(Persons)	46,739	50,438	+ 2,567	+ 5.5	+ 1,132	+ 2.4	+ 3,699	+ 7.9
Cookstown	(Persons)	28,257	31,082	+ 2,695	+ 9.5	+ 130	+ 0.5	+ 2,825	+ 10.0
Craigavon	(Persons)	73,260	74,986	+ 7,432	+ 10.1	- 5,706	- 7.8	+ 1,726	+ 2.4
Derry	(Persons)	89,101	95,371	+ 13,553	+ 15.2	- 7,283	- 8.2	+ 6,270	+ 7.0
Down	(Persons)	53,193	58,008	+ 4,562	+ 8.6	+ 253	+ 0.5	+ 4,815	+ 9.1
Dungannon	(Persons)	43,883	45,428	+ 4,522	+ 10.3	- 2,977	- 6.8	+ 1,545	+ 3.5
Fermanagh	(Persons)	51,594	54,033	+ 3,729	+ 7.2	- 1,290	- 2.5	+ 2,439	+ 4.7
Larne	(Persons)	29,076	29,419	+ 983	+ 3.4	- 640	- 2.2	+ 343	+ 1.2
Limavady	(Persons)	26,964	29,567	+ 3,263	+ 12.1	- 660	- 2.4	+ 2,603	+ 9.7
Lisburn	(Persons)	84,007	99,458	+ 8,001	+ 9.5	+ 7,450	+ 8.9	+ 15,451	+ 18.4
Magherafelt	(Persons)	32,494	36,293	+ 3,628	+ 11.2	+ 171	+ 0.5	+ 3,799	+ 11.7
Moyle	(Persons)	14,396	14,789	+ 780	+ 5.4	- 387	- 2.7	+ 393	+ 2.7
Newry and Mourne	(Persons)	76,574	82,943	+ 10,209	+ 13.3	- 3,840	- 5.0	+ 6,369	+ 8.3
Newtownabbey	(Persons)	72,246	74,035	+ 5,568	+ 7.7	- 3,779	- 5.2	+ 1,789	+ 2.5
North Down	(Persons)	66,264	71,832	+ 2,546	+ 3.8	+ 3,022	+ 4.6	+ 5,568	+ 8.4
Omagh	(Persons)	44,288	45,809	+ 4,509	+ 10.2	- 2,988	- 6.7	+ 1,521	+ 3.4
Strabane	(Persons)	36,279	36,141	+ 3,373	+ 9.3	- 3,511	- 9.7	- 138	- 0.4

* 1981 figures, as revised, take account of non-response

Table 3 Population, dwellings, private households and area — Local Government Districts

Local Government Districts	Usually resident population			Unoccupied dwellings		Number of private households	Area (in hectares) *
	Persons	Males	Females	Vacant	Other		
NORTHERN IRELAND	**1,577,836**	**769,071**	**808,765**	**30,370**	**11,927**	**530,369**	**1,416,039**
Antrim	44,516	22,135	22,381	836	191	14,166	57,793
Ards	64,764	31,527	33,237	1,232	794	22,832	38,067
Armagh	51,817	25,741	26,076	1,141	211	15,720	67,128
Ballymena	56,641	27,830	28,811	907	204	19,137	63,195
Ballymoney	24,198	12,022	12,176	425	66	7,730	41,855
Banbridge	33,482	16,568	16,914	731	147	10,984	44,556
Belfast	279,237	130,820	148,417	6,905	2,929	107,394	11,489
Carrickfergus	32,750	15,871	16,879	557	192	11,870	8,193
Castlereagh	60,799	28,946	31,853	679	230	22,910	8,500
Coleraine	50,438	24,369	26,069	1,075	993	17,870	48,555
Cookstown	31,082	15,503	15,579	672	148	9,222	62,171
Craigavon	74,986	36,511	38,475	1,621	309	24,915	37,925
Derry	95,371	46,708	48,663	1,208	561	28,015	38,742
Down	58,008	28,835	29,173	1,230	625	18,061	64,953
Dungannon	45,428	22,556	22,872	1,018	224	13,653	78,323
Fermanagh	54,033	27,095	26,938	1,272	490	16,901	187,677
Larne	29,419	14,318	15,101	698	421	10,409	33,646
Limavady	29,567	15,042	14,525	426	95	8,489	58,635
Lisburn	99,458	48,653	50,805	1,366	554	33,277	44,638
Magherafelt	36,293	18,177	18,116	580	112	10,398	57,239
Moyle	14,789	7,355	7,434	452	432	4,721	49,440
Newry and Mourne	82,943	41,307	41,636	1,470	776	24,418	90,937
Newtownabbey	74,035	35,760	38,275	1,072	309	26,491	15,069
North Down	71,832	34,284	37,548	1,404	503	26,619	8,158
Omagh	45,809	23,022	22,787	819	219	13,417	112,990
Strabane	36,141	18,116	18,025	574	192	10,750	86,165

* As supplied by OSNI 1992

Table 4 Population, dwellings, private households and area

Local Government Districts and Wards	Usually resident population: Persons	Males	Females	Unoccupied dwellings: Vacant	Other	Number of private households	Area (in hectares) *
NORTHERN IRELAND	**1,577,836**	**769,071**	**808,765**	**30,370**	**11,927**	**530,369**	**1,420,468**
Antrim	**44,516**	**22,135**	**22,381**	**836**	**191**	**14,166**	**57,793**
Wards							
Aldergrove	4,150	2,360	1,790	50	9	982	15,854
Balloo	1,658	799	859	18	9	684	503
Ballycraigy	1,669	808	861	47	9	656	52
Clady	2,263	1,141	1,122	31	9	712	7,830
Cranfield	2,441	1,230	1,211	26	3	732	5,521
Crumlin	2,875	1,430	1,445	43	8	913	2,461
Drumanaway	2,058	1,015	1,043	20	10	695	2,365
Fountain Hill	2,073	931	1,142	21	18	724	55
Greystone	2,328	1,169	1,159	50	15	708	73
Massereene	2,304	1,128	1,176	23	13	805	500
New Park	2,077	1,015	1,062	45	7	690	90
Randalstown	2,061	980	1,081	43	10	674	2,769
Rathenraw	1,431	687	744	44	7	483	354
Springfarm	3,276	1,580	1,696	148	19	994	451
Steeple	1,922	941	981	33	13	678	39
Stiles	2,286	1,132	1,154	42	9	733	55
Tardree	2,374	1,178	1,196	68	6	716	7,982
Templepatrick	2,913	1,446	1,467	55	12	987	4,341
Toome	2,357	1,165	1,192	29	5	600	6,498
Ards	**64,764**	**31,527**	**33,237**	**1,232**	**794**	**22,832**	**38,067**
Wards							
Ballygowan	4,027	2,018	2,009	55	10	1,299	3,831
Ballywalter	3,071	1,509	1,562	61	60	1,105	4,111
Bradshaw's Brae	2,882	1,397	1,485	42	13	1,007	1,136
Central	2,320	1,093	1,227	108	21	1,040	262
Comber North	2,606	1,268	1,338	27	5	895	362
Comber South	3,136	1,567	1,569	13	11	1,109	1,061
Comber West	3,456	1,712	1,744	64	11	1,200	855
Donaghadee North	2,435	1,154	1,281	80	46	946	1,670
Donaghadee South	3,328	1,548	1,780	69	44	1,356	554
Glen	3,042	1,470	1,572	57	21	1,085	462
Killinchy	3,204	1,588	1,616	52	38	1,115	4,902
Kircubbin	3,095	1,518	1,577	98	25	1,062	3,775
Loughries	4,723	2,286	2,437	35	15	1,583	1,379
Millisle	3,100	1,505	1,595	79	135	1,061	2,947
Movilla	4,833	2,365	2,468	86	15	1,575	1,150
Portaferry	3,508	1,763	1,745	128	65	1,049	4,747
Portavogie	3,459	1,697	1,762	93	227	1,210	3,253
Scrabo	2,366	1,128	1,238	30	10	984	915
West Winds	2,587	1,214	1,373	33	15	942	417
Whitespots	3,586	1,727	1,859	22	7	1,209	278
Armagh	**51,817**	**25,741**	**26,076**	**1,141**	**211**	**15,720**	**67,128**
Wards							
Abbey Park	2,389	1,150	1,239	18	6	559	335
Ballymartrim	2,039	1,034	1,005	54	2	539	5,561
Callan Bridge	2,377	1,175	1,202	40	7	718	124
Carrigatuke	2,150	1,110	1,040	87	13	595	5,245
Charlemont	2,184	1,088	1,096	64	1	611	3,288
Demesne	2,737	1,293	1,444	32	9	929	350
Derrynoose	2,010	1,023	987	89	4	547	6,760
Downs	2,260	1,060	1,200	34	49	746	160
Hamiltonsbawn	2,504	1,300	1,204	39	16	738	5,409
Hockley	2,395	1,179	1,216	83	7	704	4,702
Keady	2,405	1,168	1,237	46	14	708	103
Killeen	2,539	1,324	1,215	25	8	707	7,090
Killylea	2,260	1,141	1,119	34	6	608	6,399
Laurelvale	2,537	1,238	1,299	43	7	800	1,575
Loughgall	2,301	1,178	1,123	52	4	701	3,166
Markethill	2,257	1,097	1,160	65	6	757	3,153
Milford	2,328	1,228	1,100	50	6	643	4,427
Observatory	2,570	1,239	1,331	59	8	879	426
Poyntz Pass	2,028	1,003	1,025	71	9	660	5,679
Rich Hill	3,005	1,514	1,491	55	8	987	1,526
Tandragee	2,503	1,209	1,294	66	13	838	1,538
The Mall	2,039	990	1,049	35	8	746	112

* As supplied by OSNI 1992

Local Government Districts and Wards	Usually resident population			Unoccupied dwellings		Number of private households	Area (in hectares) *
	Persons	Males	Females	Vacant	Other		
Ballymena	**56,641**	**27,830**	**28,811**	**907**	**204**	**19,137**	**63,195**
Wards							
Ahoghill	2,992	1,473	1,519	49	1	1,013	2,244
Ardeevin	2,547	1,262	1,285	18	3	850	406
Ballee	2,490	1,158	1,332	29	16	925	148
Ballykeel	2,393	1,158	1,235	55	12	812	108
Ballyloughan	2,819	1,389	1,430	12	1	920	134
Broughshane	2,569	1,271	1,298	41	8	941	2,170
Castle Demesne	1,948	979	969	64	15	765	101
Craigywarren	2,087	1,037	1,050	30	3	688	5,783
Cullybackey	2,467	1,179	1,288	32	3	867	484
Dunclug	3,011	1,466	1,545	18	22	961	66
Dunminning	2,195	1,130	1,065	31	5	696	5,116
Fair Green	2,045	964	1,081	36	21	781	42
Galgorm	3,107	1,540	1,567	40	8	1,054	1,115
Glenravel	2,560	1,298	1,262	34	2	708	9,084
Glenwhirry	2,421	1,258	1,163	82	8	752	11,576
Grange	2,356	1,187	1,169	43	9	692	5,575
Harryville	2,359	1,134	1,225	70	8	938	295
Kells	2,497	1,196	1,301	38	11	864	2,180
Moat	1,952	934	1,018	11	11	781	38
Park	2,591	1,242	1,349	59	17	900	191
Portglenone	2,242	1,141	1,101	42	5	717	3,434
Slemish	1,919	968	951	36	5	617	12,714
Summerfield	3,074	1,466	1,608	35	10	895	191
Ballymoney	**24,198**	**12,022**	**12,176**	**425**	**66**	**7,730**	**41,855**
Wards							
Ballyhoe and Corkey	1,652	859	793	27	3	428	8,375
Benvardin	1,281	635	646	30	5	430	2,556
Carnany	2,004	970	1,034	32	11	726	131
Clogh Mills	1,528	741	787	36	1	459	2,427
Dervock	1,264	648	616	24	2	427	3,518
Dunloy	1,638	829	809	25	4	444	2,235
Fairhill	1,618	795	823	20	-	557	402
Glebe	1,588	731	857	28	15	558	101
Killoquin Lower	1,439	729	710	25	3	433	4,014
Killoquin Upper	1,490	753	737	40	2	423	2,429
Knockaholet	1,402	718	684	36	5	423	4,885
Newhill	1,507	720	787	12	4	533	59
Route	1,411	665	746	22	5	520	260
Seacon	1,460	742	718	11	3	459	2,515
Stranocum	1,471	739	732	25	2	477	4,458
The Vow	1,445	748	697	32	1	433	3,490
Banbridge	**33,482**	**16,568**	**16,914**	**731**	**147**	**10,984**	**44,556**
Wards							
Ballydown	2,936	1,452	1,484	111	14	1,036	789
Banbridge West	2,955	1,453	1,502	26	11	982	178
Bannside	2,142	1,061	1,081	18	6	614	7,119
Croob	2,069	1,048	1,021	56	7	660	6,030
Dromore North	2,286	1,099	1,187	42	13	839	614
Dromore South	2,244	1,077	1,167	45	12	783	2,039
Edenderry	2,316	1,110	1,206	16	2	811	101
Fort	2,103	1,006	1,097	34	16	726	145
Garran	2,100	1,054	1,046	80	15	576	7,754
Gilford	2,142	1,082	1,060	73	11	733	1,753
Katesbridge	1,745	902	843	50	10	539	6,138
Lawrencetown	1,975	994	981	50	16	610	2,558
Loughbrickland	2,094	1,055	1,039	48	6	656	4,195
Quilly	2,014	1,001	1,013	54	3	622	4,751
Seapatrick	2,361	1,174	1,187	28	5	797	392

* As supplied by OSNI 1992

Table 4 Population, dwellings, private households and area – **continued**

Local Government Districts and Wards	Usually resident population			Unoccupied dwellings		Number of private households	Area (in hectares) *
	Persons	Males	Females	Vacant	Other		
Belfast	**279,237**	**130,820**	**148,417**	**6,905**	**2,929**	**107,394**	**11,489**
Wards							
Andersonstown	5,425	2,550	2,875	20	21	1,695	84
Ardoyne	6,337	2,980	3,357	70	43	2,165	59
Ballyhackamore	5,830	2,729	3,101	216	52	2,388	117
Ballymacarrett	4,908	2,269	2,639	92	53	2,016	71
Ballynafeigh	4,925	2,233	2,692	158	67	2,239	58
Ballysillan	4,874	2,287	2,587	123	23	1,942	101
Beechmount	4,951	2,305	2,646	161	49	1,840	76
Bellevue	5,033	2,413	2,620	127	63	1,820	287
Belmont	6,470	3,019	3,451	76	33	2,465	193
Blackstaff	5,007	2,397	2,610	453	63	2,240	203
Bloomfield	4,477	2,142	2,335	194	31	1,897	59
Botanic	5,496	2,614	2,882	405	318	2,876	139
Castleview	5,416	2,539	2,877	56	51	2,087	151
Cavehill	6,080	2,947	3,133	44	24	2,082	350
Cherryvalley	5,731	2,554	3,177	76	40	2,213	204
Chichester Park	5,827	2,705	3,122	169	102	2,061	102
Cliftonville	5,857	2,791	3,066	178	43	2,130	119
Clonard	5,475	2,589	2,886	130	60	1,964	66
Crumlin	3,876	1,829	2,047	190	59	1,803	61
Duncairn	4,060	1,861	2,199	158	43	1,903	872
Falls	5,205	2,403	2,802	57	27	1,827	94
Falls Park	6,537	3,078	3,459	59	42	2,121	238
Finaghy	6,715	3,098	3,617	54	23	2,213	267
Fortwilliam	5,112	2,360	2,752	142	53	1,981	103
Glen Road	5,687	2,695	2,992	13	32	1,860	205
Glencairn	4,580	2,160	2,420	121	41	1,799	389
Glencolin	6,950	3,380	3,570	37	58	2,000	963
Highfield	5,392	2,617	2,775	64	24	1,963	272
Island	4,496	2,062	2,434	173	30	2,054	371
Knock	5,087	2,441	2,646	45	8	1,999	105
Ladybrook	7,126	3,535	3,591	99	34	1,993	162
Legoniel	5,577	2,571	3,006	108	26	2,128	884
Malone	7,466	3,405	4,061	140	64	2,780	243
New Lodge	6,370	3,033	3,337	125	117	2,247	85
Orangefield	5,309	2,449	2,860	103	21	2,224	147
Ravenhill	5,223	2,448	2,775	136	66	2,084	185
Rosetta	5,222	2,268	2,954	102	52	2,044	169
Shaftesbury	5,357	2,496	2,861	88	68	2,490	179
Shankill	4,333	2,000	2,333	151	47	1,933	59
St. Anne's	3,983	1,900	2,083	105	49	1,662	169
Stormont	6,129	2,885	3,244	125	41	2,263	723
Stranmillis	6,742	3,154	3,588	160	105	2,800	340
Sydenham	5,688	2,708	2,980	121	26	2,278	624
The Mount	5,298	2,470	2,828	365	77	2,402	71
Upper Malone	6,362	2,964	3,398	37	18	2,328	487
Upper Springfield	6,195	2,986	3,209	10	55	1,697	202
Water Works	5,759	2,717	3,042	235	144	1,971	98
Whiterock	5,295	2,504	2,791	24	40	1,524	75
Windsor	5,110	2,242	2,868	385	214	2,806	94
Woodstock	5,397	2,449	2,948	220	48	2,554	61
Woodvale	3,480	1,589	1,891	205	41	1,543	53
Carrickfergus	**32,750**	**15,871**	**16,879**	**557**	**192**	**11,870**	**8,193**
Wards							
Blackhead	2,149	1,055	1,094	36	17	847	243
Boneybefore	2,689	1,325	1,364	34	17	889	117
Clipperstown	1,899	912	987	9	3	664	41
Eden	2,843	1,427	1,416	47	18	998	2,183
Gortalee	1,468	688	780	46	11	612	25
Greenisland	1,577	714	863	33	13	577	442
Killycrot	1,498	667	831	103	9	644	80
Knockagh	1,947	976	971	62	8	705	331
Love Lane	2,071	971	1,100	37	21	786	111
Milebush	2,206	1,081	1,125	26	2	677	39
Northland	1,746	859	887	15	6	606	18
Sunnylands	1,686	809	877	8	7	700	33
Victoria	2,374	1,136	1,238	19	5	874	120
Whitehead	1,819	873	946	32	32	655	648
Woodburn	4,778	2,378	2,400	50	23	1,636	3,762

* As supplied by OSNI 1992

Table 4 Population, dwellings, private households and area – **continued**

Local Government Districts and Wards	Usually resident population			Unoccupied dwellings		Number of private households	Area (in hectares) *
	Persons	Males	Females	Vacant	Other		
Castlereagh	**60,799**	**28,946**	**31,853**	**679**	**230**	**22,910**	**8,500**
Wards							
Ballyhanwood	3,451	1,672	1,779	34	12	1,264	878
Beechill	3,253	1,531	1,722	22	15	1,138	396
Carrowreagh	2,313	1,103	1,210	20	9	835	584
Carryduff	4,770	2,293	2,477	60	14	1,649	571
Cregagh	2,130	968	1,162	14	14	975	30
Downshire	2,552	1,179	1,373	33	9	1,081	49
Dundonald	3,093	1,444	1,649	72	15	1,201	404
Enler	2,783	1,325	1,458	32	9	1,102	44
Four Winds	3,250	1,580	1,670	14	4	1,155	84
Gilnahirk	2,935	1,419	1,516	35	7	1,104	92
Graham's Bridge	1,838	859	979	42	14	830	57
Hillfoot	2,928	1,411	1,517	22	6	998	180
Knockbracken	4,346	2,145	2,201	53	8	1,497	431
Lisnasharragh	2,361	1,153	1,208	10	3	856	95
Lower Braniel	2,369	1,106	1,263	27	12	1,044	87
Minnowburn	2,536	1,117	1,419	25	23	1,050	144
Moneyreagh	3,047	1,533	1,514	44	6	1,021	3,625
Newtownbreda	3,091	1,414	1,677	41	7	1,178	183
Tullycarnet	2,561	1,239	1,322	35	19	985	39
Upper Braniel	2,899	1,397	1,502	25	10	1,069	483
Wynchurch	2,293	1,058	1,235	19	14	878	44
Coleraine	**50,438**	**24,369**	**26,069**	**1,075**	**993**	**17,870**	**48,555**
Wards							
Agivey	1,891	928	963	65	8	608	6,807
Atlantic	2,491	1,187	1,304	55	97	1,010	470
Ballysally	2,703	1,306	1,397	65	15	959	92
Castlerock	2,359	1,149	1,210	53	72	816	2,913
Central	1,948	885	1,063	122	40	824	85
Churchland	1,625	759	866	9	5	642	69
Cross Glebe	2,537	1,202	1,335	20	15	876	163
Dunluce	2,213	1,089	1,124	42	213	790	5,069
Garvagh	2,435	1,205	1,230	59	5	772	5,337
Hopefield	2,639	1,233	1,406	54	69	982	204
Kilrea	2,224	1,100	1,124	50	5	696	2,648
Knockantern	1,906	954	952	18	6	614	3,973
Macosquin	2,214	1,134	1,080	33	4	692	7,310
Mount Sandel	4,061	1,920	2,141	54	28	1,375	298
Portstewart	2,250	1,024	1,226	98	119	964	87
Ringsend	2,078	1,079	999	31	13	586	10,490
Royal Portrush	2,054	930	1,124	149	113	894	406
Strand	3,078	1,461	1,617	34	132	1,193	1,014
The Cuts	2,811	1,351	1,460	16	12	943	616
University	1,843	929	914	10	11	657	219
Waterside	3,078	1,544	1,534	38	11	977	285
Cookstown	**31,082**	**15,503**	**15,579**	**672**	**148**	**9,222**	**62,171**
Wards							
Ardboe	2,208	1,140	1,068	35	9	554	6,181
Coagh	1,835	886	949	47	25	549	2,980
Dunnamore	1,946	968	978	65	5	506	9,822
Gortalowry	2,469	1,239	1,230	23	2	737	191
Killycolpy	2,205	1,124	1,081	36	10	566	9,437
Killymoon	2,103	1,018	1,085	30	2	641	175
Lissan	1,724	891	833	43	8	490	7,302
Moneymore	1,863	894	969	36	2	571	2,198
Newbuildings	1,622	782	840	52	40	633	206
Oaklands	1,747	919	828	52	3	529	5,583
Oldtown	1,695	814	881	25	13	620	80
Pomeroy	1,721	879	842	70	9	486	3,277
Sandholes	1,892	964	928	47	2	590	4,333
Stewartstown	1,683	814	869	56	9	510	4,177
The Loop	2,107	1,061	1,046	31	1	564	6,099
Tullagh	2,262	1,110	1,152	24	8	676	130

* As supplied by OSNI 1992

Table 4 Population, dwellings, private households and area – **continued**

Local Government Districts and Wards	Usually resident population			Unoccupied dwellings		Number of private households	Area (in hectares) *
	Persons	Males	Females	Vacant	Other		
Craigavon	**74,986**	**36,511**	**38,475**	**1,621**	**309**	**24,915**	**37,925**
Wards							
Aghagallon	2,900	1,443	1,457	54	14	797	8,694
Annagh	2,367	1,131	1,236	183	21	963	943
Ballybay	2,417	1,165	1,252	47	9	942	452
Ballyoran	2,754	1,356	1,398	15	6	783	847
Bleary	3,902	1,914	1,988	79	6	1,243	2,811
Brownstown	3,126	1,512	1,614	34	10	1,095	748
Church	1,815	840	975	35	12	751	42
Corcrain	2,964	1,442	1,522	64	17	1,008	110
Court	2,815	1,321	1,494	89	12	1,070	129
Drumgask	2,293	1,091	1,202	52	37	709	237
Drumgor	3,332	1,585	1,747	57	13	1,043	305
Drumnamoe	3,230	1,618	1,612	21	6	840	41
Edenderry	2,989	1,386	1,603	89	6	1,126	174
Kernan	3,252	1,612	1,640	55	11	1,091	1,701
Killycomain	2,448	1,183	1,265	38	8	903	87
Kinnegoe	3,710	1,897	1,813	80	8	1,049	8,737
Knocknashane	2,828	1,372	1,456	44	7	996	192
Magheralin	3,288	1,639	1,649	93	5	1,116	2,868
Mourneview	2,229	1,107	1,122	26	7	771	75
Parklake	2,215	1,022	1,193	49	14	942	278
Taghnevan	2,816	1,411	1,405	29	8	833	93
Tavanagh	2,511	1,197	1,314	68	3	951	50
The Birches	3,070	1,535	1,535	94	10	868	5,953
Tullygally	2,424	1,213	1,211	34	22	691	86
Waringstown	3,755	1,817	1,938	74	18	1,255	2,132
Woodville	3,536	1,702	1,834	118	19	1,079	140
Derry	**95,371**	**46,708**	**48,663**	**1,208**	**561**	**28,015**	**38,742**
Wards							
Altnagelvin	4,826	2,379	2,447	73	28	1,551	284
Ballynashallog	4,231	2,097	2,134	27	13	1,115	305
Banagher	2,425	1,224	1,201	24	6	654	9,688
Beechwood	2,298	1,070	1,228	19	8	655	32
Brandywell	2,299	1,113	1,186	29	25	771	63
Carn Hill	3,502	1,699	1,803	7	9	858	95
Caw	4,189	2,007	2,182	46	20	1,461	168
Claudy	2,552	1,292	1,260	31	24	707	9,298
Clondermot	2,718	1,280	1,438	16	16	956	91
Corrody	3,125	1,528	1,597	32	8	923	3,207
Creggan Central	2,559	1,225	1,334	13	17	741	79
Creggan South	2,353	1,132	1,221	38	11	673	59
Crevagh and Springtown	9,753	4,857	4,896	40	42	2,473	2,790
Culmore	3,978	2,002	1,976	26	18	1,068	972
Ebrington	2,275	1,223	1,052	111	22	749	117
Eglinton	3,675	1,844	1,831	89	23	1,095	4,984
Enagh	3,352	1,667	1,685	46	23	902	2,142
Faughan	2,900	1,482	1,418	28	5	831	2,549
Glen	2,796	1,326	1,470	42	18	919	46
Lisnagelvin	2,054	961	1,093	14	3	783	53
New Buildings	3,284	1,598	1,686	23	12	953	520
Pennyburn	3,449	1,686	1,763	39	15	917	221
Rosemount	2,621	1,293	1,328	31	25	792	42
St. Peter's	2,141	1,045	1,096	30	6	571	47
Shantallow East	2,441	1,219	1,222	3	5	611	28
Shantallow West	4,065	1,961	2,104	16	13	1,035	584
Strand	2,242	1,097	1,145	71	52	859	94
The Diamond	2,822	1,308	1,514	126	46	982	83
Victoria	2,097	997	1,100	83	30	688	76
Westland	2,349	1,096	1,253	35	18	722	25

* As supplied by OSNI 1992

Table 4 Population, dwellings, private households and area – **continued**

Local Government Districts and Wards	Usually resident population			Unoccupied dwellings		Number of private households	Area (in hectares) *
	Persons	Males	Females	Vacant	Other		
Down	**58,008**	**28,835**	**29,173**	**1,230**	**625**	**18,061**	**64,953**
Wards							
Ardglass	2,728	1,382	1,346	76	88	776	3,621
Audleys Acre	2,722	1,318	1,404	17	15	786	188
Ballymaglave	2,706	1,303	1,403	31	9	914	804
Ballynahinch East	2,540	1,235	1,305	45	11	830	207
Castlewellan	2,496	1,236	1,260	50	10	694	1,653
Cathedral	3,079	1,510	1,569	65	6	916	562
Crossgar	2,589	1,296	1,293	49	17	833	3,597
Derryboy	2,040	1,063	977	64	8	714	4,944
Donard	2,466	1,189	1,277	92	69	844	1,012
Drumaness	2,723	1,367	1,356	68	16	791	3,248
Dundrum	2,109	1,059	1,050	62	19	650	2,101
Dunmore	2,460	1,230	1,230	68	14	714	5,619
Flying Horse	2,235	1,055	1,180	28	21	649	355
Killough	3,540	1,911	1,629	77	93	959	5,871
Killyleagh	2,358	1,179	1,179	41	14	842	538
Kilmore	2,416	1,208	1,208	76	12	753	6,433
Murlough	2,508	1,203	1,305	24	35	799	1,214
Quoile	2,491	1,225	1,266	28	11	791	1,251
Saintfield	2,780	1,370	1,410	49	14	965	1,929
Seaforde	2,188	1,119	1,069	39	12	676	6,975
Shimna	2,421	1,122	1,299	74	38	864	134
Strangford	2,222	1,124	1,098	47	58	656	5,995
Tollymore	2,191	1,131	1,060	60	35	645	6,702
Dungannon	**45,428**	**22,556**	**22,872**	**1,018**	**224**	**13,653**	**78,323**
Wards							
Altmore	2,095	1,073	1,022	52	7	559	6,044
Augher	2,036	1,039	997	67	5	585	7,381
Aughnacloy	1,818	938	880	92	6	588	6,337
Ballygawley	2,140	1,121	1,019	72	5	638	5,834
Ballysaggart	2,063	1,012	1,051	23	18	651	227
Benburb	2,239	1,147	1,092	46	6	650	4,473
Caledon	1,907	956	951	56	12	582	8,168
Castlecaulfield	2,444	1,238	1,206	52	15	731	4,437
Clogher	1,774	888	886	34	8	522	9,623
Coalisland North	2,249	1,130	1,119	35	5	597	1,071
Coalisland South	2,019	955	1,064	54	6	558	390
Coalisland West and Newmills	2,358	1,162	1,196	44	14	661	937
Coolhill	2,180	1,048	1,132	25	10	726	236
Donaghmore	2,123	1,032	1,091	24	7	610	2,751
Drumglass	1,475	724	751	17	23	476	460
Fivemiletown	1,912	949	963	29	4	648	7,798
Killyman	2,265	1,119	1,146	33	5	693	3,948
Killymeal	2,211	1,028	1,183	96	17	720	617
Moy	2,018	1,004	1,014	51	5	634	2,405
Moygashel	1,982	968	1,014	31	10	691	647
Mullaghmore	1,575	743	832	36	27	510	396
Washing Bay	2,545	1,282	1,263	49	9	623	4,143

* As supplied by OSNI 1992

Table 4 Population, dwellings, private households and area - **continued**

Local Government Districts and Wards	Usually resident population			Unoccupied dwellings		Number of private households	Area (in hectares) *
	Persons	Males	Females	Vacant	Other		
Fermanagh	**54,033**	**27,095**	**26,938**	**1,272**	**490**	**16,901**	**187,677**
Wards							
Ballinamallard	2,439	1,260	1,179	57	23	794	5,622
Belcoo and Garrison	2,351	1,213	1,138	85	56	724	20,283
Belleek and Boa	2,101	1,055	1,046	77	32	652	16,403
Boho, Cleenish and Letterbreen	2,370	1,207	1,163	76	10	691	13,557
Brookeborough	2,229	1,139	1,090	68	17	666	12,562
Castlecoole	3,167	1,549	1,618	58	17	996	985
Derrygonnelly	2,304	1,152	1,152	77	40	706	15,689
Derrylin	2,254	1,191	1,063	82	17	672	10,567
Devenish	1,908	965	943	35	8	668	388
Donagh	2,003	1,068	935	28	21	551	9,815
Ederny and Lack	1,949	1,000	949	24	16	603	8,085
Erne	2,146	999	1,147	40	27	649	882
Florencecourt and Kinawley	2,151	1,146	1,005	54	10	649	15,406
Irvinestown	2,244	1,090	1,154	35	12	758	1,727
Island	2,010	925	1,085	50	43	783	241
Kesh and Lisnarrick	2,373	1,190	1,183	46	38	750	9,630
Lisbellaw	2,590	1,305	1,285	64	4	805	6,913
Lisnaskea	2,710	1,288	1,422	39	18	881	859
Maguires Bridge	2,304	1,175	1,129	68	9	714	8,872
Newtownbutler	2,287	1,127	1,160	55	36	675	7,671
Rosslea	2,204	1,166	1,038	50	1	620	8,864
Rossorry	3,654	1,733	1,921	39	30	1,176	2,539
Tempo	2,285	1,152	1,133	65	5	718	10,117
Larne	**29,419**	**14,318**	**15,101**	**698**	**421**	**10,409**	**33,646**
Wards							
Antiville	1,952	957	995	26	5	723	62
Ballycarry	1,964	991	973	35	18	661	3,031
Ballyloran	2,216	1,075	1,141	14	19	767	31
Blackcave	2,206	1,028	1,178	21	7	713	91
Carncastle	1,983	954	1,029	29	23	707	908
Carnlough	1,970	978	992	55	49	589	5,828
Central	1,537	705	832	122	55	680	60
Craigy Hill	1,660	808	852	16	11	655	25
Gardenmore	2,094	983	1,111	24	12	738	121
Glenarm	1,650	820	830	56	18	537	9,552
Glynn	2,430	1,201	1,229	60	17	880	3,699
Harbour	1,868	863	1,005	53	12	696	156
Island Magee	1,835	939	896	102	148	662	2,658
Kilwaughter	2,121	1,103	1,018	37	18	695	7,379
Town Parks	1,933	913	1,020	48	9	706	45
Limavady	**29,567**	**15,042**	**14,525**	**426**	**95**	**8,489**	**58,635**
Wards							
Aghanloo	1,691	857	834	46	4	511	7,613
Ballykelly	2,634	1,534	1,100	22	1	622	2,321
Binevenagh	1,485	734	751	8	4	495	36
Coolessan	1,721	833	888	12	6	522	62
Dungiven	2,041	1,031	1,010	14	4	564	259
Enagh	2,978	1,444	1,534	25	7	904	86
Feeny	1,801	921	880	48	9	455	9,137
Forest	1,916	956	960	22	4	555	3,889
Glack	1,683	859	824	14	-	460	5,613
Gresteel	2,906	1,478	1,428	28	4	809	1,948
Magilligan	1,786	957	829	76	12	500	7,886
Rathbrady	2,157	1,044	1,113	12	5	694	96
Roeside	1,387	666	721	34	22	527	120
The Highlands	1,463	745	718	13	7	399	5,565
Upper Glenshane	1,918	983	935	52	6	472	14,004

* As supplied by OSNI 1992

Table 4 Population, dwellings, private households and area – **continued**

Local Government Districts and Wards	Usually resident population			Unoccupied dwellings		Number of private households	Area (in hectares) *
	Persons	Males	Females	Vacant	Other		
Lisburn	**99,458**	**48,653**	**50,805**	**1,366**	**554**	**33,277**	**44,638**
Wards							
Ballymacash	3,661	1,773	1,888	33	20	1,173	203
Ballymacbrennan	2,711	1,382	1,329	58	10	893	6,244
Ballymacoss	5,402	2,530	2,872	71	29	1,879	1,685
Blaris	2,821	1,359	1,462	57	13	1,074	595
Collin Glen	9,504	4,433	5,071	32	15	2,466	1,013
Derryaghy	2,668	1,276	1,392	28	10	1,048	453
Dromara	3,771	1,867	1,904	74	14	1,281	6,091
Drumbo	2,762	1,366	1,396	79	12	974	1,886
Dunmurry	3,585	1,683	1,902	92	12	1,288	205
Glenavy	3,971	1,997	1,974	78	17	1,212	9,104
Harmony Hill	3,853	1,828	2,025	39	17	1,362	116
Hilden	2,223	1,076	1,147	79	11	914	60
Hillhall	3,068	1,466	1,602	36	18	1,140	681
Hillsborough	3,459	1,712	1,747	56	14	1,193	3,490
Kilwee	4,772	2,313	2,459	14	20	1,287	125
Knockmore	2,364	1,169	1,195	50	52	917	184
Lagan Valley	2,816	1,270	1,546	36	14	1,086	116
Lambeg	2,072	1,019	1,053	34	5	813	392
Lisnagarvy	3,984	1,932	2,052	39	17	1,350	90
Magheragall	4,246	2,208	2,038	58	9	1,325	5,867
Magheralave	3,803	1,870	1,933	19	15	1,259	175
Maze	3,682	2,016	1,666	78	55	1,177	1,867
Moira	4,268	2,138	2,130	69	58	1,386	3,599
Old Warren	2,194	1,024	1,170	75	45	877	49
Seymour Hill	2,403	1,090	1,313	17	15	1,095	93
Tonagh	2,566	1,207	1,359	40	11	970	65
Twinbrook	2,400	1,114	1,286	8	18	780	31
Wallace Park	4,429	2,535	1,894	17	8	1,058	159
Magherafelt	**36,293**	**18,177**	**18,116**	**580**	**112**	**10,398**	**57,239**
Wards							
Ballymaguigan	2,311	1,177	1,134	51	7	624	4,369
Bellaghy	2,624	1,325	1,299	40	5	680	3,191
Castledawson	2,277	1,129	1,148	28	7	731	1,469
Draperstown	2,704	1,369	1,335	41	11	751	7,602
Gulladuff	2,532	1,306	1,226	57	2	703	4,265
Knockcloghrim	2,249	1,106	1,143	51	8	663	4,086
Lecumpher	2,457	1,250	1,207	20	6	686	6,369
Lower Glenshane	2,644	1,324	1,320	24	10	649	6,697
Maghera	2,348	1,150	1,198	20	7	713	187
Swatragh	2,244	1,169	1,075	32	4	557	6,970
Tobermore	1,802	933	869	34	4	547	4,794
Townparks East	3,034	1,464	1,570	52	9	957	131
Townparks West	2,863	1,361	1,502	43	19	906	260
Upperlands	1,843	923	920	50	7	582	3,185
Valley	2,361	1,191	1,170	37	6	649	3,664
Moyle	**14,789**	**7,355**	**7,434**	**452**	**432**	**4,721**	**49,440**
Wards							
Armoy	1,012	508	504	27	2	284	2,796
Ballylough	950	483	467	10	7	330	1,565
Bonamargy and Rathlin	938	450	488	62	28	296	1,666
Bushmills	854	413	441	52	25	333	790
Carnmoon	847	439	408	13	7	283	3,049
Dalriada	1,466	696	770	27	57	459	113
Dunseverick	796	410	386	41	29	274	3,652
Glenaan	1,343	671	672	37	69	388	1,594
Glenariff	1,179	583	596	37	58	339	5,302
Glendun	1,137	579	558	68	59	327	10,866
Glenshesk	831	423	408	23	35	250	10,135
Glentaisie	775	369	406	8	18	291	36
Kinbane	824	405	419	25	28	268	3,817
Knocklayd	1,033	506	527	5	5	330	162
Moss-Side and Moyarget	804	420	384	17	5	269	3,897

* As supplied by OSNI 1992

Local Government Districts and Wards	Usually resident population			Unoccupied dwellings		Number of private households	Area (in hectares) *
	Persons	Males	Females	Vacant	Other		
Newry and Mourne	**82,943**	**41,307**	**41,636**	**1,470**	**776**	**24,418**	**90,937**
Wards							
Annalong	2,684	1,312	1,372	78	105	875	3,853
Ballybot	2,041	1,005	1,036	74	17	741	113
Ballycrossan	3,295	1,679	1,616	31	10	854	3,038
Bessbrook	2,888	1,673	1,215	39	12	800	624
Binnian	3,159	1,564	1,595	44	48	907	6,688
Camlough	2,508	1,231	1,277	46	17	675	4,043
Clonallan	2,975	1,475	1,500	36	18	959	394
Creggan	2,464	1,255	1,209	45	21	661	6,169
Crossmaglen	2,423	1,188	1,235	38	44	704	1,666
Daisy Hill	2,876	1,401	1,475	36	14	845	132
Derrymore	2,948	1,445	1,503	35	9	840	912
Donaghmore	3,011	1,522	1,489	49	18	876	5,436
Drumalane	3,450	1,616	1,834	34	22	1,047	234
Drumgullion	3,028	1,472	1,556	59	16	911	170
Fathom	2,868	1,453	1,415	53	18	780	3,998
Forkhill	2,578	1,284	1,294	45	53	728	4,442
Kilkeel Central	2,679	1,285	1,394	54	14	872	502
Kilkeel South	2,791	1,354	1,437	25	10	837	446
Lisnacree	3,005	1,558	1,447	69	70	792	9,442
Mayobridge	2,585	1,308	1,277	37	10	688	5,550
Newtownhamilton	2,322	1,193	1,129	42	12	675	7,625
Rathfriland	2,299	1,106	1,193	51	26	783	619
Rostrevor	3,168	1,587	1,581	58	49	936	4,049
St. Mary's	2,772	1,320	1,452	49	15	796	199
St. Patrick's	2,534	1,217	1,317	66	38	857	160
Seaview	3,015	1,445	1,570	47	36	978	384
Silver Bridge	2,607	1,317	1,290	39	9	750	5,630
Spelga	2,509	1,260	1,249	73	14	689	8,174
Tullyhappy	2,120	1,117	1,003	67	13	602	6,032
Windsor Hill	3,341	1,665	1,676	51	18	960	213
Newtownabbey	**74,035**	**35,760**	**38,275**	**1,072**	**309**	**26,491**	**15,069**
Wards							
Abbey	2,553	1,215	1,338	52	17	1,010	188
Ballyclare North	3,016	1,473	1,543	42	12	1,121	178
Ballyclare South	2,882	1,374	1,508	48	2	1,097	178
Ballyduff	3,262	1,612	1,650	18	4	1,025	52
Ballyhenry	3,099	1,491	1,608	23	7	1,072	86
Ballynure	3,390	1,650	1,740	66	11	1,152	5,209
Bradan	2,317	1,086	1,231	104	20	991	48
Burnthill	2,842	1,397	1,445	28	4	920	42
Carnmoney	3,387	1,623	1,764	21	4	1,162	92
Cloughfern	3,189	1,570	1,619	49	6	1,087	334
Collinbridge	3,529	1,760	1,769	44	5	1,095	459
Coole	2,488	1,133	1,355	25	33	986	41
Doagh	3,926	1,948	1,978	67	5	1,351	2,964
Dunanney	2,152	1,029	1,123	34	19	899	56
Glebe	3,381	1,679	1,702	19	9	1,025	78
Glengormley	2,586	1,264	1,322	40	8	919	47
Hawthorne	3,131	1,459	1,672	21	5	1,060	101
Hightown	2,611	1,265	1,346	28	8	971	50
Jordanstown	2,985	1,438	1,547	13	21	1,042	153
Mallusk	4,059	2,053	2,006	93	20	1,370	4,015
Monkstown	2,716	1,329	1,387	39	6	1,011	128
Mossley	3,527	1,669	1,858	40	14	1,242	150
Rostulla	2,753	1,313	1,440	32	11	1,027	194
Valley	2,311	1,054	1,257	41	31	867	165
Whitehouse	1,943	876	1,067	85	27	989	61

* As supplied by OSNI 1992

Table 4 Population, dwellings, private households and area – **continued**

Local Government Districts and Wards

Local Government Districts and Wards	Usually resident population			Unoccupied dwellings		Number of private households	Area (in hectares) *
	Persons	Males	Females	Vacant	Other		
North Down	**71,832**	**34,284**	**37,548**	**1,404**	**503**	**26,619**	**8,158**
Wards							
Ballyholme	2,332	1,047	1,285	64	27	815	78
Ballymaconnell	3,273	1,569	1,704	22	14	1,084	225
Ballymagee	7,477	3,736	3,741	218	34	2,407	534
Bangor Castle	2,665	1,217	1,448	62	21	1,125	167
Bloomfield	3,071	1,454	1,617	33	8	1,176	145
Broadway	3,073	1,446	1,627	40	13	1,152	116
Bryansburn	2,830	1,282	1,548	30	16	1,092	62
Churchill	2,691	1,233	1,458	44	15	1,051	74
Clandeboye	3,259	1,607	1,652	36	20	1,141	667
Conlig	2,728	1,295	1,433	27	21	1,054	615
Craigavad	2,698	1,342	1,356	44	17	929	1,928
Crawfordsburn	2,561	1,239	1,322	39	16	956	641
Cultra	2,689	1,334	1,355	32	11	892	649
Dufferin	2,578	1,178	1,400	20	22	1,021	84
Groomsport	2,838	1,410	1,428	24	53	1,049	731
Harbour	2,375	1,144	1,231	320	62	1,128	58
Holywood Demesne	2,978	1,400	1,578	87	16	1,127	180
Holywood Priory	2,663	1,270	1,393	36	13	974	451
Loughview	3,076	1,481	1,595	21	19	1,186	339
Princetown	2,540	1,183	1,357	37	18	893	151
Rathgael	2,906	1,403	1,503	43	10	1,023	52
Silverstream	2,747	1,297	1,450	76	17	1,144	56
Spring Hill	3,507	1,629	1,878	33	15	1,258	117
Whitehill	2,277	1,088	1,189	16	25	942	38
Omagh	**45,809**	**23,022**	**22,787**	**819**	**219**	**13,417**	**112,990**
Wards							
Beragh	2,145	1,108	1,037	34	5	627	6,516
Camowen	1,578	769	809	41	25	567	149
Clanabogan	2,239	1,165	1,074	29	6	604	8,781
Coolnagard	2,852	1,361	1,491	46	18	806	266
Dergmoney	2,094	1,020	1,074	62	11	757	140
Dromore	2,225	1,127	1,098	24	18	622	4,794
Drumnakilly	2,276	1,175	1,101	33	6	594	7,339
Drumquin	1,831	933	898	46	12	541	12,550
Drumragh	1,548	774	774	11	5	405	376
Fairy Water	1,862	977	885	44	4	524	9,413
Fintona	2,120	1,062	1,058	38	8	703	3,871
Gortin	2,007	966	1,041	41	4	588	9,060
Gortrush	2,123	1,004	1,119	27	10	676	211
Killyclogher	3,689	1,755	1,934	41	14	1,115	271
Lisanelly	2,743	1,482	1,261	26	17	788	170
Newtownsaville	2,095	1,082	1,013	60	12	587	7,154
Owenkillew	2,021	1,070	951	54	8	528	17,498
Sixmilecross	1,905	999	906	35	6	536	7,435
Strule	2,109	1,009	1,100	27	14	683	157
Termon	2,238	1,110	1,128	42	8	567	8,445
Trillick	2,109	1,074	1,035	58	8	599	8,394
Strabane	**36,141**	**18,116**	**18,025**	**574**	**192**	**10,750**	**86,165**
Wards							
Artigarvan	2,353	1,175	1,178	35	7	719	5,277
Castlederg	2,706	1,284	1,422	34	15	887	712
Clare	2,072	1,056	1,016	37	9	596	8,597
Dunnamanagh	2,042	1,053	989	38	5	616	10,040
East	2,435	1,212	1,223	34	5	739	86
Finn	1,690	844	846	18	11	468	3,544
Glenderg	2,207	1,176	1,031	66	29	654	17,714
Newtownstewart	2,261	1,134	1,127	37	12	735	4,165
North	2,120	994	1,126	94	28	673	479
Plumbridge	1,805	988	817	62	21	531	18,911
Sion Mills	2,777	1,399	1,378	51	7	855	1,003
Slievekirk	2,034	1,080	954	31	5	618	6,442
South	3,519	1,683	1,836	7	10	940	135
Victoria Bridge	2,088	1,110	978	19	10	584	8,879
West	4,032	1,928	2,104	11	18	1,135	181

* As supplied by OSNI 1992

Table 4A Population and private households

Towns with 1,000 or more persons within Local Government Districts

Town	South-West Grid Reference	North-East Grid Reference	Total private households	Usually resident population		
				Persons	Males	Females
Antrim						
Antrim	J140855	J180892	7,100	20,878	10,121	10,757
Crumlin	J146756	J160770	575	1,762	854	908
Randalstown	J070895	J095920	1,324	3,925	1,853	2,072
Templepatrick	J220850	J237858	479	1,383	676	707
Ards						
Ballygowan	J423633	J440644	761	2,289	1,140	1,149
Ballywalter	J623686	J630698	411	1,073	512	561
Comber	J445683	J470702	2,913	8,333	4,098	4,235
Donaghadee	J580788	J600810	1,873	4,455	2,073	2,382
Millisle	J588754	J600763	551	1,531	743	788
Newtownards	J476720	J514760	8,610	23,869	11,421	12,448
Portaferry	J590500	J610520	725	2,324	1,160	1,164
Portavogie	J650590	J663610	503	1,482	731	751
Armagh						
Armagh	H860432	H898473	4,540	14,265	6,875	7,390
Keady	H840330	H850350	726	2,467	1,203	1,264
Markethill	H958390	H970410	477	1,337	635	702
Richhill	H930470	H950490	898	2,709	1,360	1,349
Tandragee	J025456	J042471	971	2,871	1,398	1,473
Ballymena						
Ahoghill	D044012	D060022	590	1,686	825	861
Ballymena	D085010	D125056	9,814	28,112	13,605	14,507
Broughshane	D140056	D160072	695	1,873	911	962
Cullybackey	D053052	D066066	766	2,167	1,026	1,141
Portglenone	C970034	C990046	391	1,193	598	595
Ballymoney						
Ballymoney	C936248	C967270	2,786	7,818	3,735	4,083
Banbridge						
Banbridge	J110440	J140471	3,959	11,448	5,567	5,881
Dromore	J190520	J212540	1,292	3,434	1,618	1,816
Gilford	J058480	J070500	540	1,551	787	764
Carrickfergus						
Carrickfergus	J390864	J440910	8,164	22,786	11,059	11,727
Greenisland	J360840	J390864	1,862	4,967	2,357	2,610
Whitehead	J460910	J480930	1,429	3,761	1,823	1,938

Table 4A Population and private households – **continued**

Towns with 1,000 or more persons within Local Government Districts

Town	South-West Grid Reference	North-East Grid Reference	Total private households	Usually resident population		
				Persons	Males	Females
Castlereagh						
Carryduff	J360642	J374656	1,505	4,270	2,037	2,233
Dundonald	J410725	J436750	5,068	12,943	6,135	6,808
Coleraine						
Castlerock	C760350	C780370	378	1,023	483	540
Coleraine	C830296	C870350	7,290	20,721	9,956	10,765
Garvagh	C830150	C850170	388	1,091	520	571
Kilrea	C916120	C934130	431	1,271	620	651
Portrush	C840390	C872416	2,256	5,598	2,592	3,006
Portstewart	C810360	C832400	2,628	6,459	3,030	3,429
Cookstown						
Cookstown	H794764	H820798	3,210	9,842	4,707	5,015
Moneymore	H856830	H864842	382	1,231	583	648
Craigavon						
Bleary	J070530	J080550	332	1,029	491	538
Craigavon	J030550	J070580	2,831	9,201	4,436	4,765
Lurgan	J070565	J100602	7,387	21,905	10,601	11,304
Magheralin	J120580	J135592	369	1,075	523	552
Portadown	H994520	J030560	7,728	21,299	10,215	11,084
Waringstown	J100544	J110560	637	1,831	896	935
Derry						
Culmore	C460220	C480230	296	1,116	569	547
Drumahoe	C461145	C474153	361	1,146	594	552
Eglinton	C517193	C535208	524	1,658	841	817
Londonderry	C410150	C464212	21,485	72,334	35,125	37,209
Newbuildings	C408120	C420130	597	2,025	969	1,056
Prehen	C415140	C430153	324	1,143	578	565
Strathfoyle	C464204	C472212	514	1,703	840	863
Tullyalley	C454138	C461150	606	1,971	968	1,003

Table 4A Population and private households – **continued**

Towns with 1,000 or more persons within Local Government Districts

Town	South-West Grid Reference	North-East Grid Reference	Total private households	Usually resident population		
				Persons	Males	Females
Down						
Ardglass	J550360	J570380	455	1,651	803	848
Ballynahinch	J355515	J378537	1,533	4,591	2,203	2,388
Castlewellan	J328350	J350370	602	2,133	1,061	1,072
Crossgar	J451515	J462525	406	1,246	615	631
Downpatrick	J480428	J508464	3,015	10,113	4,901	5,212
Dundrum	J398356	J410370	318	1,004	483	521
Killyleagh	J517520	J530535	802	2,221	1,108	1,113
Newcastle	J360290	J390330	2,451	7,214	3,425	3,789
Saintfield	J398580	J414600	761	2,168	1,046	1,122
Dungannon						
Coalisland	H830650	H850670	1,066	3,802	1,848	1,954
Dungannon	H780610	H816640	3,005	9,190	4,407	4,783
Fivemiletown	H440476	H448483	393	1,107	533	574
Moygashel	H800590	H820610	421	1,178	551	627
Fermanagh						
Enniskillen	H220420	H260460	3,840	11,436	5,470	5,966
Irvinestown	H220570	H250590	661	1,906	911	995
Lisnaskea	H350330	H370348	781	2,367	1,120	1,247
Larne						
Ballycarry	J440930	J460950	346	1,010	504	506
Carnlough	D280160	D290190	454	1,493	737	756
Larne	D380010	D416050	6,432	17,575	8,337	9,238
Limavady						
Ballykelly	C620218	C637228	489	2,140	1,291	849
Dungiven	C680080	C700100	747	2,812	1,420	1,392
Greysteel	C560200	C570210	280	1,029	521	508
Limavady	C668214	C688240	3,332	10,350	5,021	5,329
Lisburn						
Derriaghy	J263672	J280680	573	1,696	831	865
Dunmurry	J280672	J298703	4,492	12,771	6,056	6,715
Hillsborough	J232580	J256598	856	2,407	1,161	1,246
Lisburn	J236624	J284672	14,741	42,110	20,489	21,621
Magheraberry	J168630	J178636	335	1,009	512	497
Moira	J140594	J160612	950	2,772	1,368	1,404

Table 4A Population and private households – **continued**

Towns with 1,000 or more persons within Local Government Districts

Town	South-West Grid Reference	North-East Grid Reference	Total private households	Usually resident population		
				Persons	Males	Females
Magherafelt						
Bellaghy	H950960	H960980	293	1,041	501	540
Castledawson	H923920	H940940	551	1,691	817	874
Draperstown	H775940	H790951	414	1,409	689	720
Maghera	H840997	C861012	855	2,876	1,413	1,463
Magherafelt	H885890	H908916	2,105	6,682	3,191	3,491
Moyle						
Ballycastle	D105399	D126420	1,304	4,005	1,915	2,090
Bushmills	C936400	C950412	501	1,348	655	693
Cushendall	D230268	D248282	386	1,285	633	652
Newry and Mourne						
Annalong	J360188	J380210	595	1,832	903	929
Bessbrook	J036274	J056290	851	3,132	1,781	1,351
Cloughreagh	J060270	J070290	438	1,484	733	751
Crossmaglen	H900140	H920160	480	1,586	780	806
Kilkeel	J290130	J320156	1,881	6,024	2,923	3,101
Newry	J070236	J104288	6,631	21,633	10,501	11,132
Rathfriland	J192328	J204340	732	2,126	1,030	1,096
Rostrevor	J170176	J190195	692	2,269	1,119	1,150
Warrenpoint	J135176	J152198	1,763	5,408	2,612	2,796
Newtownabbey						
Ballyclare	J275900	J300924	2,615	7,108	3,431	3,677
Mossley	J318845	J325854	511	1,420	684	736
Newtownabbey	[J305812 J340800	J340850] J370850]	20,395	56,811	27,298	29,513
North Down						
Bangor	J475788	J538828	19,526	52,437	24,913	27,524
Craigavad	J416800	J444822	565	1,669	821	848
Helens Bay	J451819	J464834	487	1,268	609	659
Holywood	J390772	J416798	3,475	9,252	4,430	4,822
Omagh						
Fintona	H436608	H450618	469	1,324	661	663
Omagh	H435710	H472744	5,473	17,280	8,448	8,832
Strabane						
Castlederg	H250840	H270860	844	2,579	1,221	1,358
Newtownstewart	H390850	H410860	496	1,520	751	769
Sion Mills	H336926	H344940	550	1,676	833	843
Strabane	H330950	H358990	3,364	11,670	5,624	6,046

Table 5 Age by single years, sex and marital status — Northern Ireland

Age	Persons	Males Total	Males Single	Males Married	Males Remarried	Males Widowed	Males Divorced	Females Total	Females Single	Females Married	Females Remarried	Females Widowed	Females Divorced
ALL AGES	**1,577,836**	**769,071**	**405,414**	**324,968**	**9,111**	**18,276**	**11,302**	**808,765**	**368,256**	**336,104**	**8,664**	**78,447**	**17,294**
0	24,747	12,736	12,736					12,011	12,011				
1	25,239	12,990	12,990					12,249	12,249				
2	25,465	13,064	13,064					12,401	12,401				
3	26,082	13,394	13,394					12,688	12,688				
4	26,720	13,737	13,737					12,983	12,983				
0 - 4	128,253	65,921	65,921					62,332	62,332				
5	26,278	13,462	13,462					12,816	12,816				
6	25,856	13,396	13,396					12,460	12,460				
7	26,073	13,346	13,346					12,727	12,727				
8	25,495	13,056	13,056					12,439	12,439				
9	25,451	12,956	12,956					12,495	12,495				
5 - 9	129,153	66,216	66,216					62,937	62,937				
10	26,699	13,611	13,611					13,088	13,088				
11	26,772	13,743	13,743					13,029	13,029				
12	25,330	12,774	12,774					12,556	12,556				
13	24,711	12,531	12,531					12,180	12,180				
14	24,357	12,470	12,470					11,887	11,887				
10 - 14	127,869	65,129	65,129					62,740	62,740				
15	24,623	12,634	12,634					11,989	11,989				
16	25,075	12,849	12,834	15	-	-	-	12,226	12,211	15	-	-	-
17	25,642	13,220	13,206	13	-	1	-	12,422	12,369	52	-	1	-
18	26,273	13,576	13,528	47	-	1	-	12,697	12,465	231	-	1	-
19	25,968	13,488	13,335	151	-	-	2	12,480	11,961	512	-	-	7
15 - 19	127,581	65,767	65,537	226	-	2	2	61,814	60,995	810	-	2	7
20	26,384	13,515	13,123	388	1	-	3	12,869	11,680	1,178	1	1	9
21	25,240	12,851	12,021	818	1	2	9	12,389	10,294	2,061	5	6	23
22	25,462	12,906	11,384	1,508	1	1	12	12,556	9,422	3,052	15	12	55
23	24,728	12,502	10,133	2,337	5	-	27	12,226	7,834	4,282	15	14	81
24	24,306	12,122	8,791	3,262	7	1	61	12,184	6,542	5,466	21	21	134
20 - 24	126,120	63,896	55,452	8,313	15	4	112	62,224	45,772	16,039	57	54	302
25	24,689	12,317	7,867	4,333	20	5	92	12,372	5,594	6,539	32	27	180
26	25,065	12,412	6,755	5,509	25	8	115	12,653	4,728	7,545	66	21	293
27	24,388	12,071	5,582	6,283	35	6	165	12,317	3,859	8,026	87	27	318
28	24,348	12,155	4,906	7,010	60	13	166	12,193	3,248	8,401	110	44	390
29	23,749	11,519	3,943	7,258	87	13	218	12,230	2,825	8,779	148	47	431
25 - 29	122,239	60,474	29,053	30,393	227	45	756	61,765	20,254	39,290	443	166	1,612
30	23,787	11,745	3,500	7,849	109	16	271	12,042	2,369	8,960	178	68	467
31	23,419	11,533	3,155	7,938	136	15	289	11,886	2,063	8,971	213	72	567
32	22,227	10,831	2,510	7,845	161	18	297	11,396	1,785	8,764	252	65	530
33	22,386	11,008	2,229	8,207	210	16	346	11,378	1,515	8,906	250	82	625
34	21,642	10,655	2,089	7,981	209	18	358	10,987	1,460	8,525	278	88	636
30 - 34	113,461	55,772	13,483	39,820	825	83	1,561	57,689	9,192	44,126	1,171	375	2,825
35	21,040	10,517	1,937	7,954	246	30	350	10,523	1,236	8,274	313	93	607
36	19,781	9,970	1,667	7,676	256	29	342	9,811	1,094	7,784	271	95	567
37	19,944	10,028	1,576	7,795	269	26	362	9,916	1,012	7,925	282	125	572
38	19,813	9,908	1,510	7,718	293	30	357	9,905	999	7,851	321	145	589
39	18,733	9,355	1,297	7,418	251	30	359	9,378	886	7,523	324	135	510
35 - 39	99,311	49,778	7,987	38,561	1,315	145	1,770	49,533	5,227	39,357	1,511	593	2,845
40	19,683	9,913	1,418	7,808	268	48	371	9,770	908	7,854	309	138	561
41	19,311	9,602	1,235	7,675	289	58	345	9,709	782	7,915	278	164	570
42	19,236	9,588	1,271	7,639	282	50	346	9,648	748	7,818	284	216	582
43	19,711	9,672	1,207	7,750	296	58	361	10,039	753	8,244	273	238	531
44	19,969	9,833	1,211	7,893	295	72	362	10,136	794	8,235	315	245	547
40 - 44	97,910	48,608	6,342	38,765	1,430	286	1,785	49,302	3,985	40,066	1,459	1,001	2,791
45	18,102	9,042	1,100	7,241	298	74	329	9,060	708	7,325	255	283	489
46	18,566	9,090	1,070	7,351	258	87	324	9,476	729	7,679	238	335	495
47	18,477	9,154	1,027	7,452	250	91	334	9,323	684	7,606	226	367	440
48	18,395	9,103	986	7,360	278	115	364	9,292	692	7,533	245	396	426
49	16,380	8,123	947	6,549	221	88	318	8,257	671	6,595	186	417	388
45 - 49	89,920	44,512	5,130	35,953	1,305	455	1,669	45,408	3,484	36,738	1,150	1,798	2,238

Table 5 Age by single years, sex and marital status – **continued**

Northern Ireland

Age	Persons	Males						Females					
		Total	Single	Married	Remarried	Widowed	Divorced	Total	Single	Married	Remarried	Widowed	Divorced
50	15,405	7,623	871	6,152	202	112	286	7,782	579	6,187	197	446	373
51	15,228	7,457	838	6,046	186	128	259	7,771	580	6,179	170	503	339
52	15,595	7,579	838	6,122	205	145	269	8,016	669	6,231	176	592	348
53	15,067	7,417	842	5,971	188	169	247	7,650	672	5,868	158	627	325
54	15,276	7,458	887	5,940	193	182	256	7,818	695	5,991	117	729	286
50 - 54	76,571	37,534	4,276	30,231	974	736	1,317	39,037	3,195	30,456	818	2,897	1,671
55	14,892	7,242	881	5,773	169	207	212	7,650	677	5,800	140	776	257
56	13,977	6,793	867	5,377	156	184	209	7,184	683	5,311	116	838	236
57	13,994	6,770	807	5,433	123	227	180	7,224	750	5,214	104	935	221
58	14,197	6,736	918	5,299	144	230	145	7,461	785	5,289	105	1,074	208
59	14,009	6,657	872	5,232	133	260	160	7,352	781	5,064	116	1,209	182
55 - 59	71,069	34,198	4,345	27,114	725	1,108	906	36,871	3,676	26,678	581	4,832	1,104
60	14,275	6,618	912	5,099	127	325	155	7,657	824	5,179	98	1,362	194
61	14,234	6,569	925	5,029	134	332	149	7,665	892	4,932	112	1,553	176
62	13,698	6,327	904	4,816	123	357	127	7,371	913	4,593	94	1,630	141
63	13,329	6,104	878	4,613	117	371	125	7,225	908	4,413	73	1,694	137
64	13,791	6,360	880	4,781	132	458	109	7,431	966	4,259	102	1,967	137
60 - 64	69,327	31,978	4,499	24,338	633	1,843	665	37,349	4,503	23,376	479	8,206	785
65	13,690	6,265	925	4,619	121	504	96	7,425	929	4,161	90	2,122	123
66	12,924	5,967	891	4,352	121	515	88	6,957	990	3,664	88	2,108	107
67	13,107	5,897	871	4,272	121	564	69	7,210	996	3,638	89	2,378	109
68	12,573	5,540	847	3,994	102	545	52	7,033	1,043	3,286	85	2,506	113
69	12,661	5,564	859	3,919	117	606	63	7,097	1,051	3,237	70	2,653	86
65 - 69	64,955	29,233	4,393	21,156	582	2,734	368	35,722	5,009	17,986	422	11,767	538
70	12,611	5,478	811	3,788	131	679	69	7,133	1,077	2,993	83	2,888	92
71	11,909	5,176	729	3,611	98	687	51	6,733	971	2,752	63	2,860	87
72	9,868	4,230	642	2,871	85	594	38	5,638	895	2,118	53	2,527	45
73	8,897	3,672	583	2,387	83	580	39	5,225	844	1,809	52	2,477	43
74	8,838	3,686	598	2,362	90	603	33	5,152	791	1,627	55	2,626	53
70 - 74	52,123	22,242	3,363	15,019	487	3,143	230	29,881	4,578	11,299	306	13,378	320
75	8,619	3,388	486	2,170	75	626	31	5,231	877	1,580	41	2,698	35
76	8,843	3,469	560	2,096	69	706	38	5,374	943	1,406	32	2,944	49
77	8,166	3,123	475	1,889	65	677	17	5,043	848	1,282	36	2,849	28
78	7,685	2,879	444	1,691	62	660	22	4,806	820	1,105	33	2,825	23
79	6,973	2,560	374	1,502	48	624	12	4,413	794	901	20	2,676	22
75 - 79	40,286	15,419	2,339	9,348	319	3,293	120	24,867	4,282	6,274	162	13,992	157
80	6,399	2,265	354	1,198	52	652	9	4,134	787	760	14	2,554	19
81	5,569	1,854	258	976	50	559	11	3,715	690	594	22	2,390	19
82	5,017	1,692	266	868	34	516	8	3,325	672	501	15	2,123	14
83	4,299	1,330	214	638	36	439	3	2,969	627	426	14	1,893	9
84	3,778	1,158	180	529	26	422	1	2,620	544	329	9	1,727	11
80 - 84	25,062	8,299	1,272	4,209	198	2,588	32	16,763	3,320	2,610	74	10,687	72
85	3,352	937	155	385	16	378	3	2,415	518	261	7	1,620	9
86	2,888	763	133	311	12	304	3	2,125	462	185	7	1,466	5
87	2,284	607	104	237	12	254	-	1,677	354	149	3	1,169	2
88	1,923	464	70	181	11	201	1	1,459	340	106	6	1,006	1
89	1,541	351	65	116	9	159	2	1,190	291	90	1	803	5
85 - 89	11,988	3,122	527	1,230	60	1,296	9	8,866	1,965	791	24	6,064	22
90	1,224	288	49	103	6	130	-	936	189	64	3	680	-
91	904	191	23	64	3	101	-	713	164	41	4	503	1
92	719	138	20	46	1	71	-	581	128	21	-	432	-
93	480	103	20	24	3	56	-	377	82	20	-	274	1
94	410	83	14	20	1	48	-	327	78	21	-	226	2
90 - 94	3,737	803	126	257	14	406	-	2,934	641	167	7	2,115	4
95 and over	901	170	24	35	2	109	-	731	169	41	-	520	1

Table 6 Population under 25 years by individual years and 25 years and over by quinquennial groups, sex and marital status

Age	Persons	Males						Females					
		Total	Single	Married	Remarried	Widowed	Divorced	Total	Single	Married	Remarried	Widowed	Divorced
Antrim													
ALL AGES	**44,516**	**22,135**	**11,776**	**9,126**	**362**	**455**	**416**	**22,381**	**10,321**	**9,409**	**338**	**1,737**	**576**
0	726	364	364					362	362				
1	676	338	338					338	338				
2	685	368	368					317	317				
3	761	404	404					357	357				
4	707	361	361					346	346				
0 - 4	3,555	1,835	1,835					1,720	1,720				
5	707	363	363					344	344				
6	665	326	326					339	339				
7	684	356	356					328	328				
8	725	377	377					348	348				
9	749	375	375					374	374				
5 - 9	3,530	1,797	1,797					1,733	1,733				
10	758	383	383					375	375				
11	798	381	381					417	417				
12	747	397	397					350	350				
13	710	388	388					322	322				
14	689	363	363					326	326				
10 - 14	3,702	1,912	1,912					1,790	1,790				
15	774	381	381					393	393				
16	746	379	379	-	-	-	-	367	367	-	-	-	-
17	760	387	387	-	-	-	-	373	370	3	-	-	-
18	809	404	401	3	-	-	-	405	393	12	-	-	-
19	760	387	379	8	-	-	-	373	359	13	-	-	1
15 - 19	3,849	1,938	1,927	11	-	-	-	1,911	1,882	28	-	-	1
20	785	405	391	14	-	-	-	380	329	51	-	-	-
21	815	426	391	32	-	1	2	389	328	59	-	-	2
22	775	405	344	60	-	-	1	370	262	102	2	2	2
23	794	422	333	87	-	-	2	372	203	165	2	-	2
24	775	419	298	115	2	-	4	356	165	184	2	1	4
20 - 24	3,944	2,077	1,757	308	2	1	9	1,867	1,287	561	6	3	10
25 - 29	3,617	1,871	915	916	12	-	28	1,746	541	1,127	19	1	58
30 - 34	3,290	1,647	398	1,157	38	-	54	1,643	260	1,236	47	2	98
35 - 39	2,995	1,488	248	1,109	61	5	65	1,507	170	1,163	66	14	94
40 - 44	3,102	1,537	203	1,207	57	6	64	1,565	121	1,242	70	27	105
45 - 49	2,828	1,400	155	1,118	66	10	51	1,428	109	1,128	46	61	84
50 - 54	2,190	1,078	104	859	44	20	51	1,112	78	863	33	82	56
55 - 59	1,863	930	112	729	28	26	35	933	90	680	15	116	32
60 - 64	1,671	831	115	619	19	47	31	840	104	533	14	176	13
65 - 69	1,445	679	118	463	14	69	15	766	108	389	8	251	10
70 - 74	1,153	505	77	334	10	76	8	648	110	252	8	272	6
75 - 79	876	331	51	189	4	84	3	545	98	133	4	303	7
80 - 84	524	182	36	81	6	58	1	342	66	56	1	217	2
85 - 89	281	72	13	20	1	37	1	209	40	18	1	150	-
90 - 94	88	21	3	5	-	13	-	67	13	-	-	54	-
95 and over	13	4	-	1	-	3	-	9	1	-	-	8	-

Table 6 Population under 25 years by individual years and 25 years and over by quinquennial groups, sex and marital status – **continued**

Age	Persons	Males						Females					
		Total	Single	Married	Remarried	Widowed	Divorced	Total	Single	Married	Remarried	Widowed	Divorced
Ards													
ALL AGES	**64,764**	**31,527**	**14,755**	**14,811**	**648**	**728**	**585**	**33,237**	**13,321**	**15,192**	**582**	**3,248**	**894**
0	883	447	447					436	436				
1	902	491	491					411	411				
2	935	478	478					457	457				
3	968	516	516					452	452				
4	950	485	485					465	465				
0 - 4	4,638	2,417	2,417					2,221	2,221				
5	922	463	463					459	459				
6	943	482	482					461	461				
7	953	505	505					448	448				
8	947	485	485					462	462				
9	924	478	478					446	446				
5 - 9	4,689	2,413	2,413					2,276	2,276				
10	1,012	507	507					505	505				
11	1,025	525	525					500	500				
12	942	477	477					465	465				
13	995	495	495					500	500				
14	962	483	483					479	479				
10 - 14	4,936	2,487	2,487					2,449	2,449				
15	1,042	540	540					502	502				
16	1,008	535	535	-	-	-	-	473	472	1	-	-	-
17	1,020	564	564	-	-	-	-	456	455	1	-	-	-
18	1,025	495	493	2	-	-	-	530	523	7	-	-	-
19	968	511	507	4	-	-	-	457	436	21	-	-	-
15 - 19	5,063	2,645	2,639	6	-	-	-	2,418	2,388	30	-	-	-
20	942	453	441	12	-	-	-	489	439	50	-	-	-
21	892	439	402	37	-	-	-	453	359	91	1	1	1
22	982	504	433	70	-	1	-	478	356	119	-	-	3
23	913	460	371	85	-	-	4	453	263	185	-	1	4
24	943	480	321	151	-	-	8	463	218	235	1	1	8
20 - 24	4,672	2,336	1,968	355	-	1	12	2,336	1,635	680	2	3	16
25 - 29	4,636	2,273	960	1,256	14	3	40	2,363	615	1,645	21	6	76
30 - 34	4,770	2,366	488	1,743	62	3	70	2,404	307	1,891	69	8	129
35 - 39	4,418	2,170	274	1,712	80	6	98	2,248	171	1,800	106	17	154
40 - 44	4,916	2,432	219	1,990	110	14	99	2,484	143	2,056	98	40	147
45 - 49	4,418	2,259	184	1,866	90	18	101	2,159	111	1,748	97	66	137
50 - 54	3,234	1,634	127	1,342	81	32	52	1,600	98	1,274	64	92	72
55 - 59	2,920	1,382	122	1,120	55	41	44	1,538	107	1,154	33	188	56
60 - 64	2,851	1,276	111	1,018	47	66	34	1,575	129	1,058	34	311	43
65 - 69	2,780	1,251	121	977	51	89	13	1,529	161	815	20	503	30
70 - 74	2,329	1,005	104	736	22	133	10	1,324	145	547	23	585	24
75 - 79	1,691	647	68	411	19	141	8	1,044	141	313	9	578	3
80 - 84	1,130	371	41	201	11	114	4	759	112	144	4	492	7
85 - 89	477	129	9	67	5	48	-	348	75	27	2	244	-
90 - 94	160	28	2	10	1	15	-	132	30	9	-	93	-
95 and over	36	6	1	1	-	4	-	30	7	1	-	22	-

Table 6 Population under 25 years by individual years and 25 years and over by quinquennial groups, sex and marital status – **continued**

Age	Persons	Males						Females					
		Total	Single	Married	Remarried	Widowed	Divorced	Total	Single	Married	Remarried	Widowed	Divorced
Armagh													
ALL AGES	**51,817**	**25,741**	**14,296**	**10,515**	**164**	**553**	**213**	**26,076**	**12,376**	**10,744**	**155**	**2,514**	**287**
0	838	420	420					418	418				
1	904	481	481					423	423				
2	860	442	442					418	418				
3	890	460	460					430	430				
4	914	461	461					453	453				
0 - 4	4,406	2,264	2,264					2,142	2,142				
5	895	454	454					441	441				
6	940	485	485					455	455				
7	925	468	468					457	457				
8	883	457	457					426	426				
9	899	443	443					456	456				
5 - 9	4,542	2,307	2,307					2,235	2,235				
10	995	487	487					508	508				
11	934	495	495					439	439				
12	931	486	486					445	445				
13	885	455	455					430	430				
14	856	479	479					377	377				
10 - 14	4,601	2,402	2,402					2,199	2,199				
15	907	462	462					445	445				
16	924	472	472	-	-	-	-	452	451	1	-	-	-
17	921	486	486	-	-	-	-	435	434	1	-	-	-
18	926	461	459	2	-	-	-	465	456	9	-	-	-
19	923	477	473	4	-	-	-	446	423	23	-	-	-
15 - 19	4,601	2,358	2,352	6	-	-	-	2,243	2,209	34	-	-	-
20	913	453	445	8	-	-	-	460	416	44	-	-	-
21	858	467	445	22	-	-	-	391	331	60	-	-	-
22	822	429	371	58	-	-	-	393	285	107	-	-	1
23	749	397	299	98	-	-	-	352	228	123	-	-	1
24	771	371	280	90	-	-	1	400	177	218	-	3	2
20 - 24	4,113	2,117	1,840	276	-	-	1	1,996	1,437	552	-	3	4
25 - 29	3,883	2,011	932	1,055	3	-	21	1,872	518	1,318	12	6	18
30 - 34	3,579	1,856	427	1,371	16	5	37	1,723	233	1,412	19	10	49
35 - 39	3,115	1,558	259	1,247	21	5	26	1,557	168	1,294	22	26	47
40 - 44	3,277	1,633	243	1,308	29	10	43	1,644	148	1,387	23	40	46
45 - 49	2,856	1,460	201	1,192	24	15	28	1,396	75	1,212	22	46	41
50 - 54	2,425	1,189	186	957	14	10	22	1,236	110	972	12	107	35
55 - 59	2,190	1,085	173	860	13	27	12	1,105	102	794	12	184	13
60 - 64	2,143	988	193	721	9	52	13	1,155	159	669	9	303	15
65 - 69	2,044	952	195	649	14	88	6	1,092	191	532	8	350	11
70 - 74	1,583	685	143	428	10	101	3	898	160	298	8	426	6
75 - 79	1,204	473	87	282	5	98	1	731	118	177	5	430	1
80 - 84	737	262	54	119	4	85	-	475	97	73	2	302	1
85 - 89	375	109	30	36	1	42	-	266	55	17	1	193	-
90 - 94	118	30	8	7	1	14	-	88	15	1	-	72	-
95 and over	25	2	-	1	-	1	-	23	5	2	-	16	-

Table 6 Population under 25 years by individual years and 25 years and over by quinquennial groups, sex and marital status – **continued**

Age	Persons	Males						Females					
		Total	Single	Married	Remarried	Widowed	Divorced	Total	Single	Married	Remarried	Widowed	Divorced
Ballymena													
ALL AGES	**56,641**	**27,830**	**14,001**	**12,349**	**346**	**651**	**483**	**28,811**	**12,579**	**12,667**	**311**	**2,624**	**630**
0	743	382	382					361	361				
1	819	407	407					412	412				
2	832	430	430					402	402				
3	909	470	470					439	439				
4	880	452	452					428	428				
0 - 4	4,183	2,141	2,141					2,042	2,042				
5	836	451	451					385	385				
6	861	453	453					408	408				
7	865	424	424					441	441				
8	906	466	466					440	440				
9	809	422	422					387	387				
5 - 9	4,277	2,216	2,216					2,061	2,061				
10	907	471	471					436	436				
11	885	451	451					434	434				
12	927	481	481					446	446				
13	795	404	404					391	391				
14	853	457	457					396	396				
10 - 14	4,367	2,264	2,264					2,103	2,103				
15	821	417	417					404	404				
16	869	425	424	1	-	-	-	444	444	-	-	-	-
17	979	529	529	-	-	-	-	450	448	2	-	-	-
18	993	527	524	3	-	-	-	466	461	5	-	-	-
19	947	475	468	7	-	-	-	472	448	24	-	-	-
15 - 19	4,609	2,373	2,362	11	-	-	-	2,236	2,205	31	-	-	-
20	998	559	543	16	-	-	-	439	397	42	-	-	-
21	934	471	446	24	-	-	1	463	388	73	-	-	2
22	898	470	408	62	-	-	-	428	290	135	3	-	-
23	946	475	384	91	-	-	-	471	283	184	1	-	3
24	890	446	306	135	-	-	5	444	236	202	-	1	5
20 - 24	4,666	2,421	2,087	328	-	-	6	2,245	1,594	636	4	1	10
25 - 29	4,114	2,058	945	1,056	10	2	45	2,056	609	1,363	16	5	63
30 - 34	3,747	1,862	402	1,371	31	2	56	1,885	276	1,482	40	11	76
35 - 39	3,798	1,893	269	1,498	45	6	75	1,905	162	1,543	71	20	109
40 - 44	3,754	1,885	224	1,507	65	13	76	1,869	130	1,544	56	28	111
45 - 49	3,527	1,717	162	1,401	57	14	83	1,810	153	1,479	39	59	80
50 - 54	3,047	1,505	158	1,236	33	22	56	1,542	142	1,227	27	81	65
55 - 59	2,714	1,317	151	1,076	31	27	32	1,397	143	1,022	20	159	53
60 - 64	2,577	1,184	164	906	24	61	29	1,393	200	888	12	267	26
65 - 69	2,297	1,060	181	764	17	84	14	1,237	167	653	9	383	25
70 - 74	1,840	812	114	580	16	98	4	1,028	190	402	9	422	5
75 - 79	1,518	604	94	368	8	129	5	914	174	241	7	488	4
80 - 84	958	325	39	179	7	99	1	633	127	128	1	375	2
85 - 89	472	150	26	56	1	66	1	322	66	20	-	235	1
90 - 94	144	39	2	12	1	24	-	105	27	7	-	71	-
95 and over	32	4	-	-	-	4	-	28	8	1	-	19	-

Table 6 Population under 25 years by individual years and 25 years and over by quinquennial groups, sex and marital status – **continued**

Age	Persons	Males						Females					
		Total	Single	Married	Remarried	Widowed	Divorced	Total	Single	Married	Remarried	Widowed	Divorced
Ballymoney													
ALL AGES	**24,198**	**12,022**	**6,408**	**5,135**	**81**	**257**	**141**	**12,176**	**5,546**	**5,249**	**73**	**1,116**	**192**
0	367	176	176					191	191				
1	399	219	219					180	180				
2	360	189	189					171	171				
3	377	191	191					186	186				
4	419	223	223					196	196				
0 - 4	1,922	998	998					924	924				
5	391	221	221					170	170				
6	413	218	218					195	195				
7	398	190	190					208	208				
8	412	198	198					214	214				
9	405	211	211					194	194				
5 - 9	2,019	1,038	1,038					981	981				
10	444	245	245					199	199				
11	399	206	206					193	193				
12	392	190	190					202	202				
13	386	206	206					180	180				
14	368	187	187					181	181				
10 - 14	1,989	1,034	1,034					955	955				
15	407	192	192					215	215				
16	367	183	183	-	-	-	-	184	184	-	-	-	-
17	383	215	215	-	-	-	-	168	167	1	-	-	-
18	396	216	216	-	-	-	-	180	176	4	-	-	-
19	402	213	212	1	-	-	-	189	179	10	-	-	-
15 - 19	1,955	1,019	1,018	1	-	-	-	936	921	15	-	-	-
20	390	213	208	5	-	-	-	177	155	22	-	-	-
21	410	198	182	16	-	-	-	212	175	37	-	-	-
22	405	207	182	25	-	-	-	198	150	48	-	-	-
23	384	200	161	39	-	-	-	184	116	67	-	-	1
24	351	176	124	52	-	-	-	175	90	84	1	-	-
20 - 24	1,940	994	857	137	-	-	-	946	686	258	1	-	1
25 - 29	1,830	911	461	437	2	-	11	919	233	657	3	1	25
30 - 34	1,704	865	190	646	7	2	20	839	133	657	13	6	30
35 - 39	1,513	771	129	603	15	2	22	742	89	607	10	11	25
40 - 44	1,445	755	102	614	13	5	21	690	58	565	11	15	41
45 - 49	1,482	717	100	577	11	7	22	765	62	636	9	26	32
50 - 54	1,218	611	79	500	8	11	13	607	42	500	11	39	15
55 - 59	1,086	530	81	417	4	13	15	556	69	395	5	77	10
60 - 64	1,101	505	83	378	9	28	7	596	87	385	4	118	2
65 - 69	1,042	494	85	352	4	50	3	548	98	250	2	192	6
70 - 74	845	356	64	237	3	47	5	489	86	183	1	217	2
75 - 79	543	237	50	148	4	35	-	306	47	86	1	170	2
80 - 84	334	128	23	67	1	35	2	206	43	40	1	121	1
85 - 89	188	49	13	20	-	16	-	139	26	14	-	99	-
90 - 94	35	9	3	1	-	5	-	26	5	1	1	19	-
95 and over	7	1	-	-	-	1	-	6	1	-	-	5	-

Table 6 Population under 25 years by individual years and 25 years and over by quinquennial groups, sex and marital status – **continued**

Age	Persons	Males						Females					
		Total	Single	Married	Remarried	Widowed	Divorced	Total	Single	Married	Remarried	Widowed	Divorced
Banbridge													
ALL AGES	**33,482**	**16,568**	**8,523**	**7,298**	**169**	**375**	**203**	**16,914**	**7,435**	**7,404**	**185**	**1,608**	**282**
0	492	279	279					213	213				
1	511	268	268					243	243				
2	551	287	287					264	264				
3	529	256	256					273	273				
4	540	287	287					253	253				
0 - 4	2,623	1,377	1,377					1,246	1,246				
5	527	252	252					275	275				
6	553	288	288					265	265				
7	519	278	278					241	241				
8	521	262	262					259	259				
9	600	303	303					297	297				
5 - 9	2,720	1,383	1,383					1,337	1,337				
10	616	332	332					284	284				
11	586	275	275					311	311				
12	501	253	253					248	248				
13	539	293	293					246	246				
14	520	259	259					261	261				
10 - 14	2,762	1,412	1,412					1,350	1,350				
15	485	269	269					216	216				
16	509	261	261	-	-	-	-	248	248	-	-	-	-
17	522	275	274	1	-	-	-	247	244	3	-	-	-
18	567	284	282	2	-	-	-	283	276	7	-	-	-
19	546	279	278	1	-	-	-	267	261	6	-	-	-
15 - 19	2,629	1,368	1,364	4	-	-	-	1,261	1,245	16	-	-	-
20	517	270	265	5	-	-	-	247	225	22	-	-	-
21	510	267	250	17	-	-	-	243	200	43	-	-	-
22	531	268	239	29	-	-	-	263	193	67	-	-	3
23	500	259	220	38	-	-	1	241	155	85	-	-	1
24	503	258	188	66	-	1	3	245	130	112	-	-	3
20 - 24	2,561	1,322	1,162	155	-	1	4	1,239	903	329	-	-	7
25 - 29	2,567	1,287	613	660	-	1	13	1,280	384	859	9	2	26
30 - 34	2,576	1,296	279	964	18	2	33	1,280	161	1,019	26	7	67
35 - 39	2,183	1,147	183	904	25	2	33	1,036	98	864	30	10	34
40 - 44	2,151	1,059	136	860	24	3	36	1,092	75	916	29	33	39
45 - 49	2,014	1,016	101	853	30	10	22	998	67	822	28	43	38
50 - 54	1,656	794	81	669	14	15	15	862	57	682	22	71	30
55 - 59	1,484	699	93	563	14	15	14	785	66	596	7	98	18
60 - 64	1,395	686	89	531	13	38	15	709	75	474	11	142	7
65 - 69	1,366	630	94	460	12	57	7	736	86	391	12	241	6
70 - 74	1,136	480	65	329	7	71	8	656	108	230	7	305	6
75 - 79	848	346	46	215	5	78	2	502	70	139	3	287	3
80 - 84	515	178	28	96	6	47	1	337	70	51	1	215	-
85 - 89	226	74	13	33	1	27	-	152	28	14	-	110	-
90 - 94	60	10	3	2	-	5	-	50	9	2	-	38	1
95 and over	10	4	1	-	-	3	-	6	-	-	-	6	-

Table 6 Population under 25 years by individual years and 25 years and over by quinquennial groups, sex and marital status – **continued**

Age	Persons	Males						Females					
		Total	Single	Married	Remarried	Widowed	Divorced	Total	Single	Married	Remarried	Widowed	Divorced
Belfast													
ALL AGES	**279,237**	**130,820**	**68,802**	**53,480**	**1,581**	**4,357**	**2,600**	**148,417**	**67,646**	**56,818**	**1,539**	**18,154**	**4,260**
0	4,207	2,161	2,161					2,046	2,046				
1	4,220	2,125	2,125					2,095	2,095				
2	4,426	2,233	2,233					2,193	2,193				
3	4,369	2,225	2,225					2,144	2,144				
4	4,537	2,349	2,349					2,188	2,188				
0 - 4	21,759	11,093	11,093					10,666	10,666				
5	4,448	2,272	2,272					2,176	2,176				
6	4,260	2,207	2,207					2,053	2,053				
7	4,165	2,100	2,100					2,065	2,065				
8	4,015	2,059	2,059					1,956	1,956				
9	3,922	1,978	1,978					1,944	1,944				
5 - 9	20,810	10,616	10,616					10,194	10,194				
10	4,017	2,100	2,100					1,917	1,917				
11	4,058	2,129	2,129					1,929	1,929				
12	3,811	1,896	1,896					1,915	1,915				
13	3,746	1,879	1,879					1,867	1,867				
14	3,700	1,921	1,921					1,779	1,779				
10 - 14	19,332	9,925	9,925					9,407	9,407				
15	3,614	1,823	1,823					1,791	1,791				
16	3,756	1,869	1,865	4	-	-	-	1,887	1,883	4	-	-	-
17	3,818	1,939	1,937	1	-	1	-	1,879	1,873	6	-	-	-
18	3,950	2,038	2,032	5	-	1	-	1,912	1,890	22	-	-	-
19	4,045	2,027	2,004	22	-	-	1	2,018	1,960	58	-	-	-
15 - 19	19,183	9,696	9,661	32	-	2	1	9,487	9,397	90	-	-	-
20	4,424	2,151	2,086	65	-	-	-	2,273	2,108	164	1	-	-
21	4,338	2,147	2,023	121	1	-	2	2,191	1,899	285	-	2	5
22	4,669	2,222	1,990	229	-	-	3	2,447	1,961	463	4	3	16
23	4,776	2,337	1,985	348	1	-	3	2,439	1,794	624	2	3	16
24	4,720	2,236	1,768	460	1	-	7	2,484	1,613	825	1	5	40
20 - 24	22,927	11,093	9,852	1,223	3	-	15	11,834	9,375	2,361	8	13	77
25 - 29	23,264	10,873	6,128	4,532	36	8	169	12,391	5,486	6,388	68	38	411
30 - 34	20,066	9,491	3,015	6,015	119	21	321	10,575	2,508	7,053	211	91	712
35 - 39	15,911	7,841	1,653	5,539	232	24	393	8,070	1,308	5,698	243	130	691
40 - 44	15,001	7,289	1,221	5,376	241	59	392	7,712	955	5,692	247	193	625
45 - 49	14,616	7,069	1,058	5,334	204	77	396	7,547	844	5,636	183	391	493
50 - 54	13,656	6,501	824	5,043	167	164	303	7,155	736	5,291	144	561	423
55 - 59	13,891	6,445	802	5,016	127	274	226	7,446	882	5,149	117	1,014	284
60 - 64	14,531	6,513	864	4,907	113	444	185	8,018	1,121	4,782	95	1,799	221
65 - 69	14,044	6,062	846	4,289	112	711	104	7,982	1,222	3,889	94	2,625	152
70 - 74	11,215	4,479	550	3,000	95	780	54	6,736	981	2,533	68	3,058	96
75 - 79	9,120	3,253	379	1,979	73	786	36	5,867	1,000	1,422	38	3,358	49
80 - 84	5,926	1,734	204	883	41	601	5	4,192	824	596	19	2,734	19
85 - 89	2,841	649	83	258	14	294	-	2,192	514	188	3	1,482	5
90 - 94	913	169	23	48	4	94	-	744	180	42	1	520	1
95 and over	231	29	5	6	-	18	-	202	46	8	-	147	1

Table 6 Population under 25 years by individual years and 25 years and over by quinquennial groups, sex and marital status – **continued**

Age	Persons	Males						Females					
		Total	Single	Married	Remarried	Widowed	Divorced	Total	Single	Married	Remarried	Widowed	Divorced
Carrickfergus													
ALL AGES	**32,750**	**15,871**	**7,400**	**7,375**	**366**	**378**	**352**	**16,879**	**6,831**	**7,621**	**332**	**1,600**	**495**
0	498	243	243					255	255				
1	553	285	285					268	268				
2	519	249	249					270	270				
3	530	277	277					253	253				
4	539	288	288					251	251				
0 - 4	2,639	1,342	1,342					1,297	1,297				
5	549	278	278					271	271				
6	481	250	250					231	231				
7	499	250	250					249	249				
8	483	246	246					237	237				
9	453	225	225					228	228				
5 - 9	2,465	1,249	1,249					1,216	1,216				
10	510	255	255					255	255				
11	496	257	257					239	239				
12	469	240	240					229	229				
13	453	224	224					229	229				
14	447	220	220					227	227				
10 - 14	2,375	1,196	1,196					1,179	1,179				
15	418	211	211					207	207				
16	460	251	251	-	-	-	-	209	209	-	-	-	-
17	481	257	255	2	-	-	-	224	223	1	-	-	-
18	533	285	284	1	-	-	-	248	242	6	-	-	-
19	490	222	220	2	-	-	-	268	258	10	-	-	-
15 - 19	2,382	1,226	1,221	5	-	-	-	1,156	1,139	17	-	-	-
20	492	228	217	11	-	-	-	264	234	29	-	-	1
21	497	264	247	17	-	-	-	233	184	49	-	-	-
22	525	276	233	43	-	-	-	249	159	87	1	-	2
23	508	250	191	58	-	-	1	258	130	124	1	1	2
24	548	278	175	98	1	-	4	270	122	138	1	-	9
20 - 24	2,570	1,296	1,063	227	1	-	5	1,274	829	427	3	1	14
25 - 29	2,920	1,414	555	819	9	-	31	1,506	400	1,029	23	2	52
30 - 34	2,606	1,290	219	970	38	-	63	1,316	156	1,024	46	12	78
35 - 39	2,167	1,076	148	821	47	2	58	1,091	84	845	69	11	82
40 - 44	2,082	1,022	101	794	66	2	59	1,060	56	863	46	17	78
45 - 49	2,023	1,007	65	836	64	5	37	1,016	52	822	39	41	62
50 - 54	1,654	827	45	692	32	16	42	827	40	653	32	57	45
55 - 59	1,565	751	42	624	30	31	24	814	60	603	24	90	37
60 - 64	1,469	682	43	563	20	36	20	787	50	528	22	169	18
65 - 69	1,284	573	44	436	20	64	9	711	59	376	11	251	14
70 - 74	1,038	443	28	309	20	83	3	595	56	250	11	271	7
75 - 79	724	254	20	170	10	54	-	470	65	120	5	275	5
80 - 84	474	150	13	82	6	48	1	324	51	48	1	222	2
85 - 89	228	54	5	22	1	26	-	174	30	14	-	129	1
90 - 94	69	16	1	5	2	8	-	53	8	2	-	43	-
95 and over	16	3	-	-	-	3	-	13	4	-	-	9	-

Table 6 Population under 25 years by individual years and 25 years and over by quinquennial groups, sex and marital status – **continued**

Age	Persons	Males						Females					
		Total	Single	Married	Remarried	Widowed	Divorced	Total	Single	Married	Remarried	Widowed	Divorced
Castlereagh													
ALL AGES	**60,799**	**28,946**	**12,735**	**14,372**	**528**	**788**	**523**	**31,853**	**12,253**	**14,736**	**490**	**3,540**	**834**
0	855	401	401					454	454				
1	870	434	434					436	436				
2	794	399	399					395	395				
3	800	393	393					407	407				
4	797	394	394					403	403				
0 - 4	4,116	2,021	2,021					2,095	2,095				
5	779	421	421					358	358				
6	752	370	370					382	382				
7	681	329	329					352	352				
8	697	371	371					326	326				
9	730	401	401					329	329				
5 - 9	3,639	1,892	1,892					1,747	1,747				
10	765	408	408					357	357				
11	769	398	398					371	371				
12	717	348	348					369	369				
13	699	364	364					335	335				
14	660	343	343					317	317				
10 - 14	3,610	1,861	1,861					1,749	1,749				
15	756	380	380					376	376				
16	739	391	391	-	-	-	-	348	348	-	-	-	-
17	776	407	407	-	-	-	-	369	367	2	-	-	-
18	837	429	428	1	-	-	-	408	405	3	-	-	-
19	883	465	462	3	-	-	-	418	408	10	-	-	-
15 - 19	3,991	2,072	2,068	4	-	-	-	1,919	1,904	15	-	-	-
20	941	510	498	12	-	-	-	431	401	30	-	-	-
21	895	429	406	22	-	-	1	466	405	61	-	-	-
22	884	454	420	34	-	-	-	430	345	82	-	-	3
23	893	442	387	54	-	-	1	451	309	138	-	1	3
24	933	436	331	103	-	-	2	497	304	187	-	1	5
20 - 24	4,546	2,271	2,042	225	-	-	4	2,275	1,764	498	-	2	11
25 - 29	4,999	2,432	1,110	1,269	13	2	38	2,567	840	1,633	21	3	70
30 - 34	4,824	2,382	552	1,726	42	3	59	2,442	442	1,792	62	6	140
35 - 39	3,821	1,890	265	1,478	62	4	81	1,931	240	1,471	86	23	111
40 - 44	3,594	1,715	177	1,379	71	18	70	1,879	172	1,448	85	42	132
45 - 49	3,794	1,805	134	1,498	76	12	85	1,989	153	1,609	55	64	108
50 - 54	3,406	1,605	95	1,361	58	23	68	1,801	119	1,415	50	129	88
55 - 59	3,376	1,564	99	1,340	38	46	41	1,812	142	1,365	34	215	56
60 - 64	3,648	1,647	123	1,365	40	84	35	2,001	157	1,382	31	375	56
65 - 69	3,355	1,525	127	1,203	40	135	20	1,830	173	1,017	26	580	34
70 - 74	2,492	1,073	80	795	46	142	10	1,419	153	606	20	627	13
75 - 79	1,779	692	50	468	23	142	9	1,087	165	303	10	600	9
80 - 84	1,048	326	25	180	14	104	3	722	121	120	8	469	4
85 - 89	540	135	11	67	2	55	-	405	82	51	2	269	1
90 - 94	180	33	2	13	2	16	-	147	27	8	-	111	1
95 and over	41	5	1	1	1	2	-	36	8	3	-	25	-

Table 6 Population under 25 years by individual years and 25 years and over by quinquennial groups, sex and marital status – **continued**

Age	Persons	Males						Females					
		Total	Single	Married	Remarried	Widowed	Divorced	Total	Single	Married	Remarried	Widowed	Divorced
Coleraine													
ALL AGES	**50,438**	**24,369**	**12,399**	**10,596**	**361**	**558**	**455**	**26,069**	**11,559**	**10,939**	**328**	**2,567**	**676**
0	768	392	392					376	376				
1	738	355	355					383	383				
2	763	411	411					352	352				
3	744	372	372					372	372				
4	849	463	463					386	386				
0 - 4	3,862	1,993	1,993					1,869	1,869				
5	806	435	435					371	371				
6	767	410	410					357	357				
7	739	382	382					357	357				
8	687	362	362					325	325				
9	736	396	396					340	340				
5 - 9	3,735	1,985	1,985					1,750	1,750				
10	748	365	365					383	383				
11	830	433	433					397	397				
12	730	388	388					342	342				
13	716	373	373					343	343				
14	774	379	379					395	395				
10 - 14	3,798	1,938	1,938					1,860	1,860				
15	750	368	368					382	382				
16	791	390	388	2	-	-	-	401	401	-	-	-	-
17	852	439	439	-	-	-	-	413	411	2	-	-	-
18	894	440	439	1	-	-	-	454	447	7	-	-	-
19	845	416	408	8	-	-	-	429	422	7	-	-	-
15 - 19	4,132	2,053	2,042	11	-	-	-	2,079	2,063	16	-	-	-
20	877	420	409	11	-	-	-	457	418	39	-	-	-
21	830	392	371	21	-	-	-	438	372	65	-	-	1
22	816	382	345	37	-	-	-	434	341	90	-	1	2
23	768	363	289	73	-	-	1	405	237	163	-	-	5
24	758	359	270	85	1	-	3	399	208	183	2	-	6
20 - 24	4,049	1,916	1,684	227	1	-	4	2,133	1,576	540	2	1	14
25 - 29	3,764	1,860	923	899	7	1	30	1,904	634	1,172	15	7	76
30 - 34	3,621	1,800	461	1,220	32	3	84	1,821	320	1,341	47	8	105
35 - 39	3,244	1,629	253	1,267	45	1	63	1,615	153	1,270	49	21	122
40 - 44	3,226	1,587	204	1,247	41	8	87	1,639	118	1,326	55	26	114
45 - 49	2,958	1,489	162	1,207	55	15	50	1,469	118	1,196	46	42	67
50 - 54	2,754	1,303	146	1,031	39	22	65	1,451	145	1,094	37	104	71
55 - 59	2,338	1,140	140	899	31	38	32	1,198	113	876	16	159	34
60 - 64	2,182	1,002	120	781	32	52	17	1,180	142	747	23	240	28
65 - 69	2,129	970	130	731	20	75	14	1,159	149	608	10	372	20
70 - 74	1,778	752	93	536	20	95	8	1,026	168	399	14	429	16
75 - 79	1,429	530	61	343	15	110	1	899	148	250	7	488	6
80 - 84	846	281	42	148	16	75	-	565	125	74	3	361	2
85 - 89	416	109	17	39	6	47	-	307	67	26	3	210	1
90 - 94	146	26	4	10	-	12	-	120	35	3	1	81	-
95 and over	31	6	1	-	1	4	-	25	6	1	-	18	-

Table 6 Population under 25 years by individual years and 25 years and over by quinquennial groups, sex and marital status – **continued**

Age	Persons	Males						Females					
		Total	Single	Married	Remarried	Widowed	Divorced	Total	Single	Married	Remarried	Widowed	Divorced
Cookstown													
ALL AGES	**31,082**	**15,503**	**8,777**	**6,256**	**71**	**287**	**112**	**15,579**	**7,656**	**6,361**	**69**	**1,325**	**168**
0	546	278	278					268	268				
1	591	313	313					278	278				
2	567	288	288					279	279				
3	575	283	283					292	292				
4	600	317	317					283	283				
0 - 4	2,879	1,479	1,479					1,400	1,400				
5	582	315	315					267	267				
6	604	316	316					288	288				
7	594	280	280					314	314				
8	560	291	291					269	269				
9	587	293	293					294	294				
5 - 9	2,927	1,495	1,495					1,432	1,432				
10	633	324	324					309	309				
11	621	304	304					317	317				
12	546	286	286					260	260				
13	584	284	284					300	300				
14	531	286	286					245	245				
10 - 14	2,915	1,484	1,484					1,431	1,431				
15	575	298	298					277	277				
16	555	291	291	-	-	-	-	264	263	1	-	-	-
17	588	314	313	1	-	-	-	274	271	3	-	-	-
18	591	305	304	1	-	-	-	286	280	6	-	-	-
19	538	292	291	1	-	-	-	246	231	15	-	-	-
15 - 19	2,847	1,500	1,497	3	-	-	-	1,347	1,322	25	-	-	-
20	553	271	265	6	-	-	-	282	250	32	-	-	-
21	515	265	240	25	-	-	-	250	206	42	2	-	-
22	489	239	205	33	-	-	1	250	182	68	-	-	-
23	462	240	199	40	-	-	1	222	118	101	-	2	1
24	465	238	153	83	-	-	2	227	109	117	-	-	1
20 - 24	2,484	1,253	1,062	187	-	-	4	1,231	865	360	2	2	2
25 - 29	2,268	1,155	491	656	-	2	6	1,113	312	777	4	2	18
30 - 34	2,154	1,076	226	826	8	-	16	1,078	146	888	9	10	25
35 - 39	1,875	931	132	768	12	2	17	944	73	810	11	16	34
40 - 44	1,888	946	119	788	11	7	21	942	63	828	10	20	21
45 - 49	1,691	849	120	702	9	6	12	842	58	720	8	36	20
50 - 54	1,383	699	103	559	7	16	14	684	62	534	8	62	18
55 - 59	1,149	574	92	447	5	23	7	575	53	440	4	67	11
60 - 64	1,176	589	135	417	4	26	7	587	75	369	4	132	7
65 - 69	1,113	521	123	348	5	40	5	592	93	281	6	207	5
70 - 74	954	417	96	277	4	40	-	537	86	184	1	264	2
75 - 79	713	293	66	171	2	51	3	420	93	95	-	228	4
80 - 84	375	152	34	76	2	40	-	223	52	26	1	144	-
85 - 89	203	62	18	21	2	21	-	141	28	17	1	94	1
90 - 94	73	24	5	7	-	12	-	49	10	4	-	35	-
95 and over	15	4	-	3	-	1	-	11	2	3	-	6	-

Table 6 Population under 25 years by individual years and 25 years and over by quinquennial groups, sex and marital status – **continued**

Age	Persons	Males						Females					
		Total	Single	Married	Remarried	Widowed	Divorced	Total	Single	Married	Remarried	Widowed	Divorced
Craigavon													
ALL AGES	**74,986**	**36,511**	**18,849**	**15,926**	**401**	**799**	**536**	**38,475**	**17,295**	**16,462**	**381**	**3,439**	**898**
0	1,256	661	661					595	595				
1	1,256	650	650					606	606				
2	1,279	669	669					610	610				
3	1,294	657	657					637	637				
4	1,315	683	683					632	632				
0 - 4	6,400	3,320	3,320					3,080	3,080				
5	1,257	659	659					598	598				
6	1,265	616	616					649	649				
7	1,264	645	645					619	619				
8	1,181	604	604					577	577				
9	1,165	587	587					578	578				
5 - 9	6,132	3,111	3,111					3,021	3,021				
10	1,251	667	667					584	584				
11	1,275	650	650					625	625				
12	1,251	615	615					636	636				
13	1,136	568	568					568	568				
14	1,091	580	580					511	511				
10 - 14	6,004	3,080	3,080					2,924	2,924				
15	1,147	582	582					565	565				
16	1,211	642	640	2	-	-	-	569	566	3	-	-	-
17	1,209	607	607	-	-	-	-	602	601	1	-	-	-
18	1,233	664	662	2	-	-	-	569	553	16	-	-	-
19	1,296	652	640	12	-	-	-	644	600	44	-	-	-
15 - 19	6,096	3,147	3,131	16	-	-	-	2,949	2,885	64	-	-	-
20	1,291	654	633	19	1	-	1	637	568	69	-	-	-
21	1,241	647	590	57	-	-	-	594	467	124	2	-	1
22	1,287	636	545	90	-	-	1	651	451	195	1	1	3
23	1,257	605	464	139	1	-	1	652	419	231	-	-	2
24	1,230	599	427	170	-	-	2	631	316	306	-	1	8
20 - 24	6,306	3,141	2,659	475	2	-	5	3,165	2,221	925	3	2	14
25 - 29	6,170	3,093	1,345	1,702	14	2	30	3,077	910	2,062	17	11	77
30 - 34	5,380	2,651	561	1,988	32	5	65	2,729	362	2,150	52	25	140
35 - 39	4,608	2,268	303	1,811	60	8	86	2,340	244	1,825	85	28	158
40 - 44	4,700	2,304	266	1,873	71	12	82	2,396	208	1,920	76	43	149
45 - 49	4,390	2,134	205	1,750	71	24	84	2,256	156	1,840	47	82	131
50 - 54	3,769	1,854	141	1,554	46	46	67	1,915	128	1,523	31	150	83
55 - 59	3,431	1,642	183	1,341	27	44	47	1,789	154	1,321	28	220	66
60 - 64	3,131	1,458	165	1,160	22	79	32	1,673	217	1,040	17	358	41
65 - 69	2,797	1,238	141	930	28	121	18	1,559	187	806	12	534	20
70 - 74	2,173	907	106	648	9	127	17	1,266	185	517	4	548	12
75 - 79	1,802	679	68	456	11	142	2	1,123	172	309	6	632	4
80 - 84	1,051	334	44	166	5	118	1	717	142	116	2	454	3
85 - 89	467	113	17	45	3	48	-	354	72	33	1	248	-
90 - 94	136	30	3	11	-	16	-	106	18	11	-	77	-
95 and over	43	7	-	-	-	7	-	36	9	-	-	27	-

Table 6 Population under 25 years by individual years and 25 years and over by quinquennial groups, sex and marital status – **continued**

Age	Persons	Males						Females					
		Total	Single	Married	Remarried	Widowed	Divorced	Total	Single	Married	Remarried	Widowed	Divorced
Derry													
ALL AGES	**95,371**	**46,708**	**27,478**	**17,501**	**293**	**938**	**498**	**48,663**	**25,374**	**18,618**	**310**	**3,454**	**907**
0	1,799	905	905					894	894				
1	1,787	915	915					872	872				
2	1,835	929	929					906	906				
3	1,973	1,021	1,021					952	952				
4	1,946	992	992					954	954				
0 - 4	9,340	4,762	4,762					4,578	4,578				
5	1,944	1,017	1,017					927	927				
6	1,925	1,024	1,024					901	901				
7	2,001	1,049	1,049					952	952				
8	1,899	954	954					945	945				
9	1,856	948	948					908	908				
5 - 9	9,625	4,992	4,992					4,633	4,633				
10	1,968	984	984					984	984				
11	1,958	1,005	1,005					953	953				
12	1,840	949	949					891	891				
13	1,787	926	926					861	861				
14	1,790	933	933					857	857				
10 - 14	9,343	4,797	4,797					4,546	4,546				
15	1,766	917	917					849	849				
16	1,768	903	902	1	-	-	-	865	864	1	-	-	-
17	1,751	878	878	-	-	-	-	873	871	2	-	-	-
18	1,762	908	905	3	-	-	-	854	838	16	-	-	-
19	1,717	916	906	10	-	-	-	801	773	28	-	-	-
15 - 19	8,764	4,522	4,508	14	-	-	-	4,242	4,195	47	-	-	-
20	1,720	872	848	23	-	-	1	848	777	70	-	-	1
21	1,640	863	805	58	-	-	-	777	624	152	-	-	1
22	1,709	914	807	105	-	-	2	795	608	186	1	-	-
23	1,658	818	647	168	-	-	3	840	518	312	2	-	8
24	1,474	724	493	230	-	-	1	750	408	335	2	-	5
20 - 24	8,201	4,191	3,600	584	-	-	7	4,010	2,935	1,055	5	-	15
25 - 29	7,546	3,611	1,640	1,924	11	3	33	3,935	1,322	2,481	24	20	88
30 - 34	6,824	3,256	780	2,366	34	3	73	3,568	537	2,786	50	25	170
35 - 39	5,919	2,863	429	2,295	45	14	80	3,056	341	2,467	51	35	162
40 - 44	5,519	2,791	388	2,267	42	15	79	2,728	223	2,245	43	50	167
45 - 49	4,763	2,329	277	1,895	43	32	82	2,434	201	1,996	32	96	109
50 - 54	4,105	2,041	263	1,636	24	58	60	2,064	203	1,596	35	170	60
55 - 59	3,639	1,763	268	1,362	32	63	38	1,876	238	1,322	25	229	62
60 - 64	3,348	1,568	256	1,155	15	120	22	1,780	293	1,055	10	390	32
65 - 69	2,871	1,204	190	851	10	141	12	1,667	319	751	14	564	19
70 - 74	2,281	945	163	606	16	150	10	1,336	276	442	7	596	15
75 - 79	1,628	597	93	335	14	153	2	1,031	238	235	10	541	7
80 - 84	1,006	325	50	158	7	110	-	681	154	94	3	429	1
85 - 89	487	114	17	43	-	54	-	373	104	36	1	232	-
90 - 94	125	29	4	8	-	17	-	96	29	8	-	59	-
95 and over	37	8	1	2	-	5	-	29	9	2	-	18	-

Table 6 Population under 25 years by individual years and 25 years and over by quinquennial groups, sex and marital status – **continued**

Age	Persons	Males Total	Males Single	Males Married	Males Remarried	Males Widowed	Males Divorced	Females Total	Females Single	Females Married	Females Remarried	Females Widowed	Females Divorced
Down													
ALL AGES	**58,008**	**28,835**	**15,833**	**11,820**	**270**	**619**	**293**	**29,173**	**13,575**	**12,096**	**283**	**2,776**	**443**
0	980	512	512					468	468				
1	1,001	518	518					483	483				
2	915	483	483					432	432				
3	1,028	528	528					500	500				
4	1,029	506	506					523	523				
0 - 4	4,953	2,547	2,547					2,406	2,406				
5	1,015	539	539					476	476				
6	1,018	520	520					498	498				
7	1,005	537	537					468	468				
8	1,033	520	520					513	513				
9	994	504	504					490	490				
5 - 9	5,065	2,620	2,620					2,445	2,445				
10	1,097	589	589					508	508				
11	1,052	553	553					499	499				
12	986	474	474					512	512				
13	985	525	525					460	460				
14	[illegible]	475	475					448	448				
10 - 14	5,043	2,616	2,616					2,427	2,427				
15	933	509	509					424	424				
16	967	493	490	3	-	-	-	474	473	1	-	-	-
17	968	479	479	-	-	-	-	489	488	1	-	-	-
18	1,038	564	561	3	-	-	-	474	464	10	-	-	-
19	968	550	544	6	-	-	-	418	391	26	-	-	1
15 - 19	4,874	2,595	2,583	12	-	-	-	2,279	2,240	38	-	-	1
20	1,019	549	528	21	-	-	-	470	429	41	-	-	-
21	912	485	453	32	-	-	-	427	340	87	-	-	-
22	978	530	468	61	-	-	1	448	334	106	1	1	6
23	852	446	354	91	-	-	1	406	232	171	-	-	3
24	842	462	321	139	-	-	2	380	195	179	1	1	4
20 - 24	4,603	2,472	2,124	344	-	-	4	2,131	1,530	584	2	2	13
25 - 29	4,272	2,171	1,042	1,100	11	1	17	2,101	616	1,424	17	4	40
30 - 34	3,993	1,971	440	1,471	18	4	38	2,022	250	1,670	35	12	55
35 - 39	3,690	1,863	277	1,500	31	5	50	1,827	165	1,504	51	21	86
40 - 44	3,688	1,885	271	1,512	44	15	43	1,803	130	1,513	45	31	84
45 - 49	3,218	1,637	241	1,310	34	12	40	1,581	101	1,338	35	57	50
50 - 54	2,749	1,354	163	1,095	25	31	40	1,395	132	1,082	24	108	49
55 - 59	2,386	1,154	172	896	28	37	21	1,232	128	887	22	173	22
60 - 64	2,314	1,072	176	799	19	57	21	1,242	150	757	16	302	17
65 - 69	2,247	1,026	180	729	19	90	8	1,221	207	605	16	387	6
70 - 74	1,834	811	156	529	19	99	8	1,023	189	360	8	455	11
75 - 79	1,415	543	110	310	14	107	2	872	182	210	5	468	7
80 - 84	958	345	82	162	4	96	1	613	129	82	3	398	1
85 - 89	498	111	23	40	2	46	-	387	104	30	3	249	1
90 - 94	168	35	8	11	2	14	-	133	37	10	1	85	-
95 and over	40	7	2	-	-	5	-	33	7	2	-	24	-

Table 6 Population under 25 years by individual years and 25 years and over by quinquennial groups, sex and marital status – **continued**

Age	Persons	Males						Females					
		Total	Single	Married	Remarried	Widowed	Divorced	Total	Single	Married	Remarried	Widowed	Divorced
Dungannon													
ALL AGES	**45,428**	**22,556**	**12,814**	**9,055**	**99**	**444**	**144**	**22,872**	**11,155**	**9,285**	**98**	**2,117**	**217**
0	773	389	389					384	384				
1	804	426	426					378	378				
2	786	410	410					376	376				
3	755	370	370					385	385				
4	866	460	460					406	406				
0 - 4	3,984	2,055	2,055					1,929	1,929				
5	827	431	431					396	396				
6	796	429	429					367	367				
7	868	439	439					429	429				
8	839	405	405					434	434				
9	839	424	424					415	415				
5 - 9	4,169	2,128	2,128					2,041	2,041				
10	859	427	427					432	432				
11	865	454	454					411	411				
12	880	446	446					434	434				
13	817	404	404					413	413				
14	839	398	398					441	441				
10 - 14	4,260	2,129	2,129					2,131	2,131				
15	842	430	430					412	412				
16	863	454	454	-	-	-	-	409	409	-	-	-	-
17	839	416	415	1	-	-	-	423	422	1	-	-	-
18	875	459	459	-	-	-	-	416	410	6	-	-	-
19	813	422	414	8	-	-	-	391	368	23	-	-	-
15 - 19	4,232	2,181	2,172	9	-	-	-	2,051	2,021	30	-	-	-
20	798	425	411	14	-	-	-	373	332	39	-	1	1
21	680	359	329	30	-	-	-	321	250	69	-	2	-
22	668	318	285	33	-	-	-	350	251	99	-	-	-
23	656	358	301	57	-	-	-	298	194	101	-	-	3
24	600	305	218	86	-	-	1	295	157	137	1	-	-
20 - 24	3,402	1,765	1,544	220	-	-	1	1,637	1,184	445	1	3	4
25 - 29	3,243	1,644	801	834	2	1	6	1,599	472	1,096	2	3	26
30 - 34	3,075	1,562	353	1,174	10	2	23	1,513	197	1,249	16	9	42
35 - 39	2,740	1,402	244	1,123	12	2	21	1,338	140	1,136	10	19	33
40 - 44	2,721	1,362	226	1,098	12	6	20	1,359	90	1,189	11	32	37
45 - 49	2,377	1,209	177	984	4	21	23	1,168	88	981	20	54	25
50 - 54	2,122	1,042	153	842	14	14	19	1,080	97	857	10	96	20
55 - 59	2,000	977	177	748	7	34	11	1,023	111	727	6	168	11
60 - 64	1,912	899	165	675	10	44	5	1,013	136	615	4	254	4
65 - 69	1,707	789	155	554	9	63	8	918	129	439	9	333	8
70 - 74	1,442	630	164	385	7	70	4	812	141	285	7	377	2
75 - 79	1,029	420	96	252	7	65	-	609	98	141	2	366	2
80 - 84	636	239	51	116	4	66	2	397	91	69	-	235	2
85 - 89	271	92	21	32	1	37	1	179	47	16	-	115	1
90 - 94	88	23	3	8	-	12	-	65	10	10	-	45	-
95 and over	18	8	-	1	-	7	-	10	2	-	-	8	-

Table 6 Population under 25 years by individual years and 25 years and over by quinquennial groups, sex and marital status – **continued**

Age	Persons	Males						Females					
		Total	Single	Married	Remarried	Widowed	Divorced	Total	Single	Married	Remarried	Widowed	Divorced
Fermanagh													
ALL AGES	**54,033**	**27,095**	**15,535**	**10,606**	**153**	**572**	**229**	**26,938**	**12,958**	**10,921**	**137**	**2,663**	**259**
0	795	397	397					398	398				
1	862	441	441					421	421				
2	911	451	451					460	460				
3	878	491	491					387	387				
4	992	507	507					485	485				
0 - 4	4,438	2,287	2,287					2,151	2,151				
5	972	487	487					485	485				
6	922	461	461					461	461				
7	1,020	533	533					487	487				
8	973	476	476					497	497				
9	946	493	493					453	453				
5 - 9	4,833	2,450	2,450					2,383	2,383				
10	997	498	498					499	499				
11	1,026	536	536					490	490				
12	959	477	477					482	482				
13	929	468	468					461	461				
14	932	463	463					469	469				
10 - 14	4,843	2,442	2,442					2,401	2,401				
15	953	476	476					477	477				
16	893	483	483	-	-	-	-	410	410	-	-	-	-
17	976	506	505	1	-	-	-	470	468	2	-	-	-
18	949	503	502	1	-	-	-	446	436	10	-	-	-
19	943	476	470	6	-	-	-	467	449	18	-	-	-
15 - 19	4,714	2,444	2,436	8	-	-	-	2,270	2,240	30	-	-	-
20	860	447	442	5	-	-	-	413	380	33	-	-	-
21	813	388	375	12	-	1	-	425	362	60	-	1	2
22	720	386	354	32	-	-	-	334	267	64	-	1	2
23	716	365	319	46	-	-	-	351	223	126	-	1	1
24	673	333	258	73	-	-	2	340	181	158	-	-	1
20 - 24	3,762	1,919	1,748	168	-	1	2	1,863	1,413	441	-	3	6
25 - 29	3,677	1,910	1,018	883	2	1	6	1,767	569	1,178	2	3	15
30 - 34	3,597	1,787	488	1,250	13	5	31	1,810	249	1,487	15	11	48
35 - 39	3,471	1,818	338	1,412	24	3	41	1,653	165	1,406	20	13	49
40 - 44	3,437	1,736	321	1,347	19	8	41	1,701	143	1,450	26	38	44
45 - 49	2,876	1,483	261	1,151	20	13	38	1,393	116	1,155	22	63	37
50 - 54	2,414	1,232	247	926	18	19	22	1,182	100	945	12	103	22
55 - 59	2,321	1,162	276	835	6	30	15	1,159	123	817	8	200	11
60 - 64	2,301	1,126	297	764	8	46	11	1,175	167	719	10	266	13
65 - 69	2,318	1,072	304	663	14	84	7	1,246	193	585	11	450	7
70 - 74	1,972	961	278	577	12	86	8	1,011	176	361	7	464	3
75 - 79	1,544	700	203	375	10	106	6	844	162	207	3	469	3
80 - 84	924	384	96	174	6	107	1	540	114	95	1	329	1
85 - 89	428	135	36	57	1	41	-	293	71	37	-	185	-
90 - 94	112	35	7	13	-	15	-	77	18	5	-	54	-
95 and over	31	12	2	3	-	7	-	19	4	3	-	12	-

Table 6 Population under 25 years by individual years and 25 years and over by quinquennial groups, sex and marital status – **continued**

Age	Persons	Males						Females					
		Total	Single	Married	Remarried	Widowed	Divorced	Total	Single	Married	Remarried	Widowed	Divorced
Larne													
ALL AGES	**29,419**	**14,318**	**7,092**	**6,369**	**219**	**372**	**266**	**15,101**	**6,468**	**6,523**	**190**	**1,593**	**327**
0	425	226	226					199	199				
1	398	212	212					186	186				
2	449	241	241					208	208				
3	432	221	221					211	211				
4	428	210	210					218	218				
0 - 4	2,132	1,110	1,110					1,022	1,022				
5	418	197	197					221	221				
6	404	204	204					200	200				
7	427	224	224					203	203				
8	409	201	201					208	208				
9	431	222	222					209	209				
5 - 9	2,089	1,048	1,048					1,041	1,041				
10	435	221	221					214	214				
11	428	201	201					227	227				
12	406	187	187					219	219				
13	394	191	191					203	203				
14	396	210	210					186	186				
10 - 14	2,059	1,010	1,010					1,049	1,049				
15	428	215	215					213	213				
16	472	227	227	-	-	-	-	245	245	-	-	-	-
17	467	251	250	1	-	-	-	216	214	2	-	-	-
18	489	253	253	-	-	-	-	236	230	6	-	-	-
19	465	230	229	1	-	-	-	235	222	13	-	-	-
15 - 19	2,321	1,176	1,174	2	-	-	-	1,145	1,124	21	-	-	-
20	496	255	245	10	-	-	-	241	227	13	-	-	1
21	468	232	221	11	-	-	-	236	206	30	-	-	-
22	490	238	210	28	-	-	-	252	191	59	-	-	2
23	452	235	199	35	-	-	1	217	145	70	-	1	1
24	436	218	173	44	-	-	1	218	121	96	1	-	-
20 - 24	2,342	1,178	1,048	128	-	-	2	1,164	890	268	1	1	4
25 - 29	2,192	1,068	537	510	6	2	13	1,124	346	738	10	4	26
30 - 34	2,152	1,112	288	776	11	1	36	1,040	181	765	28	6	60
35 - 39	1,815	942	178	683	38	-	43	873	81	682	44	20	46
40 - 44	1,932	951	133	733	34	7	44	981	74	814	32	12	49
45 - 49	1,835	953	95	763	34	19	42	882	56	722	18	28	58
50 - 54	1,566	780	85	626	23	15	31	786	54	642	17	46	27
55 - 59	1,525	749	78	594	23	29	25	776	57	583	14	95	27
60 - 64	1,429	651	72	512	17	36	14	778	77	508	7	171	15
65 - 69	1,321	619	88	452	13	61	5	702	96	352	8	240	6
70 - 74	1,093	457	71	306	10	62	8	636	94	230	9	301	2
75 - 79	793	292	45	174	4	66	3	501	92	126	1	279	3
80 - 84	529	160	21	85	3	51	-	369	83	55	1	228	2
85 - 89	206	52	10	23	3	16	-	154	31	13	-	108	2
90 - 94	67	6	-	2	-	4	-	61	12	2	-	47	-
95 and over	21	4	1	-	-	3	-	17	8	2	-	7	-

Table 6 Population under 25 years by individual years and 25 years and over by quinquennial groups, sex and marital status – **continued**

Age	Persons	Males						Females					
		Total	Single	Married	Remarried	Widowed	Divorced	Total	Single	Married	Remarried	Widowed	Divorced
Limavady													
ALL AGES	**29,567**	**15,042**	**8,557**	**5,907**	**127**	**279**	**172**	**14,525**	**7,205**	**5,953**	**139**	**1,029**	**199**
0	518	279	279					239	239				
1	555	299	299					256	256				
2	551	273	273					278	278				
3	519	265	265					254	254				
4	578	293	293					285	285				
0 - 4	2,721	1,409	1,409					1,312	1,312				
5	541	286	286					255	255				
6	506	264	264					242	242				
7	557	293	293					264	264				
8	576	297	297					279	279				
9	573	288	288					285	285				
5 - 9	2,753	1,428	1,428					1,325	1,325				
10	545	278	278					267	267				
11	584	297	297					287	287				
12	490	255	255					235	235				
13	551	279	279					272	272				
14	526	260	260					266	266				
10 - 14	2,696	1,369	1,369					1,327	1,327				
15	582	308	308					274	274				
16	559	271	270	1	-	-	-	288	288	-	-	-	-
17	578	287	286	1	-	-	-	291	291	-	-	-	-
18	581	322	319	3	-	-	-	259	254	5	-	-	-
19	582	309	306	3	-	-	-	273	255	16	-	-	2
15 - 19	2,882	1,497	1,489	8	-	-	-	1,385	1,362	21	-	-	2
20	631	348	331	17	-	-	-	283	241	42	-	-	-
21	537	294	268	26	-	-	-	243	180	62	-	-	1
22	570	300	264	36	-	-	-	270	171	98	-	-	1
23	504	285	203	81	-	-	1	219	128	90	-	-	1
24	517	279	189	89	-	-	1	238	110	125	1	-	2
20 - 24	2,759	1,506	1,255	249	-	-	2	1,253	830	417	1	-	5
25 - 29	2,448	1,278	521	720	11	3	23	1,170	284	843	19	4	20
30 - 34	2,103	1,075	229	799	15	-	32	1,028	116	842	27	8	35
35 - 39	1,929	994	147	795	23	4	25	935	90	779	26	13	27
40 - 44	1,794	923	110	758	22	7	26	871	60	734	23	14	40
45 - 49	1,564	767	92	637	12	9	17	797	69	660	14	28	26
50 - 54	1,259	655	98	513	12	13	19	604	46	480	11	50	17
55 - 59	996	479	80	367	9	16	7	517	57	375	9	63	13
60 - 64	1,000	482	84	353	8	27	10	518	64	313	1	133	7
65 - 69	919	429	95	292	8	29	5	490	89	240	3	153	5
70 - 74	706	334	67	207	3	53	4	372	52	139	3	176	2
75 - 79	514	216	34	142	1	38	1	298	63	65	1	169	-
80 - 84	318	134	35	48	3	47	1	184	32	28	-	124	-
85 - 89	141	47	9	13	-	25	-	94	20	11	1	62	-
90 - 94	48	17	5	6	-	6	-	31	6	4	-	21	-
95 and over	17	3	1	-	-	2	-	14	1	2	-	11	-

Table 6 Population under 25 years by individual years and 25 years and over by quinquennial groups, sex and marital status – **continued**

Age	Persons	Males Total	Males Single	Males Married	Males Remarried	Males Widowed	Males Divorced	Females Total	Females Single	Females Married	Females Remarried	Females Widowed	Females Divorced
Lisburn													
ALL AGES	**99,458**	**48,653**	**24,588**	**21,420**	**796**	**978**	**871**	**50,805**	**22,338**	**22,172**	**744**	**4,298**	**1,253**
0	1,643	838	838					805	805				
1	1,687	854	854					833	833				
2	1,711	898	898					813	813				
3	1,724	882	882					842	842				
4	1,701	869	869					832	832				
0 - 4	8,466	4,341	4,341					4,125	4,125				
5	1,777	888	888					889	889				
6	1,738	916	916					822	822				
7	1,676	863	863					813	813				
8	1,655	864	864					791	791				
9	1,630	851	851					779	779				
5 - 9	8,476	4,382	4,382					4,094	4,094				
10	1,760	850	850					910	910				
11	1,655	880	880					775	775				
12	1,540	754	754					786	786				
13	1,464	722	722					742	742				
14	1,550	776	776					774	774				
10 - 14	7,969	3,982	3,982					3,987	3,987				
15	1,465	752	752					713	713				
16	1,470	748	748	-	-	-	-	722	721	1	-	-	-
17	1,449	760	759	1	-	-	-	689	688	1	-	-	-
18	1,540	773	773	-	-	-	-	767	753	14	-	-	-
19	1,564	837	828	9	-	-	-	727	700	27	-	-	-
15 - 19	7,488	3,870	3,860	10	-	-	-	3,618	3,575	43	-	-	-
20	1,641	835	813	22	-	-	-	806	734	72	-	-	-
21	1,575	823	778	43	-	-	2	752	623	128	-	-	1
22	1,568	805	710	95	-	-	-	763	549	210	-	1	3
23	1,595	849	671	177	-	-	1	746	481	258	3	1	3
24	1,688	838	596	237	1	-	4	850	419	418	3	1	9
20 - 24	8,067	4,150	3,568	574	1	-	7	3,917	2,806	1,086	6	3	16
25 - 29	8,335	4,168	1,859	2,222	20	4	63	4,167	1,154	2,827	46	10	130
30 - 34	7,840	3,862	786	2,863	67	5	141	3,978	508	3,140	99	21	210
35 - 39	6,821	3,452	449	2,711	129	8	155	3,369	271	2,737	144	32	185
40 - 44	6,537	3,249	287	2,661	156	18	127	3,288	209	2,655	136	74	214
45 - 49	5,919	2,937	226	2,434	115	30	132	2,982	166	2,454	94	113	155
50 - 54	4,822	2,323	161	1,936	86	43	97	2,499	178	1,976	62	149	134
55 - 59	4,316	2,078	168	1,729	57	61	63	2,238	175	1,694	51	242	76
60 - 64	3,907	1,775	147	1,445	50	93	40	2,132	173	1,390	37	480	52
65 - 69	3,501	1,560	145	1,205	45	147	18	1,941	191	1,043	37	628	42
70 - 74	2,756	1,154	99	847	38	152	18	1,602	238	622	21	700	21
75 - 79	2,041	745	77	463	14	186	5	1,296	207	295	6	780	8
80 - 84	1,324	425	38	245	13	126	3	899	165	154	4	569	7
85 - 89	647	150	8	56	5	79	2	497	87	49	1	357	3
90 - 94	183	43	4	17	-	22	-	140	21	5	-	114	-
95 and over	43	7	1	2	-	4	-	36	8	2	-	26	-

Table 6 Population under 25 years by individual years and 25 years and over by quinquennial groups, sex and marital status – **continued**

Age	Persons	Males						Females					
		Total	Single	Married	Remarried	Widowed	Divorced	Total	Single	Married	Remarried	Widowed	Divorced
Magherafelt													
ALL AGES	**36,293**	**18,177**	**10,496**	**7,121**	**80**	**369**	**111**	**18,116**	**9,112**	**7,309**	**65**	**1,460**	**170**
0	601	328	328					273	273				
1	669	328	328					341	341				
2	652	354	354					298	298				
3	676	359	359					317	317				
4	703	356	356					347	347				
0 - 4	3,301	1,725	1,725					1,576	1,576				
5	676	335	335					341	341				
6	674	353	353					321	321				
7	667	333	333					334	334				
8	666	351	351					315	315				
9	657	340	340					317	317				
5 - 9	3,340	1,712	1,712					1,628	1,628				
10	722	352	352					370	370				
11	670	308	308					362	362				
12	706	357	357					349	349				
13	641	340	340					301	301				
14	646	316	316					330	330				
10 - 14	3,385	1,673	1,673					1,712	1,712				
15	633	310	310					323	323				
16	658	337	337	-	-	-	-	321	321	-	-	-	-
17	682	373	373	-	-	-	-	309	307	2	-	-	-
18	660	335	335	-	-	-	-	325	319	6	-	-	-
19	699	370	367	3	-	-	-	329	318	10	-	-	1
15 - 19	3,332	1,725	1,722	3	-	-	-	1,607	1,588	18	-	-	1
20	675	365	356	9	-	-	-	310	275	34	-	-	1
21	692	356	338	18	-	-	-	336	278	58	-	-	-
22	620	335	288	46	-	-	1	285	201	84	-	-	-
23	588	303	249	54	-	-	-	285	181	102	-	-	2
24	524	294	201	92	-	-	1	230	106	120	1	2	1
20 - 24	3,099	1,653	1,432	219	-	-	2	1,446	1,041	398	1	2	4
25 - 29	2,680	1,363	640	712	1	1	9	1,317	399	899	4	2	13
30 - 34	2,537	1,254	294	934	13	-	13	1,283	198	1,034	12	7	32
35 - 39	2,216	1,155	211	912	9	5	18	1,061	119	891	9	9	33
40 - 44	2,161	1,077	163	873	11	5	25	1,084	102	909	9	29	35
45 - 49	1,871	919	121	761	10	12	15	952	79	811	8	34	20
50 - 54	1,565	765	125	610	11	12	7	800	76	636	5	73	10
55 - 59	1,459	719	125	555	7	25	7	740	83	542	4	103	8
60 - 64	1,390	667	133	481	3	45	5	723	89	449	1	176	8
65 - 69	1,247	621	136	435	3	42	5	626	100	311	7	205	3
70 - 74	1,108	517	123	314	10	67	3	591	114	226	4	246	1
75 - 79	836	350	83	195	2	70	-	486	102	134	1	248	1
80 - 84	450	180	49	88	-	42	1	270	57	36	-	176	1
85 - 89	233	78	26	22	-	29	1	155	34	11	-	110	-
90 - 94	74	21	3	6	-	12	-	53	14	4	-	35	-
95 and over	9	3	-	1	-	2	-	6	1	-	-	5	-

Table 6 Population under 25 years by individual years and 25 years and over by quinquennial groups, sex and marital status – **continued**

Age	Persons	Males						Females					
		Total	Single	Married	Remarried	Widowed	Divorced	Total	Single	Married	Remarried	Widowed	Divorced
Moyle													
ALL AGES	**14,789**	**7,355**	**4,191**	**2,831**	**54**	**201**	**78**	**7,434**	**3,572**	**2,914**	**48**	**785**	**115**
0	227	115	115					112	112				
1	234	126	126					108	108				
2	233	113	113					120	120				
3	233	129	129					104	104				
4	267	142	142					125	125				
0 - 4	1,194	625	625					569	569				
5	237	112	112					125	125				
6	262	150	150					112	112				
7	248	123	123					125	125				
8	240	129	129					111	111				
9	245	126	126					119	119				
5 - 9	1,232	640	640					592	592				
10	267	133	133					134	134				
11	269	141	141					128	128				
12	291	139	139					152	152				
13	232	113	113					119	119				
14	233	117	117					116	116				
10 - 14	1,292	643	643					649	649				
15	267	135	135					132	132				
16	280	162	162	-	-	-	-	118	118	-	-	-	-
17	263	129	129	-	-	-	-	134	134	-	-	-	-
18	287	155	153	2	-	-	-	132	129	3	-	-	-
19	259	135	134	1	-	-	-	124	119	5	-	-	-
15 - 19	1,356	716	713	3	-	-	-	640	632	8	-	-	-
20	233	119	113	5	-	-	1	114	101	12	-	-	1
21	231	127	117	10	-	-	-	104	89	15	-	-	-
22	208	128	111	16	-	-	1	80	61	19	-	-	-
23	187	88	76	12	-	-	-	99	58	41	-	-	-
24	202	94	76	17	-	-	1	108	53	54	-	-	1
20 - 24	1,061	556	493	60	-	-	3	505	362	141	-	-	2
25 - 29	983	499	258	236	1	-	4	484	161	306	1	1	15
30 - 34	950	474	152	305	7	-	10	476	77	375	5	5	14
35 - 39	907	464	108	331	11	3	11	443	46	362	10	3	22
40 - 44	885	479	76	378	7	6	12	406	38	341	5	6	16
45 - 49	807	388	69	297	3	3	16	419	45	325	8	23	18
50 - 54	722	361	60	288	3	2	8	361	41	274	4	33	9
55 - 59	642	321	73	231	4	7	6	321	54	212	4	45	6
60 - 64	637	290	69	196	4	17	4	347	53	207	3	78	6
65 - 69	662	307	74	202	4	25	2	355	57	178	5	112	3
70 - 74	544	258	60	155	5	38	-	286	60	97	-	129	-
75 - 79	459	191	50	98	4	37	2	268	58	59	2	146	3
80 - 84	278	98	14	35	1	48	-	180	41	22	1	115	1
85 - 89	128	38	12	15	-	11	-	90	24	6	-	60	-
90 - 94	34	5	-	1	-	4	-	29	7	1	-	21	-
95 and over	16	2	2	-	-	-	-	14	6	-	-	8	-

Table 6 Population under 25 years by individual years and 25 years and over by quinquennial groups, sex and marital status – **continued**

Age	Persons	Males						Females					
		Total	Single	Married	Remarried	Widowed	Divorced	Total	Single	Married	Remarried	Widowed	Divorced
Newry and Mourne													
ALL AGES	**82,943**	**41,307**	**23,708**	**16,180**	**225**	**850**	**344**	**41,636**	**20,841**	**16,468**	**222**	**3,557**	**548**
0	1,423	758	758					665	665				
1	1,472	768	768					704	704				
2	1,483	784	784					699	699				
3	1,574	804	804					770	770				
4	1,540	792	792					748	748				
0 - 4	7,492	3,906	3,906					3,586	3,586				
5	1,514	742	742					772	772				
6	1,519	776	776					743	743				
7	1,610	841	841					769	769				
8	1,597	827	827					770	770				
9	1,563	763	763					800	800				
5 - 9	7,803	3,949	3,949					3,854	3,854				
10	1,616	798	798					818	818				
11	1,645	827	827					818	818				
12	1,531	775	775					756	756				
13	1,555	795	795					760	760				
14	1,479	772	772					707	707				
10 - 14	7,826	3,967	3,967					3,859	3,859				
15	1,408	743	743					665	665				
16	1,470	783	782	1	-	-	-	687	687	-	-	-	-
17	1,507	766	764	2	-	-	-	741	736	4	-	1	-
18	1,525	787	785	2	-	-	-	738	724	14	-	-	-
19	1,517	847	839	8	-	-	-	670	642	28	-	-	-
15 - 19	7,427	3,926	3,913	13	-	-	-	3,501	3,454	46	-	1	-
20	1,543	846	816	30	-	-	-	697	631	65	-	-	1
21	1,430	716	657	58	-	-	1	714	614	99	-	-	1
22	1,407	745	650	94	1	-	-	662	512	147	-	-	3
23	1,313	673	516	157	-	-	-	640	380	252	1	2	5
24	1,227	637	460	174	-	-	3	590	294	293	1	1	1
20 - 24	6,920	3,617	3,099	513	1	-	4	3,303	2,431	856	2	3	11
25 - 29	6,174	3,183	1,515	1,636	11	3	18	2,991	952	1,968	16	6	49
30 - 34	5,769	2,879	646	2,146	23	7	57	2,890	430	2,297	32	22	109
35 - 39	5,197	2,643	402	2,157	31	7	46	2,554	237	2,169	35	22	91
40 - 44	4,880	2,466	343	2,021	30	12	60	2,414	186	2,052	33	56	87
45 - 49	4,173	2,057	278	1,676	28	22	53	2,116	165	1,764	27	88	72
50 - 54	3,604	1,818	259	1,445	22	51	41	1,786	160	1,417	20	141	48
55 - 59	3,455	1,682	320	1,270	18	43	31	1,773	207	1,261	9	266	30
60 - 64	3,134	1,446	279	1,052	13	88	14	1,688	238	1,026	18	383	23
65 - 69	3,015	1,405	283	961	20	129	12	1,610	298	748	9	542	13
70 - 74	2,415	1,051	247	636	11	155	2	1,364	248	462	14	632	8
75 - 79	1,885	746	175	412	9	144	6	1,139	242	250	5	639	3
80 - 84	1,055	381	75	183	6	117	-	674	160	107	1	402	4
85 - 89	507	135	38	46	2	49	-	372	95	34	1	242	-
90 - 94	158	37	13	9	-	15	-	121	26	8	-	87	-
95 and over	54	13	1	4	-	8	-	41	13	3	-	25	-

Table 6 Population under 25 years by individual years and 25 years and over by quinquennial groups, sex and marital status – **continued**

Age	Persons	Males						Females					
		Total	Single	Married	Remarried	Widowed	Divorced	Total	Single	Married	Remarried	Widowed	Divorced
Newtownabbey													
ALL AGES	**74,035**	**35,760**	**16,725**	**16,885**	**665**	**819**	**666**	**38,275**	**15,508**	**17,396**	**642**	**3,626**	**1,103**
0	1,125	587	587					538	538				
1	1,035	561	561					474	474				
2	1,050	508	508					542	542				
3	1,155	597	597					558	558				
4	1,062	555	555					507	507				
0 - 4	5,427	2,808	2,808					2,619	2,619				
5	1,085	528	528					557	557				
6	1,101	548	548					553	553				
7	1,059	521	521					538	538				
8	1,040	567	567					473	473				
9	1,104	557	557					547	547				
5 - 9	5,389	2,721	2,721					2,668	2,668				
10	1,112	576	576					536	536				
11	1,138	585	585					553	553				
12	1,122	601	601					521	521				
13	1,152	574	574					578	578				
14	1,084	540	540					544	544				
10 - 14	5,608	2,876	2,876					2,732	2,732				
15	1,124	591	591					533	533				
16	1,163	576	576	-	-	-	-	587	587	-	-	-	-
17	1,169	603	603	-	-	-	-	566	566	-	-	-	-
18	1,137	575	574	1	-	-	-	562	551	11	-	-	-
19	1,201	606	600	5	-	-	1	595	564	29	-	-	2
15 - 19	5,794	2,951	2,944	6	-	-	1	2,843	2,801	40	-	-	2
20	1,171	585	568	17	-	-	-	586	532	53	-	-	1
21	1,123	559	533	26	-	-	-	564	454	107	-	-	3
22	1,119	558	495	62	-	-	1	561	408	149	2	-	2
23	1,086	501	393	103	1	-	4	585	385	193	1	-	6
24	1,078	536	372	163	-	-	1	542	260	271	1	1	9
20 - 24	5,577	2,739	2,361	371	1	-	6	2,838	2,039	773	4	1	21
25 - 29	5,861	2,923	1,267	1,596	11	2	47	2,938	831	1,976	22	6	103
30 - 34	5,616	2,697	517	2,011	77	3	89	2,919	380	2,240	99	20	180
35 - 39	4,968	2,465	301	1,945	118	8	93	2,503	179	2,010	104	31	179
40 - 44	4,939	2,410	190	2,017	98	7	98	2,529	133	2,082	113	44	157
45 - 49	4,656	2,290	142	1,934	94	25	95	2,366	115	1,917	99	82	153
50 - 54	4,020	1,946	129	1,619	78	30	90	2,074	89	1,673	58	139	115
55 - 59	3,774	1,828	100	1,559	51	53	65	1,946	131	1,477	45	226	67
60 - 64	3,701	1,708	121	1,400	46	104	37	1,993	174	1,307	35	424	53
65 - 69	3,181	1,417	99	1,141	29	130	18	1,764	165	967	26	570	36
70 - 74	2,212	952	60	695	32	149	16	1,260	124	524	19	568	25
75 - 79	1,651	615	49	388	17	151	10	1,036	125	277	9	618	7
80 - 84	961	276	25	144	12	95	-	685	109	100	7	466	3
85 - 89	501	108	9	47	1	50	1	393	66	26	1	298	2
90 - 94	163	24	6	10	-	8	-	139	24	7	1	107	-
95 and over	36	6	-	2	-	4	-	30	4	-	-	26	-

Table 6 Population under 25 years by individual years and 25 years and over by quinquennial groups, sex and marital status - **continued**

Age	Persons	Males						Females					
		Total	Single	Married	Remarried	Widowed	Divorced	Total	Single	Married	Remarried	Widowed	Divorced
North Down													
ALL AGES	**71,832**	**34,284**	**15,374**	**16,508**	**869**	**826**	**707**	**37,548**	**14,674**	**16,853**	**807**	**4,130**	**1,084**
0	931	503	503					428	428				
1	856	429	429					427	427				
2	916	444	444					472	472				
3	922	477	477					445	445				
4	993	504	504					489	489				
0 - 4	4,618	2,357	2,357					2,261	2,261				
5	1,016	514	514					502	502				
6	971	498	498					473	473				
7	1,067	559	559					508	508				
8	976	514	514					462	462				
9	1,055	535	535					520	520				
5 - 9	5,085	2,620	2,620					2,465	2,465				
10	1,090	583	583					507	507				
11	1,196	618	618					578	578				
12	1,067	539	539					528	528				
13	1,032	498	498					534	534				
14	1,036	518	518					518	518				
10 - 14	5,421	2,756	2,756					2,665	2,665				
15	1,044	547	547					497	497				
16	1,060	542	542	-	-	-	-	518	516	2	-	-	-
17	1,097	547	546	1	-	-	-	550	547	3	-	-	-
18	1,073	546	541	5	-	-	-	527	517	10	-	-	-
19	1,036	540	534	6	-	-	-	496	486	10	-	-	-
15 - 19	5,310	2,722	2,710	12	-	-	-	2,588	2,563	25	-	-	-
20	1,024	526	517	9	-	-	-	498	458	39	-	-	1
21	1,031	502	471	31	-	-	-	529	455	73	-	-	1
22	971	486	441	45	-	-	-	485	382	103	-	-	-
23	923	478	391	86	1	-	-	445	275	166	1	-	3
24	946	472	335	136	1	-	-	474	259	210	-	1	4
20 - 24	4,895	2,464	2,155	307	2	-	-	2,431	1,829	591	1	1	9
25 - 29	4,795	2,345	1,048	1,245	16	1	35	2,450	717	1,608	42	10	73
30 - 34	5,078	2,455	514	1,760	78	3	100	2,623	349	2,030	82	13	149
35 - 39	4,870	2,420	292	1,873	126	7	122	2,450	195	1,930	134	18	173
40 - 44	5,427	2,644	203	2,195	128	7	111	2,783	168	2,252	142	43	178
45 - 49	5,065	2,507	166	2,094	125	20	102	2,558	132	2,060	129	74	163
50 - 54	3,618	1,801	113	1,496	93	16	83	1,817	105	1,428	76	104	104
55 - 59	3,350	1,611	89	1,340	64	58	60	1,739	140	1,267	54	202	76
60 - 64	3,225	1,433	103	1,143	71	71	45	1,792	160	1,166	47	352	67
65 - 69	3,385	1,445	92	1,170	60	94	29	1,940	197	1,085	46	564	48
70 - 74	2,844	1,161	71	901	45	136	8	1,683	177	719	28	732	27
75 - 79	2,306	843	42	580	37	174	10	1,463	193	443	15	801	11
80 - 84	1,542	456	26	276	17	136	1	1,086	200	193	8	681	4
85 - 89	721	193	13	97	6	76	1	528	117	49	1	359	2
90 - 94	231	41	4	17	1	19	-	190	34	5	2	149	-
95 and over	46	10	-	2	-	8	-	36	7	2	-	27	-

Table 6 Population under 25 years by individual years and 25 years and over by quinquennial groups, sex and marital status – **continued**

Age	Persons	Males						Females					
		Total	Single	Married	Remarried	Widowed	Divorced	Total	Single	Married	Remarried	Widowed	Divorced
Omagh													
ALL AGES	**45,809**	**23,022**	**13,652**	**8,642**	**111**	**449**	**168**	**22,787**	**11,603**	**8,842**	**111**	**1,956**	**275**
0	745	394	394					351	351				
1	793	416	416					377	377				
2	809	430	430					379	379				
3	822	418	418					404	404				
4	859	427	427					432	432				
0 - 4	4,028	2,085	2,085					1,943	1,943				
5	868	447	447					421	421				
6	860	463	463					397	397				
7	920	470	470					450	450				
8	891	440	440					451	451				
9	899	452	452					447	447				
5 - 9	4,438	2,272	2,272					2,166	2,166				
10	921	449	449					472	472				
11	920	464	464					456	456				
12	882	419	419					463	463				
13	847	433	433					414	414				
14	783	383	383					400	400				
10 - 14	4,353	2,148	2,148					2,205	2,205				
15	804	404	404					400	400				
16	803	419	419	-	-	-	-	384	384	-	-	-	-
17	861	437	437	-	-	-	-	424	418	6	-	-	-
18	878	449	447	2	-	-	-	429	419	10	-	-	-
19	861	460	452	8	-	-	-	401	379	22	-	-	-
15 - 19	4,207	2,169	2,159	10	-	-	-	2,038	2,000	38	-	-	-
20	787	433	417	16	-	-	-	354	318	36	-	-	-
21	770	429	394	35	-	-	-	341	274	66	-	-	1
22	765	363	318	45	-	-	-	402	307	95	-	-	-
23	670	349	278	70	-	-	1	321	217	102	-	1	1
24	641	337	247	90	-	-	-	304	158	145	1	-	-
20 - 24	3,633	1,911	1,654	256	-	-	1	1,722	1,274	444	1	1	2
25 - 29	3,317	1,696	884	798	3	1	10	1,621	536	1,048	8	4	25
30 - 34	3,301	1,656	454	1,172	8	2	20	1,645	241	1,343	14	9	38
35 - 39	3,022	1,569	300	1,224	11	6	28	1,453	132	1,230	15	16	60
40 - 44	2,644	1,375	240	1,078	18	9	30	1,269	110	1,068	17	30	44
45 - 49	2,316	1,166	199	925	14	9	19	1,150	94	956	13	53	34
50 - 54	1,950	972	187	734	12	23	16	978	86	774	11	76	31
55 - 59	1,725	884	199	637	11	22	15	841	103	588	9	124	17
60 - 64	1,706	814	209	542	10	45	8	892	95	548	8	233	8
65 - 69	1,614	774	204	501	6	56	7	840	162	362	6	305	5
70 - 74	1,357	627	181	350	12	75	9	730	159	235	4	327	5
75 - 79	1,131	496	155	255	5	79	2	635	142	125	4	360	4
80 - 84	643	273	79	120	-	72	2	370	84	58	-	228	-
85 - 89	311	97	35	27	1	33	1	214	54	21	1	137	1
90 - 94	93	30	6	8	-	16	-	63	16	3	-	43	1
95 and over	20	8	2	5	-	1	-	12	1	1	-	10	-

Table 6 Population under 25 years by individual years and 25 years and over by quinquennial groups, sex and marital status – **continued**

Local Government Districts

Age	Persons	Males						Females					
		Total	Single	Married	Remarried	Widowed	Divorced	Total	Single	Married	Remarried	Widowed	Divorced
Strabane													
ALL AGES	**36,141**	**18,116**	**10,650**	**6,884**	**72**	**374**	**136**	**18,025**	**9,055**	**7,152**	**85**	**1,531**	**202**
0	583	301	301					282	282				
1	647	331	331					316	316				
2	593	303	303					290	290				
3	645	328	328					317	317				
4	709	361	361					348	348				
0 - 4	3,177	1,624	1,624					1,553	1,553				
5	689	355	355					334	334				
6	656	369	369					287	287				
7	662	354	354					308	308				
8	684	333	333					351	351				
9	680	341	341					339	339				
5 - 9	3,371	1,752	1,752					1,619	1,619				
10	654	329	329					325	325				
11	690	370	370					320	320				
12	666	345	345					321	321				
13	681	330	330					351	351				
14	689	352	352					337	337				
10 - 14	3,380	1,726	1,726					1,654	1,654				
15	678	374	374					304	304				
16	714	362	362	-	-	-	-	352	352	-	-	-	-
17	726	369	369	-	-	-	-	357	355	2	-	-	-
18	725	399	397	2	-	-	-	326	319	6	-	1	-
19	700	374	370	4	-	-	-	326	310	16	-	-	-
15 - 19	3,543	1,878	1,872	6	-	-	-	1,665	1,640	24	-	1	-
20	663	323	317	6	-	-	-	340	305	35	-	-	-
21	603	306	289	17	-	-	-	297	231	66	-	-	-
22	586	308	268	40	-	-	-	278	205	70	-	2	1
23	578	304	253	50	1	-	-	274	162	108	1	-	3
24	571	297	211	84	-	-	2	274	133	134	-	1	6
20 - 24	3,001	1,538	1,338	197	1	-	2	1,463	1,036	413	1	3	10
25 - 29	2,684	1,377	645	720	1	1	10	1,307	413	868	2	5	19
30 - 34	2,309	1,150	324	796	8	2	20	1,159	175	923	16	11	34
35 - 39	2,098	1,066	195	843	2	6	20	1,032	106	864	10	14	38
40 - 44	2,210	1,096	176	884	10	7	19	1,114	72	975	18	18	31
45 - 49	1,883	948	139	758	12	15	24	935	99	751	12	48	25
50 - 54	1,663	844	144	662	10	12	16	819	71	648	2	74	24
55 - 59	1,474	732	130	559	5	25	13	742	88	531	6	109	8
60 - 64	1,448	686	183	455	7	37	4	762	118	461	6	174	3
65 - 69	1,271	610	143	398	5	60	4	661	112	313	7	225	4
70 - 74	1,023	470	103	302	5	58	2	553	102	196	1	251	3
75 - 79	807	326	87	169	2	67	1	481	87	119	3	271	1
80 - 84	520	200	48	97	3	51	1	320	71	45	1	201	2
85 - 89	195	67	15	28	1	23	-	128	28	13	-	87	-
90 - 94	71	22	4	10	-	8	-	49	10	5	-	34	-
95 and over	13	4	2	-	-	2	-	9	1	3	-	5	-

Table 7 Population by sex, marital status, area of enumeration, country of birth, and whether visitor to Northern Ireland

Birthplace	All persons	Males						Females					
		Total	Single	Married	Re-married	Widowed	Divorced	Total	Single	Married	Re-married	Widowed	Divorced
NORTHERN IRELAND													
TOTAL	**1,588,794**	**775,836**	**410,112**	**326,702**	**9,243**	**18,343**	**11,436**	**812,958**	**371,133**	**337,046**	**8,707**	**78,691**	**17,381**
Resident in Northern Ireland	**1,577,836**	**769,071**	**405,414**	**324,968**	**9,111**	**18,276**	**11,302**	**808,765**	**368,256**	**336,104**	**8,664**	**78,447**	**17,294**
Northern Ireland	1,452,509	709,605	380,775	295,197	7,354	16,324	9,955	742,904	346,069	304,544	7,360	69,357	15,574
Great Britain	64,734	34,010	13,782	16,953	1,347	964	964	30,724	10,946	14,487	863	3,405	1,023
Republic of Ireland	35,380	13,277	3,757	8,362	216	755	187	22,103	4,953	12,085	217	4,466	382
Commonwealth countries	8,427	4,232	2,080	1,956	82	45	69	4,195	1,725	1,998	79	288	105
Other countries and at sea	8,872	4,162	2,376	1,580	89	56	61	4,710	2,238	1,876	121	355	120
Birthplace not stated	7,914	3,785	2,644	920	23	132	66	4,129	2,325	1,114	24	576	90
Visitors to Northern Ireland	**10,958**	**6,765**	**4,698**	**1,734**	**132**	**67**	**134**	**4,193**	**2,877**	**942**	**43**	**244**	**87**
Northern Ireland	3,654	1,751	1,274	399	20	24	34	1,903	1,149	559	19	130	46
Great Britain	4,462	3,541	2,335	1,003	90	29	84	921	622	197	14	64	24
Republic of Ireland	1,201	450	362	76	3	7	2	751	647	64	3	34	3
Commonwealth countries	663	389	319	61	2	4	3	274	212	50	3	4	5
Other countries and at sea	842	546	342	181	14	1	8	296	218	59	3	8	8
Birthplace not stated	136	88	66	14	3	2	3	48	29	13	1	4	1
Antrim													
TOTAL	**44,851**	**22,383**	**11,919**	**9,215**	**371**	**456**	**422**	**22,468**	**10,364**	**9,437**	**342**	**1,747**	**578**
Resident in Northern Ireland	**44,516**	**22,135**	**11,776**	**9,126**	**362**	**455**	**416**	**22,381**	**10,321**	**9,409**	**338**	**1,737**	**576**
Northern Ireland	39,885	19,623	10,637	7,974	261	403	348	20,262	9,529	8,381	279	1,563	510
Great Britain	3,101	1,816	819	830	82	31	54	1,285	495	633	46	70	41
Republic of Ireland	671	268	74	166	6	18	4	403	79	228	4	81	11
Commonwealth countries	342	179	76	91	5	-	7	163	66	80	2	9	6
Other countries and at sea	346	163	107	48	6	-	2	183	101	67	7	4	4
Birthplace not stated	171	86	63	17	2	3	1	85	51	20	-	10	4
Visitors to Northern Ireland	**335**	**248**	**143**	**89**	**9**	**1**	**6**	**87**	**43**	**28**	**4**	**10**	**2**
Northern Ireland	99	60	45	12	1	1	1	39	19	13	2	4	1
Great Britain	197	169	87	69	8	-	5	28	12	12	1	2	1
Republic of Ireland	13	3	2	1	-	-	-	10	7	1	-	2	-
Commonwealth countries	10	7	3	4	-	-	-	3	1	2	-	-	-
Other countries and at sea	12	7	4	3	-	-	-	5	3	-	1	1	-
Birthplace not stated	4	2	2	-	-	-	-	2	1	-	-	1	-
Ards													
TOTAL	**64,994**	**31,635**	**14,817**	**14,848**	**651**	**732**	**587**	**33,359**	**13,383**	**15,236**	**583**	**3,259**	**898**
Resident in Northern Ireland	**64,764**	**31,527**	**14,755**	**14,811**	**648**	**728**	**585**	**33,237**	**13,321**	**15,192**	**582**	**3,248**	**894**
Northern Ireland	60,365	29,519	14,117	13,675	542	657	528	30,846	12,735	13,906	507	2,894	804
Great Britain	2,668	1,294	376	746	88	38	46	1,374	353	728	55	169	69
Republic of Ireland	884	304	46	221	8	25	4	580	65	355	7	142	11
Commonwealth countries	377	169	73	85	5	3	3	208	68	116	5	14	5
Other countries and at sea	317	164	83	69	5	4	3	153	59	65	8	17	4
Birthplace not stated	153	77	60	15	-	1	1	76	41	22	-	12	1
Visitors to Northern Ireland	**230**	**108**	**62**	**37**	**3**	**4**	**2**	**122**	**62**	**44**	**1**	**11**	**4**
Northern Ireland	132	58	37	19	1	1	-	74	39	30	1	3	1
Great Britain	62	33	17	12	2	1	1	29	11	10	-	5	3
Republic of Ireland	11	4	1	1	-	2	-	7	5	1	-	1	-
Commonwealth countries	10	5	2	3	-	-	-	5	3	2	-	-	-
Other countries and at sea	13	8	5	2	-	-	1	5	3	-	-	2	-
Birthplace not stated	2	-	-	-	-	-	-	2	1	1	-	-	-

Note: This table is on a usually resident + visitors base

Table 7 Population by sex, marital status, area of enumeration, country of birth, and whether visitor to Northern Ireland - **continued**

Birthplace	All persons	Males						Females					
		Total	Single	Married	Re-married	Widowed	Divorced	Total	Single	Married	Re-married	Widowed	Divorced
Armagh													
TOTAL	**52,180**	**26,003**	**14,458**	**10,603**	**171**	**554**	**217**	**26,177**	**12,452**	**10,761**	**155**	**2,520**	**289**
Resident in Northern Ireland	**51,817**	**25,741**	**14,296**	**10,515**	**164**	**553**	**213**	**26,076**	**12,376**	**10,744**	**155**	**2,514**	**287**
Northern Ireland	47,877	23,942	13,549	9,567	133	508	185	23,935	11,736	9,613	121	2,198	267
Great Britain	1,587	799	363	380	23	14	19	788	293	382	20	80	13
Republic of Ireland	1,708	685	170	476	4	27	8	1,023	184	631	9	192	7
Commonwealth countries	189	102	70	31	1	-	-	87	45	37	-	5	-
Other countries and at sea	174	76	44	30	1	-	1	98	44	45	3	6	-
Birthplace not stated	282	137	100	31	2	4	-	145	74	36	2	33	-
Visitors to Northern Ireland	**363**	**262**	**162**	**88**	**7**	**1**	**4**	**101**	**76**	**17**	**-**	**6**	**2**
Northern Ireland	142	72	55	15	-	1	1	70	51	12	-	5	2
Great Britain	181	170	94	66	7	-	3	11	9	2	-	-	-
Republic of Ireland	17	6	4	2	-	-	-	11	7	3	-	1	-
Commonwealth countries	8	4	3	1	-	-	-	4	4	-	-	-	-
Other countries and at sea	15	10	6	4	-	-	-	5	5	-	-	-	-
Birthplace not stated	-	-	-	-	-	-	-	-	-	-	-	-	-
Ballymena													
TOTAL	**56,822**	**27,923**	**14,064**	**12,372**	**346**	**656**	**485**	**28,899**	**12,636**	**12,685**	**313**	**2,633**	**632**
Resident in Northern Ireland	**56,641**	**27,830**	**14,001**	**12,349**	**346**	**651**	**483**	**28,811**	**12,579**	**12,667**	**311**	**2,624**	**630**
Northern Ireland	53,468	26,297	13,329	11,626	293	616	433	27,171	12,034	11,857	271	2,433	576
Great Britain	1,864	942	405	442	41	24	30	922	299	455	31	101	36
Republic of Ireland	567	236	75	142	5	5	9	331	60	199	5	60	7
Commonwealth countries	287	143	63	69	4	3	4	144	49	78	2	11	4
Other countries and at sea	267	124	71	47	3	1	2	143	73	54	2	12	2
Birthplace not stated	188	88	58	23	-	2	5	100	64	24	-	7	5
Visitors to Northern Ireland	**181**	**93**	**63**	**23**	**-**	**5**	**2**	**88**	**57**	**18**	**2**	**9**	**2**
Northern Ireland	123	64	48	13	-	2	1	59	45	9	1	4	-
Great Britain	28	15	8	4	-	2	1	13	4	4	1	3	1
Republic of Ireland	10	4	1	2	-	1	-	6	3	2	-	1	-
Commonwealth countries	11	5	3	2	-	-	-	6	2	3	-	1	-
Other countries and at sea	7	5	3	2	-	-	-	2	1	-	-	-	1
Birthplace not stated	2	-	-	-	-	-	-	2	2	-	-	-	-
Ballymoney													
TOTAL	**24,281**	**12,059**	**6,435**	**5,144**	**82**	**257**	**141**	**12,222**	**5,574**	**5,261**	**73**	**1,120**	**194**
Resident in Northern Ireland	**24,198**	**12,022**	**6,408**	**5,135**	**81**	**257**	**141**	**12,176**	**5,546**	**5,249**	**73**	**1,116**	**192**
Northern Ireland	23,158	11,572	6,232	4,902	66	238	134	11,586	5,362	4,955	58	1,037	174
Great Britain	598	272	106	137	10	13	6	326	92	172	9	41	12
Republic of Ireland	198	74	14	54	3	2	1	124	27	62	3	27	5
Commonwealth countries	88	32	12	19	1	-	-	56	19	30	3	3	1
Other countries and at sea	44	17	6	9	1	1	-	27	8	16	-	3	-
Birthplace not stated	112	55	38	14	-	3	-	57	38	14	-	5	-
Visitors to Northern Ireland	**83**	**37**	**27**	**9**	**1**	**-**	**-**	**46**	**28**	**12**	**-**	**4**	**2**
Northern Ireland	61	30	25	5	-	-	-	31	20	7	-	2	2
Great Britain	14	5	1	3	1	-	-	9	4	4	-	1	-
Republic of Ireland	2	-	-	-	-	-	-	2	1	-	-	1	-
Commonwealth countries	2	1	-	1	-	-	-	1	-	1	-	-	-
Other countries and at sea	4	1	1	-	-	-	-	3	3	-	-	-	-
Birthplace not stated	-	-	-	-	-	-	-	-	-	-	-	-	-

Note: This table is on a usually resident + visitors base

Table 7 Population by sex, marital status, area of enumeration, country of birth, and whether visitor to Northern Ireland – **continued**

Birthplace	All persons	Males						Females					
		Total	Single	Married	Re-married	Widowed	Divorced	Total	Single	Married	Re-married	Widowed	Divorced
Banbridge													
TOTAL	**33,578**	**16,611**	**8,550**	**7,308**	**170**	**380**	**203**	**16,967**	**7,471**	**7,418**	**185**	**1,611**	**282**
Resident in Northern Ireland	**33,482**	**16,568**	**8,523**	**7,298**	**169**	**375**	**203**	**16,914**	**7,435**	**7,404**	**185**	**1,608**	**282**
Northern Ireland	31,840	15,826	8,240	6,902	148	352	184	16,014	7,164	6,937	164	1,491	258
Great Britain	904	459	167	248	15	16	13	445	154	225	14	38	14
Republic of Ireland	404	127	30	88	4	4	1	277	45	160	3	62	7
Commonwealth countries	116	56	26	23	2	1	4	60	25	28	2	4	1
Other countries and at sea	107	48	26	21	-	1	-	59	16	35	2	5	1
Birthplace not stated	111	52	34	16	-	1	1	59	31	19	-	8	1
Visitors to Northern Ireland	**96**	**43**	**27**	**10**	**1**	**5**	**-**	**53**	**36**	**14**	**-**	**3**	**-**
Northern Ireland	66	30	23	4	1	2	-	36	25	9	-	2	-
Great Britain	16	8	1	5	-	2	-	8	5	3	-	-	-
Republic of Ireland	3	1	1	-	-	-	-	2	1	-	-	1	-
Commonwealth countries	2	1	1	-	-	-	-	1	1	-	-	-	-
Other countries and at sea	8	2	1	1	-	-	-	6	4	2	-	-	-
Birthplace not stated	1	1	-	-	-	1	-	-	-	-	-	-	-
Belfast													
TOTAL	**281,547**	**132,155**	**69,762**	**53,796**	**1,608**	**4,367**	**2,622**	**149,392**	**68,352**	**57,017**	**1,550**	**18,193**	**4,280**
Resident in Northern Ireland	**279,237**	**130,820**	**68,802**	**53,480**	**1,581**	**4,357**	**2,600**	**148,417**	**67,646**	**56,818**	**1,539**	**18,154**	**4,260**
Northern Ireland	259,214	121,776	64,904	49,238	1,345	3,928	2,361	137,438	63,279	52,594	1,367	16,302	3,896
Great Britain	9,316	4,607	1,753	2,315	175	205	159	4,709	1,821	1,839	106	749	194
Republic of Ireland	4,962	1,723	599	930	25	140	29	3,239	1,115	1,285	23	741	75
Commonwealth countries	1,916	984	517	424	17	14	12	932	422	405	14	62	29
Other countries and at sea	1,818	827	417	359	14	17	20	991	447	407	22	82	33
Birthplace not stated	2,011	903	612	214	5	53	19	1,108	562	288	7	218	33
Visitors to Northern Ireland	**2,310**	**1,335**	**960**	**316**	**27**	**10**	**22**	**975**	**706**	**199**	**11**	**39**	**20**
Northern Ireland	646	301	206	80	3	4	8	345	180	123	3	28	11
Great Britain	748	520	358	129	16	5	12	228	179	34	3	7	5
Republic of Ireland	333	162	145	17	-	-	-	171	161	8	-	2	-
Commonwealth countries	265	140	130	9	-	1	-	125	109	10	2	2	2
Other countries and at sea	298	201	114	77	8	-	2	97	73	20	2	-	2
Birthplace not stated	20	11	7	4	-	-	-	9	4	4	1	-	-
Carrickfergus													
TOTAL	**32,953**	**15,978**	**7,471**	**7,406**	**371**	**378**	**352**	**16,975**	**6,890**	**7,648**	**333**	**1,607**	**497**
Resident in Northern Ireland	**32,750**	**15,871**	**7,400**	**7,375**	**366**	**378**	**352**	**16,879**	**6,831**	**7,621**	**332**	**1,600**	**495**
Northern Ireland	30,152	14,654	6,985	6,732	303	325	309	15,498	6,414	6,954	290	1,401	439
Great Britain	1,746	877	271	476	52	43	35	869	271	419	32	113	34
Republic of Ireland	388	136	31	86	7	7	5	252	52	123	4	61	12
Commonwealth countries	208	102	52	45	2	2	1	106	30	60	5	7	4
Other countries and at sea	215	89	54	32	1	1	1	126	50	57	1	12	6
Birthplace not stated	41	13	7	4	1	-	1	28	14	8	-	6	-
Visitors to Northern Ireland	**203**	**107**	**71**	**31**	**5**	**-**	**-**	**96**	**59**	**27**	**1**	**7**	**2**
Northern Ireland	98	45	32	12	1	-	-	53	27	17	1	6	2
Great Britain	51	34	17	13	4	-	-	17	12	4	-	1	-
Republic of Ireland	27	10	10	-	-	-	-	17	16	1	-	-	-
Commonwealth countries	9	6	2	4	-	-	-	3	1	2	-	-	-
Other countries and at sea	17	11	9	2	-	-	-	6	3	3	-	-	-
Birthplace not stated	1	1	1	-	-	-	-	-	-	-	-	-	-

Note: This table is on a usually resident + visitors base

Table 7 Population by sex, marital status, area of enumeration, country of birth, and whether visitor to Northern Ireland – **continued**

Birthplace	All persons	Males						Females					
		Total	Single	Married	Re-married	Widowed	Divorced	Total	Single	Married	Re-married	Widowed	Divorced
Castlereagh													
TOTAL	**61,063**	**29,098**	**12,835**	**14,413**	**534**	**789**	**527**	**31,965**	**12,305**	**14,778**	**492**	**3,554**	**836**
Resident in Northern Ireland	**60,799**	**28,946**	**12,735**	**14,372**	**528**	**788**	**523**	**31,853**	**12,253**	**14,736**	**490**	**3,540**	**834**
Northern Ireland	56,496	26,957	12,167	13,155	448	704	483	29,539	11,638	13,535	455	3,142	769
Great Britain	2,383	1,197	296	756	61	51	33	1,186	313	613	21	195	44
Republic of Ireland	992	358	66	249	11	28	4	634	116	354	6	149	9
Commonwealth countries	391	202	78	118	2	2	2	189	56	111	4	13	5
Other countries and at sea	366	160	85	70	5	-	-	206	89	90	4	18	5
Birthplace not stated	171	72	43	24	1	3	1	99	41	33	-	23	2
Visitors to Northern Ireland	**264**	**152**	**100**	**41**	**6**	**1**	**4**	**112**	**52**	**42**	**2**	**14**	**2**
Northern Ireland	123	63	44	16	-	1	2	60	26	26	-	7	1
Great Britain	57	34	19	11	3	-	1	23	9	8	1	4	1
Republic of Ireland	12	4	3	-	1	-	-	8	4	-	1	3	-
Commonwealth countries	18	11	8	3	-	-	-	7	4	3	-	-	-
Other countries and at sea	47	36	26	9	-	-	1	11	8	3	-	-	-
Birthplace not stated	7	4	-	2	2	-	-	3	1	2	-	-	-
Coleraine													
TOTAL	**51,366**	**24,750**	**12,720**	**10,648**	**364**	**561**	**457**	**26,616**	**12,032**	**10,991**	**332**	**2,584**	**677**
Resident in Northern Ireland	**50,438**	**24,369**	**12,399**	**10,596**	**361**	**558**	**455**	**26,069**	**11,559**	**10,939**	**328**	**2,567**	**676**
Northern Ireland	46,281	22,425	11,630	9,623	292	480	400	23,856	10,788	9,952	269	2,240	607
Great Britain	2,420	1,214	471	601	56	44	42	1,206	439	528	44	146	49
Republic of Ireland	920	343	72	231	9	26	5	577	136	280	5	145	11
Commonwealth countries	339	169	89	71	3	2	4	170	71	82	1	13	3
Other countries and at sea	330	137	78	53	-	3	3	193	88	81	8	12	4
Birthplace not stated	148	81	59	17	1	3	1	67	37	16	1	11	2
Visitors to Northern Ireland	**928**	**381**	**321**	**52**	**3**	**3**	**2**	**547**	**473**	**52**	**4**	**17**	**1**
Northern Ireland	180	82	65	16	1	-	-	98	64	24	2	7	1
Great Britain	284	133	112	15	2	3	1	151	127	15	2	7	-
Republic of Ireland	308	83	69	14	-	-	-	225	219	4	-	2	-
Commonwealth countries	79	48	47	1	-	-	-	31	27	4	-	-	-
Other countries and at sea	71	34	27	6	-	-	1	37	31	5	-	1	-
Birthplace not stated	6	1	1	-	-	-	-	5	5	-	-	-	-
Cookstown													
TOTAL	**31,258**	**15,637**	**8,870**	**6,289**	**73**	**289**	**116**	**15,621**	**7,690**	**6,368**	**69**	**1,326**	**168**
Resident in Northern Ireland	**31,082**	**15,503**	**8,777**	**6,256**	**71**	**287**	**112**	**15,579**	**7,656**	**6,361**	**69**	**1,325**	**168**
Northern Ireland	29,709	14,866	8,471	5,963	59	268	105	14,843	7,413	5,975	62	1,242	151
Great Britain	728	359	178	160	8	9	4	369	138	180	7	31	13
Republic of Ireland	329	111	36	65	3	6	1	218	42	136	-	39	1
Commonwealth countries	80	37	18	18	-	-	1	43	9	30	-	3	1
Other countries and at sea	98	57	24	31	1	1	-	41	17	21	-	3	-
Birthplace not stated	138	73	50	19	-	3	1	65	37	19	-	7	2
Visitors to Northern Ireland	**176**	**134**	**93**	**33**	**2**	**2**	**4**	**42**	**34**	**7**	**-**	**1**	**-**
Northern Ireland	53	19	16	2	-	1	-	34	28	5	-	1	-
Great Britain	114	110	75	28	2	1	4	4	2	2	-	-	-
Republic of Ireland	1	1	1	-	-	-	-	-	-	-	-	-	-
Commonwealth countries	3	1	1	-	-	-	-	2	2	-	-	-	-
Other countries and at sea	5	3	-	3	-	-	-	2	2	-	-	-	-
Birthplace not stated	-	-	-	-	-	-	-	-	-	-	-	-	-

Note: This table is on a usually resident + visitors base

Table 7 Population by sex, marital status, area of enumeration, country of birth, and whether visitor to Northern Ireland – **continued**

Birthplace	All persons	Males						Females					
		Total	Single	Married	Re-married	Widowed	Divorced	Total	Single	Married	Re-married	Widowed	Divorced
Craigavon													
TOTAL	**75,252**	**36,647**	**18,935**	**15,968**	**402**	**800**	**542**	**38,605**	**17,376**	**16,498**	**382**	**3,449**	**900**
Resident in Northern Ireland	**74,986**	**36,511**	**18,849**	**15,926**	**401**	**799**	**536**	**38,475**	**17,295**	**16,462**	**381**	**3,439**	**898**
Northern Ireland	70,180	34,281	17,984	14,745	335	741	476	35,899	16,449	15,177	329	3,139	805
Great Britain	2,513	1,246	454	673	51	31	37	1,267	422	638	32	113	62
Republic of Ireland	1,168	457	130	285	10	22	10	711	149	390	12	142	18
Commonwealth countries	352	179	68	106	1	1	3	173	54	100	4	12	3
Other countries and at sea	369	161	89	63	3	1	5	208	93	93	2	13	7
Birthplace not stated	404	187	124	54	1	3	5	217	128	64	2	20	3
Visitors to Northern Ireland	**266**	**136**	**86**	**42**	**1**	**1**	**6**	**130**	**81**	**36**	**1**	**10**	**2**
Northern Ireland	133	64	49	12	1	-	2	69	35	24	1	7	2
Great Britain	59	43	13	25	-	1	4	16	10	4	-	2	-
Republic of Ireland	44	7	6	1	-	-	-	37	35	1	-	1	-
Commonwealth countries	10	5	5	-	-	-	-	5	1	4	-	-	-
Other countries and at sea	15	13	10	3	-	-	-	2	-	2	-	-	-
Birthplace not stated	5	4	3	1	-	-	-	1	-	1	-	-	-
Derry													
TOTAL	**95,950**	**46,999**	**27,677**	**17,581**	**297**	**941**	**503**	**48,951**	**25,593**	**18,665**	**310**	**3,464**	**919**
Resident in Northern Ireland	**95,371**	**46,708**	**27,478**	**17,501**	**293**	**938**	**498**	**48,663**	**25,374**	**18,618**	**310**	**3,454**	**907**
Northern Ireland	85,044	41,969	25,380	15,164	217	781	427	43,075	23,356	15,960	245	2,716	798
Great Britain	3,954	2,179	1,065	964	51	57	42	1,775	765	792	31	147	40
Republic of Ireland	4,633	1,701	497	1,082	15	86	21	2,932	729	1,587	24	535	57
Commonwealth countries	407	195	85	99	6	3	2	212	100	90	3	15	4
Other countries and at sea	462	244	141	96	3	3	1	218	123	78	4	11	2
Birthplace not stated	871	420	310	96	1	8	5	451	301	111	3	30	6
Visitors to Northern Ireland	**579**	**291**	**199**	**80**	**4**	**3**	**5**	**288**	**219**	**47**	**-**	**10**	**12**
Northern Ireland	236	110	85	21	1	1	2	126	85	32	-	6	3
Great Britain	149	98	60	31	2	2	3	51	37	7	-	1	6
Republic of Ireland	117	32	24	7	1	-	-	85	76	6	-	2	1
Commonwealth countries	11	9	5	4	-	-	-	2	1	1	-	-	-
Other countries and at sea	54	37	20	17	-	-	-	17	15	1	-	-	1
Birthplace not stated	12	5	5	-	-	-	-	7	5	-	-	1	1
Down													
TOTAL	**58,264**	**28,972**	**15,920**	**11,859**	**273**	**621**	**299**	**29,292**	**13,644**	**12,132**	**286**	**2,783**	**447**
Resident in Northern Ireland	**58,008**	**28,835**	**15,833**	**11,820**	**270**	**619**	**293**	**29,173**	**13,575**	**12,096**	**283**	**2,776**	**443**
Northern Ireland	53,084	26,411	14,773	10,635	201	549	253	26,673	12,707	10,889	216	2,470	391
Great Britain	3,023	1,608	675	817	48	37	31	1,415	498	696	47	136	38
Republic of Ireland	957	361	98	222	13	25	3	596	121	330	9	132	4
Commonwealth countries	315	161	93	60	4	1	3	154	75	61	4	11	3
Other countries and at sea	370	172	112	55	3	1	1	198	96	82	6	11	3
Birthplace not stated	259	122	82	31	1	6	2	137	78	38	1	16	4
Visitors to Northern Ireland	**256**	**137**	**87**	**39**	**3**	**2**	**6**	**119**	**69**	**36**	**3**	**7**	**4**
Northern Ireland	137	64	47	12	1	1	3	73	39	24	2	5	3
Great Britain	72	49	23	22	1	1	2	23	14	7	1	-	1
Republic of Ireland	11	4	3	1	-	-	-	7	5	1	-	1	-
Commonwealth countries	12	5	4	1	-	-	-	7	5	2	-	-	-
Other countries and at sea	17	10	6	3	1	-	-	7	5	1	-	1	-
Birthplace not stated	7	5	4	-	-	-	1	2	1	1	-	-	-

Note: This table is on a usually resident + visitors base

Table 7 Population by sex, marital status, area of enumeration, country of birth, and whether visitor to Northern Ireland – **continued**

Birthplace	All persons	Males						Females					
		Total	Single	Married	Re-married	Widowed	Divorced	Total	Single	Married	Re-married	Widowed	Divorced
Dungannon													
TOTAL	**45,811**	**22,834**	**13,008**	**9,129**	**106**	**445**	**146**	**22,977**	**11,236**	**9,303**	**98**	**2,122**	**218**
Resident in Northern Ireland	**45,428**	**22,556**	**12,814**	**9,055**	**99**	**444**	**144**	**22,872**	**11,155**	**9,285**	**98**	**2,117**	**217**
Northern Ireland	42,714	21,358	12,238	8,507	88	393	132	21,356	10,662	8,514	85	1,900	195
Great Britain	1,129	527	281	219	7	15	5	602	245	276	4	61	16
Republic of Ireland	1,028	400	124	244	-	28	4	628	110	385	6	123	4
Commonwealth countries	123	58	27	29	1	1	-	65	30	27	1	7	-
Other countries and at sea	136	62	31	27	1	2	1	74	22	42	-	10	-
Birthplace not stated	298	151	113	29	2	5	2	147	86	41	2	16	2
Visitors to Northern Ireland	**383**	**278**	**194**	**74**	**7**	**1**	**2**	**105**	**81**	**18**	**-**	**5**	**1**
Northern Ireland	105	42	33	7	1	1	-	63	42	16	-	4	1
Great Britain	217	201	131	62	6	-	2	16	16	-	-	-	-
Republic of Ireland	11	5	5	-	-	-	-	6	5	-	-	1	-
Commonwealth countries	35	21	20	1	-	-	-	14	12	2	-	-	-
Other countries and at sea	11	7	4	3	-	-	-	4	4	-	-	-	-
Birthplace not stated	4	2	1	1	-	-	-	2	2	-	-	-	-
Fermanagh													
TOTAL	**54,907**	**27,803**	**15,964**	**10,843**	**172**	**577**	**247**	**27,104**	**13,070**	**10,956**	**139**	**2,677**	**262**
Resident in Northern Ireland	**54,033**	**27,095**	**15,535**	**10,606**	**153**	**572**	**229**	**26,938**	**12,958**	**10,921**	**137**	**2,663**	**259**
Northern Ireland	48,167	24,578	14,525	9,290	105	469	189	23,589	12,046	9,124	100	2,104	215
Great Britain	1,807	883	436	379	25	22	21	924	397	401	12	93	21
Republic of Ireland	3,426	1,341	401	837	17	74	12	2,085	349	1,282	22	413	19
Commonwealth countries	125	66	34	30	1	1	-	59	21	29	-	9	-
Other countries and at sea	221	99	51	37	5	2	4	122	53	47	2	17	3
Birthplace not stated	287	128	88	33	-	4	3	159	92	38	1	27	1
Visitors to Northern Ireland	**874**	**708**	**429**	**237**	**19**	**5**	**18**	**166**	**112**	**35**	**2**	**14**	**3**
Northern Ireland	177	83	65	14	1	2	1	94	64	22	1	5	2
Great Britain	559	517	283	202	15	3	14	42	24	7	1	9	1
Republic of Ireland	29	14	8	6	-	-	-	15	13	2	-	-	-
Commonwealth countries	31	23	16	6	1	-	-	8	7	1	-	-	-
Other countries and at sea	34	28	22	4	1	-	1	6	4	2	-	-	-
Birthplace not stated	44	43	35	5	1	-	2	1	-	1	-	-	-
Larne													
TOTAL	**29,606**	**14,429**	**7,157**	**6,406**	**222**	**372**	**272**	**15,177**	**6,505**	**6,551**	**190**	**1,601**	**330**
Resident in Northern Ireland	**29,419**	**14,318**	**7,092**	**6,369**	**219**	**372**	**266**	**15,101**	**6,468**	**6,523**	**190**	**1,593**	**327**
Northern Ireland	27,560	13,440	6,798	5,869	186	347	240	14,120	6,184	6,037	158	1,456	285
Great Britain	1,245	614	201	346	28	18	21	631	178	324	22	77	30
Republic of Ireland	302	106	25	70	3	6	2	196	32	112	6	42	4
Commonwealth countries	133	61	23	34	2	1	1	72	33	26	1	7	5
Other countries and at sea	127	65	23	40	-	-	2	62	29	17	3	10	3
Birthplace not stated	52	32	22	10	-	-	-	20	12	7	-	1	-
Visitors to Northern Ireland	**187**	**111**	**65**	**37**	**3**	**-**	**6**	**76**	**37**	**28**	**-**	**8**	**3**
Northern Ireland	85	46	35	10	1	-	-	39	26	12	-	1	-
Great Britain	69	47	18	23	2	-	4	22	8	8	-	5	1
Republic of Ireland	8	3	3	-	-	-	-	5	1	3	-	1	-
Commonwealth countries	6	3	2	1	-	-	-	3	-	2	-	1	-
Other countries and at sea	17	10	5	3	-	-	2	7	2	3	-	-	2
Birthplace not stated	2	2	2	-	-	-	-	-	-	-	-	-	-

Note: This table is on a usually resident + visitors base

Table 7 Population by sex, marital status, area of enumeration, country of birth, and whether visitor to Northern Ireland – **continued**

Birthplace	All persons	Males						Females					
		Total	Single	Married	Re-married	Widowed	Divorced	Total	Single	Married	Re-married	Widowed	Divorced
Limavady													
TOTAL	**29,671**	**15,091**	**8,591**	**5,918**	**127**	**279**	**176**	**14,580**	**7,237**	**5,971**	**139**	**1,033**	**200**
Resident in Northern Ireland	**29,567**	**15,042**	**8,557**	**5,907**	**127**	**279**	**172**	**14,525**	**7,205**	**5,953**	**139**	**1,029**	**199**
Northern Ireland	26,360	13,255	7,666	5,129	79	243	138	13,105	6,680	5,247	87	917	174
Great Britain	2,211	1,330	642	600	38	22	28	881	332	464	42	29	14
Republic of Ireland	452	180	57	102	5	12	4	272	39	161	3	63	6
Commonwealth countries	140	74	35	35	2	1	1	66	29	25	3	8	1
Other countries and at sea	263	129	100	25	3	1	-	134	90	34	4	5	1
Birthplace not stated	141	74	57	16	-	-	1	67	35	22	-	7	3
Visitors to Northern Ireland	**104**	**49**	**34**	**11**	**-**	**-**	**4**	**55**	**32**	**18**	**-**	**4**	**1**
Northern Ireland	61	26	19	6	-	-	1	35	19	12	-	4	-
Great Britain	28	14	10	2	-	-	2	14	9	4	-	-	1
Republic of Ireland	7	5	2	2	-	-	1	2	1	1	-	-	-
Commonwealth countries	6	3	2	1	-	-	-	3	2	1	-	-	-
Other countries and at sea	2	1	1	-	-	-	-	1	1	-	-	-	-
Birthplace not stated	-	-	-	-	-	-	-	-	-	-	-	-	-
Lisburn													
TOTAL	**100,663**	**49,685**	**25,405**	**21,612**	**810**	**981**	**877**	**50,978**	**22,434**	**22,226**	**747**	**4,311**	**1,260**
Resident in Northern Ireland	**99,458**	**48,653**	**24,588**	**21,420**	**796**	**978**	**871**	**50,805**	**22,338**	**22,172**	**744**	**4,298**	**1,253**
Northern Ireland	89,656	43,349	22,271	18,901	585	874	718	46,307	20,704	19,987	606	3,861	1,149
Great Britain	6,122	3,628	1,513	1,775	168	50	122	2,494	889	1,273	95	174	63
Republic of Ireland	1,748	731	215	438	21	38	19	1,017	228	556	16	201	16
Commonwealth countries	679	344	177	152	8	2	5	335	165	147	5	10	8
Other countries and at sea	947	452	313	121	12	2	4	495	276	170	20	18	11
Birthplace not stated	306	149	99	33	2	12	3	157	76	39	2	34	6
Visitors to Northern Ireland	**1,205**	**1,032**	**817**	**192**	**14**	**3**	**6**	**173**	**96**	**54**	**3**	**13**	**7**
Northern Ireland	150	68	42	20	3	1	2	82	46	28	-	5	3
Great Britain	934	885	724	148	7	2	4	49	29	13	1	6	-
Republic of Ireland	21	7	4	2	1	-	-	14	6	4	1	2	1
Commonwealth countries	46	32	22	9	1	-	-	14	7	4	1	-	2
Other countries and at sea	50	39	24	13	2	-	-	11	6	4	-	-	1
Birthplace not stated	4	1	1	-	-	-	-	3	2	1	-	-	-
Magherafelt													
TOTAL	**36,381**	**18,215**	**10,527**	**7,127**	**80**	**369**	**112**	**18,166**	**9,154**	**7,315**	**65**	**1,461**	**171**
Resident in Northern Ireland	**36,293**	**18,177**	**10,496**	**7,121**	**80**	**369**	**111**	**18,116**	**9,112**	**7,309**	**65**	**1,460**	**170**
Northern Ireland	34,804	17,536	10,166	6,838	75	351	106	17,268	8,824	6,891	61	1,336	156
Great Britain	712	326	161	147	5	9	4	386	128	191	4	53	10
Republic of Ireland	365	122	55	63	-	4	-	243	62	139	-	39	3
Commonwealth countries	116	53	24	29	-	-	-	63	18	34	-	11	-
Other countries and at sea	92	38	19	19	-	-	-	54	21	25	-	8	-
Birthplace not stated	204	102	71	25	-	5	1	102	59	29	-	13	1
Visitors to Northern Ireland	**88**	**38**	**31**	**6**	**-**	**-**	**1**	**50**	**42**	**6**	**-**	**1**	**1**
Northern Ireland	61	29	24	4	-	-	1	32	27	4	-	-	1
Great Britain	12	4	3	1	-	-	-	8	7	1	-	-	-
Republic of Ireland	4	2	1	1	-	-	-	2	1	-	-	1	-
Commonwealth countries	2	1	1	-	-	-	-	1	1	-	-	-	-
Other countries and at sea	7	2	2	-	-	-	-	5	5	-	-	-	-
Birthplace not stated	2	-	-	-	-	-	-	2	1	1	-	-	-

Note: This table is on a usually resident + visitors base

Table 7 Population by sex, marital status, area of enumeration, country of birth, and whether visitor to Northern Ireland – **continued**

Birthplace	All persons	Males						Females					
		Total	Single	Married	Re-married	Widowed	Divorced	Total	Single	Married	Re-married	Widowed	Divorced
Moyle													
TOTAL	**14,858**	**7,391**	**4,215**	**2,843**	**54**	**201**	**78**	**7,467**	**3,594**	**2,922**	**48**	**787**	**116**
Resident in Northern Ireland	**14,789**	**7,355**	**4,191**	**2,831**	**54**	**201**	**78**	**7,434**	**3,572**	**2,914**	**48**	**785**	**115**
Northern Ireland	13,829	6,937	3,990	2,647	39	186	75	6,892	3,375	2,678	37	703	99
Great Britain	563	261	121	117	13	8	2	302	109	132	9	39	13
Republic of Ireland	227	68	28	34	2	4	-	159	48	78	2	31	-
Commonwealth countries	56	31	17	14	-	-	-	25	11	11	-	2	1
Other countries and at sea	59	32	15	14	-	2	1	27	12	9	-	4	2
Birthplace not stated	55	26	20	5	-	1	-	29	17	6	-	6	-
Visitors to Northern Ireland	**69**	**36**	**24**	**12**	**-**	**-**	**-**	**33**	**22**	**8**	**-**	**2**	**1**
Northern Ireland	48	27	18	9	-	-	-	21	16	3	-	1	1
Great Britain	13	6	3	3	-	-	-	7	1	5	-	1	-
Republic of Ireland	2	2	2	-	-	-	-	-	-	-	-	-	-
Commonwealth countries	2	1	1	-	-	-	-	1	1	-	-	-	-
Other countries and at sea	3	-	-	-	-	-	-	3	3	-	-	-	-
Birthplace not stated	1	-	-	-	-	-	-	1	1	-	-	-	-
Newry and Mourne													
TOTAL	**83,486**	**41,651**	**23,946**	**16,275**	**228**	**852**	**350**	**41,835**	**20,975**	**16,517**	**223**	**3,570**	**550**
Resident in Northern Ireland	**82,943**	**41,307**	**23,708**	**16,180**	**225**	**850**	**344**	**41,636**	**20,841**	**16,468**	**222**	**3,557**	**548**
Northern Ireland	75,200	37,607	22,037	14,357	170	754	289	37,593	19,485	14,377	171	3,090	470
Great Britain	3,125	1,738	845	783	39	39	32	1,387	550	625	29	146	37
Republic of Ireland	3,356	1,317	410	834	10	45	18	2,039	465	1,260	14	266	34
Commonwealth countries	263	135	92	39	2	2	-	128	76	43	2	7	-
Other countries and at sea	356	179	97	72	3	5	2	177	82	63	5	26	1
Birthplace not stated	643	331	227	95	1	5	3	312	183	100	1	22	6
Visitors to Northern Ireland	**543**	**344**	**238**	**95**	**3**	**2**	**6**	**199**	**134**	**49**	**1**	**13**	**2**
Northern Ireland	213	104	79	22	1	-	2	109	83	21	-	5	-
Great Britain	215	180	126	49	1	-	4	35	27	6	1	-	1
Republic of Ireland	61	28	15	12	-	1	-	33	11	16	-	5	1
Commonwealth countries	12	9	7	2	-	-	-	3	2	1	-	-	-
Other countries and at sea	33	19	9	9	1	-	-	14	8	4	-	2	-
Birthplace not stated	9	4	2	1	-	1	-	5	3	1	-	1	-
Newtownabbey													
TOTAL	**74,408**	**35,951**	**16,864**	**16,928**	**665**	**824**	**670**	**38,457**	**15,630**	**17,439**	**644**	**3,636**	**1,108**
Resident in Northern Ireland	**74,035**	**35,760**	**16,725**	**16,885**	**665**	**819**	**666**	**38,275**	**15,508**	**17,396**	**642**	**3,626**	**1,103**
Northern Ireland	69,474	33,528	15,943	15,664	572	739	610	35,946	14,792	16,256	586	3,285	1,027
Great Britain	2,756	1,440	442	827	76	56	39	1,316	404	643	38	181	50
Republic of Ireland	754	254	58	166	7	17	6	500	99	262	7	121	11
Commonwealth countries	465	239	101	129	3	1	5	226	77	122	6	14	7
Other countries and at sea	388	202	116	74	7	3	2	186	87	78	5	10	6
Birthplace not stated	198	97	65	25	-	3	4	101	49	35	-	15	2
Visitors to Northern Ireland	**373**	**191**	**139**	**43**	**-**	**5**	**4**	**182**	**122**	**43**	**2**	**10**	**5**
Northern Ireland	149	81	57	20	-	3	1	68	29	27	2	5	5
Great Britain	83	44	29	12	-	1	2	39	28	8	-	3	-
Republic of Ireland	77	27	26	1	-	-	-	50	44	4	-	2	-
Commonwealth countries	32	21	15	4	-	1	1	11	9	2	-	-	-
Other countries and at sea	32	18	12	6	-	-	-	14	12	2	-	-	-
Birthplace not stated	-	-	-	-	-	-	-	-	-	-	-	-	-

Note: This table is on a usually resident + visitors base

Table 7 Population by sex, marital status, area of enumeration, country of birth, and whether visitor to Northern Ireland – **continued**

Birthplace	All persons	Males						Females					
		Total	Single	Married	Re-married	Widowed	Divorced	Total	Single	Married	Re-married	Widowed	Divorced
North Down													
TOTAL	**72,365**	**34,608**	**15,557**	**16,612**	**880**	**833**	**726**	**37,757**	**14,787**	**16,925**	**813**	**4,146**	**1,086**
Resident in Northern Ireland	**71,832**	**34,284**	**15,374**	**16,508**	**869**	**826**	**707**	**37,548**	**14,674**	**16,853**	**807**	**4,130**	**1,084**
Northern Ireland	63,399	30,253	14,085	14,238	672	695	563	33,146	13,389	14,726	671	3,422	938
Great Britain	5,132	2,688	778	1,541	161	87	121	2,444	707	1,212	99	339	87
Republic of Ireland	1,758	620	120	438	16	37	9	1,138	218	571	15	307	27
Commonwealth countries	678	328	163	145	9	3	8	350	132	174	12	20	12
Other countries and at sea	709	331	188	126	10	2	5	378	175	146	10	28	19
Birthplace not stated	156	64	40	20	1	2	1	92	53	24	-	14	1
Visitors to Northern Ireland	**533**	**324**	**183**	**104**	**11**	**7**	**19**	**209**	**113**	**72**	**6**	**16**	**2**
Northern Ireland	208	102	67	29	1	-	5	106	50	42	3	9	2
Great Britain	195	146	60	61	9	4	12	49	25	18	2	4	-
Republic of Ireland	46	23	18	3	-	1	1	23	17	4	1	1	-
Commonwealth countries	32	22	16	4	-	1	1	10	8	2	-	-	-
Other countries and at sea	51	31	22	7	1	1	-	20	13	6	-	1	-
Birthplace not stated	1	-	-	-	-	-	-	1	-	-	-	1	-
Omagh													
TOTAL	**46,015**	**23,148**	**13,754**	**8,659**	**113**	**451**	**171**	**22,867**	**11,658**	**8,859**	**111**	**1,959**	**280**
Resident in Northern Ireland	**45,809**	**23,022**	**13,652**	**8,642**	**111**	**449**	**168**	**22,787**	**11,603**	**8,842**	**111**	**1,956**	**275**
Northern Ireland	41,883	21,010	12,563	7,813	86	403	145	20,873	10,803	7,962	94	1,769	245
Great Britain	2,049	1,199	698	453	18	16	14	850	420	362	10	43	15
Republic of Ireland	1,162	457	151	274	3	27	2	705	169	399	3	126	8
Commonwealth countries	162	87	47	38	1	-	1	75	33	35	-	5	2
Other countries and at sea	233	107	77	26	2	1	1	126	76	40	3	5	2
Birthplace not stated	320	162	116	38	1	2	5	158	102	44	1	8	3
Visitors to Northern Ireland	**206**	**126**	**102**	**17**	**2**	**2**	**3**	**80**	**55**	**17**	**-**	**3**	**5**
Northern Ireland	85	35	27	8	-	-	-	50	38	10	-	-	2
Great Britain	86	70	60	4	2	1	3	16	9	5	-	1	1
Republic of Ireland	12	3	2	1	-	-	-	9	6	1	-	2	-
Commonwealth countries	6	4	3	-	-	1	-	2	-	1	-	-	1
Other countries and at sea	15	12	8	4	-	-	-	3	2	-	-	-	1
Birthplace not stated	2	2	2	-	-	-	-	-	-	-	-	-	-
Strabane													
TOTAL	**36,264**	**18,180**	**10,691**	**6,900**	**73**	**378**	**138**	**18,084**	**9,091**	**7,167**	**85**	**1,538**	**203**
Resident in Northern Ireland	**36,141**	**18,116**	**10,650**	**6,884**	**72**	**374**	**136**	**18,025**	**9,055**	**7,152**	**85**	**1,531**	**202**
Northern Ireland	32,710	16,636	10,095	6,043	54	320	124	16,074	8,521	6,060	71	1,246	176
Great Britain	1,078	507	265	221	8	9	4	571	234	284	4	41	8
Republic of Ireland	2,021	797	175	565	9	42	6	1,224	214	760	9	226	15
Commonwealth countries	80	46	20	23	-	1	2	34	11	17	-	6	-
Other countries and at sea	58	27	9	16	-	2	-	31	11	14	-	5	1
Birthplace not stated	194	103	86	16	1	-	-	91	64	17	1	7	2
Visitors to Northern Ireland	**123**	**64**	**41**	**16**	**1**	**4**	**2**	**59**	**36**	**15**	**-**	**7**	**1**
Northern Ireland	83	46	31	11	1	2	1	37	26	7	-	4	-
Great Britain	19	6	3	3	-	-	-	13	4	6	-	2	1
Republic of Ireland	14	10	6	2	-	2	-	4	2	1	-	1	-
Commonwealth countries	3	1	-	-	-	-	1	2	2	-	-	-	-
Other countries and at sea	4	1	1	-	-	-	-	3	2	1	-	-	-
Birthplace not stated	-	-	-	-	-	-	-	-	-	-	-	-	-

Note: This table is on a usually resident + visitors base

Table 8 Religion

Local Government Districts	Population			Roman Catholic			Presbyterian			Church of Ireland		
	Persons	Males	Females	Persons	Males	Females	Persons	Males	Females	Persons	Males	Females
NORTHERN IRELAND	**1,577,836**	**769,071**	**808,765**	**605,639**	**295,095**	**310,544**	**336,891**	**161,648**	**175,243**	**279,280**	**134,758**	**144,522**
Antrim	44,516	22,135	22,381	14,117	6,864	7,253	13,614	6,727	6,887	6,384	3,121	3,263
Ards	64,764	31,527	33,237	7,341	3,551	3,790	25,219	12,212	13,007	12,137	5,763	6,374
Armagh	51,817	25,741	26,076	23,518	11,631	11,887	8,627	4,353	4,274	10,604	5,189	5,415
Ballymena	56,641	27,830	28,811	10,392	5,121	5,271	26,067	12,737	13,330	6,869	3,371	3,498
Ballymoney	24,198	12,022	12,176	7,311	3,672	3,639	9,411	4,617	4,794	3,151	1,570	1,581
Banbridge	33,482	16,568	16,914	9,256	4,574	4,682	9,608	4,712	4,896	6,362	3,115	3,247
Belfast	279,237	130,820	148,417	108,954	51,057	57,897	47,743	21,409	26,334	50,242	23,377	26,865
Carrickfergus	32,750	15,871	16,879	2,269	1,060	1,209	10,166	4,898	5,268	7,698	3,734	3,964
Castlereagh	60,799	28,946	31,853	5,743	2,652	3,091	17,445	8,172	9,273	14,638	6,882	7,756
Coleraine	50,438	24,369	26,069	11,323	5,406	5,917	15,946	7,611	8,335	12,550	6,052	6,498
Cookstown	31,082	15,503	15,579	16,522	8,198	8,324	4,779	2,376	2,403	5,288	2,657	2,631
Craigavon	74,986	36,511	38,475	30,060	14,722	15,338	7,718	3,706	4,012	18,666	8,951	9,715
Derry	95,371	46,708	48,663	66,260	32,132	34,128	10,539	5,146	5,393	8,503	4,169	4,334
Down	58,008	28,835	29,173	32,507	16,090	16,417	9,025	4,507	4,518	6,183	2,959	3,224
Dungannon	45,428	22,556	22,872	25,299	12,540	12,759	5,822	2,916	2,906	8,245	4,060	4,185
Fermanagh	54,033	27,095	26,938	29,657	14,910	14,747	1,549	757	792	14,283	7,127	7,156
Larne	29,419	14,318	15,101	6,510	3,140	3,370	11,136	5,385	5,751	4,083	1,937	2,146
Limavady	29,567	15,042	14,525	15,281	7,745	7,536	5,683	2,834	2,849	4,699	2,440	2,259
Lisburn	99,458	48,653	50,805	26,786	12,882	13,904	20,980	10,072	10,908	26,286	12,926	13,360
Magherafelt	36,293	18,177	18,116	21,377	10,713	10,664	5,466	2,693	2,773	4,372	2,196	2,176
Moyle	14,789	7,355	7,434	7,723	3,828	3,895	2,766	1,368	1,398	2,587	1,271	1,316
Newry and Mourne	82,943	41,307	41,636	59,555	29,385	30,170	8,890	4,412	4,478	3,861	1,896	1,965
Newtownabbey	74,035	35,760	38,275	9,635	4,604	5,031	23,610	11,236	12,374	14,976	7,210	7,766
North Down	71,832	34,284	37,548	6,435	2,937	3,498	23,658	11,014	12,644	16,591	7,736	8,855
Omagh	45,809	23,022	22,787	29,469	14,636	14,833	5,141	2,577	2,564	5,766	2,879	2,887
Strabane	36,141	18,116	18,025	22,339	11,045	11,294	6,283	3,201	3,082	4,256	2,170	2,086

Methodist			Other denominations			None			Not stated			Local Government Districts
Persons	Males	Females	Persons	Males	Females	Persons	Males	Females	Persons	Males	Females	
59,517	**27,634**	**31,883**	**122,448**	**59,430**	**63,018**	**59,234**	**33,318**	**25,916**	**114,827**	**57,188**	**57,639**	**NORTHERN IRELAND**
786	404	382	3,600	1,853	1,747	2,025	1,144	881	3,990	2,022	1,968	Antrim
3,386	1,568	1,818	7,069	3,386	3,683	3,904	2,186	1,718	5,708	2,861	2,847	Ards
1,236	617	619	3,964	1,938	2,026	825	475	350	3,043	1,538	1,505	Armagh
1,442	688	754	6,115	2,958	3,157	1,845	997	848	3,911	1,958	1,953	Ballymena
123	59	64	2,184	1,066	1,118	524	292	232	1,494	746	748	Ballymoney
624	296	328	3,977	1,948	2,029	929	532	397	2,726	1,391	1,335	Banbridge
14,667	6,468	8,199	20,113	9,317	10,796	14,756	8,195	6,561	22,762	10,997	11,765	Belfast
3,162	1,451	1,711	4,390	2,052	2,338	2,476	1,373	1,103	2,589	1,303	1,286	Carrickfergus
5,323	2,481	2,842	8,481	3,970	4,511	3,797	2,173	1,624	5,372	2,616	2,756	Castlereagh
784	348	436	4,214	2,018	2,196	2,104	1,191	913	3,517	1,743	1,774	Coleraine
331	152	179	2,131	1,050	1,081	382	203	179	1,649	867	782	Cookstown
3,904	1,850	2,054	7,190	3,445	3,745	1,955	1,106	849	5,493	2,731	2,762	Craigavon
853	404	449	2,629	1,434	1,195	1,353	817	536	5,234	2,606	2,628	Derry
559	248	311	3,454	1,725	1,729	1,658	954	704	4,622	2,352	2,270	Down
912	430	482	2,416	1,209	1,207	384	215	169	2,350	1,186	1,164	Dungannon
2,724	1,345	1,379	2,534	1,204	1,330	745	430	315	2,541	1,322	1,219	Fermanagh
1,107	521	586	2,771	1,335	1,436	1,291	720	571	2,521	1,280	1,241	Larne
203	94	109	1,035	542	493	512	294	218	2,154	1,093	1,061	Limavady
4,095	1,955	2,140	9,154	4,492	4,662	4,780	2,668	2,112	7,377	3,658	3,719	Lisburn
165	82	83	2,632	1,298	1,334	313	188	125	1,968	1,007	961	Magherafelt
29	16	13	452	226	226	254	135	119	978	511	467	Moyle
314	166	148	3,376	1,883	1,493	947	555	392	6,000	3,010	2,990	Newry and Mourne
6,437	2,952	3,485	8,125	3,867	4,258	4,476	2,529	1,947	6,776	3,362	3,414	Newtownabbey
5,077	2,381	2,696	7,500	3,606	3,894	6,140	3,436	2,704	6,431	3,174	3,257	North Down
785	397	388	1,910	1,089	821	570	323	247	2,168	1,121	1,047	Omagh
489	261	228	1,032	519	513	289	187	102	1,453	733	720	Strabane

Table 8A Analysis of column headed "Other Denominations" in Table 8 **Northern Ireland**

Denominations	Persons	Males	Females
Baptist	19,484	9,147	10,337
Brethren	12,446	5,626	6,820
Protestant	12,386	6,240	6,146
Free Presbyterian Church of Ulster	12,363	6,091	6,272
Christian	10,556	5,127	5,429
Congregational Church	8,176	3,798	4,378
Elim Church	5,537	2,541	2,996
Church of England	4,869	3,293	1,576
Pentecostal	4,312	1,960	2,352
Non - Subscribing Presbyterian or Unitarian	3,213	1,562	1,651
Reformed Presbyterian	3,184	1,535	1,649
Indefinite Answer	2,373	1,252	1,121
Jehovah's Witness	2,121	945	1,176
Salvation Army	1,918	846	1,072
Church of God	1,613	738	875
Church of Jesus Christ of Latter Day Saints	1,437	637	800
Undenominational or Unsectarian	1,401	663	738
Christian Fellowship	1,300	602	698
Church of the Nazarene	1,149	510	639
Free Methodist	1,119	522	597
Mohammedan	972	583	389
Independent Methodist	835	391	444
Society of Friends	804	375	429
Agnostic	742	454	288
Hindu	742	396	346
Evangelical Presbyterian Church	730	313	417
Moravian	714	329	385
Fellowship of Independent Evangelical Churches	623	291	332
Atheist	470	311	159
Jew	410	195	215
Interdenominational	352	169	183
Assemblies of God	326	147	179
Baha'i World Faith	319	155	164
Churches of God	297	133	164
Buddhist	270	160	110
Church of Christ	255	120	135
Apostolic Church	254	123	131
Seventh Day Adventist	230	109	121
Sikh	157	81	76
Apostolic Pentecostal	156	64	92
Non - Subscribing Old Presbyterian	152	71	81
Spiritualist	146	63	83
Lutheran	123	41	82
Christian Scientist	114	40	74
Nonconformist	102	61	41
Episcopal Church of Scotland	100	63	37
Faith Mission	80	30	50
Charismatic	72	32	40
Greek Orthodox	72	46	26
Humanist	69	44	25
Christadelphian	66	28	38
Free Thinker	56	33	23
Dutch Reform Church	51	25	26
Agape	48	17	31
Bible Pattern Church	42	22	20
Combined Methodist and Presbyterian Church	39	15	24
Independent Baptist	36	18	18
Emmanuel Mission	33	19	14
Free Church of God - Pentecostal Movement	29	14	15
Independent Evangelist	29	15	14
Presbyterian Apostolic	28	15	13
Cooneyite	26	12	14
Free Baptist	25	13	12
Church of the First Born	21	9	12
Church on the Way	19	10	9
Free Evangelical Church	15	8	7
British Israelite	14	7	7
United Church of Canada	14	5	9
Norwegian State Religion	12	5	7
Seceding Presbyterian	11	5	6
Zoroastrians	10	4	6
Other Denominations*	179	106	73
TOTAL	122,448	59,430	63,018

* This heading comprises denominations each of which had less than ten adherents usually resident in Northern Ireland; 74 different terms were used in describing these denominations on the Census returns

Table 9 Households by tenure and rooms

Tenure	Number of rooms occupied by household										Total households	Total rooms	Total persons
	1 room	2 rooms	3 rooms	4 rooms	5 rooms	6 rooms	7 rooms	8 rooms	9 rooms	10 or more rooms			
NORTHERN IRELAND													
All tenures	1,525	9,308	27,568	76,802	178,291	129,229	56,210	27,919	12,434	11,083	530,369	2,927,375	1,554,538
Owner occupied	181	1,364	6,233	29,729	97,367	98,996	48,687	25,706	11,640	10,295	330,198	1,985,447	1,036,896
Rented from a local or public authority	457	4,374	15,576	37,306	69,169	23,355	4,647	734	143	56	155,817	731,431	423,155
Rented from a housing association or charitable trust	159	1,862	2,212	1,742	1,516	565	213	78	28	30	8,405	31,200	15,500
Rented unfurnished from a private person or company	100	522	1,476	4,456	5,467	3,551	1,268	608	275	305	18,028	91,621	41,862
Rented furnished from a private person or company	564	1,016	1,750	2,827	3,001	1,891	955	501	195	155	12,855	59,709	24,317
Other and not stated tenures	64	170	321	742	1,771	871	440	292	153	242	5,066	27,967	12,808
Antrim													
All tenures	40	181	702	1,654	5,168	3,412	1,569	790	349	301	14,166	79,191	42,782
Owner occupied	2	29	135	603	2,591	2,431	1,271	716	326	287	8,391	51,118	27,291
Rented from a local or public authority	21	107	482	865	2,223	810	209	29	3	-	4,749	22,838	12,786
Rented from a housing association or charitable trust	11	28	30	13	36	7	3	1	-	1	130	470	240
Rented unfurnished from a private person or company	5	11	34	105	169	105	51	26	10	8	524	2,774	1,443
Rented furnished from a private person or company	1	6	17	48	86	32	27	4	3	2	226	1,153	624
Other and not stated tenures	-	-	4	20	63	27	8	14	7	3	146	838	398
Ards													
All tenures	19	281	1,116	3,443	8,019	5,252	2,253	1,230	613	606	22,832	127,044	64,179
Owner occupied	5	39	234	1,373	5,138	4,220	2,044	1,167	588	569	15,377	92,437	46,225
Rented from a local or public authority	3	183	689	1,601	2,458	815	109	17	4	2	5,881	26,975	14,604
Rented from a housing association or charitable trust	-	31	65	36	26	6	3	-	-	-	167	588	279
Rented unfurnished from a private person or company	5	12	79	321	259	139	63	28	12	16	934	4,620	2,087
Rented furnished from a private person or company	6	14	39	89	92	45	21	11	3	5	325	1,553	618
Other and not stated tenures	-	2	10	23	46	27	13	7	6	14	148	871	366
Armagh													
All tenures	19	206	625	1,866	5,438	3,731	2,004	999	433	399	15,720	89,710	50,617
Owner occupied	7	52	201	812	3,110	3,067	1,808	944	410	364	10,775	65,852	37,000
Rented from a local or public authority	8	95	304	845	2,032	463	107	11	1	2	3,868	18,296	10,998
Rented from a housing association or charitable trust	1	26	24	33	41	7	1	-	1	-	134	520	247
Rented unfurnished from a private person or company	1	11	47	105	128	117	43	24	7	12	495	2,618	1,293
Rented furnished from a private person or company	1	18	30	47	79	40	15	9	5	8	252	1,266	577
Other and not stated tenures	1	4	19	24	48	37	30	11	9	13	196	1,158	502

Tenure	Number of rooms occupied by household: 1 room	2 rooms	3 rooms	4 rooms	5 rooms	6 rooms	7 rooms	8 rooms	9 rooms	10 or more rooms	Total households	Total rooms	Total persons
Ballymena													
All tenures	20	294	822	2,298	5,388	5,522	2,636	1,182	542	433	19,137	109,789	56,064
Owner occupied	6	36	161	1,012	3,095	4,052	2,251	1,087	513	404	12,617	77,826	39,329
Rented from a local or public authority	6	180	546	1,071	2,012	1,217	275	38	2	1	5,348	25,907	13,878
Rented from a housing association or charitable trust	-	35	26	9	9	11	5	-	1	-	96	339	177
Rented unfurnished from a private person or company	1	19	39	119	158	152	64	26	19	18	615	3,349	1,671
Rented furnished from a private person or company	4	15	35	62	52	51	22	18	2	3	264	1,300	560
Other and not stated tenures	3	9	15	25	62	39	19	13	5	7	197	1,068	449
Ballymoney													
All tenures	12	133	290	1,146	2,722	1,658	831	479	235	224	7,730	43,542	24,075
Owner occupied	2	25	76	348	1,226	1,160	754	452	221	207	4,471	27,951	14,785
Rented from a local or public authority	4	61	188	719	1,401	401	45	6	-	1	2,826	13,350	8,200
Rented from a housing association or charitable trust	-	30	7	4	9	4	-	-	1	-	55	175	111
Rented unfurnished from a private person or company	2	8	10	56	58	63	23	14	9	11	254	1,412	683
Rented furnished from a private person or company	1	6	7	15	16	15	3	2	-	2	67	321	151
Other and not stated tenures	3	3	2	4	12	15	6	5	4	3	57	333	145
Banbridge													
All tenures	23	159	533	1,494	3,630	2,557	1,228	699	360	301	10,984	62,127	33,341
Owner occupied	5	43	134	672	1,973	2,002	1,132	656	340	286	7,243	44,418	23,657
Rented from a local or public authority	6	75	323	690	1,468	426	53	15	-	-	3,056	14,272	8,066
Rented from a housing association or charitable trust	7	25	24	3	6	6	1	-	-	1	73	227	111
Rented unfurnished from a private person or company	2	7	34	90	113	77	26	14	8	5	376	1,926	1,001
Rented furnished from a private person or company	3	4	7	25	29	23	9	5	4	2	111	574	232
Other and not stated tenures	-	5	11	14	41	23	7	9	8	7	125	710	274
Belfast													
All tenures	622	2,509	7,018	23,913	33,429	23,044	9,119	4,312	1,846	1,582	107,394	560,082	275,172
Owner occupied	13	209	1,563	9,072	16,076	16,906	7,455	3,719	1,652	1,449	58,114	335,913	161,503
Rented from a local or public authority	190	1,011	3,506	11,149	14,101	4,442	879	169	36	12	35,495	162,442	88,795
Rented from a housing association or charitable trust	21	662	767	855	641	264	105	38	6	8	3,367	13,039	6,624
Rented unfurnished from a private person or company	36	127	352	1,495	1,434	758	232	116	45	37	4,632	22,413	8,673
Rented furnished from a private person or company	333	465	782	1,171	860	547	377	236	85	40	4,896	21,603	7,632
Other and not stated tenures	29	35	48	171	317	127	71	34	22	36	890	4,672	1,945

Tenure	1 room	2 rooms	3 rooms	4 rooms	5 rooms	6 rooms	7 rooms	8 rooms	9 rooms	10 or more rooms	Total house-holds	Total rooms	Total persons
	Number of rooms occupied by household												
Carrickfergus													
All tenures	17	191	601	1,369	4,124	3,289	1,231	525	272	251	11,870	66,078	32,450
Owner occupied	-	10	60	463	2,566	2,537	1,022	501	261	236	7,656	46,226	22,735
Rented from a local or public authority	10	109	416	754	1,392	641	170	6	3	-	3,501	16,563	8,421
Rented from a housing association or charitable trust	-	46	75	32	12	12	9	-	1	-	187	649	258
Rented unfurnished from a private person or company	-	12	21	70	77	50	13	8	4	6	261	1,312	528
Rented furnished from a private person or company	7	12	28	44	57	29	9	7	-	5	198	926	341
Other and not stated tenures	-	2	1	6	20	20	8	3	3	4	67	402	167
Castlereagh													
All tenures	57	405	1,180	2,777	7,250	7,634	2,271	858	294	184	22,910	124,946	59,644
Owner occupied	3	20	154	1,008	4,792	6,498	2,058	814	282	172	15,801	92,780	44,013
Rented from a local or public authority	25	292	908	1,646	2,232	957	162	18	3	-	6,243	28,124	13,924
Rented from a housing association or charitable trust	3	74	86	45	43	19	7	2	-	-	279	983	440
Rented unfurnished from a private person or company	-	6	9	29	110	93	28	13	7	6	301	1,690	703
Rented furnished from a private person or company	26	12	15	34	44	43	10	7	2	3	196	890	370
Other and not stated tenures	-	1	8	15	29	24	6	4	-	3	90	479	194
Coleraine													
All tenures	41	326	872	2,074	6,019	4,159	2,050	1,205	569	555	17,870	102,030	49,824
Owner occupied	3	29	128	649	2,919	3,033	1,757	1,118	526	499	10,661	67,418	31,992
Rented from a local or public authority	10	118	468	1,116	2,650	826	169	17	1	1	5,376	25,658	14,534
Rented from a housing association or charitable trust	8	83	101	42	57	10	4	1	1	-	307	1,035	523
Rented unfurnished from a private person or company	3	21	43	96	151	125	48	27	17	19	550	2,976	1,332
Rented furnished from a private person or company	17	69	123	147	179	140	61	31	15	24	806	3,951	1,053
Other and not stated tenures	-	6	9	24	63	25	11	11	9	12	170	992	390
Cookstown													
All tenures	9	121	386	1,259	2,986	2,234	1,100	620	279	228	9,222	52,413	30,859
Owner occupied	4	40	161	573	1,681	1,830	1,003	581	269	215	6,357	38,655	22,615
Rented from a local or public authority	2	44	117	535	1,078	284	55	8	3	-	2,126	10,151	6,446
Rented from a housing association or charitable trust	-	9	38	29	27	7	3	1	4	1	119	501	242
Rented unfurnished from a private person or company	1	9	35	77	113	74	20	18	1	10	358	1,844	958
Rented furnished from a private person or company	2	16	29	35	44	22	10	5	-	1	164	733	331
Other and not stated tenures	-	3	6	10	43	17	9	7	2	1	98	529	267

Table 9 Households by tenure and rooms – **continued**

Tenure	Number of rooms occupied by household: 1 room	2 rooms	3 rooms	4 rooms	5 rooms	6 rooms	7 rooms	8 rooms	9 rooms	10 or more rooms	Total house-holds	Total rooms	Total persons
Craigavon													
All tenures	49	470	1,055	2,828	9,318	6,570	2,683	1,111	409	422	24,915	137,423	74,443
Owner occupied	6	43	204	1,049	5,395	4,821	2,153	995	376	387	15,429	91,428	50,148
Rented from a local or public authority	38	281	609	1,324	3,271	1,432	404	73	20	4	7,456	36,304	19,916
Rented from a housing association or charitable trust	-	99	118	173	112	29	5	3	1	-	540	2,046	917
Rented unfurnished from a private person or company	1	18	70	165	327	190	68	22	7	15	883	4,561	2,023
Rented furnished from a private person or company	1	23	42	85	95	59	29	6	1	1	342	1,621	726
Other and not stated tenures	3	6	12	32	118	39	24	12	4	15	265	1,463	713
Derry													
All tenures	47	616	1,533	3,603	11,541	6,095	2,495	1,169	486	430	28,015	150,544	93,695
Owner occupied	11	46	215	931	4,877	4,058	2,104	1,078	459	402	14,181	85,120	50,633
Rented from a local or public authority	11	240	998	2,355	6,179	1,772	279	43	7	4	11,888	56,839	38,875
Rented from a housing association or charitable trust	10	252	156	78	90	51	20	5	3	6	671	2,359	1,197
Rented unfurnished from a private person or company	4	15	50	85	125	76	40	18	7	7	427	2,175	1,077
Rented furnished from a private person or company	10	50	89	115	134	101	33	18	6	4	560	2,584	1,120
Other and not stated tenures	1	13	25	39	136	37	19	7	4	7	288	1,467	793
Down													
All tenures	42	309	845	2,309	5,945	4,367	2,137	1,083	514	510	18,061	102,311	56,616
Owner occupied	15	66	230	934	3,565	3,354	1,877	994	484	474	11,993	73,261	39,591
Rented from a local or public authority	5	144	430	1,048	1,893	741	138	22	8	3	4,432	20,930	12,996
Rented from a housing association or charitable trust	-	39	59	33	21	6	5	1	-	3	167	607	275
Rented unfurnished from a private person or company	5	19	66	149	215	127	49	29	8	11	678	3,434	1,751
Rented furnished from a private person or company	15	33	50	105	159	92	49	15	5	7	530	2,595	1,296
Other and not stated tenures	2	8	10	40	92	47	19	22	9	12	261	1,484	707
Dungannon													
All tenures	19	197	652	1,658	4,738	3,172	1,586	849	396	386	13,653	77,460	45,062
Owner occupied	4	68	239	666	2,708	2,505	1,392	798	368	354	9,102	55,453	31,971
Rented from a local or public authority	6	71	303	774	1,641	470	90	15	4	-	3,374	15,964	9,987
Rented from a housing association or charitable trust	1	18	29	24	42	8	2	-	2	1	127	520	274
Rented unfurnished from a private person or company	4	14	37	114	205	119	60	19	15	19	606	3,263	1,691
Rented furnished from a private person or company	1	13	29	41	55	43	16	5	3	5	211	1,043	476
Other and not stated tenures	3	13	15	39	87	27	26	12	4	7	233	1,217	663

Tenure	Number of rooms occupied by household										Total households	Total rooms	Total persons
	1 room	2 rooms	3 rooms	4 rooms	5 rooms	6 rooms	7 rooms	8 rooms	9 rooms	10 or more rooms			
Fermanagh													
All tenures	37	276	841	2,073	5,405	3,913	2,146	1,197	557	456	16,901	96,619	53,568
Owner occupied	17	125	357	874	3,004	3,124	1,914	1,104	518	433	11,470	70,327	38,506
Rented from a local or public authority	5	44	286	958	2,034	533	105	22	4	1	3,992	19,110	11,598
Rented from a housing association or charitable trust	-	29	46	37	21	13	4	2	3	1	156	608	326
Rented unfurnished from a private person or company	4	25	53	83	167	135	57	30	17	10	581	3,091	1,589
Rented furnished from a private person or company	8	42	79	100	106	59	35	17	8	2	456	2,086	963
Other and not stated tenures	3	11	20	21	73	49	31	22	7	9	246	1,397	586
Larne													
All tenures	13	121	517	1,459	3,062	2,875	1,207	606	272	277	10,409	58,946	29,159
Owner occupied	2	22	101	714	1,980	2,171	1,014	568	259	251	7,082	42,809	21,166
Rented from a local or public authority	2	50	326	591	901	567	140	13	3	1	2,594	12,473	6,446
Rented from a housing association or charitable trust	6	29	48	23	14	9	-	-	-	-	129	424	218
Rented unfurnished from a private person or company	1	9	22	92	116	97	33	20	6	9	405	2,156	896
Rented furnished from a private person or company	2	10	14	25	27	16	11	2	1	1	109	508	230
Other and not stated tenures	-	1	6	14	24	15	9	3	3	15	90	576	203
Limavady													
All tenures	18	125	409	1,070	3,313	1,913	783	485	194	179	8,489	46,896	28,892
Owner occupied	9	33	93	306	1,570	1,331	649	446	176	154	4,767	28,803	16,898
Rented from a local or public authority	4	45	235	593	1,496	409	76	15	4	2	2,879	13,814	9,521
Rented from a housing association or charitable trust	-	26	18	15	13	6	-	-	-	2	80	289	131
Rented unfurnished from a private person or company	1	13	20	54	82	77	24	12	6	9	298	1,588	905
Rented furnished from a private person or company	3	7	35	86	112	67	23	8	5	8	354	1,795	1,057
Other and not stated tenures	1	1	8	16	40	23	11	4	3	4	111	607	380
Lisburn													
All tenures	31	420	1,645	4,287	11,422	8,235	3,814	1,855	868	700	33,277	186,351	97,109
Owner occupied	7	41	270	1,550	6,010	6,206	3,347	1,696	824	647	20,598	125,733	63,187
Rented from a local or public authority	17	261	1,124	2,254	4,783	1,602	308	61	9	11	10,430	49,299	28,369
Rented from a housing association or charitable trust	2	84	144	103	84	27	12	14	-	1	471	1,802	958
Rented unfurnished from a private person or company	-	18	62	230	256	199	71	40	15	17	908	4,758	2,262
Rented furnished from a private person or company	3	11	32	129	231	154	56	23	16	9	664	3,533	1,749
Other and not stated tenures	2	5	13	21	58	47	20	21	4	15	206	1,226	584

Tenure	Number of rooms occupied by household: 1 room	2 rooms	3 rooms	4 rooms	5 rooms	6 rooms	7 rooms	8 rooms	9 rooms	10 or more rooms	Total house-holds	Total rooms	Total persons
Magherafelt													
All tenures	26	136	466	1,212	3,597	2,512	1,237	691	279	242	10,398	58,982	36,111
Owner occupied	8	50	214	537	1,877	1,922	1,133	645	259	219	6,864	41,665	25,424
Rented from a local or public authority	7	26	166	501	1,448	456	57	16	2	1	2,680	13,094	8,554
Rented from a housing association or charitable trust	1	28	21	12	17	2	-	1	-	-	82	273	135
Rented unfurnished from a private person or company	1	10	33	89	120	75	28	14	6	9	385	1,985	1,003
Rented furnished from a private person or company	6	16	21	42	63	25	9	5	6	-	193	891	434
Other and not stated tenures	3	6	11	31	72	32	10	10	6	13	194	1,074	561
Moyle													
All tenures	2	70	300	685	1,519	1,069	513	288	150	125	4,721	26,436	14,574
Owner occupied	2	22	79	251	700	746	433	256	136	115	2,740	16,856	8,888
Rented from a local or public authority	-	29	150	346	706	256	51	6	3	-	1,547	7,390	4,664
Rented from a housing association or charitable trust	-	6	33	2	13	2	3	-	-	-	59	217	90
Rented unfurnished from a private person or company	-	4	20	55	57	36	10	11	7	6	206	1,079	546
Rented furnished from a private person or company	-	9	14	27	33	18	12	9	1	1	124	617	280
Other and not stated tenures	-	-	4	4	10	11	4	6	3	3	45	277	106
Newry and Mourne													
All tenures	49	544	1,339	3,038	8,646	5,694	2,762	1,300	534	512	24,418	134,880	81,436
Owner occupied	21	136	429	1,391	4,988	4,218	2,309	1,194	504	474	15,664	92,880	55,857
Rented from a local or public authority	7	269	744	1,308	3,192	1,226	342	48	9	3	7,148	34,214	21,696
Rented from a housing association or charitable trust	1	60	32	17	31	8	2	2	1	1	155	538	291
Rented unfurnished from a private person or company	2	22	41	160	203	125	48	18	6	13	638	3,245	1,655
Rented furnished from a private person or company	14	41	61	106	102	64	30	15	8	6	447	2,064	910
Other and not stated tenures	4	16	32	56	130	53	31	23	6	15	366	1,939	1,027
Newtownabbey													
All tenures	53	358	1,365	3,243	9,271	7,947	2,556	971	426	301	26,491	144,588	73,413
Owner occupied	3	17	126	1,103	5,899	6,585	2,305	921	400	288	17,647	104,022	53,409
Rented from a local or public authority	33	273	1,108	1,848	2,867	1,016	175	24	8	-	7,352	33,215	17,138
Rented from a housing association or charitable trust	10	47	64	45	77	28	8	2	1	1	283	1,120	505
Rented unfurnished from a private person or company	-	8	40	187	319	247	40	10	7	4	862	4,426	1,749
Rented furnished from a private person or company	5	11	19	44	67	51	17	7	2	3	226	1,126	334
Other and not stated tenures	2	2	8	16	42	20	11	7	8	5	121	679	278

Tenure	Number of rooms occupied by household										Total house-holds	Total rooms	Total persons
	1 room	2 rooms	3 rooms	4 rooms	5 rooms	6 rooms	7 rooms	8 rooms	9 rooms	10 or more rooms			
North Down													
All tenures	187	417	1,321	2,981	7,738	6,888	3,380	1,961	889	857	26,619	153,694	70,777
Owner occupied	8	28	281	1,658	5,517	6,185	3,225	1,912	864	826	20,504	126,941	57,941
Rented from a local or public authority	18	237	636	871	1,833	465	46	4	2	3	4,115	18,245	9,349
Rented from a housing association or charitable trust	77	52	176	64	30	10	1	-	2	-	412	1,200	560
Rented unfurnished from a private person or company	13	50	148	258	186	117	49	20	9	15	865	3,982	1,564
Rented furnished from a private person or company	70	46	73	92	125	80	44	18	6	5	559	2,413	1,025
Other and not stated tenures	1	4	7	38	47	31	15	7	6	8	164	913	338
Omagh													
All tenures	42	227	624	1,593	4,460	3,088	1,678	921	406	378	13,417	76,432	44,669
Owner occupied	10	68	241	674	2,338	2,442	1,478	855	383	354	8,843	54,364	31,642
Rented from a local or public authority	8	77	271	723	1,763	454	113	21	3	1	3,434	16,405	10,056
Rented from a housing association or charitable trust	-	19	6	3	15	2	-	3	-	1	49	189	89
Rented unfurnished from a private person or company	5	26	50	80	169	100	48	17	9	7	511	2,612	1,494
Rented furnished from a private person or company	18	31	49	82	116	57	20	14	5	5	397	1,829	893
Other and not stated tenures	1	6	7	31	59	33	19	11	6	10	183	1,033	495
Strabane													
All tenures	31	216	511	1,470	4,143	2,399	941	533	262	244	10,750	58,861	36,007
Owner occupied	8	67	147	506	1,772	1,592	799	489	242	229	5,851	35,191	20,490
Rented from a local or public authority	11	52	243	821	2,115	674	90	17	1	3	4,027	19,559	13,338
Rented from a housing association or charitable trust	-	25	19	12	29	11	10	2	-	2	110	482	282
Rented unfurnished from a private person or company	3	28	61	92	150	78	32	14	11	6	475	2,332	1,285
Rented furnished from a private person or company	7	36	31	31	38	18	7	4	3	3	178	734	335
Other and not stated tenures	2	8	10	8	39	26	3	7	5	1	109	563	277

Table 10 Private households by size, rooms, dwelling type and population

Number of usually resident persons	Number of rooms occupied by household: 1 room	2 rooms	3 rooms	4 rooms	5 rooms	6 rooms	7 rooms	8 rooms	9 rooms	10 or more rooms	Total house-holds	Total persons	Total rooms	Average number of persons per room
NORTHERN IRELAND														
All households														
1 person	1,166	7,230	17,471	32,914	32,474	19,125	5,832	2,311	756	701	119,980	119,980	550,778	0.22
2 persons	141	1,423	6,379	24,764	47,003	33,749	12,667	5,304	2,236	1,729	135,395	270,790	728,920	0.37
3 persons	30	274	1,861	9,427	34,092	24,159	9,956	4,644	1,987	1,568	87,998	263,994	501,202	0.53
4 persons	13	140	851	5,424	32,380	26,003	12,670	6,740	3,067	2,629	89,917	359,668	541,417	0.66
5 persons	13	43	390	2,244	18,250	14,319	7,932	4,742	2,252	2,226	52,411	262,055	325,368	0.81
6 persons	10	19	184	965	8,616	6,966	4,122	2,475	1,268	1,318	25,943	155,658	164,074	0.95
7 persons	1	6	60	309	2,888	2,619	1,545	856	448	483	9,215	64,505	58,620	1.10
8 persons	2	7	33	110	1,184	1,095	693	369	198	216	3,907	31,256	25,003	1.25
9 persons	1	3	15	42	437	423	319	182	88	80	1,590	14,310	10,293	1.39
10 or more persons	2	5	8	44	281	310	205	136	79	82	1,152	12,322	7,614	1.62
Other households *	146	158	316	559	686	461	269	160	55	51	2,861	-	14,086	-
Total households	1,525	9,308	27,568	76,802	178,291	129,229	56,210	27,919	12,434	11,083	530,369			
Total persons	1,767	11,969	43,177	153,332	537,837	410,719	197,507	104,404	48,681	45,145		1,554,538		0.53
Total rooms	1,525	18,616	82,704	307,208	891,455	775,374	393,470	223,352	111,906	121,765			2,927,375	
Households in shared dwellings														
Total households	273	171	120	98	66	40	26	17	12	11	834			
Total persons	265	173	155	163	128	64	43	39	24	31		1,085		0.44
Total rooms	273	342	360	392	330	240	182	136	108	129			2,492	
Households in non-permanent dwellings														
Total households	172	471	486	506	468	95	31	13	7	5	2,254			
Total persons	330	1,034	1,115	1,406	1,562	311	99	55	26	15		5,953		0.75
Total rooms	172	942	1,458	2,024	2,340	570	217	104	63	56			7,946	
Antrim														
All households														
1 person	37	144	477	716	816	368	114	51	16	15	2,754	2,754	12,415	0.22
2 persons	1	31	149	519	1,369	849	366	148	74	53	3,559	7,118	19,523	0.36
3 persons	-	6	33	222	1,114	689	294	159	48	47	2,612	7,836	14,983	0.52
4 persons	1	-	24	114	1,012	766	374	203	84	74	2,652	10,608	16,007	0.66
5 persons	-	-	8	37	508	409	238	139	76	66	1,481	7,405	9,343	0.79
6 persons	-	-	4	15	216	203	102	58	29	33	660	3,960	4,172	0.95
7 persons	-	-	-	11	78	80	51	16	12	8	256	1,792	1,602	1.12
8 persons	-	-	-	4	21	27	14	10	6	4	86	688	557	1.24
9 persons	-	-	1	4	14	10	6	2	3	1	41	369	245	1.51
10 or more persons	-	-	-	-	3	6	9	4	1	-	23	252	155	1.63
Other households *	1	-	6	12	17	5	1	-	-	-	42	-	189	-
Total households	40	181	702	1,654	5,168	3,412	1,569	790	349	301	14,166			
Total persons	43	224	1,043	3,296	15,654	11,390	5,646	2,934	1,369	1,183		42,782		0.54
Total rooms	40	362	2,106	6,616	25,840	20,472	10,983	6,320	3,141	3,311			79,191	
Households in shared dwellings														
Total households	1	-	2	5	-	-	-	-	-	-	8			
Total persons	-	-	4	7	-	-	-	-	-	-		11		0.41
Total rooms	1	-	6	20	-	-	-	-	-	-			27	
Households in non-permanent dwellings														
Total households	2	16	31	24	24	3	2	1	-	-	103			
Total persons	5	33	76	62	68	9	16	3	-	-		272		0.71
Total rooms	2	32	93	96	120	18	14	8	-	-			383	

* Households where the persons present were not usually resident

Table 10 Private households by size, rooms, dwelling type and population – **continued**

Number of usually resident persons	Number of rooms occupied by household: 1 room	2 rooms	3 rooms	4 rooms	5 rooms	6 rooms	7 rooms	8 rooms	9 rooms	10 or more rooms	Total households	Total persons	Total rooms	Average number of persons per room
Ards														
All households														
1 person	15	223	726	1,384	1,338	702	238	82	35	42	4,785	4,785	22,178	0.22
2 persons	2	47	259	1,306	2,336	1,445	585	299	124	108	6,511	13,022	35,229	0.37
3 persons	-	4	69	428	1,613	1,071	391	193	116	88	3,973	11,919	22,708	0.52
4 persons	1	1	32	205	1,658	1,227	603	358	182	162	4,429	17,716	27,060	0.65
5 persons	1	4	7	73	732	566	297	207	99	115	2,101	10,505	13,228	0.79
6 persons	-	-	9	23	232	155	94	71	47	63	694	4,164	4,568	0.91
7 persons	-	-	1	3	59	44	28	13	6	16	170	1,190	1,099	1.08
8 persons	-	-	-	3	24	21	6	3	3	6	66	528	416	1.27
9 persons	-	-	-	-	6	10	4	1	1	2	24	216	156	1.38
10 or more persons	-	-	-	-	2	3	3	2	-	2	12	134	85	1.58
Other households *	-	2	13	18	19	8	4	1	-	2	67	-	317	-
Total households	19	281	1,116	3,443	8,019	5,252	2,253	1,230	613	606	22,832			
Total persons	28	353	1,675	6,648	23,213	16,072	7,355	4,297	2,211	2,327		64,179		0.51
Total rooms	19	562	3,348	13,772	40,095	31,512	15,771	9,840	5,517	6,608			127,044	
Households in shared dwellings														
Total households	1	1	-	1	2	1	1	-	-	-	7			
Total persons	1	1	-	4	4	3	2	-	-	-		15		0.50
Total rooms	1	2	-	4	10	6	7	-	-	-			30	
Households in non-permanent dwellings														
Total households	4	11	20	9	5	4	-	-	-	-	53			
Total persons	12	30	54	17	15	13	-	-	-	-		141		0.82
Total rooms	4	22	60	36	25	24	-	-	-	-			171	
Armagh														
All households														
1 person	9	165	401	827	929	534	181	72	26	19	3,163	3,163	14,983	0.21
2 persons	2	24	130	541	1,316	863	357	171	72	39	3,515	7,030	19,298	0.36
3 persons	3	8	50	210	974	681	356	159	57	50	2,548	7,644	14,799	0.52
4 persons	1	4	20	148	959	738	436	216	94	84	2,700	10,800	16,442	0.66
5 persons	2	2	10	73	657	475	326	176	84	88	1,893	9,465	11,874	0.80
6 persons	1	2	7	38	363	275	193	125	61	65	1,130	6,780	7,282	0.93
7 persons	-	-	3	12	118	99	84	41	22	23	402	2,814	2,618	1.07
8 persons	-	-	1	5	71	39	49	18	4	18	205	1,640	1,343	1.22
9 persons	-	-	-	5	28	15	13	9	5	3	78	702	503	1.40
10 or more persons	-	-	-	2	8	8	7	12	7	10	54	579	414	1.40
Other households *	1	1	3	5	15	4	2	-	1	-	32	-	154	-
Total households	19	206	625	1,866	5,438	3,731	2,004	999	433	399	15,720			
Total persons	42	275	1,012	3,914	17,517	12,503	7,673	4,024	1,805	1,852		50,617		0.56
Total rooms	19	412	1,875	7,464	27,190	22,386	14,028	7,992	3,897	4,447			89,710	
Households in shared dwellings														
Total households	-	4	1	1	1	3	-	-	-	-	10			
Total persons	-	5	1	5	4	7	-	-	-	-		22		0.58
Total rooms	-	8	3	4	5	18	-	-	-	-			38	
Households in non-permanent dwellings														
Total households	13	21	37	34	25	7	1	-	-	-	138			
Total persons	31	40	87	93	87	23	1	-	-	-		362		0.76
Total rooms	13	42	111	136	125	42	7	-	-	-			476	

* Households where the persons present were not usually resident

Table 10 Private households by size, rooms, dwelling type and population – **continued**

Number of usually resident persons	Number of rooms occupied by household: 1 room	2 rooms	3 rooms	4 rooms	5 rooms	6 rooms	7 rooms	8 rooms	9 rooms	10 or more rooms	Total house-holds	Total persons	Total rooms	Average number of persons per room
Ballymena														
All households														
1 person	16	231	552	976	1,030	755	240	80	20	27	3,927	3,927	18,503	0.21
2 persons	2	48	188	759	1,576	1,502	630	227	88	76	5,096	10,192	28,421	0.36
3 persons	-	6	46	321	1,102	1,110	511	226	94	67	3,483	10,449	20,545	0.51
4 persons	1	6	23	149	954	1,166	617	287	158	92	3,453	13,812	21,480	0.64
5 persons	-	-	5	58	425	599	366	207	111	94	1,865	9,325	12,194	0.76
6 persons	-	1	2	22	205	229	183	101	43	42	828	4,968	5,429	0.92
7 persons	-	-	-	3	58	91	54	35	19	21	281	1,967	1,910	1.03
8 persons	-	-	-	1	20	34	16	11	6	7	95	760	643	1.18
9 persons	-	-	-	-	5	21	8	4	2	3	43	387	291	1.33
10 or more persons	-	-	1	-	4	6	6	4	1	4	26	277	183	1.51
Other households *	1	2	5	9	9	9	5	-	-	-	40	-	190	-
Total households	20	294	822	2,298	5,388	5,522	2,636	1,182	542	433	19,137			
Total persons	24	375	1,207	4,504	15,311	17,283	9,067	4,414	2,134	1,745		56,064		0.51
Total rooms	20	588	2,466	9,192	26,940	33,132	18,452	9,456	4,878	4,665			109,789	
Households in shared dwellings														
Total households	-	3	-	2	1	-	1	-	-	-	7			
Total persons	-	5	-	5	4	-	2	-	-	-		16		0.62
Total rooms	-	6	-	8	5	-	7	-	-	-			26	
Households in non-permanent dwellings														
Total households	6	6	21	31	16	7	2	1	-	-	90			
Total persons	10	6	48	71	53	24	5	3	-	-		220		0.63
Total rooms	6	12	63	124	80	42	14	8	-	-			349	
Ballymoney														
All households														
1 person	11	97	141	370	444	243	65	35	15	15	1,436	1,436	6,813	0.21
2 persons	1	20	85	351	722	414	179	85	39	42	1,938	3,876	10,552	0.37
3 persons	-	11	31	180	523	351	158	76	47	40	1,417	4,251	8,137	0.52
4 persons	-	2	25	126	508	324	184	108	47	46	1,370	5,480	8,153	0.67
5 persons	-	-	4	67	287	166	142	92	36	38	832	4,160	5,178	0.80
6 persons	-	1	2	32	125	96	51	42	23	24	396	2,376	2,513	0.95
7 persons	-	-	-	10	61	31	27	24	17	14	184	1,288	1,228	1.05
8 persons	-	-	-	1	29	17	8	9	5	4	73	584	464	1.26
9 persons	-	-	-	2	13	11	8	6	2	-	42	378	261	1.45
10 or more persons	-	-	-	4	4	2	7	1	3	1	22	246	142	1.73
Other households *	-	2	2	3	6	3	2	1	1	-	20	-	101	-
Total households	12	133	290	1,146	2,722	1,658	831	479	235	224	7,730			
Total persons	13	184	536	2,789	8,498	5,298	3,046	1,881	949	881		24,075		0.55
Total rooms	12	266	870	4,584	13,610	9,948	5,817	3,832	2,115	2,488			43,542	
Households in shared dwellings														
Total households	-	1	2	-	-	-	-	-	-	-	3			
Total persons	-	1	4	-	-	-	-	-	-	-		5		0.62
Total rooms	-	2	6	-	-	-	-	-	-	-			8	
Households in non-permanent dwellings														
Total households	4	11	9	17	5	-	-	-	-	-	46			
Total persons	4	22	16	58	10	-	-	-	-	-		110		0.75
Total rooms	4	22	27	68	25	-	-	-	-	-			146	

* Households where the persons present were not usually resident

Number of usually resident persons	Number of rooms occupied by household: 1 room	2 rooms	3 rooms	4 rooms	5 rooms	6 rooms	7 rooms	8 rooms	9 rooms	10 or more rooms	Total house-holds	Total persons	Total rooms	Average number of persons per room
Banbridge														
All households														
1 person	21	121	339	627	564	323	98	53	19	14	2,179	2,179	9,988	0.22
2 persons	2	30	134	483	980	638	292	133	69	55	2,816	5,632	15,461	0.36
3 persons	-	3	32	172	726	490	203	115	50	46	1,837	5,511	10,650	0.52
4 persons	-	4	20	122	692	542	295	182	91	64	2,012	8,048	12,305	0.65
5 persons	-	1	3	56	402	320	187	111	68	57	1,205	6,025	7,590	0.79
6 persons	-	-	3	21	167	163	94	64	40	46	598	3,588	3,940	0.91
7 persons	-	-	1	6	64	51	39	23	11	14	209	1,463	1,362	1.07
8 persons	-	-	-	1	12	16	10	12	6	4	61	488	423	1.15
9 persons	-	-	-	-	7	4	8	6	5	1	31	279	218	1.28
10 or more persons	-	-	-	1	4	5	1	-	1	-	12	128	70	1.83
Other households *	-	-	1	5	12	5	1	-	-	-	24	-	120	-
Total households	23	159	533	1,494	3,630	2,557	1,228	699	360	301	10,984			
Total persons	25	211	823	3,063	11,131	8,391	4,406	2,642	1,431	1,218		33,341		0.54
Total rooms	23	318	1,599	5,976	18,150	15,342	8,596	5,592	3,240	3,291			62,127	
Households in shared dwellings														
Total households	-	-	1	3	1	-	-	-	-	-	5			
Total persons	-	-	1	9	4	-	-	-	-	-		14		0.70
Total rooms	-	-	3	12	5	-	-	-	-	-			20	
Households in non-permanent dwellings														
Total households	4	12	18	25	26	4	1	2	1	-	93			
Total persons	6	24	40	63	91	7	4	10	4	-		249		0.68
Total rooms	4	24	54	100	130	24	7	16	9	-			368	
Belfast														
All households														
1 person	459	1,918	4,165	10,417	7,972	4,741	1,383	542	164	134	31,895	31,895	143,726	0.22
2 persons	49	385	1,744	7,697	9,291	6,325	2,329	894	371	253	29,338	58,676	150,799	0.39
3 persons	7	78	576	3,012	6,016	4,105	1,576	706	290	218	16,584	49,752	90,339	0.55
4 persons	1	22	242	1,654	5,197	4,069	1,718	968	416	377	14,664	58,656	85,454	0.69
5 persons	3	7	99	590	2,843	2,137	1,086	615	306	311	7,997	39,985	48,399	0.83
6 persons	1	2	32	211	1,290	990	562	309	179	181	3,757	22,542	23,343	0.97
7 persons	-	2	11	56	365	311	176	103	47	49	1,120	7,840	6,987	1.12
8 persons	-	1	3	15	133	103	69	29	17	24	394	3,152	2,478	1.27
9 persons	-	-	1	3	42	41	36	21	8	8	160	1,440	1,050	1.37
10 or more persons	-	1	-	3	39	25	25	11	7	7	118	1,234	764	1.62
Other households *	102	93	145	255	241	197	159	114	41	20	1,367	-	6,743	-
Total households	622	2,509	7,018	23,913	33,429	23,044	9,119	4,312	1,846	1,582	107,394			
Total persons	603	3,089	11,146	46,248	91,746	66,236	28,813	14,504	6,658	6,129		275,172		0.49
Total rooms	622	5,018	21,054	95,652	167,145	138,264	63,833	34,496	16,614	17,384			560,082	
Households in shared dwellings														
Total households	147	78	49	48	29	20	10	14	11	5	411			
Total persons	133	74	65	66	48	31	20	29	21	16		503		0.41
Total rooms	147	156	147	192	145	120	70	112	99	53			1,241	
Households in non-permanent dwellings														
Total households	4	4	5	7	80	2	1	1	1	-	105			
Total persons	7	25	14	15	383	4	5	1	4	-		458		0.93
Total rooms	4	8	15	28	400	12	7	8	9	-			491	

* Households where the persons present were not usually resident

Table 10 Private households by size, rooms, dwelling type and population – **continued**

Number of usually resident persons	Number of rooms occupied by household: 1 room	2 rooms	3 rooms	4 rooms	5 rooms	6 rooms	7 rooms	8 rooms	9 rooms	10 or more rooms	Total house-holds	Total persons	Total rooms	Average number of persons per room
Carrickfergus														
All households														
1 person	15	167	444	626	686	460	116	40	14	19	2,587	2,587	11,844	0.22
2 persons	2	21	121	510	1,233	1,021	334	105	45	39	3,431	6,862	18,750	0.37
3 persons	-	3	18	138	908	710	235	98	52	42	2,204	6,612	12,765	0.52
4 persons	-	-	6	61	830	667	330	158	86	67	2,205	8,820	13,493	0.65
5 persons	-	-	5	23	330	291	151	83	53	56	992	4,960	6,319	0.78
6 persons	-	-	2	2	86	93	46	31	16	15	291	1,746	1,894	0.92
7 persons	-	-	-	2	21	29	10	8	5	10	85	595	589	1.01
8 persons	-	-	-	1	8	4	5	1	-	3	22	176	146	1.21
9 persons	-	-	-	-	5	2	1	-	-	-	8	72	44	1.64
10 or more persons	-	-	-	-	-	1	-	-	1	-	2	20	15	1.33
Other households *	-	-	5	6	17	11	3	1	-	-	43	-	219	-
Total households	17	191	601	1,369	4,124	3,289	1,231	525	272	251	11,870			
Total persons	19	218	801	2,453	11,618	9,576	3,959	1,841	1,010	955		32,450		0.49
Total rooms	17	382	1,803	5,476	20,620	19,734	8,617	4,200	2,448	2,781			66,078	
Households in shared dwellings														
Total households	4	3	3	1	1	1	-	-	-	-	13			
Total persons	5	3	3	3	5	1	-	-	-	-		20		0.59
Total rooms	4	6	9	4	5	6	-	-	-	-			34	
Households in non-permanent dwellings														
Total households	1	2	2	2	1	2	1	-	-	-	11			
Total persons	1	3	9	6	2	8	3	-	-	-		32		0.74
Total rooms	1	4	6	8	5	12	7	-	-	-			43	
Castlereagh														
All households														
1 person	45	349	853	1,315	1,351	1,292	238	52	15	6	5,516	5,516	25,351	0.22
2 persons	2	41	252	995	2,333	2,522	608	170	63	32	7,018	14,036	38,150	0.37
3 persons	1	2	34	277	1,480	1,563	486	148	54	24	4,069	12,207	23,326	0.52
4 persons	-	5	13	125	1,356	1,558	586	267	78	58	4,046	16,184	24,236	0.67
5 persons	1	1	6	38	552	532	248	162	62	38	1,640	8,200	10,118	0.81
6 persons	-	1	3	12	136	125	74	44	16	16	427	2,562	2,670	0.96
7 persons	-	-	-	4	22	26	20	11	5	5	93	651	610	1.07
8 persons	-	-	-	1	7	6	5	2	1	2	24	192	155	1.24
9 persons	-	-	1	-	-	1	2	-	-	2	6	54	43	1.26
10 or more persons	-	-	-	-	1	1	1	1	-	-	4	42	26	1.62
Other households *	8	6	18	10	12	8	3	1	-	1	67	-	261	-
Total households	57	405	1,180	2,777	7,250	7,634	2,271	858	294	184	22,910			
Total persons	57	468	1,568	4,934	19,677	20,916	7,148	3,083	1,064	729		59,644		0.48
Total rooms	57	810	3,540	11,108	36,250	45,804	15,897	6,864	2,646	1,970			124,946	
Households in shared dwellings														
Total households	-	2	4	1	-	-	-	-	-	-	7			
Total persons	-	4	4	2	-	-	-	-	-	-		10		0.50
Total rooms	-	4	12	4	-	-	-	-	-	-			20	
Households in non-permanent dwellings														
Total households	1	2	11	7	2	-	-	1	-	-	24			
Total persons	-	7	9	14	4	-	-	12	-	-		46		0.55
Total rooms	1	4	33	28	10	-	-	8	-	-			84	

* Households where the persons present were not usually resident

Table 10 Private households by size, rooms, dwelling type and population – **continued**

Number of usually resident persons	Number of rooms occupied by household: 1 room	2 rooms	3 rooms	4 rooms	5 rooms	6 rooms	7 rooms	8 rooms	9 rooms	10 or more rooms	Total house-holds	Total persons	Total rooms	Average number of persons per room
Coleraine														
All households														
1 person	32	239	553	860	1,162	728	266	121	40	44	4,045	4,045	19,502	0.21
2 persons	4	53	206	709	1,617	1,186	503	276	116	108	4,778	9,556	26,768	0.36
3 persons	-	13	44	264	1,213	717	352	216	94	84	2,997	8,991	17,551	0.51
4 persons	-	3	17	142	1,074	796	460	285	130	123	3,030	12,120	18,805	0.64
5 persons	-	-	16	36	565	392	262	174	89	93	1,627	8,135	10,420	0.78
6 persons	-	-	3	19	185	178	118	75	63	64	705	4,230	4,810	0.88
7 persons	-	-	4	4	62	61	42	21	17	16	227	1,589	1,489	1.07
8 persons	-	-	1	-	25	22	12	6	8	6	80	640	531	1.21
9 persons	-	-	-	-	6	9	5	7	2	-	29	261	193	1.35
10 or more persons	-	-	-	1	7	9	1	2	2	2	24	257	159	1.62
Other households *	5	18	28	39	103	61	29	22	8	15	328	-	1,802	-
Total households	41	326	872	2,074	6,019	4,159	2,050	1,205	569	555	17,870			
Total persons	40	396	1,299	3,970	17,028	12,242	6,634	4,059	2,121	2,035		49,824		0.49
Total rooms	41	652	2,616	8,296	30,095	24,954	14,350	9,640	5,121	6,265			102,030	
Households in shared dwellings														
Total households	13	11	7	5	4	2	-	-	-	3	45			
Total persons	13	2	6	3	9	1	-	-	-	6		40		0.27
Total rooms	13	22	21	20	20	12	-	-	-	40			148	
Households in non-permanent dwellings														
Total households	5	10	9	12	10	1	5	1	-	-	53			
Total persons	6	17	20	36	13	3	6	1	-	-		102		0.51
Total rooms	5	20	27	48	50	6	35	8	-	-			199	
Cookstown														
All households														
1 person	4	89	222	509	485	260	86	39	17	15	1,726	1,726	8,118	0.21
2 persons	1	17	85	351	689	460	210	93	34	31	1,971	3,942	10,746	0.37
3 persons	1	10	31	162	515	369	200	103	51	31	1,473	4,419	8,565	0.52
4 persons	-	4	18	130	530	466	226	134	65	34	1,607	6,428	9,627	0.67
5 persons	-	-	12	69	389	319	173	110	47	52	1,171	5,855	7,253	0.81
6 persons	1	-	8	27	231	195	120	74	43	37	736	4,416	4,665	0.95
7 persons	-	-	3	4	92	88	52	33	13	16	301	2,107	1,928	1.09
8 persons	-	-	4	2	30	41	20	18	3	6	124	992	799	1.24
9 persons	-	-	1	1	9	15	9	6	3	2	46	414	301	1.38
10 or more persons	-	-	1	-	15	16	3	10	3	4	52	560	346	1.62
Other households *	2	1	1	4	1	5	1	-	-	-	15	-	65	-
Total households	9	121	386	1,259	2,986	2,234	1,100	620	279	228	9,222			
Total persons	15	169	738	2,777	9,983	8,171	4,233	2,601	1,165	1,007		30,859		0.59
Total rooms	9	242	1,158	5,036	14,930	13,404	7,700	4,960	2,511	2,463			52,413	
Households in shared dwellings														
Total households	-	-	1	-	-	-	-	-	-	-	1			
Total persons	-	-	1	-	-	-	-	-	-	-		1		0.33
Total rooms	-	-	3	-	-	-	-	-	-	-			3	
Households in non-permanent dwellings														
Total households	3	22	20	22	10	1	1	-	-	-	79			
Total persons	3	44	33	55	32	5	5	-	-	-		177		0.69
Total rooms	3	44	60	88	50	6	7	-	-	-			258	

* Households where the persons present were not usually resident

Table 10 Private households by size, rooms, dwelling type and population - **continued**

Number of usually resident persons	Number of rooms occupied by household: 1 room	2 rooms	3 rooms	4 rooms	5 rooms	6 rooms	7 rooms	8 rooms	9 rooms	10 or more rooms	Total house-holds	Total persons	Total rooms	Average number of persons per room
Craigavon														
All households														
1 person	43	392	724	1,287	1,585	853	244	89	17	20	5,254	5,254	23,985	0.22
2 persons	5	55	213	885	2,466	1,632	607	221	61	55	6,200	12,400	33,591	0.37
3 persons	1	10	59	316	1,910	1,269	478	182	70	54	4,349	13,047	24,645	0.53
4 persons	-	5	27	199	1,774	1,441	629	255	107	119	4,556	18,224	27,098	0.67
5 persons	-	5	15	74	927	778	378	205	69	87	2,538	12,690	15,500	0.82
6 persons	-	-	5	30	418	385	207	103	49	66	1,263	7,578	7,963	0.95
7 persons	-	-	3	11	132	125	68	35	21	8	403	2,821	2,500	1.13
8 persons	-	-	-	5	53	39	38	11	10	5	161	1,288	1,018	1.27
9 persons	-	-	-	2	14	16	24	4	4	2	66	594	430	1.38
10 or more persons	-	-	-	-	15	17	6	6	1	6	51	547	346	1.58
Other households *	-	3	9	19	24	15	4	-	-	-	74	-	347	-
Total households	49	470	1,055	2,828	9,318	6,570	2,683	1,111	409	422	24,915			
Total persons	56	577	1,561	5,486	28,114	21,399	9,603	4,179	1,689	1,779		74,443		0.54
Total rooms	49	940	3,165	11,312	46,590	39,420	18,781	8,888	3,681	4,597			137,423	
Households in shared dwellings														
Total households	-	6	4	1	-	-	-	-	-	-	11			
Total persons	-	7	7	3	-	-	-	-	-	-		17		0.61
Total rooms	-	12	12	4	-	-	-	-	-	-			28	
Households in non-permanent dwellings														
Total households	5	21	18	19	15	9	-	-	-	-	87			
Total persons	8	42	45	65	52	37	-	-	-	-		249		0.81
Total rooms	5	42	54	76	75	54	-	-	-	-			306	
Derry														
All households														
1 person	27	493	937	1,449	1,473	685	209	61	29	18	5,381	5,381	23,520	0.23
2 persons	8	89	358	1,157	2,307	1,137	364	181	59	57	5,717	11,434	29,421	0.39
3 persons	3	10	115	442	2,224	988	405	184	72	50	4,493	13,479	24,696	0.55
4 persons	-	12	55	288	2,253	1,263	532	270	131	99	4,903	19,612	28,347	0.69
5 persons	1	1	30	119	1,580	900	425	226	92	89	3,463	17,315	20,461	0.85
6 persons	2	-	11	73	998	566	310	150	56	55	2,221	13,326	13,191	1.01
7 persons	-	-	2	29	387	289	130	49	16	33	935	6,545	5,602	1.17
8 persons	1	1	1	10	176	140	59	23	18	13	442	3,536	2,667	1.33
9 persons	-	-	5	6	62	59	28	14	5	5	184	1,656	1,110	1.49
10 or more persons	1	-	-	6	40	40	22	7	6	8	130	1,411	819	1.72
Other households *	4	10	19	24	41	28	11	4	2	3	146	-	710	-
Total households	47	616	1,533	3,603	11,541	6,095	2,495	1,169	486	430	28,015			
Total persons	87	762	2,501	7,673	40,767	22,981	10,142	4,812	2,049	1,921		93,695		0.62
Total rooms	47	1,232	4,599	14,412	57,705	36,570	17,465	9,352	4,374	4,788			150,544	
Households in shared dwellings														
Total households	7	9	6	4	7	2	4	-	-	1	40			
Total persons	9	11	6	8	14	4	6	-	-	4		62		0.43
Total rooms	7	18	18	16	35	12	28	-	-	11			145	
Households in non-permanent dwellings														
Total households	14	9	9	10	11	2	2	-	-	1	58			
Total persons	50	17	25	22	30	3	4	-	-	4		155		0.81
Total rooms	14	18	27	40	55	12	14	-	-	11			191	

* Households where the persons present were not usually resident

Table 10 Private households by size, rooms, dwelling type and population – **continued**

Number of usually resident persons	1 room	2 rooms	3 rooms	4 rooms	5 rooms	6 rooms	7 rooms	8 rooms	9 rooms	10 or more rooms	Total house-holds	Total persons	Total rooms	Average number of persons per room
	Number of rooms occupied by household													
Down														
All households														
1 person	26	239	503	880	996	572	234	95	34	36	3,615	3,615	17,063	0.21
2 persons	7	52	194	687	1,449	1,022	448	207	96	83	4,245	8,490	23,415	0.36
3 persons	1	9	76	333	1,087	794	380	170	73	64	2,987	8,961	17,158	0.52
4 persons	2	5	30	216	1,147	888	467	265	111	109	3,240	12,960	19,633	0.66
5 persons	1	1	14	95	676	544	334	166	95	105	2,031	10,155	12,733	0.80
6 persons	1	1	16	53	367	324	158	119	57	60	1,156	6,936	7,298	0.95
7 persons	-	-	1	15	129	127	53	35	27	32	419	2,933	2,731	1.07
8 persons	-	-	1	8	49	46	33	19	10	10	176	1,408	1,148	1.23
9 persons	-	-	1	-	19	18	18	4	7	7	74	666	501	1.33
10 or more persons	-	-	-	2	12	18	8	1	4	1	46	492	288	1.71
Other households *	4	2	9	20	14	14	4	2	-	3	72	-	343	-
Total households	42	309	845	2,309	5,945	4,367	2,137	1,083	514	510	18,061			
Total persons	62	401	1,429	5,099	18,923	14,820	7,634	4,067	2,088	2,093		56,616		0.55
Total rooms	42	618	2,535	9,236	29,725	26,202	14,959	8,664	4,626	5,704			102,311	
Households in shared dwellings														
Total households	11	3	1	6	1	1	-	1	-	-	24			
Total persons	11	3	1	14	1	1	-	2	-	-		33		0.52
Total rooms	11	6	3	24	5	6	-	8	-	-			63	
Households in non-permanent dwellings														
Total households	10	20	35	32	28	4	2	-	-	-	131			
Total persons	18	34	76	73	85	25	4	-	-	-		315		0.68
Total rooms	10	40	105	128	140	24	14	-	-	-			461	
Dungannon														
All households														
1 person	12	127	389	690	832	405	160	61	17	28	2,721	2,721	12,884	0.21
2 persons	2	44	162	447	1,091	672	323	145	70	53	3,009	6,018	16,494	0.36
3 persons	-	11	50	229	800	559	262	118	52	45	2,126	6,378	12,169	0.52
4 persons	-	9	23	149	835	565	282	174	95	75	2,207	8,828	13,289	0.66
5 persons	1	3	15	76	604	468	241	160	61	73	1,702	8,510	10,511	0.81
6 persons	-	1	5	36	340	280	165	104	55	62	1,048	6,288	6,720	0.94
7 persons	-	1	6	11	130	119	82	43	26	27	445	3,115	2,869	1.09
8 persons	-	-	2	9	58	63	43	23	9	11	218	1,744	1,396	1.25
9 persons	1	-	-	4	21	21	13	11	5	4	80	720	513	1.40
10 or more persons	-	-	-	1	11	20	13	10	5	8	68	740	483	1.53
Other households *	3	1	-	6	16	-	2	-	1	-	29	-	132	-
Total households	19	197	652	1,658	4,738	3,172	1,586	849	396	386	13,653			
Total persons	30	312	1,118	3,658	15,496	11,449	6,085	3,521	1,681	1,712		45,062		0.58
Total rooms	19	394	1,956	6,632	23,690	19,032	11,102	6,792	3,564	4,279			77,460	
Households in shared dwellings														
Total households	2	-	1	3	1	-	-	-	-	-	7			
Total persons	-	-	1	3	3	-	-	-	-	-		7		0.32
Total rooms	2	-	3	12	5	-	-	-	-	-			22	
Households in non-permanent dwellings														
Total households	5	33	32	29	32	10	3	1	-	-	145			
Total persons	17	80	71	103	102	25	13	2	-	-		413		0.78
Total rooms	5	66	96	116	160	60	21	8	-	-			532	

* Households where the persons present were not usually resident

Table 10 Private households by size, rooms, dwelling type and population – **continued**

Number of usually resident persons	Number of rooms occupied by household: 1 room	2 rooms	3 rooms	4 rooms	5 rooms	6 rooms	7 rooms	8 rooms	9 rooms	10 or more rooms	Total house-holds	Total persons	Total rooms	Average number of persons per room
Fermanagh														
All households														
1 person	33	205	532	954	979	554	210	126	36	38	3,667	3,667	17,295	0.21
2 persons	2	49	184	605	1,287	967	465	206	98	69	3,932	7,864	21,872	0.36
3 persons	-	9	73	217	912	657	338	215	98	73	2,592	7,776	15,391	0.51
4 persons	-	6	24	148	967	701	431	227	110	98	2,712	10,848	16,674	0.65
5 persons	-	3	6	64	647	477	310	174	98	74	1,853	9,265	11,640	0.80
6 persons	-	-	13	47	354	312	212	128	59	56	1,181	7,086	7,533	0.94
7 persons	-	2	1	17	147	124	94	66	31	20	502	3,514	3,232	1.09
8 persons	-	1	1	4	56	76	42	28	15	20	243	1,944	1,619	1.20
9 persons	-	-	1	1	23	24	24	18	6	4	101	909	675	1.35
10 or more persons	-	-	1	3	14	16	15	7	6	3	65	695	429	1.62
Other households *	2	1	5	13	19	5	5	2	-	1	53	-	259	-
Total households	37	276	841	2,073	5,405	3,913	2,146	1,197	557	456	16,901			
Total persons	37	391	1,357	4,203	17,350	13,390	8,066	4,651	2,262	1,861		53,568		0.55
Total rooms	37	552	2,523	8,292	27,025	23,478	15,022	9,576	5,013	5,101			96,619	
Households in shared dwellings														
Total households	3	9	-	-	2	1	-	-	-	-	15			
Total persons	3	10	-	-	2	4	-	-	-	-		19		0.51
Total rooms	3	18	-	-	10	6	-	-	-	-			37	
Households in non-permanent dwellings														
Total households	18	51	33	24	24	2	2	-	1	1	156			
Total persons	19	79	67	76	74	6	6	-	1	3		331		0.69
Total rooms	18	102	99	96	120	12	14	-	9	10			480	
Larne														
All households														
1 person	9	94	358	670	573	439	151	58	21	32	2,405	2,405	11,523	0.21
2 persons	2	22	116	468	915	812	290	125	61	41	2,852	5,704	15,745	0.36
3 persons	1	1	24	173	613	576	213	111	52	50	1,814	5,442	10,670	0.51
4 persons	-	1	11	97	569	574	276	143	56	65	1,792	7,168	10,986	0.65
5 persons	-	2	4	34	277	307	164	102	44	50	984	4,920	6,280	0.78
6 persons	-	1	-	11	76	106	71	50	30	24	369	2,214	2,484	0.89
7 persons	-	-	-	2	25	39	26	10	7	7	116	812	768	1.06
8 persons	-	-	1	1	5	10	13	4	1	3	38	304	254	1.20
9 persons	-	-	-	-	2	5	1	1	-	3	12	108	86	1.26
10 or more persons	-	-	-	-	1	2	1	2	-	2	8	82	61	1.34
Other households *	1	-	3	3	6	5	1	-	-	-	19	-	89	-
Total households	13	121	517	1,459	3,062	2,875	1,207	606	272	277	10,409			
Total persons	16	161	734	2,771	8,602	8,676	4,025	2,156	980	1,038		29,159		0.49
Total rooms	13	242	1,551	5,836	15,310	17,250	8,449	4,848	2,448	2,999			58,946	
Households in shared dwellings														
Total households	-	-	1	1	-	-	-	-	-	-	2			
Total persons	-	-	1	2	-	-	-	-	-	-		3		0.43
Total rooms	-	-	3	4	-	-	-	-	-	-			7	
Households in non-permanent dwellings														
Total households	4	9	12	18	5	1	-	-	-	-	49			
Total persons	4	26	31	42	14	4	-	-	-	-		121		0.75
Total rooms	4	18	36	72	25	6	-	-	-	-			161	

* Households where the persons present were not usually resident

Table 10 Private households by size, rooms, dwelling type and population - **continued**

Number of usually resident persons	1 room	2 rooms	3 rooms	4 rooms	5 rooms	6 rooms	7 rooms	8 rooms	9 rooms	10 or more rooms	Total house-holds	Total persons	Total rooms	Average number of persons per room
	Number of rooms occupied by household													
Limavady														
All households														
1 person	12	90	233	350	366	196	54	40	10	13	1,364	1,364	6,225	0.22
2 persons	2	20	88	374	678	423	132	87	40	33	1,877	3,754	10,087	0.37
3 persons	2	12	45	170	634	346	144	71	30	16	1,470	4,410	8,110	0.54
4 persons	-	2	19	86	730	415	174	106	38	30	1,600	6,400	9,277	0.69
5 persons	1	-	12	37	467	232	122	76	33	41	1,021	5,105	6,125	0.83
6 persons	-	-	3	25	245	162	88	53	22	21	619	3,714	3,774	0.98
7 persons	-	-	3	9	105	62	31	30	12	11	263	1,841	1,623	1.13
8 persons	1	-	2	8	49	42	15	7	7	6	137	1,096	826	1.33
9 persons	-	1	1	2	20	14	9	10	1	1	59	531	359	1.48
10 or more persons	-	-	1	5	16	20	11	5	1	5	64	677	403	1.68
Other households *	-	-	2	4	3	1	3	-	-	2	15	-	87	-
Total households	18	125	409	1,070	3,313	1,913	783	485	194	179	8,489			
Total persons	35	183	754	2,486	11,825	6,972	3,118	1,962	790	767		28,892		0.62
Total rooms	18	250	1,227	4,280	16,565	11,478	5,481	3,880	1,746	1,971			46,896	
Households in shared dwellings														
Total households	-	-	-	-	1	-	-	-	-	-	1			
Total persons	-	-	-	-	3	-	-	-	-	-		3		0.60
Total rooms	-	-	-	-	5	-	-	-	-	-			5	
Households in non-permanent dwellings														
Total households	9	12	7	7	6	1	-	1	-	-	43			
Total persons	13	14	17	14	22	5	-	11	-	-		96		0.76
Total rooms	9	24	21	28	30	6	-	8	-	-			126	
Lisburn														
All households														
1 person	21	335	1,099	1,849	1,941	1,052	334	101	38	28	6,798	6,798	31,192	0.22
2 persons	5	66	369	1,466	3,073	2,281	906	324	143	111	8,744	17,488	47,569	0.37
3 persons	2	5	95	533	2,396	1,689	719	328	155	94	6,016	18,048	34,618	0.52
4 persons	-	11	44	275	2,213	1,794	954	561	266	218	6,336	25,344	38,961	0.65
5 persons	-	-	18	102	1,166	884	548	341	175	153	3,387	16,935	21,345	0.79
6 persons	2	-	4	38	449	357	232	133	62	69	1,346	8,076	8,590	0.94
7 persons	-	-	3	6	122	115	83	31	22	12	394	2,758	2,495	1.11
8 persons	-	-	1	1	31	36	21	22	2	10	124	992	820	1.21
9 persons	-	-	-	-	10	12	6	5	3	4	40	360	277	1.30
10 or more persons	-	-	-	-	5	9	6	8	1	1	30	310	205	1.51
Other households *	1	3	12	17	16	6	5	1	1	-	62	-	279	-
Total households	31	420	1,645	4,287	11,422	8,235	3,814	1,855	868	700	33,277			
Total persons	49	526	2,441	8,268	33,894	25,716	13,116	6,998	3,308	2,793		97,109		0.52
Total rooms	31	840	4,935	17,148	57,110	49,410	26,698	14,840	7,812	7,527			186,351	
Households in shared dwellings														
Total households	2	2	6	2	2	3	2	-	-	-	19			
Total persons	1	2	7	3	2	3	5	-	-	-		23		0.31
Total rooms	2	4	18	8	10	18	14	-	-	-			74	
Households in non-permanent dwellings														
Total households	5	21	26	42	27	10	-	2	2	-	135			
Total persons	19	43	64	92	70	33	-	7	4	-		332		0.64
Total rooms	5	42	78	168	135	60	-	16	18	-			522	

* Households where the persons present were not usually resident

Table 10 Private households by size, rooms, dwelling type and population - **continued**

Number of usually resident persons	Number of rooms occupied by household: 1 room	2 rooms	3 rooms	4 rooms	5 rooms	6 rooms	7 rooms	8 rooms	9 rooms	10 or more rooms	Total house-holds	Total persons	Total rooms	Average number of persons per room
Magherafelt														
All households														
1 person	18	88	254	502	526	242	89	55	15	12	1,801	1,801	8,385	0.21
2 persons	2	29	118	341	818	532	197	106	49	23	2,215	4,430	11,972	0.37
3 persons	2	7	42	149	617	434	203	100	38	24	1,616	4,848	9,250	0.52
4 persons	1	6	19	95	671	489	255	130	43	48	1,757	7,028	10,478	0.67
5 persons	-	4	17	66	484	356	188	127	50	58	1,350	6,750	8,299	0.81
6 persons	2	-	10	29	280	251	149	101	37	40	899	5,394	5,717	0.94
7 persons	-	-	4	13	110	111	70	39	19	18	384	2,688	2,444	1.10
8 persons	-	1	-	7	53	54	39	16	9	9	188	1,504	1,198	1.26
9 persons	-	-	-	3	26	22	31	10	6	7	105	945	699	1.35
10 or more persons	1	-	-	4	7	18	15	7	13	3	68	723	470	1.54
Other households *	-	1	2	3	5	3	1	-	-	-	15	-	70	-
Total households	26	136	466	1,212	3,597	2,512	1,237	691	279	242	10,398			
Total persons	54	219	865	2,731	12,300	9,452	5,188	2,892	1,267	1,143		36,111		0.61
Total rooms	26	272	1,398	4,848	17,985	15,072	8,659	5,528	2,511	2,683			58,982	
Households in shared dwellings														
Total households	-	-	-	-	-	-	-	-	-	-	-			
Total persons	-	-	-	-	-	-	-	-	-	-		-		-
Total rooms	-	-	-	-	-	-	-	-	-	-			-	
Households in non-permanent dwellings														
Total households	15	20	27	29	15	5	-	1	-	-	112			
Total persons	41	57	73	90	42	15	-	2	-	-		320		0.88
Total rooms	15	40	81	116	75	30	-	8	-	-			365	
Moyle														
All households														
1 person	1	52	185	262	298	174	68	43	15	10	1,108	1,108	5,315	0.21
2 persons	1	13	62	212	331	243	101	50	31	16	1,060	2,120	5,737	0.37
3 persons	-	2	22	84	281	186	70	46	24	21	736	2,208	4,240	0.52
4 persons	-	1	14	66	278	193	116	41	27	24	760	3,040	4,497	0.68
5 persons	-	-	7	39	183	145	67	58	30	26	555	2,775	3,458	0.80
6 persons	-	-	6	11	87	78	58	21	15	14	290	1,740	1,836	0.95
7 persons	-	-	-	5	26	23	23	19	3	8	107	749	712	1.05
8 persons	-	-	-	3	21	17	4	6	2	2	55	440	341	1.29
9 persons	-	1	2	1	9	6	3	1	1	2	26	234	151	1.55
10 or more persons	-	-	-	1	5	1	2	3	2	1	15	160	101	1.58
Other households *	-	1	2	1	-	3	1	-	-	1	9	-	48	-
Total households	2	70	300	685	1,519	1,069	513	288	150	125	4,721			
Total persons	3	97	520	1,541	4,840	3,545	1,867	1,081	565	515		14,574		0.55
Total rooms	2	140	900	2,740	7,595	6,414	3,591	2,304	1,350	1,400			26,436	
Households in shared dwellings														
Total households	-	-	1	1	-	2	-	-	-	1	5			
Total persons	-	-	2	3	-	5	-	-	-	1		11		0.34
Total rooms	-	-	3	4	-	12	-	-	-	13			32	
Households in non-permanent dwellings														
Total households	1	2	8	10	3	-	1	-	-	-	25			
Total persons	2	4	19	24	13	-	6	-	-	-		68		0.75
Total rooms	1	4	24	40	15	-	7	-	-	-			91	

* Households where the persons present were not usually resident

Number of usually resident persons	1 room	2 rooms	3 rooms	4 rooms	5 rooms	6 rooms	7 rooms	8 rooms	9 rooms	10 or more rooms	Total house-holds	Total persons	Total rooms	Average number of persons per room
Newry and Mourne														
All households														
1 person	37	398	800	1,215	1,432	651	245	94	26	27	4,925	4,925	22,167	0.22
2 persons	6	83	319	863	1,935	1,123	484	195	76	76	5,160	10,320	27,459	0.38
3 persons	2	25	102	375	1,437	908	421	203	80	47	3,600	10,800	20,301	0.53
4 persons	1	15	58	289	1,569	1,067	549	224	115	105	3,992	15,968	23,435	0.68
5 persons	1	7	32	155	1,156	911	467	259	91	99	3,178	15,890	19,218	0.83
6 persons	-	6	12	74	699	580	330	173	76	84	2,034	12,204	12,625	0.97
7 persons	1	1	4	33	243	270	142	70	35	38	837	5,859	5,265	1.11
8 persons	-	1	5	8	95	104	71	40	24	20	368	2,944	2,402	1.23
9 persons	-	-	1	3	42	46	32	21	10	9	164	1,476	1,085	1.36
10 or more persons	-	4	-	5	21	26	18	17	1	6	98	1,050	626	1.68
Other households *	1	4	6	18	17	8	3	4	-	1	62	-	297	-
Total households	49	544	1,339	3,038	8,646	5,694	2,762	1,300	534	512	24,418			
Total persons	71	832	2,285	6,828	28,920	21,342	11,025	5,499	2,326	2,308		81,436		0.60
Total rooms	49	1,088	4,017	12,152	43,230	34,164	19,334	10,400	4,806	5,640			134,880	
Households in shared dwellings														
Total households	2	9	6	1	-	-	-	2	-	-	20			
Total persons	2	12	10	1	-	-	-	8	-	-		33		0.57
Total rooms	2	18	18	4	-	-	-	16	-	-			58	
Households in non-permanent dwellings														
Total households	13	59	38	43	39	8	3	-	-	1	204			
Total persons	23	210	96	154	124	25	7	-	-	5		644		0.93
Total rooms	13	118	114	172	195	48	21	-	-	14			695	
Newtownabbey														
All households														
1 person	36	306	975	1,497	1,521	1,004	209	63	10	18	5,639	5,639	25,438	0.22
2 persons	11	44	289	1,092	2,733	2,359	627	169	64	31	7,419	14,838	39,799	0.37
3 persons	1	3	62	371	2,025	1,701	520	181	59	51	4,974	14,922	28,166	0.53
4 persons	-	2	17	168	1,815	1,773	677	294	138	95	4,979	19,916	29,793	0.67
5 persons	-	1	11	61	818	773	351	191	106	68	2,380	11,900	14,674	0.81
6 persons	-	1	1	20	256	226	124	51	36	24	739	4,434	4,579	0.97
7 persons	-	-	-	5	50	52	23	13	9	8	160	1,120	1,018	1.10
8 persons	-	-	-	2	17	20	11	4	3	4	61	488	393	1.24
9 persons	-	-	-	-	2	2	1	3	1	1	10	90	72	1.25
10 or more persons	-	-	-	-	3	3	-	-	-	-	6	66	33	2.00
Other households *	5	1	10	27	31	34	13	2	-	1	124	-	623	-
Total households	53	358	1,365	3,243	9,271	7,947	2,556	971	426	301	26,491			
Total persons	61	422	1,868	5,942	26,483	23,715	8,488	3,531	1,709	1,194		73,413		0.51
Total rooms	53	716	4,095	12,972	46,355	47,682	17,892	7,768	3,834	3,221			144,588	
Households in shared dwellings														
Total households	9	1	-	5	5	2	6	-	-	-	28			
Total persons	15	4	-	13	15	1	5	-	-	-		53		0.48
Total rooms	9	2	-	20	25	12	42	-	-	-			110	
Households in non-permanent dwellings														
Total households	-	5	5	10	9	3	2	-	-	-	34			
Total persons	-	12	11	25	20	10	3	-	-	-		81		0.57
Total rooms	-	10	15	40	45	18	14	-	-	-			142	

* Households where the persons present were not usually resident

Table 10 Private households by size, rooms, dwelling type and population – **continued**

Number of usually resident persons	1 room	2 rooms	3 rooms	4 rooms	5 rooms	6 rooms	7 rooms	8 rooms	9 rooms	10 or more rooms	Total house-holds	Total persons	Total rooms	Average number of persons per room
	Number of rooms occupied by household													
North Down														
All households														
1 person	166	346	979	1,437	1,679	1,213	390	141	49	43	6,443	6,443	29,992	0.21
2 persons	14	62	286	1,092	2,600	2,236	861	441	167	157	7,916	15,832	44,547	0.36
3 persons	1	3	29	255	1,499	1,287	617	322	150	149	4,312	12,936	26,245	0.49
4 persons	2	2	16	128	1,270	1,441	922	583	268	229	4,861	19,444	31,573	0.62
5 persons	-	-	4	34	480	528	432	348	162	176	2,164	10,820	14,909	0.73
6 persons	-	-	1	11	138	134	119	102	72	75	652	3,912	4,676	0.84
7 persons	-	-	-	3	33	27	23	15	11	21	133	931	947	0.98
8 persons	-	-	-	-	7	5	9	4	8	3	36	288	272	1.06
9 persons	-	-	-	-	4	2	2	1	2	1	12	108	85	1.27
10 or more persons	-	-	-	-	2	1	1	-	-	2	6	63	48	1.31
Other households *	4	4	6	21	26	14	4	4	-	1	84	-	400	-
Total households	187	417	1,321	2,981	7,738	6,888	3,380	1,961	889	857	26,619			
Total persons	205	487	1,728	5,155	20,028	19,011	10,787	6,819	3,306	3,251		70,777		0.46
Total rooms	187	834	3,963	11,924	38,690	41,328	23,660	15,688	8,001	9,419			153,694	
Households in shared dwellings														
Total households	57	25	16	4	5	2	2	-	-	1	112			
Total persons	58	25	21	5	7	3	3	-	-	4		126		0.54
Total rooms	57	50	48	16	25	12	14	-	-	12			234	
Households in non-permanent dwellings														
Total households	1	1	-	3	1	-	1	1	-	-	8			
Total persons	1	1	-	4	4	-	5	3	-	-		18		0.51
Total rooms	1	2	-	12	5	-	7	8	-	-			35	
Omagh														
All households														
1 person	38	180	375	680	852	400	140	68	28	14	2,775	2,775	12,831	0.22
2 persons	1	32	137	443	971	622	300	146	76	51	2,779	5,558	15,345	0.36
3 persons	1	6	41	197	743	513	253	130	49	52	1,985	5,955	11,536	0.52
4 persons	2	6	29	129	765	627	388	190	83	83	2,302	9,208	14,072	0.65
5 persons	-	1	14	72	576	426	268	156	70	75	1,658	8,290	10,334	0.80
6 persons	-	1	13	37	330	275	159	128	53	53	1,049	6,294	6,677	0.94
7 persons	-	-	5	16	121	120	68	50	23	32	435	3,045	2,847	1.07
8 persons	-	-	3	6	60	67	59	31	15	11	252	2,016	1,648	1.22
9 persons	-	-	-	2	16	15	20	11	4	5	73	657	493	1.33
10 or more persons	-	-	4	2	20	18	21	10	5	2	82	871	520	1.67
Other households *	-	1	3	9	6	5	2	1	-	-	27	-	129	-
Total households	42	227	624	1,593	4,460	3,088	1,678	921	406	378	13,417			
Total persons	51	297	1,140	3,456	14,627	11,175	6,688	3,864	1,696	1,675		44,669		0.58
Total rooms	42	454	1,872	6,372	22,300	18,528	11,746	7,368	3,654	4,096			76,432	
Households in shared dwellings														
Total households	14	2	4	2	2	-	-	-	-	-	24			
Total persons	14	2	4	2	2	-	-	-	-	-		24		0.50
Total rooms	14	4	12	8	10	-	-	-	-	-			48	
Households in non-permanent dwellings														
Total households	12	37	26	25	32	5	-	-	1	-	138			
Total persons	14	55	59	86	99	13	-	-	9	-		335		0.72
Total rooms	12	74	78	100	160	30	-	-	9	-			463	

* Households where the persons present were not usually resident

Table 10 Private households by size, rooms, dwelling type and population – **continued**

Number of usually resident persons	Number of rooms occupied by household: 1 room	2 rooms	3 rooms	4 rooms	5 rooms	6 rooms	7 rooms	8 rooms	9 rooms	10 or more rooms	Total house-holds	Total persons	Total rooms	Average number of persons per room
Strabane														
All households														
1 person	23	142	255	565	644	279	70	49	30	14	2,071	2,071	9,542	0.22
2 persons	5	46	131	411	887	463	169	100	50	37	2,299	4,598	12,170	0.38
3 persons	1	17	62	197	730	396	171	84	32	41	1,731	5,193	9,639	0.54
4 persons	-	6	25	115	754	453	189	111	48	51	1,752	7,008	10,242	0.68
5 persons	1	-	16	96	519	384	161	77	45	44	1,343	6,715	7,965	0.84
6 persons	-	1	9	48	343	228	103	65	29	29	855	5,130	5,125	1.00
7 persons	-	-	5	19	128	105	46	23	12	16	354	2,478	2,145	1.16
8 persons	-	2	7	4	74	46	22	12	6	5	178	1,424	1,046	1.36
9 persons	-	1	-	3	32	22	7	6	2	3	76	684	452	1.51
10 or more persons	-	-	-	4	22	19	3	6	8	4	66	706	423	1.67
Other households *	1	1	1	8	10	4	-	-	-	-	25	-	112	-
Total households	31	216	511	1,470	4,143	2,399	941	533	262	244	10,750			
Total persons	41	340	1,028	3,439	14,292	8,998	3,695	2,092	1,048	1,034		36,007		0.61
Total rooms	31	432	1,533	5,880	20,715	14,394	6,587	4,264	2,358	2,667			58,861	
Households in shared dwellings														
Total households	-	2	4	1	1	-	-	-	1	-	9			
Total persons	-	2	6	2	1	-	-	-	3	-		14		0.41
Total rooms	-	4	12	4	5	-	-	-	9	-			34	
Households in non-permanent dwellings														
Total households	13	54	27	15	17	4	1	-	1	2	134			
Total persons	16	109	55	46	53	14	6	-	4	3		306		0.75
Total rooms	13	108	81	60	85	24	7	-	9	21			408	

* Households where the persons present were not usually resident

Table 11 Private households by size, dwelling type and density of occupation (persons per room)

Number of usually resident persons	Total	All households									
		Over 1.5	Over 1 and up to 1.5	Over 0.75 and up to 1	0.5 and over and up to 0.75	Less than 0.5	Over 1.5	Over 1 and up to 1.5	Over 0.75 and up to 1	0.5 and over and up to 0.75	Less than 0.5
		Number					Percentage				
NORTHERN IRELAND											
All households											
1 person	119,980	-	-	1,166	7,230	111,584	-	-	1.0	6.0	93.0
2 persons	135,395	141	-	1,423	31,143	102,688	0.1	-	1.1	23.0	75.8
3 persons	87,998	30	274	1,861	67,678	18,155	0.0	0.3	2.1	76.9	20.6
4 persons	89,917	153	851	37,804	45,413	5,696	0.2	0.9	42.0	50.5	6.3
5 persons	52,411	446	2,244	32,569	16,174	978	0.9	4.3	62.1	30.9	1.9
6 persons	25,943	213	9,581	11,088	4,878	183	0.8	36.9	42.7	18.8	0.7
7 persons	9,215	376	5,507	2,849	464	19	4.1	59.8	30.9	5.0	0.2
8 persons	3,907	1,336	1,788	683	97	3	34.2	45.8	17.5	2.5	0.1
9 persons	1,590	498	924	153	14	1	31.3	58.1	9.6	0.9	0.1
10 or more persons	1,152	731	366	54	1	-	63.5	31.8	4.7	0.1	-
Other households *	2,861	-	-	-	-	2,861	-	-	-	-	100.0
Total households	530,369	3,924	21,535	89,650	173,092	242,168	0.7	4.1	16.9	32.6	45.7
Total persons	1,554,538	30,229	137,921	417,524	568,501	400,363	1.9	8.9	26.9	36.6	25.8
Households in shared dwellings											
Total households	834	26	9	255	217	327	3.1	1.1	30.6	26.0	39.2
Total persons	1,085	60	35	342	381	267	5.5	3.2	31.5	35.1	24.6
Households in non-permanent dwellings											
Total households	2,254	218	207	529	726	574	9.7	9.2	23.5	32.2	25.5
Total persons	5,953	1,217	966	1,577	1,499	694	20.4	16.2	26.5	25.2	11.7
Antrim											
All households											
1 person	2,754	-	-	37	144	2,573	-	-	1.3	5.2	93.4
2 persons	3,559	1	-	31	668	2,859	0.0	-	0.9	18.8	80.3
3 persons	2,612	-	6	33	2,025	548	-	0.2	1.3	77.5	21.0
4 persons	2,652	1	24	1,126	1,343	158	0.0	0.9	42.5	50.6	6.0
5 persons	1,481	8	37	917	490	29	0.5	2.5	61.9	33.1	2.0
6 persons	660	4	231	305	115	5	0.6	35.0	46.2	17.4	0.8
7 persons	256	11	158	79	7	1	4.3	61.7	30.9	2.7	0.4
8 persons	86	25	41	19	1	-	29.1	47.7	22.1	1.2	-
9 persons	41	19	18	4	-	-	46.3	43.9	9.8	-	-
10 or more persons	23	15	8	-	-	-	65.2	34.8	-	-	-
Other households *	42	-	-	-	-	42	-	-	-	-	100.0
Total households	14,166	84	523	2,551	4,793	6,215	0.6	3.7	18.0	33.8	43.9
Total persons	42,782	686	3,365	11,858	16,124	10,749	1.6	7.9	27.7	37.7	25.1
Households in shared dwellings											
Total households	8	-	-	-	4	4	-	-	-	50.0	50.0
Total persons	11	-	-	-	8	3	-	-	-	72.7	27.3
Households in non-permanent dwellings											
Total households	103	7	10	21	37	28	6.8	9.7	20.4	35.9	27.2
Total persons	272	43	39	67	85	38	15.8	14.3	24.6	31.2	14.0

* Households where the persons present were not usually resident

Table 11 Private households by size, dwelling type and density of occupation (persons per room) – **continued**

Number of usually resident persons	Total	All households: Over 1.5	Over 1 and up to 1.5	Over 0.75 and up to 1	0.5 and over and up to 0.75	Less than 0.5	Over 1.5	Over 1 and up to 1.5	Over 0.75 and up to 1	0.5 and over and up to 0.75	Less than 0.5
		Number					Percentage				
Ards											
All households											
1 person	4,785	-	-	15	223	4,547	-	-	0.3	4.7	95.0
2 persons	6,511	2	-	47	1,565	4,897	0.0	-	0.7	24.0	75.2
3 persons	3,973	-	4	69	3,112	788	-	0.1	1.7	78.3	19.8
4 persons	4,429	2	32	1,863	2,188	344	0.0	0.7	42.1	49.4	7.8
5 persons	2,101	12	73	1,298	675	43	0.6	3.5	61.8	32.1	2.0
6 persons	694	9	255	249	169	12	1.3	36.7	35.9	24.4	1.7
7 persons	170	4	103	47	16	-	2.4	60.6	27.6	9.4	-
8 persons	66	27	27	8	4	-	40.9	40.9	12.1	6.1	-
9 persons	24	6	15	3	-	-	25.0	62.5	12.5	-	-
10 or more persons	12	8	3	1	-	-	66.7	25.0	8.3	-	-
Other households *	67	-	-	-	-	67	-	-	-	-	100.0
Total households	22,832	70	512	3,600	7,952	10,698	0.3	2.2	15.8	34.8	46.9
Total persons	64,179	517	3,138	16,182	25,974	18,368	0.8	4.9	25.2	40.5	28.6
Households in shared dwellings											
Total households	7	-	-	2	3	2	-	-	28.6	42.9	28.6
Total persons	15	-	-	5	7	3	-	-	33.3	46.7	20.0
Households in non-permanent dwellings											
Total households	53	10	5	11	14	13	18.9	9.4	20.8	26.4	24.5
Total persons	141	47	19	33	33	9	33.3	13.5	23.4	23.4	6.4
Armagh											
All households											
1 person	3,163	-	-	9	165	2,989	-	-	0.3	5.2	94.5
2 persons	3,515	2	-	24	671	2,818	0.1	-	0.7	19.1	80.2
3 persons	2,548	3	8	50	1,865	622	0.1	0.3	2.0	73.2	24.4
4 persons	2,700	5	20	1,107	1,390	178	0.2	0.7	41.0	51.5	6.6
5 persons	1,893	14	73	1,132	635	39	0.7	3.9	59.8	33.5	2.1
6 persons	1,130	10	401	468	243	8	0.9	35.5	41.4	21.5	0.7
7 persons	402	15	217	147	21	2	3.7	54.0	36.6	5.2	0.5
8 persons	205	77	88	27	12	1	37.6	42.9	13.2	5.9	0.5
9 persons	78	33	37	6	1	1	42.3	47.4	7.7	1.3	1.3
10 or more persons	54	22	25	7	-	-	40.7	46.3	13.0	-	-
Other households *	32	-	-	-	-	32	-	-	-	-	100.0
Total households	15,720	181	869	2,977	5,003	6,690	1.2	5.5	18.9	31.8	42.6
Total persons	50,617	1,428	5,692	14,473	17,547	11,477	2.8	11.2	28.6	34.7	22.7
Households in shared dwellings											
Total households	10	-	1	3	3	3	-	10.0	30.0	30.0	30.0
Total persons	22	-	5	11	3	3	-	22.7	50.0	13.6	13.6
Households in non-permanent dwellings											
Total households	138	12	15	32	50	29	8.7	10.9	23.2	36.2	21.0
Total persons	362	55	65	96	113	33	15.2	18.0	26.5	31.2	9.1

* Households where the persons present were not usually resident

Table 11 Private households by size, dwelling type and density of occupation (persons per room) – **continued**

Local Government Districts

Number of usually resident persons	Total	All households: Over 1.5	Over 1 and up to 1.5	Over 0.75 and up to 1	0.5 and over and up to 0.75	Less than 0.5	Over 1.5	Over 1 and up to 1.5	Over 0.75 and up to 1	0.5 and over and up to 0.75	Less than 0.5
		Number					Percentage				
Ballymena											
All households											
1 person	3,927	-	-	16	231	3,680	-	-	0.4	5.9	93.7
2 persons	5,096	2	-	48	947	4,099	0.0	-	0.9	18.6	80.4
3 persons	3,483	-	6	46	2,533	898	-	0.2	1.3	72.7	25.8
4 persons	3,453	7	23	1,103	2,070	250	0.2	0.7	31.9	59.9	7.2
5 persons	1,865	5	58	1,024	738	40	0.3	3.1	54.9	39.6	2.1
6 persons	828	3	227	412	184	2	0.4	27.4	49.8	22.2	0.2
7 persons	281	3	149	108	20	1	1.1	53.0	38.4	7.1	0.4
8 persons	95	21	50	17	7	-	22.1	52.6	17.9	7.4	-
9 persons	43	5	33	4	1	-	11.6	76.7	9.3	2.3	-
10 or more persons	26	11	13	2	-	-	42.3	50.0	7.7	-	-
Other households *	40	-	-	-	-	40	-	-	-	-	100.0
Total households	19,137	57	559	2,780	6,731	9,010	0.3	2.9	14.5	35.2	47.1
Total persons	56,064	425	3,643	13,202	23,003	15,791	0.8	6.5	23.5	41.0	28.2
Households in shared dwellings											
Total households	7	-	1	1	4	1	-	14.3	14.3	57.1	14.3
Total persons	16	-	3	4	7	2	-	18.7	25.0	43.7	12.5
Households in non-permanent dwellings											
Total households	90	2	6	21	37	24	2.2	6.7	23.3	41.1	26.7
Total persons	220	6	28	69	85	32	2.7	12.7	31.4	38.6	14.5
Ballymoney											
All households											
1 person	1,436	-	-	11	97	1,328	-	-	0.8	6.8	92.5
2 persons	1,938	1	-	20	436	1,481	0.1	-	1.0	22.5	76.4
3 persons	1,417	-	11	31	1,054	321	-	0.8	2.2	74.4	22.7
4 persons	1,370	2	25	634	616	93	0.1	1.8	46.3	45.0	6.8
5 persons	832	4	67	453	288	20	0.5	8.1	54.4	34.6	2.4
6 persons	396	3	157	147	85	4	0.8	39.6	37.1	21.5	1.0
7 persons	184	10	92	68	13	1	5.4	50.0	37.0	7.1	0.5
8 persons	73	30	25	18	-	-	41.1	34.2	24.7	-	-
9 persons	42	15	25	2	-	-	35.7	59.5	4.8	-	-
10 or more persons	22	11	11	-	-	-	50.0	50.0	-	-	-
Other households *	20	-	-	-	-	20	-	-	-	-	100.0
Total households	7,730	76	413	1,384	2,589	3,268	1.0	5.3	17.9	33.5	42.3
Total persons	24,075	623	2,595	6,465	8,636	5,756	2.6	10.8	26.9	35.9	23.9
Households in shared dwellings											
Total households	3	-	-	-	3	-	-	-	-	100.0	-
Total persons	5	-	-	-	5	-	-	-	-	100.0	-
Households in non-permanent dwellings											
Total households	46	1	7	11	14	13	2.2	15.2	23.9	30.4	28.3
Total persons	110	16	24	27	32	11	14.5	21.8	24.5	29.1	10.0

* Households where the persons present were not usually resident

Table 11 Private households by size, dwelling type and density of occupation (persons per room) – **continued**

Number of usually resident persons	Total	All households: Over 1.5	Over 1 and up to 1.5	Over 0.75 and up to 1	0.5 and over and up to 0.75	Less than 0.5	Over 1.5	Over 1 and up to 1.5	Over 0.75 and up to 1	0.5 and over and up to 0.75	Less than 0.5
		Number					Percentage				
Banbridge											
All households											
1 person	2,179	-	-	21	121	2,037	-	-	1.0	5.6	93.5
2 persons	2,816	2	-	30	617	2,167	0.1	-	1.1	21.9	77.0
3 persons	1,837	-	3	32	1,388	414	-	0.2	1.7	75.6	22.5
4 persons	2,012	4	20	814	1,019	155	0.2	1.0	40.5	50.6	7.7
5 persons	1,205	4	56	722	399	24	0.3	4.6	59.9	33.1	2.0
6 persons	598	3	188	257	146	4	0.5	31.4	43.0	24.4	0.7
7 persons	209	7	115	73	14	-	3.3	55.0	34.9	6.7	-
8 persons	61	13	26	20	2	-	21.3	42.6	32.8	3.3	-
9 persons	31	7	18	6	-	-	22.6	58.1	19.4	-	-
10 or more persons	12	11	1	-	-	-	91.7	8.3	-	-	-
Other households *	24	-	-	-	-	24	-	-	-	-	100.0
Total households	10,984	51	427	1,975	3,706	4,825	0.5	3.9	18.0	33.7	43.9
Total persons	33,341	392	2,682	9,310	12,580	8,377	1.2	8.0	27.9	37.7	25.1
Households in shared dwellings											
Total households	5	-	1	1	2	1	-	20.0	20.0	40.0	20.0
Total persons	14	-	5	4	4	1	-	35.7	28.6	28.6	7.1
Households in non-permanent dwellings											
Total households	93	5	7	25	27	29	5.4	7.5	26.9	29.0	31.2
Total persons	249	22	42	88	56	41	8.8	16.9	35.3	22.5	16.5
Belfast											
All households											
1 person	31,895	-	-	459	1,918	29,518	-	-	1.4	6.0	92.5
2 persons	29,338	49	-	385	9,441	19,463	0.2	-	1.3	32.2	66.3
3 persons	16,584	7	78	576	13,133	2,790	0.0	0.5	3.5	79.2	16.8
4 persons	14,664	23	242	6,851	6,755	793	0.2	1.7	46.7	46.1	5.4
5 persons	7,997	109	590	4,980	2,173	145	1.4	7.4	62.3	27.2	1.8
6 persons	3,757	35	1,501	1,552	650	19	0.9	40.0	41.3	17.3	0.5
7 persons	1,120	69	676	326	45	4	6.2	60.4	29.1	4.0	0.4
8 persons	394	152	172	61	9	-	38.6	43.7	15.5	2.3	-
9 persons	160	46	98	14	2	-	28.7	61.2	8.7	1.2	-
10 or more persons	118	76	40	1	1	-	64.4	33.9	0.8	0.8	-
Other households *	1,367	-	-	-	-	1,367	-	-	-	-	100.0
Total households	107,394	566	3,397	15,205	34,127	54,099	0.5	3.2	14.2	31.8	50.4
Total persons	275,172	3,878	20,562	67,479	102,400	80,853	1.4	7.5	24.5	37.2	29.4
Households in shared dwellings											
Total households	411	13	2	123	100	173	3.2	0.5	29.9	24.3	42.1
Total persons	503	29	7	146	191	130	5.8	1.4	29.0	38.0	25.8
Households in non-permanent dwellings											
Total households	105	21	16	21	20	27	20.0	15.2	20.0	19.0	25.7
Total persons	458	170	98	89	59	42	37.1	21.4	19.4	12.9	9.2

* Households where the persons present were not usually resident

Table 11 Private households by size, dwelling type and density of occupation (persons per room) – **continued**

Number of usually resident persons	Total	All households									
		Over 1.5	Over 1 and up to 1.5	Over 0.75 and up to 1	0.5 and over and up to 0.75	Less than 0.5	Over 1.5	Over 1 and up to 1.5	Over 0.75 and up to 1	0.5 and over and up to 0.75	Less than 0.5
		Number					Percentage				
Carrickfergus											
All households											
1 person	2,587	-	-	15	167	2,405	-	-	0.6	6.5	93.0
2 persons	3,431	2	-	21	631	2,777	0.1	-	0.6	18.4	80.9
3 persons	2,204	-	3	18	1,756	427	-	0.1	0.8	79.7	19.4
4 persons	2,205	-	6	891	1,155	153	-	0.3	40.4	52.4	6.9
5 persons	992	5	23	621	319	24	0.5	2.3	62.6	32.2	2.4
6 persons	291	2	88	139	58	4	0.7	30.2	47.8	19.9	1.4
7 persons	85	2	50	23	9	1	2.4	58.8	27.1	10.6	1.2
8 persons	22	9	9	2	2	-	40.9	40.9	9.1	9.1	-
9 persons	8	5	3	-	-	-	62.5	37.5	-	-	-
10 or more persons	2	1	1	-	-	-	50.0	50.0	-	-	-
Other households *	43	-	-	-	-	43	-	-	-	-	100.0
Total households	11,870	26	183	1,730	4,097	5,834	0.2	1.5	14.6	34.5	49.1
Total persons	32,450	182	1,135	7,791	13,339	10,003	0.6	3.5	24.0	41.1	30.8
Households in shared dwellings											
Total households	13	1	-	4	4	4	7.7	-	30.8	30.8	30.8
Total persons	20	2	-	8	6	4	10.0	-	40.0	30.0	20.0
Households in non-permanent dwellings											
Total households	11	1	-	5	3	2	9.1	-	45.5	27.3	18.2
Total persons	32	6	-	15	6	5	18.7	-	46.9	18.7	15.6
Castlereagh											
All households											
1 person	5,516	-	-	45	349	5,122	-	-	0.8	6.3	92.9
2 persons	7,018	2	-	41	1,247	5,728	0.0	-	0.6	17.8	81.6
3 persons	4,069	1	2	34	3,320	712	0.0	0.0	0.8	81.6	17.5
4 persons	4,046	5	13	1,481	2,411	136	0.1	0.3	36.6	59.6	3.4
5 persons	1,640	8	38	1,084	497	13	0.5	2.3	66.1	30.3	0.8
6 persons	427	4	148	199	75	1	0.9	34.7	46.6	17.6	0.2
7 persons	93	4	48	36	5	-	4.3	51.6	38.7	5.4	-
8 persons	24	8	11	5	-	-	33.3	45.8	20.8	-	-
9 persons	6	1	3	2	-	-	16.7	50.0	33.3	-	-
10 or more persons	4	2	2	-	-	-	50.0	50.0	-	-	-
Other households *	67	-	-	-	-	67	-	-	-	-	100.0
Total households	22,910	35	265	2,927	7,904	11,779	0.2	1.2	12.8	34.5	51.4
Total persons	59,644	212	1,609	13,077	25,417	19,329	0.4	2.7	21.9	42.6	32.4
Households in shared dwellings											
Total households	7	-	-	2	1	4	-	-	28.6	14.3	57.1
Total persons	10	-	-	4	2	4	-	-	40.0	20.0	40.0
Households in non-permanent dwellings											
Total households	24	1	2	2	5	14	4.2	8.3	8.3	20.8	58.3
Total persons	46	6	17	7	10	6	13.0	37.0	15.2	21.7	13.0

* Households where the persons present were not usually resident

Table 11 Private households by size, dwelling type and density of occupation (persons per room) – **continued**

Number of usually resident persons	Total	All households									
		Over 1.5	Over 1 and up to 1.5	Over 0.75 and up to 1	0.5 and over and up to 0.75	Less than 0.5	Over 1.5	Over 1 and up to 1.5	Over 0.75 and up to 1	0.5 and over and up to 0.75	Less than 0.5
		Number					Percentage				
Coleraine											
All households											
1 person	4,045	-	-	32	239	3,774	-	-	0.8	5.9	93.3
2 persons	4,778	4	-	53	915	3,806	0.1	-	1.1	19.2	79.7
3 persons	2,997	-	13	44	2,194	746	-	0.4	1.5	73.2	24.9
4 persons	3,030	3	17	1,216	1,541	253	0.1	0.6	40.1	50.9	8.3
5 persons	1,627	16	36	957	574	44	1.0	2.2	58.8	35.3	2.7
6 persons	705	3	204	296	191	11	0.4	28.9	42.0	27.1	1.6
7 persons	227	8	123	80	16	-	3.5	54.2	35.2	7.0	-
8 persons	80	26	34	17	3	-	32.5	42.5	21.2	3.7	-
9 persons	29	6	21	2	-	-	20.7	72.4	6.9	-	-
10 or more persons	24	18	4	2	-	-	75.0	16.7	8.3	-	-
Other households *	328	-	-	-	-	328	-	-	-	-	100.0
Total households	17,870	84	452	2,699	5,673	8,962	0.5	2.5	15.1	31.7	50.2
Total persons	49,824	628	2,876	12,431	18,967	14,922	1.3	5.8	24.9	38.1	29.9
Households in shared dwellings											
Total households	45	2	-	11	5	27	4.4	-	24.4	11.1	60.0
Total persons	40	4	-	17	8	11	10.0	-	42.5	20.0	27.5
Households in non-permanent dwellings											
Total households	53	4	3	10	15	21	7.5	5.7	18.9	28.3	39.6
Total persons	102	17	11	25	32	17	16.7	10.8	24.5	31.4	16.7
Cookstown											
All households											
1 person	1,726	-	-	4	89	1,633	-	-	0.2	5.2	94.6
2 persons	1,971	1	-	17	436	1,517	0.1	-	0.9	22.1	77.0
3 persons	1,473	1	10	31	1,046	385	0.1	0.7	2.1	71.0	26.1
4 persons	1,607	4	18	660	826	99	0.2	1.1	41.1	51.4	6.2
5 persons	1,171	12	69	708	358	24	1.0	5.9	60.5	30.6	2.0
6 persons	736	9	258	315	153	1	1.2	35.1	42.8	20.8	0.1
7 persons	301	7	180	98	16	-	2.3	59.8	32.6	5.3	-
8 persons	124	36	61	22	5	-	29.0	49.2	17.7	4.0	-
9 persons	46	11	30	5	-	-	23.9	65.2	10.9	-	-
10 or more persons	52	34	14	4	-	-	65.4	26.9	7.7	-	-
Other households *	15	-	-	-	-	15	-	-	-	-	100.0
Total households	9,222	115	640	1,864	2,929	3,674	1.2	6.9	20.2	31.8	39.8
Total persons	30,859	940	4,163	9,149	10,263	6,344	3.0	13.5	29.6	33.3	20.6
Households in shared dwellings											
Total households	1	-	-	-	-	1	-	-	-	-	100.0
Total persons	1	-	-	-	-	1	-	-	-	-	100.0
Households in non-permanent dwellings											
Total households	79	3	8	16	32	20	3.8	10.1	20.3	40.5	25.3
Total persons	177	10	29	53	64	21	5.6	16.4	29.9	36.2	11.9

* Households where the persons present were not usually resident

Table 11 Private households by size, dwelling type and density of occupation (persons per room) – **continued**

Number of usually resident persons	Total	All households: Number: Over 1.5	Over 1 and up to 1.5	Over 0.75 and up to 1	0.5 and over and up to 0.75	Less than 0.5	Percentage: Over 1.5	Over 1 and up to 1.5	Over 0.75 and up to 1	0.5 and over and up to 0.75	Less than 0.5
Craigavon											
All households											
1 person	5,254	-	-	43	392	4,819	-	-	0.8	7.5	91.7
2 persons	6,200	5	-	55	1,098	5,042	0.1	-	0.9	17.7	81.3
3 persons	4,349	1	10	59	3,495	784	0.0	0.2	1.4	80.4	18.0
4 persons	4,556	5	27	1,973	2,325	226	0.1	0.6	43.3	51.0	5.0
5 persons	2,538	20	74	1,705	701	38	0.8	2.9	67.2	27.6	1.5
6 persons	1,263	5	448	592	211	7	0.4	35.5	46.9	16.7	0.6
7 persons	403	14	257	124	7	1	3.5	63.8	30.8	1.7	0.2
8 persons	161	58	77	24	2	-	36.0	47.8	14.9	1.2	-
9 persons	66	16	44	6	-	-	24.2	66.7	9.1	-	-
10 or more persons	51	38	8	5	-	-	74.5	15.7	9.8	-	-
Other households *	74	-	-	-	-	74	-	-	-	-	100.0
Total households	24,915	162	945	4,586	8,231	10,991	0.7	3.8	18.4	33.0	44.1
Total persons	74,443	1,277	6,093	21,466	27,209	18,398	1.7	8.2	28.8	36.6	24.7
Households in shared dwellings											
Total households	11	-	-	2	7	2	-	-	18.2	63.6	18.2
Total persons	17	-	-	5	10	2	-	-	29.4	58.8	11.8
Households in non-permanent dwellings											
Total households	87	7	9	30	26	15	8.0	10.3	34.5	29.9	17.2
Total persons	249	29	46	102	50	22	11.6	18.5	41.0	20.1	8.8
Derry											
All households											
1 person	5,381	-	-	27	493	4,861	-	-	0.5	9.2	90.3
2 persons	5,717	8	-	89	1,515	4,105	0.1	-	1.6	26.5	71.8
3 persons	4,493	3	10	115	3,654	711	0.1	0.2	2.6	81.3	15.8
4 persons	4,903	12	55	2,541	2,065	230	0.2	1.1	51.8	42.1	4.7
5 persons	3,463	32	119	2,480	785	47	0.9	3.4	71.6	22.7	1.4
6 persons	2,221	13	1,071	876	256	5	0.6	48.2	39.4	11.5	0.2
7 persons	935	31	676	195	32	1	3.3	72.3	20.9	3.4	0.1
8 persons	442	189	199	49	5	-	42.8	45.0	11.1	1.1	-
9 persons	184	73	101	8	2	-	39.7	54.9	4.3	1.1	-
10 or more persons	130	97	27	6	-	-	74.6	20.8	4.6	-	-
Other households *	146	-	-	-	-	146	-	-	-	-	100.0
Total households	28,015	458	2,258	6,386	8,807	10,106	1.6	8.1	22.8	31.4	36.1
Total persons	93,695	3,761	14,788	30,262	28,488	16,396	4.0	15.8	32.3	30.4	17.5
Households in shared dwellings											
Total households	40	2	-	9	10	19	5.0	-	22.5	25.0	47.5
Total persons	62	5	-	20	15	22	8.1	-	32.3	24.2	35.5
Households in non-permanent dwellings											
Total households	58	13	5	11	11	18	22.4	8.6	19.0	19.0	31.0
Total persons	155	63	27	25	20	20	40.6	17.4	16.1	12.9	12.9

* Households where the persons present were not usually resident

Number of usually resident persons	Total	All households: Number: Over 1.5	Over 1 and up to 1.5	Over 0.75 and up to 1	0.5 and over and up to 0.75	Less than 0.5	All households: Percentage: Over 1.5	Over 1 and up to 1.5	Over 0.75 and up to 1	0.5 and over and up to 0.75	Less than 0.5
Down											
All households											
1 person	3,615	-	-	26	239	3,350	-	-	0.7	6.6	92.7
2 persons	4,245	7	-	52	881	3,305	0.2	-	1.2	20.8	77.9
3 persons	2,987	1	9	76	2,214	687	0.0	0.3	2.5	74.1	23.0
4 persons	3,240	7	30	1,363	1,620	220	0.2	0.9	42.1	50.0	6.8
5 persons	2,031	16	95	1,220	655	45	0.8	4.7	60.1	32.3	2.2
6 persons	1,156	18	420	482	225	11	1.6	36.3	41.7	19.5	1.0
7 persons	419	16	256	115	30	2	3.8	61.1	27.4	7.2	0.5
8 persons	176	58	79	34	4	1	33.0	44.9	19.3	2.3	0.6
9 persons	74	20	40	13	1	-	27.0	54.1	17.6	1.4	-
10 or more persons	46	34	11	1	-	-	73.9	23.9	2.2	-	-
Other households *	72	-	-	-	-	72	-	-	-	-	100.0
Total households	18,061	177	940	3,382	5,869	7,693	1.0	5.2	18.7	32.5	42.6
Total persons	56,616	1,356	6,040	16,007	19,999	13,214	2.4	10.7	28.3	35.3	23.3
Households in shared dwellings											
Total households	24	-	-	13	5	6	-	-	54.2	20.8	25.0
Total persons	33	-	-	19	7	7	-	-	57.6	21.2	21.2
Households in non-permanent dwellings											
Total households	131	10	11	26	40	44	7.6	8.4	19.8	30.5	33.6
Total persons	315	51	59	80	82	43	16.2	18.7	25.4	26.0	13.7
Dungannon											
All households											
1 person	2,721	-	-	12	127	2,582	-	-	0.4	4.7	94.9
2 persons	3,009	2	-	44	609	2,354	0.1	-	1.5	20.2	78.2
3 persons	2,126	-	11	50	1,588	477	-	0.5	2.4	74.7	22.4
4 persons	2,207	9	23	984	1,021	170	0.4	1.0	44.6	46.3	7.7
5 persons	1,702	19	76	1,072	495	40	1.1	4.5	63.0	29.1	2.4
6 persons	1,048	6	376	445	210	11	0.6	35.9	42.5	20.0	1.0
7 persons	445	18	249	151	27	-	4.0	56.0	33.9	6.1	-
8 persons	218	69	106	38	5	-	31.7	48.6	17.4	2.3	-
9 persons	80	26	45	9	-	-	32.5	56.2	11.2	-	-
10 or more persons	68	38	26	4	-	-	55.9	38.2	5.9	-	-
Other households *	29	-	-	-	-	29	-	-	-	-	100.0
Total households	13,653	187	912	2,809	4,082	5,663	1.4	6.7	20.6	29.9	41.5
Total persons	45,062	1,502	6,036	13,700	14,157	9,667	3.3	13.4	30.4	31.4	21.5
Households in shared dwellings											
Total households	7	-	-	-	2	5	-	-	-	28.6	71.4
Total persons	7	-	-	-	5	2	-	-	-	71.4	28.6
Households in non-permanent dwellings											
Total households	145	19	12	30	42	42	13.1	8.3	20.7	29.0	29.0
Total persons	413	114	55	96	92	56	27.6	13.3	23.2	22.3	13.6

* Households where the persons present were not usually resident

Table 11 Private households by size, dwelling type and density of occupation (persons per room) – **continued**

Number of usually resident persons	Total	All households: Number – Over 1.5	Over 1 and up to 1.5	Over 0.75 and up to 1	0.5 and over and up to 0.75	Less than 0.5	All households: Percentage – Over 1.5	Over 1 and up to 1.5	Over 0.75 and up to 1	0.5 and over and up to 0.75	Less than 0.5
Fermanagh											
All households											
1 person	3,667	-	-	33	205	3,429	-	-	0.9	5.6	93.5
2 persons	3,932	2	-	49	789	3,092	0.1	-	1.2	20.1	78.6
3 persons	2,592	-	9	73	1,786	724	-	0.3	2.8	68.9	27.9
4 persons	2,712	6	24	1,115	1,359	208	0.2	0.9	41.1	50.1	7.7
5 persons	1,853	9	64	1,124	619	37	0.5	3.5	60.7	33.4	2.0
6 persons	1,181	13	401	524	235	8	1.1	34.0	44.4	19.9	0.7
7 persons	502	20	271	191	20	-	4.0	54.0	38.0	4.0	-
8 persons	243	62	118	58	5	-	25.5	48.6	23.9	2.1	-
9 persons	101	25	66	9	1	-	24.8	65.3	8.9	1.0	-
10 or more persons	65	37	26	2	-	-	56.9	40.0	3.1	-	-
Other households *	53	-	-	-	-	53	-	-	-	-	100.0
Total households	16,901	174	979	3,178	5,019	7,551	1.0	5.8	18.8	29.7	44.7
Total persons	53,568	1,420	6,551	15,476	17,271	12,850	2.7	12.2	28.9	32.2	24.0
Households in shared dwellings											
Total households	15	-	-	5	7	3	-	-	33.3	46.7	20.0
Total persons	19	-	-	7	10	2	-	-	36.8	52.6	10.5
Households in non-permanent dwellings											
Total households	156	8	13	37	61	37	5.1	8.3	23.7	39.1	23.7
Total persons	331	44	67	85	91	44	13.3	20.2	25.7	27.5	13.3
Larne											
All households											
1 person	2,405	-	-	9	94	2,302	-	-	0.4	3.9	95.7
2 persons	2,852	2	-	22	584	2,244	0.1	-	0.8	20.5	78.7
3 persons	1,814	1	1	24	1,362	426	0.1	0.1	1.3	75.1	23.5
4 persons	1,792	1	11	666	993	121	0.1	0.6	37.2	55.4	6.8
5 persons	984	6	34	584	337	23	0.6	3.5	59.3	34.2	2.3
6 persons	369	1	87	177	101	3	0.3	23.6	48.0	27.4	0.8
7 persons	116	2	64	43	7	-	1.7	55.2	37.1	6.0	-
8 persons	38	7	23	8	-	-	18.4	60.5	21.1	-	-
9 persons	12	2	7	3	-	-	16.7	58.3	25.0	-	-
10 or more persons	8	3	3	2	-	-	37.5	37.5	25.0	-	-
Other households *	19	-	-	-	-	19	-	-	-	-	100.0
Total households	10,409	25	230	1,538	3,478	5,138	0.2	2.2	14.8	33.4	49.4
Total persons	29,159	165	1,466	7,183	11,660	8,685	0.6	5.0	24.6	40.0	29.8
Households in shared dwellings											
Total households	2	-	-	-	1	1	-	-	-	50.0	50.0
Total persons	3	-	-	-	2	1	-	-	-	66.7	33.3
Households in non-permanent dwellings											
Total households	49	6	3	9	20	11	12.2	6.1	18.4	40.8	22.4
Total persons	121	27	14	25	46	9	22.3	11.6	20.7	38.0	7.4

* Households where the persons present were not usually resident

Table 11 Private households by size, dwelling type and density of occupation (persons per room) – **continued**

Number of usually resident persons	Total	All households									
		Over 1.5	Over 1 and up to 1.5	Over 0.75 and up to 1	0.5 and over and up to 0.75	Less than 0.5	Over 1.5	Over 1 and up to 1.5	Over 0.75 and up to 1	0.5 and over and up to 0.75	Less than 0.5
		Number					Percentage				
Limavady											
All households											
1 person	1,364	-	-	12	90	1,262	-	-	0.9	6.6	92.5
2 persons	1,877	2	-	20	462	1,393	0.1	-	1.1	24.6	74.2
3 persons	1,470	2	12	45	1,150	261	0.1	0.8	3.1	78.2	17.8
4 persons	1,600	2	19	816	695	68	0.1	1.2	51.0	43.4	4.2
5 persons	1,021	13	37	699	253	19	1.3	3.6	68.5	24.8	1.9
6 persons	619	3	270	250	93	3	0.5	43.6	40.4	15.0	0.5
7 persons	263	12	167	73	11	-	4.6	63.5	27.8	4.2	-
8 persons	137	60	57	18	2	-	43.8	41.6	13.1	1.5	-
9 persons	59	24	33	2	-	-	40.7	55.9	3.4	-	-
10 or more persons	64	47	14	3	-	-	73.4	21.9	4.7	-	-
Other households *	15	-	-	-	-	15	-	-	-	-	100.0
Total households	8,489	165	609	1,938	2,756	3,021	1.9	7.2	22.8	32.5	35.6
Total persons	28,892	1,377	3,988	9,151	9,160	5,216	4.8	13.8	31.7	31.7	18.1
Households in shared dwellings											
Total households	1	-	-	-	1	-	-	-	-	100.0	-
Total persons	3	-	-	-	3	-	-	-	-	100.0	-
Households in non-permanent dwellings											
Total households	43	2	3	13	21	4	4.7	7.0	30.2	48.8	9.3
Total persons	96	6	22	27	35	6	6.2	22.9	28.1	36.5	6.2
Lisburn											
All households											
1 person	6,798	-	-	21	335	6,442	-	-	0.3	4.9	94.8
2 persons	8,744	5	-	66	1,835	6,838	0.1	-	0.8	21.0	78.2
3 persons	6,016	2	5	95	4,618	1,296	0.0	0.1	1.6	76.8	21.5
4 persons	6,336	11	44	2,488	3,309	484	0.2	0.7	39.3	52.2	7.6
5 persons	3,387	18	102	2,050	1,170	47	0.5	3.0	60.5	34.5	1.4
6 persons	1,346	6	487	589	253	11	0.4	36.2	43.8	18.8	0.8
7 persons	394	9	237	136	12	-	2.3	60.2	34.5	3.0	-
8 persons	124	33	57	33	1	-	26.6	46.0	26.6	0.8	-
9 persons	40	10	23	5	2	-	25.0	57.5	12.5	5.0	-
10 or more persons	30	16	13	1	-	-	53.3	43.3	3.3	-	-
Other households *	62	-	-	-	-	62	-	-	-	-	100.0
Total households	33,277	110	968	5,484	11,535	15,180	0.3	2.9	16.5	34.7	45.6
Total persons	97,109	772	6,076	25,445	38,573	26,243	0.8	6.3	26.2	39.7	27.0
Households in shared dwellings											
Total households	19	-	-	1	5	13	-	-	5.3	26.3	68.4
Total persons	23	-	-	1	10	12	-	-	4.3	43.5	52.2
Households in non-permanent dwellings											
Total households	135	11	10	24	48	42	8.1	7.4	17.8	35.6	31.1
Total persons	332	45	47	77	113	50	13.6	14.2	23.2	34.0	15.1

* Households where the persons present were not usually resident

Table 11 Private households by size, dwelling type and density of occupation (persons per room) – **continued**

Number of usually resident persons	Total	All households: Number: Over 1.5	Over 1 and up to 1.5	Over 0.75 and up to 1	0.5 and over and up to 0.75	Less than 0.5	Percentage: Over 1.5	Over 1 and up to 1.5	Over 0.75 and up to 1	0.5 and over and up to 0.75	Less than 0.5
Magherafelt											
All households											
1 person	1,801	-	-	18	88	1,695	-	-	1.0	4.9	94.1
2 persons	2,215	2	-	29	459	1,725	0.1	-	1.3	20.7	77.9
3 persons	1,616	2	7	42	1,200	365	0.1	0.4	2.6	74.3	22.6
4 persons	1,757	7	19	766	874	91	0.4	1.1	43.6	49.7	5.2
5 persons	1,350	21	66	840	396	27	1.6	4.9	62.2	29.3	2.0
6 persons	899	12	309	400	164	14	1.3	34.4	44.5	18.2	1.6
7 persons	384	17	221	128	18	-	4.4	57.6	33.3	4.7	-
8 persons	188	61	93	32	2	-	32.4	49.5	17.0	1.1	-
9 persons	105	29	63	12	1	-	27.6	60.0	11.4	1.0	-
10 or more persons	68	36	29	3	-	-	52.9	42.6	4.4	-	-
Other households *	15	-	-	-	-	15	-	-	-	-	100.0
Total households	10,398	187	807	2,270	3,202	3,932	1.8	7.8	21.8	30.8	37.8
Total persons	36,111	1,476	5,439	11,156	11,217	6,823	4.1	15.1	30.9	31.1	18.9
Households in shared dwellings											
Total households	-	-	-	-	-	-	-	-	-	-	-
Total persons	-	-	-	-	-	-	-	-	-	-	-
Households in non-permanent dwellings											
Total households	112	14	11	42	27	18	12.5	9.8	37.5	24.1	16.1
Total persons	320	71	47	118	58	26	22.2	14.7	36.9	18.1	8.1

Number of usually resident persons	Total	All households: Number: Over 1.5	Over 1 and up to 1.5	Over 0.75 and up to 1	0.5 and over and up to 0.75	Less than 0.5	Percentage: Over 1.5	Over 1 and up to 1.5	Over 0.75 and up to 1	0.5 and over and up to 0.75	Less than 0.5
Moyle											
All households											
1 person	1,108	-	-	1	52	1,055	-	-	0.1	4.7	95.2
2 persons	1,060	1	-	13	274	772	0.1	-	1.2	25.8	72.8
3 persons	736	-	2	22	551	161	-	0.3	3.0	74.9	21.9
4 persons	760	1	14	344	350	51	0.1	1.8	45.3	46.1	6.7
5 persons	555	7	39	328	170	11	1.3	7.0	59.1	30.6	2.0
6 persons	290	6	98	136	45	5	2.1	33.8	46.9	15.5	1.7
7 persons	107	5	49	45	8	-	4.7	45.8	42.1	7.5	-
8 persons	55	24	21	8	2	-	43.6	38.2	14.5	3.6	-
9 persons	26	13	10	3	-	-	50.0	38.5	11.5	-	-
10 or more persons	15	7	7	1	-	-	46.7	46.7	6.7	-	-
Other households *	9	-	-	-	-	9	-	-	-	-	100.0
Total households	4,721	64	240	901	1,452	2,064	1.4	5.1	19.1	30.8	43.7
Total persons	14,574	499	1,518	4,341	4,845	3,371	3.4	10.4	29.8	33.2	23.1
Households in shared dwellings											
Total households	5	-	-	-	3	2	-	-	-	60.0	40.0
Total persons	11	-	-	-	9	2	-	-	-	81.8	18.2
Households in non-permanent dwellings											
Total households	25	1	5	5	8	6	4.0	20.0	20.0	32.0	24.0
Total persons	68	2	21	22	17	6	2.9	30.9	32.4	25.0	8.8

* Households where the persons present were not usually resident

Table 11 Private households by size, dwelling type and density of occupation (persons per room) – **continued**

Number of usually resident persons	Total	All households: Number: Over 1.5	Over 1 and up to 1.5	Over 0.75 and up to 1	0.5 and over and up to 0.75	Less than 0.5	Percentage: Over 1.5	Over 1 and up to 1.5	Over 0.75 and up to 1	0.5 and over and up to 0.75	Less than 0.5
Newry and Mourne											
All households											
1 person	4,925	-	-	37	398	4,490	-	-	0.8	8.1	91.2
2 persons	5,160	6	-	83	1,182	3,889	0.1	-	1.6	22.9	75.4
3 persons	3,600	2	25	102	2,720	751	0.1	0.7	2.8	75.6	20.9
4 persons	3,992	16	58	1,858	1,840	220	0.4	1.5	46.5	46.1	5.5
5 persons	3,178	40	155	2,067	870	46	1.3	4.9	65.0	27.4	1.4
6 persons	2,034	18	773	910	324	9	0.9	38.0	44.7	15.9	0.4
7 persons	837	39	513	247	37	1	4.7	61.3	29.5	4.4	0.1
8 persons	368	109	175	73	11	-	29.6	47.6	19.8	3.0	-
9 persons	164	46	99	17	2	-	28.0	60.4	10.4	1.2	-
10 or more persons	98	63	31	4	-	-	64.3	31.6	4.1	-	-
Other households *	62	-	-	-	-	62	-	-	-	-	100.0
Total households	24,418	339	1,829	5,398	7,384	9,468	1.4	7.5	22.1	30.2	38.8
Total persons	81,436	2,639	11,922	26,242	24,941	15,692	3.2	14.6	32.2	30.6	19.3
Households in shared dwellings											
Total households	20	-	2	3	9	6	-	10.0	15.0	45.0	30.0
Total persons	33	-	7	4	15	7	-	21.2	12.1	45.5	21.2
Households in non-permanent dwellings											
Total households	204	37	21	50	60	36	18.1	10.3	24.5	29.4	17.6
Total persons	644	225	87	145	136	51	34.9	13.5	22.5	21.1	7.9
Newtownabbey											
All households											
1 person	5,639	-	-	36	306	5,297	-	-	0.6	5.4	93.9
2 persons	7,419	11	-	44	1,381	5,983	0.1	-	0.6	18.6	80.6
3 persons	4,974	1	3	62	4,097	811	0.0	0.1	1.2	82.4	16.3
4 persons	4,979	2	17	1,983	2,744	233	0.0	0.3	39.8	55.1	4.7
5 persons	2,380	12	61	1,591	687	29	0.5	2.6	66.8	28.9	1.2
6 persons	739	2	276	350	109	2	0.3	37.3	47.4	14.7	0.3
7 persons	160	5	102	45	7	1	3.1	63.7	28.1	4.4	0.6
8 persons	61	19	31	8	3	-	31.1	50.8	13.1	4.9	-
9 persons	10	2	6	2	-	-	20.0	60.0	20.0	-	-
10 or more persons	6	6	-	-	-	-	100.0	-	-	-	-
Other households *	124	-	-	-	-	124	-	-	-	-	100.0
Total households	26,491	60	496	4,121	9,334	12,480	0.2	1.9	15.6	35.2	47.1
Total persons	73,413	376	3,054	18,694	30,497	20,792	0.5	4.2	25.5	41.5	28.3
Households in shared dwellings											
Total households	28	7	1	4	5	11	25.0	3.6	14.3	17.9	39.3
Total persons	53	17	5	11	14	6	32.1	9.4	20.8	26.4	11.3
Households in non-permanent dwellings											
Total households	34	2	3	4	10	15	5.9	8.8	11.8	29.4	44.1
Total persons	81	9	13	17	22	20	11.1	16.0	21.0	27.2	24.7

* Households where the persons present were not usually resident

Table 11 Private households by size, dwelling type and density of occupation (persons per room) – **continued**

Number of usually resident persons	Total	All households: Number: Over 1.5	Over 1 and up to 1.5	Over 0.75 and up to 1	0.5 and over and up to 0.75	Less than 0.5	Percentage: Over 1.5	Over 1 and up to 1.5	Over 0.75 and up to 1	0.5 and over and up to 0.75	Less than 0.5
North Down											
All households											
1 person	6,443	-	-	166	346	5,931	-	-	2.6	5.4	92.1
2 persons	7,916	14	-	62	1,378	6,462	0.2	-	0.8	17.4	81.6
3 persons	4,312	1	3	29	3,041	1,238	0.0	0.1	0.7	70.5	28.7
4 persons	4,861	4	16	1,398	2,946	497	0.1	0.3	28.8	60.6	10.2
5 persons	2,164	4	34	1,008	1,038	80	0.2	1.6	46.6	48.0	3.7
6 persons	652	1	149	253	237	12	0.2	22.9	38.8	36.3	1.8
7 persons	133	3	60	49	20	1	2.3	45.1	36.8	15.0	0.8
8 persons	36	7	14	12	2	1	19.4	38.9	33.3	5.6	2.8
9 persons	12	4	5	2	1	-	33.3	41.7	16.7	8.3	-
10 or more persons	6	4	-	2	-	-	66.7	-	33.3	-	-
Other households *	84	-	-	-	-	84	-	-	-	-	100.0
Total households	26,619	42	281	2,981	9,009	14,306	0.2	1.1	11.2	33.8	53.7
Total persons	70,777	228	1,714	13,005	30,786	25,044	0.3	2.4	18.4	43.5	35.4
Households in shared dwellings											
Total households	112	1	1	56	28	26	0.9	0.9	50.0	25.0	23.2
Total persons	126	3	3	59	34	27	2.4	2.4	46.8	27.0	21.4
Households in non-permanent dwellings											
Total households	8	-	-	2	3	3	-	-	25.0	37.5	37.5
Total persons	18	-	-	5	8	5	-	-	27.8	44.4	27.8
Omagh											
All households											
1 person	2,775	-	-	38	180	2,557	-	-	1.4	6.5	92.1
2 persons	2,779	1	-	32	580	2,166	0.0	-	1.2	20.9	77.9
3 persons	1,985	1	6	41	1,453	484	0.1	0.3	2.1	73.2	24.4
4 persons	2,302	8	29	894	1,205	166	0.3	1.3	38.8	52.3	7.2
5 persons	1,658	15	72	1,002	541	28	0.9	4.3	60.4	32.6	1.7
6 persons	1,049	14	367	434	228	6	1.3	35.0	41.4	21.7	0.6
7 persons	435	21	241	141	30	2	4.8	55.4	32.4	6.9	0.5
8 persons	252	69	126	52	5	-	27.4	50.0	20.6	2.0	-
9 persons	73	18	46	9	-	-	24.7	63.0	12.3	-	-
10 or more persons	82	49	32	1	-	-	59.8	39.0	1.2	-	-
Other households *	27	-	-	-	-	27	-	-	-	-	100.0
Total households	13,417	196	919	2,644	4,222	5,436	1.5	6.8	19.7	31.5	40.5
Total persons	44,669	1,592	6,131	12,909	14,842	9,195	3.6	13.7	28.9	33.2	20.6
Households in shared dwellings											
Total households	24	-	-	14	2	8	-	-	58.3	8.3	33.3
Total persons	24	-	-	14	2	8	-	-	58.3	8.3	33.3
Households in non-permanent dwellings											
Total households	138	10	8	38	46	36	7.2	5.8	27.5	33.3	26.1
Total persons	335	69	37	107	75	47	20.6	11.0	31.9	22.4	14.0

* Households where the persons present were not usually resident

Table 11 Private households by size, dwelling type and density of occupation (persons per room) – **continued**

Number of usually resident persons	Total	All households									
		Over 1.5	Over 1 and up to 1.5	Over 0.75 and up to 1	0.5 and over and up to 0.75	Less than 0.5	Over 1.5	Over 1 and up to 1.5	Over 0.75 and up to 1	0.5 and over and up to 0.75	Less than 0.5
		Number					Percentage				
Strabane											
All households											
1 person	2,071	-	-	23	142	1,906	-	-	1.1	6.9	92.0
2 persons	2,299	5	-	46	542	1,706	0.2	-	2.0	23.6	74.2
3 persons	1,731	1	17	62	1,323	328	0.1	1.0	3.6	76.4	18.9
4 persons	1,752	6	25	869	753	99	0.3	1.4	49.6	43.0	5.7
5 persons	1,343	17	96	903	311	16	1.3	7.1	67.2	23.2	1.2
6 persons	855	10	391	331	118	5	1.2	45.7	38.7	13.8	0.6
7 persons	354	24	233	81	16	-	6.8	65.8	22.9	4.5	-
8 persons	178	87	68	20	3	-	48.9	38.2	11.2	1.7	-
9 persons	76	36	35	5	-	-	47.4	46.1	6.6	-	-
10 or more persons	66	47	17	2	-	-	71.2	25.8	3.0	-	-
Other households *	25	-	-	-	-	25	-	-	-	-	100.0
Total households	10,750	233	882	2,342	3,208	4,085	2.2	8.2	21.8	29.8	38.0
Total persons	36,007	1,878	5,645	11,070	10,606	6,808	5.2	15.7	30.7	29.5	18.9
Households in shared dwellings											
Total households	9	-	-	1	3	5	-	-	11.1	33.3	55.6
Total persons	14	-	-	3	4	7	-	-	21.4	28.6	50.0
Households in non-permanent dwellings											
Total households	134	11	14	33	49	27	8.2	10.4	24.6	36.6	20.1
Total persons	306	64	52	77	79	34	20.9	17.0	25.2	25.8	11.1

* Households where the persons present were not usually resident

Table 12 Households by dwelling type, number of rooms and household amenities

Households	Total households	With fixed bath or shower: Exclusive use: Number	Per cent	Shared use: Number	Per cent	With inside flush toilet (WC): Exclusive use: Number	Per cent	Shared use: Number	Per cent	With outside flush toilet (WC) only: Number	Per cent	Connected to public water supply: Number	Per cent	Connected to public sewer: Number	Per cent	With central heating: All rooms: Number	Per cent	Some rooms: Number	Per cent	No central heating: Number	Per cent
NORTHERN IRELAND																					
Households in all dwellings																					
All sizes	530,369	519,512	98.0	1,622	0.3	521,654	98.4	840	0.2	4,010	0.8	523,191	98.6	437,013	82.4	383,974	72.4	54,681	10.3	91,714	17.3
1-3 rooms	38,401	35,001	91.1	780	2.0	35,716	93.0	454	1.2	665	1.7	36,895	96.1	33,377	86.9	24,104	62.8	3,352	8.7	10,945	28.5
4 rooms	76,802	73,365	95.5	220	0.3	73,953	96.3	75	0.1	1,776	2.3	75,799	98.7	67,839	88.3	47,816	62.3	8,470	11.0	20,516	26.7
5 rooms	178,291	175,993	98.7	277	0.2	176,460	99.0	143	0.1	957	0.5	176,877	99.2	156,559	87.8	126,921	71.2	20,284	11.4	31,086	17.4
6 or more rooms	236,875	235,153	99.3	345	0.1	235,525	99.4	168	0.1	612	0.3	233,620	98.6	179,238	75.7	185,133	78.2	22,575	9.5	29,167	12.3
Households in unshared dwellings (permanent)																					
All sizes	521,400	512,066	98.2	677	0.1	513,608	98.5	379	0.1	3,894	0.7	514,773	98.7	430,157	82.5	379,766	72.8	53,725	10.3	87,909	16.9
1-3 rooms	33,438	31,054	92.9	177	0.5	31,419	94.0	102	0.3	583	1.7	32,284	96.5	29,452	88.1	21,991	65.8	2,960	8.9	8,487	25.4
4 rooms	74,611	71,333	95.6	90	0.1	71,821	96.3	44	0.1	1,763	2.4	73,671	98.7	66,138	88.6	46,643	62.5	8,144	10.9	19,824	26.6
5 rooms	177,083	175,009	98.8	183	0.1	175,398	99.0	109	0.1	942	0.5	175,791	99.3	155,784	88.0	126,324	71.3	20,134	11.4	30,625	17.3
6 or more rooms	236,268	234,670	99.3	227	0.1	234,970	99.5	124	0.1	606	0.3	233,027	98.6	178,783	75.7	184,808	78.2	22,487	9.5	28,973	12.3
Households in shared dwellings (permanent)																					
All sizes	834	-	-	813	97.5	395	47.4	419	50.2	20	2.4	832	99.8	790	94.7	246	29.5	57	6.8	531	63.7
1-3 rooms	564	-	-	549	97.3	226	40.1	332	58.9	6	1.1	562	99.6	538	95.4	136	24.1	27	4.8	401	71.1
4 rooms	98	-	-	97	99.0	70	71.4	23	23.5	5	5.1	98	100.0	92	93.9	36	36.7	14	14.3	48	49.0
5 rooms	66	-	-	63	95.5	40	60.6	23	34.8	3	4.5	66	100.0	60	90.9	23	34.8	5	7.6	38	57.6
6 or more rooms	106	-	-	104	98.1	59	55.7	41	38.7	6	5.7	106	100.0	100	94.3	51	48.1	11	10.4	44	41.5
Households in non-permanent dwellings																					
All sizes	2,254	1,673	74.2	35	1.6	1,807	80.2	11	0.5	93	4.1	1,720	76.3	393	17.4	950	42.1	195	8.7	1,109	49.2
1-3 rooms	1,129	718	63.6	20	1.8	820	72.6	6	0.5	73	6.5	789	69.9	219	19.4	272	24.1	79	7.0	778	68.9
4 rooms	506	471	93.1	8	1.6	482	95.3	1	0.2	8	1.6	446	88.1	74	14.6	323	63.8	61	12.1	122	24.1
5 rooms	468	337	72.0	7	1.5	356	76.1	4	0.9	12	2.6	346	73.9	71	15.2	252	53.8	36	7.7	180	38.5
6 or more rooms	151	147	97.4	-	-	149	98.7	-	-	-	-	139	92.1	29	19.2	103	68.2	19	12.6	29	19.2

Table 12 Households by dwelling type, number of rooms and household amenities – **continued**

Households	Total households	With fixed bath or shower: Exclusive use: Number	Per cent	Shared use: Number	Per cent	With inside flush toilet (WC): Exclusive use: Number	Per cent	Shared use: Number	Per cent	With outside flush toilet (WC) only: Number	Per cent	Connected to public water supply: Number	Per cent	Connected to public sewer: Number	Per cent	With central heating: All rooms: Number	Per cent	Some rooms: Number	Per cent	No central heating: Number	Per cent
Antrim																					
Households in all dwellings																					
All sizes	14,166	13,940	98.4	31	0.2	13,996	98.8	15	0.1	50	0.4	13,805	97.5	10,556	74.5	10,239	72.3	1,802	12.7	2,125	15.0
1-3 rooms	923	865	93.7	9	1.0	885	95.9	3	0.3	6	0.7	898	97.3	781	84.6	590	63.9	71	7.7	262	28.4
4 rooms	1,654	1,584	95.8	10	0.6	1,597	96.6	7	0.4	17	1.0	1,617	97.8	1,361	82.3	901	54.5	210	12.7	543	32.8
5 rooms	5,168	5,123	99.1	3	0.1	5,131	99.3	2	0.0	15	0.3	5,109	98.9	4,464	86.4	3,519	68.1	928	18.0	721	14.0
6 or more rooms	6,421	6,368	99.2	9	0.1	6,383	99.4	3	0.0	12	0.2	6,181	96.3	3,950	61.5	5,229	81.4	593	9.2	599	9.3
Households in unshared dwellings (permanent)																					
All sizes	13,987	13,786	98.6	20	0.1	13,831	98.9	9	0.1	48	0.3	13,646	97.6	10,475	74.9	10,135	72.5	1,781	12.7	2,071	14.8
1-3 rooms	845	806	95.4	3	0.4	816	96.6	1	0.1	4	0.5	831	98.3	752	89.0	559	66.2	67	7.9	219	25.9
4 rooms	1,591	1,526	95.9	5	0.3	1,539	96.7	3	0.2	17	1.1	1,559	98.0	1,322	83.1	859	54.0	197	12.4	535	33.6
5 rooms	5,138	5,093	99.1	3	0.1	5,101	99.3	2	0.0	15	0.3	5,082	98.9	4,453	86.7	3,492	68.0	926	18.0	720	14.0
6 or more rooms	6,413	6,361	99.2	9	0.1	6,375	99.4	3	0.0	12	0.2	6,174	96.3	3,948	61.6	5,225	81.5	591	9.2	597	9.3
Households in shared dwellings (permanent)																					
All sizes	8	-	-	8	100.0	3	37.5	5	62.5	-	-	8	100.0	6	75.0	6	75.0	1	12.5	1	12.5
1-3 rooms	3	-	-	3	100.0	1	33.3	2	66.7	-	-	3	100.0	2	66.7	3	100.0	-	-	-	-
4 rooms	5	-	-	5	100.0	2	40.0	3	60.0	-	-	5	100.0	4	80.0	3	60.0	1	20.0	1	20.0
5 rooms	-	-	-	-	-	-	-	-	-	-	-	-	-	-	-	-	-	-	-	-	-
6 or more rooms	-	-	-	-	-	-	-	-	-	-	-	-	-	-	-	-	-	-	-	-	-
Households in non-permanent dwellings																					
All sizes	103	88	85.4	1	1.0	95	92.2	1	1.0	1	1.0	83	80.6	9	8.7	56	54.4	5	4.9	42	40.8
1-3 rooms	49	35	71.4	1	2.0	43	87.8	-	-	1	2.0	38	77.6	2	4.1	14	28.6	1	2.0	34	69.4
4 rooms	24	24	100.0	-	-	22	91.7	1	4.2	-	-	19	79.2	2	8.3	17	70.8	2	8.3	5	20.8
5 rooms	24	24	100.0	-	-	24	100.0	-	-	-	-	21	87.5	5	20.8	22	91.7	1	4.2	1	4.2
6 or more rooms	6	5	83.3	-	-	6	100.0	-	-	-	-	5	83.3	-	-	3	50.0	1	16.7	2	33.3

Table 12 Households by dwelling type, number of rooms and household amenities – **continued**

Households	Total households	With fixed bath or shower				With inside flush toilet (WC)				With outside flush toilet (WC) only		Connected to public water supply		Connected to public sewer		With central heating				No central heating	
		Exclusive use		Shared use		Exclusive use		Shared use								All rooms		Some rooms			
		Number	Per cent	Number	Per cent	Number	Per cent	Number	Per cent	Number	Per cent	Number	Per cent	Number	Per cent	Number	Per cent	Number	Per cent	Number	Per cent
Ards																					
Households in all dwellings																					
All sizes	22,832	22,408	98.1	23	0.1	22,480	98.5	9	0.0	268	1.2	22,759	99.7	18,827	82.5	16,476	72.2	2,253	9.9	4,103	18.0
1-3 rooms	1,416	1,348	95.2	2	0.1	1,351	95.4	3	0.2	36	2.5	1,397	98.7	1,266	89.4	921	65.0	116	8.2	379	26.8
4 rooms	3,443	3,258	94.6	5	0.1	3,285	95.4	-	-	134	3.9	3,429	99.6	3,021	87.7	2,118	61.5	279	8.1	1,046	30.4
5 rooms	8,019	7,916	98.7	9	0.1	7,941	99.0	5	0.1	60	0.7	8,004	99.8	7,201	89.8	5,691	71.0	822	10.3	1,506	18.8
6 or more rooms	9,954	9,886	99.3	7	0.1	9,903	99.5	1	0.0	38	0.4	9,929	99.7	7,339	73.7	7,746	77.8	1,036	10.4	1,172	11.8
Households in unshared dwellings (permanent)																					
All sizes	22,702	22,293	98.2	17	0.1	22,363	98.5	4	0.0	266	1.2	22,638	99.7	18,752	82.6	16,428	72.4	2,231	9.8	4,043	17.8
1-3 rooms	1,347	1,287	95.5	1	0.1	1,290	95.8	1	0.1	34	2.5	1,334	99.0	1,231	91.4	902	67.0	108	8.0	337	25.0
4 rooms	3,409	3,226	94.6	4	0.1	3,252	95.4	-	-	134	3.9	3,396	99.6	2,997	87.9	2,099	61.6	270	7.9	1,040	30.5
5 rooms	8,001	7,901	98.8	7	0.1	7,926	99.1	3	0.0	60	0.7	7,988	99.8	7,191	89.9	5,685	71.1	819	10.2	1,497	18.7
6 or more rooms	9,945	9,879	99.3	5	0.1	9,895	99.5	-	-	38	0.4	9,920	99.7	7,333	73.7	7,742	77.8	1,034	10.4	1,169	11.8
Households in shared dwellings (permanent)																					
All sizes	7	-	-	6	85.7	2	28.6	5	71.4	-	-	7	100.0	5	71.4	1	14.3	-	-	6	85.7
1-3 rooms	2	-	-	1	50.0	-	-	2	100.0	-	-	2	100.0	2	100.0	-	-	-	-	2	100.0
4 rooms	1	-	-	1	100.0	1	100.0	-	-	-	-	1	100.0	1	100.0	-	-	-	-	1	100.0
5 rooms	2	-	-	2	100.0	-	-	2	100.0	-	-	2	100.0	-	-	-	-	-	-	2	100.0
6 or more rooms	2	-	-	2	100.0	1	50.0	1	50.0	-	-	2	100.0	2	100.0	1	50.0	-	-	1	50.0
Households in non-permanent dwellings																					
All sizes	53	45	84.9	-	-	45	84.9	-	-	2	3.8	44	83.0	3	5.7	17	32.1	7	13.2	29	54.7
1-3 rooms	35	29	82.9	-	-	29	82.9	-	-	2	5.7	29	82.9	2	5.7	6	17.1	2	5.7	27	77.1
4 rooms	9	8	88.9	-	-	8	88.9	-	-	-	-	8	88.9	-	-	7	77.8	2	22.2	-	-
5 rooms	5	4	80.0	-	-	4	80.0	-	-	-	-	3	60.0	-	-	3	60.0	1	20.0	1	20.0
6 or more rooms	4	4	100.0	-	-	4	100.0	-	-	-	-	4	100.0	1	25.0	1	25.0	2	50.0	1	25.0

Table 12 Households by dwelling type, number of rooms and household amenities – **continued**

Households	Total households	With fixed bath or shower: Exclusive use Number	Exclusive use Per cent	Shared use Number	Shared use Per cent	With inside flush toilet (WC): Exclusive use Number	Exclusive use Per cent	Shared use Number	Shared use Per cent	With outside flush toilet (WC) only Number	Per cent	Connected to public water supply Number	Per cent	Connected to public sewer Number	Per cent	With central heating: All rooms Number	All rooms Per cent	Some rooms Number	Some rooms Per cent	No central heating Number	Per cent
Armagh																					
Households in all dwellings																					
All sizes	15,720	15,255	97.0	43	0.3	15,342	97.6	16	0.1	111	0.7	15,535	98.8	9,989	63.5	11,028	70.2	1,651	10.5	3,041	19.3
1-3 rooms	850	720	84.7	12	1.4	743	87.4	2	0.2	23	2.7	797	93.8	579	68.1	458	53.9	60	7.1	332	39.1
4 rooms	1,866	1,732	92.8	4	0.2	1,754	94.0	3	0.2	33	1.8	1,821	97.6	1,370	73.4	1,093	58.6	202	10.8	571	30.6
5 rooms	5,438	5,319	97.8	13	0.2	5,348	98.3	5	0.1	28	0.5	5,398	99.3	4,101	75.4	3,513	64.6	696	12.8	1,229	22.6
6 or more rooms	7,566	7,484	98.9	14	0.2	7,497	99.1	6	0.1	27	0.4	7,519	99.4	3,939	52.1	5,964	78.8	693	9.2	909	12.0
Households in unshared dwellings (permanent)																					
All sizes	15,438	15,009	97.2	24	0.2	15,080	97.7	12	0.1	107	0.7	15,267	98.9	9,840	63.7	10,865	70.4	1,619	10.5	2,954	19.1
1-3 rooms	697	594	85.2	2	0.3	604	86.7	2	0.3	21	3.0	657	94.3	492	70.6	377	54.1	44	6.3	276	39.6
4 rooms	1,804	1,672	92.7	2	0.1	1,694	93.9	2	0.1	32	1.8	1,760	97.6	1,342	74.4	1,054	58.4	191	10.6	559	31.0
5 rooms	5,388	5,273	97.9	9	0.2	5,299	98.3	4	0.1	28	0.5	5,348	99.3	4,076	75.6	3,480	64.6	691	12.8	1,217	22.6
6 or more rooms	7,549	7,470	99.0	11	0.1	7,483	99.1	4	0.1	26	0.3	7,502	99.4	3,930	52.1	5,954	78.9	693	9.2	902	11.9
Households in shared dwellings (permanent)																					
All sizes	10	-	-	10	100.0	7	70.0	2	20.0	1	10.0	10	100.0	8	80.0	8	80.0	1	10.0	1	10.0
1-3 rooms	5	-	-	5	100.0	5	100.0	-	-	-	-	5	100.0	5	100.0	3	60.0	1	20.0	1	20.0
4 rooms	1	-	-	1	100.0	1	100.0	-	-	-	-	1	100.0	-	-	1	100.0	-	-	-	-
5 rooms	1	-	-	1	100.0	1	100.0	-	-	-	-	1	100.0	-	-	1	100.0	-	-	-	-
6 or more rooms	3	-	-	3	100.0	-	-	2	66.7	1	33.3	3	100.0	3	100.0	3	100.0	-	-	-	-
Households in non-permanent dwellings																					
All sizes	138	118	85.5	3	2.2	123	89.1	-	-	3	2.2	124	89.9	14	10.1	64	46.4	16	11.6	58	42.0
1-3 rooms	71	51	71.8	3	4.2	57	80.3	-	-	2	2.8	58	81.7	9	12.7	22	31.0	8	11.3	41	57.7
4 rooms	34	34	100.0	-	-	33	97.1	-	-	1	2.9	33	97.1	2	5.9	19	55.9	6	17.6	9	26.5
5 rooms	25	25	100.0	-	-	25	100.0	-	-	-	-	25	100.0	3	12.0	19	76.0	2	8.0	4	16.0
6 or more rooms	8	8	100.0	-	-	8	100.0	-	-	-	-	8	100.0	-	-	4	50.0	-	-	4	50.0

Table 12 Households by dwelling type, number of rooms and household amenities – **continued**

Households	Total households	With fixed bath or shower				With inside flush toilet (WC)				With outside flush toilet (WC) only		Connected to public water supply		Connected to public sewer		With central heating				No central heating	
		Exclusive use		Shared use		Exclusive use		Shared use								All rooms		Some rooms			
		Number	Per cent	Number	Per cent	Number	Per cent	Number	Per cent	Number	Per cent	Number	Per cent	Number	Per cent	Number	Per cent	Number	Per cent	Number	Per cent
Ballymena																					
Households in all dwellings																					
All sizes	19,137	18,731	97.9	31	0.2	18,792	98.2	10	0.1	127	0.7	18,354	95.9	14,340	74.9	13,455	70.3	1,865	9.7	3,817	19.9
1-3 rooms	1,136	1,047	92.2	3	0.3	1,055	92.9	2	0.2	15	1.3	1,071	94.3	964	84.9	710	62.5	86	7.6	340	29.9
4 rooms	2,298	2,170	94.4	7	0.3	2,191	95.3	1	0.0	50	2.2	2,220	96.6	1,903	82.8	1,260	54.8	249	10.8	789	34.3
5 rooms	5,388	5,289	98.2	9	0.2	5,309	98.5	2	0.0	33	0.6	5,237	97.2	4,440	82.4	3,609	67.0	531	9.9	1,248	23.2
6 or more rooms	10,315	10,225	99.1	12	0.1	10,237	99.2	5	0.0	29	0.3	9,826	95.3	7,033	68.2	7,876	76.4	999	9.7	1,440	14.0
Households in unshared dwellings (permanent)																					
All sizes	18,858	18,470	97.9	21	0.1	18,521	98.2	8	0.0	125	0.7	18,089	95.9	14,151	75.0	13,277	70.4	1,835	9.7	3,746	19.9
1-3 rooms	995	917	92.2	-	-	921	92.6	1	0.1	13	1.3	938	94.3	852	85.6	623	62.6	75	7.5	297	29.8
4 rooms	2,212	2,087	94.3	4	0.2	2,105	95.2	1	0.0	50	2.3	2,137	96.6	1,848	83.5	1,199	54.2	236	10.7	777	35.1
5 rooms	5,355	5,257	98.2	8	0.1	5,276	98.5	2	0.0	33	0.6	5,205	97.2	4,423	82.6	3,590	67.0	526	9.8	1,239	23.1
6 or more rooms	10,296	10,209	99.2	9	0.1	10,219	99.3	4	0.0	29	0.3	9,809	95.3	7,028	68.3	7,865	76.4	998	9.7	1,433	13.9
Households in shared dwellings (permanent)																					
All sizes	7	-	-	7	100.0	6	85.7	1	14.3	-	-	7	100.0	6	85.7	3	42.9	1	14.3	3	42.9
1-3 rooms	3	-	-	3	100.0	3	100.0	-	-	-	-	3	100.0	3	100.0	1	33.3	-	-	2	66.7
4 rooms	2	-	-	2	100.0	2	100.0	-	-	-	-	2	100.0	2	100.0	1	50.0	1	50.0	-	-
5 rooms	1	-	-	1	100.0	1	100.0	-	-	-	-	1	100.0	1	100.0	-	-	-	-	1	100.0
6 or more rooms	1	-	-	1	100.0	-	-	1	100.0	-	-	1	100.0	-	-	1	100.0	-	-	-	-
Households in non-permanent dwellings																					
All sizes	90	82	91.1	-	-	83	92.2	1	1.1	2	2.2	76	84.4	6	6.7	61	67.8	9	10.0	20	22.2
1-3 rooms	33	25	75.8	-	-	26	78.8	1	3.0	2	6.1	25	75.8	5	15.2	16	48.5	3	9.1	14	42.4
4 rooms	31	31	100.0	-	-	31	100.0	-	-	-	-	28	90.3	1	3.2	26	83.9	4	12.9	1	3.2
5 rooms	16	16	100.0	-	-	16	100.0	-	-	-	-	15	93.7	-	-	13	81.2	1	6.2	2	12.5
6 or more rooms	10	10	100.0	-	-	10	100.0	-	-	-	-	8	80.0	-	-	6	60.0	1	10.0	3	30.0

Table 12 Households by dwelling type, number of rooms and household amenities – **continued**

Households	Total households	With fixed bath or shower: Exclusive use: Number	Per cent	Shared use: Number	Per cent	With inside flush toilet (WC): Exclusive use: Number	Per cent	Shared use: Number	Per cent	With outside flush toilet (WC) only: Number	Per cent	Connected to public water supply: Number	Per cent	Connected to public sewer: Number	Per cent	With central heating: All rooms: Number	Per cent	Some rooms: Number	Per cent	No central heating: Number	Per cent
Ballymoney																					
Households in all dwellings																					
All sizes	7,730	7,562	97.8	23	0.3	7,586	98.1	8	0.1	50	0.6	7,454	96.4	5,039	65.2	4,549	58.8	1,025	13.3	2,156	27.9
1-3 rooms	435	375	86.2	16	3.7	390	89.7	3	0.7	15	3.4	400	92.0	343	78.9	190	43.7	39	9.0	206	47.4
4 rooms	1,146	1,096	95.6	2	0.2	1,101	96.1	-	-	25	2.2	1,113	97.1	903	78.8	483	42.1	141	12.3	522	45.5
5 rooms	2,722	2,689	98.8	2	0.1	2,692	98.9	3	0.1	5	0.2	2,672	98.2	2,075	76.2	1,460	53.6	434	15.9	828	30.4
6 or more rooms	3,427	3,402	99.3	3	0.1	3,403	99.3	2	0.1	5	0.1	3,269	95.4	1,718	50.1	2,416	70.5	411	12.0	600	17.5
Households in unshared dwellings (permanent)																					
All sizes	7,651	7,497	98.0	17	0.2	7,520	98.3	4	0.1	47	0.6	7,388	96.6	5,004	65.4	4,505	58.9	1,019	13.3	2,127	27.8
1-3 rooms	386	337	87.3	12	3.1	352	91.2	-	-	13	3.4	361	93.5	316	81.9	164	42.5	37	9.6	185	47.9
4 rooms	1,127	1,079	95.7	1	0.1	1,083	96.1	-	-	24	2.1	1,096	97.2	901	79.9	472	41.9	139	12.3	516	45.8
5 rooms	2,712	2,679	98.8	2	0.1	2,682	98.9	3	0.1	5	0.2	2,663	98.2	2,069	76.3	1,453	53.6	432	15.9	827	30.5
6 or more rooms	3,426	3,402	99.3	2	0.1	3,403	99.3	1	0.0	5	0.1	3,268	95.4	1,718	50.1	2,416	70.5	411	12.0	599	17.5
Households in shared dwellings (permanent)																					
All sizes	3	-	-	3	100.0	1	33.3	2	66.7	-	-	3	100.0	3	100.0	-	-	-	-	3	100.0
1-3 rooms	3	-	-	3	100.0	1	33.3	2	66.7	-	-	3	100.0	3	100.0	-	-	-	-	3	100.0
4 rooms	-	-	-	-	-	-	-	-	-	-	-	-	-	-	-	-	-	-	-	-	-
5 rooms	-	-	-	-	-	-	-	-	-	-	-	-	-	-	-	-	-	-	-	-	-
6 or more rooms	-	-	-	-	-	-	-	-	-	-	-	-	-	-	-	-	-	-	-	-	-
Households in non-permanent dwellings																					
All sizes	46	36	78.3	2	4.3	36	78.3	1	2.2	3	6.5	33	71.7	6	13.0	23	50.0	4	8.7	19	41.3
1-3 rooms	24	16	66.7	1	4.2	15	62.5	1	4.2	2	8.3	14	58.3	4	16.7	9	37.5	2	8.3	13	54.2
4 rooms	17	15	88.2	1	5.9	16	94.1	-	-	1	5.9	15	88.2	-	-	10	58.8	2	11.8	5	29.4
5 rooms	5	5	100.0	-	-	5	100.0	-	-	-	-	4	80.0	2	40.0	4	80.0	-	-	1	20.0
6 or more rooms	-	-	-	-	-	-	-	-	-	-	-	-	-	-	-	-	-	-	-	-	-

Table 12 Households by dwelling type, number of rooms and household amenities – **continued**

Local Government Districts

Households	Total households	With fixed bath or shower				With inside flush toilet (WC)				With outside flush toilet (WC) only		Connected to public water supply		Connected to public sewer		With central heating				No central heating	
		Exclusive use		Shared use		Exclusive use		Shared use								All rooms		Some rooms			
		Number	Per cent	Number	Per cent	Number	Per cent	Number	Per cent	Number	Per cent	Number	Per cent	Number	Per cent	Number	Per cent	Number	Per cent	Number	Per cent
Banbridge																					
Households in all dwellings																					
All sizes	10,984	10,697	97.4	13	0.1	10,754	97.9	6	0.1	96	0.9	10,838	98.7	7,057	64.2	8,041	73.2	1,003	9.1	1,940	17.7
1-3 rooms	715	646	90.3	1	0.1	661	92.4	-	-	16	2.2	686	95.9	541	75.7	443	62.0	35	4.9	237	33.1
4 rooms	1,494	1,386	92.8	4	0.3	1,411	94.4	2	0.1	40	2.7	1,457	97.5	1,094	73.2	915	61.2	99	6.6	480	32.1
5 rooms	3,630	3,570	98.3	4	0.1	3,580	98.6	3	0.1	19	0.5	3,606	99.3	2,787	76.8	2,579	71.0	460	12.7	591	16.3
6 or more rooms	5,145	5,095	99.0	4	0.1	5,102	99.2	1	0.0	21	0.4	5,089	98.9	2,635	51.2	4,104	79.8	409	7.9	632	12.3
Households in unshared dwellings (permanent)																					
All sizes	10,818	10,548	97.5	7	0.1	10,598	98.0	3	0.0	95	0.9	10,681	98.7	6,982	64.5	7,920	73.2	993	9.2	1,905	17.6
1-3 rooms	648	589	90.9	-	-	600	92.6	-	-	15	2.3	626	96.6	508	78.4	401	61.9	30	4.6	217	33.5
4 rooms	1,438	1,335	92.8	-	-	1,357	94.4	-	-	40	2.8	1,401	97.4	1,064	74.0	870	60.5	97	6.7	471	32.8
5 rooms	3,598	3,540	98.4	3	0.1	3,550	98.7	2	0.1	19	0.5	3,575	99.4	2,778	77.2	2,554	71.0	458	12.7	586	16.3
6 or more rooms	5,134	5,084	99.0	4	0.1	5,091	99.2	1	0.0	21	0.4	5,079	98.9	2,632	51.3	4,095	79.8	408	7.9	631	12.3
Households in shared dwellings (permanent)																					
All sizes	5	-	-	5	100.0	3	60.0	2	40.0	-	-	5	100.0	4	80.0	4	80.0	1	20.0	-	-
1-3 rooms	1	-	-	1	100.0	1	100.0	-	-	-	-	1	100.0	-	-	-	-	1	100.0	-	-
4 rooms	3	-	-	3	100.0	2	66.7	1	33.3	-	-	3	100.0	3	100.0	3	100.0	-	-	-	-
5 rooms	1	-	-	1	100.0	-	-	1	100.0	-	-	1	100.0	1	100.0	1	100.0	-	-	-	-
6 or more rooms	-	-	-	-	-	-	-	-	-	-	-	-	-	-	-	-	-	-	-	-	-
Households in non-permanent dwellings																					
All sizes	93	82	88.2	-	-	86	92.5	-	-	1	1.1	84	90.3	10	10.8	58	62.4	5	5.4	30	32.3
1-3 rooms	34	25	73.5	-	-	28	82.4	-	-	1	2.9	27	79.4	3	8.8	12	35.3	3	8.8	19	55.9
4 rooms	25	24	96.0	-	-	25	100.0	-	-	-	-	25	100.0	2	8.0	19	76.0	1	4.0	5	20.0
5 rooms	26	25	96.2	-	-	25	96.2	-	-	-	-	25	96.2	3	11.5	20	76.9	1	3.8	5	19.2
6 or more rooms	8	8	100.0	-	-	8	100.0	-	-	-	-	7	87.5	2	25.0	7	87.5	-	-	1	12.5

Table 12 Households by dwelling type, number of rooms and household amenities – **continued**

Households	Total households	With fixed bath or shower: Exclusive use: Number	Per cent	Shared use: Number	Per cent	With inside flush toilet (WC): Exclusive use: Number	Per cent	Shared use: Number	Per cent	With outside flush toilet (WC) only: Number	Per cent	Connected to public water supply: Number	Per cent	Connected to public sewer: Number	Per cent	With central heating: All rooms: Number	Per cent	Some rooms: Number	Per cent	No central heating: Number	Per cent
Belfast																					
Households in all dwellings																					
All sizes	107,394	104,877	97.7	595	0.6	105,208	98.0	334	0.3	1,681	1.6	107,239	99.9	105,898	98.6	74,946	69.8	13,149	12.2	19,299	18.0
1-3 rooms	10,149	9,549	94.1	378	3.7	9,723	95.8	237	2.3	170	1.7	10,125	99.8	9,960	98.1	6,762	66.6	934	9.2	2,453	24.2
4 rooms	23,913	22,791	95.3	77	0.3	22,898	95.8	26	0.1	941	3.9	23,890	99.9	23,568	98.6	15,304	64.0	2,912	12.2	5,697	23.8
5 rooms	33,429	32,908	98.4	47	0.1	32,926	98.5	27	0.1	385	1.2	33,337	99.7	32,881	98.4	23,587	70.6	4,262	12.7	5,580	16.7
6 or more rooms	39,903	39,629	99.3	93	0.2	39,661	99.4	44	0.1	185	0.5	39,887	100.0	39,489	99.0	29,293	73.4	5,041	12.6	5,569	14.0
Households in unshared dwellings (permanent)																					
All sizes	104,129	102,124	98.1	177	0.2	102,254	98.2	126	0.1	1,664	1.6	104,064	99.9	102,801	98.7	73,612	70.7	12,837	12.3	17,680	17.0
1-3 rooms	8,302	7,990	96.2	104	1.3	8,050	97.0	77	0.9	164	2.0	8,287	99.8	8,168	98.4	6,025	72.6	806	9.7	1,471	17.7
4 rooms	23,148	22,078	95.4	27	0.1	22,151	95.7	13	0.1	937	4.0	23,128	99.9	22,824	98.6	14,956	64.6	2,807	12.1	5,385	23.3
5 rooms	33,016	32,603	98.7	17	0.1	32,602	98.7	17	0.1	383	1.2	33,001	100.0	32,552	98.6	23,444	71.0	4,216	12.8	5,356	16.2
6 or more rooms	39,663	39,453	99.5	29	0.1	39,451	99.5	19	0.0	180	0.5	39,648	100.0	39,257	99.0	29,187	73.6	5,008	12.6	5,468	13.8
Households in shared dwellings (permanent)																					
All sizes	411	-	-	402	97.8	194	47.2	200	48.7	17	4.1	410	99.8	394	95.9	104	25.3	24	5.8	283	68.9
1-3 rooms	274	-	-	267	97.4	112	40.9	156	56.9	6	2.2	273	99.6	261	95.3	58	21.2	7	2.6	209	76.3
4 rooms	48	-	-	47	97.9	32	66.7	12	25.0	4	8.3	48	100.0	46	95.8	13	27.1	5	10.4	30	62.5
5 rooms	29	-	-	28	96.6	18	62.1	9	31.0	2	6.9	29	100.0	29	100.0	7	24.1	4	13.8	18	62.1
6 or more rooms	60	-	-	60	100.0	32	53.3	23	38.3	5	8.3	60	100.0	58	96.7	26	43.3	8	13.3	26	43.3
Households in non-permanent dwellings																					
All sizes	105	20	19.0	-	-	19	18.1	-	-	-	-	19	18.1	16	15.2	16	15.2	-	-	89	84.8
1-3 rooms	13	6	46.2	-	-	5	38.5	-	-	-	-	6	46.2	5	38.5	4	30.8	-	-	9	69.2
4 rooms	7	6	85.7	-	-	6	85.7	-	-	-	-	6	85.7	5	71.4	5	71.4	-	-	2	28.6
5 rooms	80	3	3.7	-	-	3	3.7	-	-	-	-	3	3.7	3	3.7	2	2.5	-	-	78	97.5
6 or more rooms	5	5	100.0	-	-	5	100.0	-	-	-	-	4	80.0	3	60.0	5	100.0	-	-	-	-

Table 12 Households by dwelling type, number of rooms and household amenities – **continued**

Households	Total households	With fixed bath or shower				With inside flush toilet (WC)				With outside flush toilet (WC) only		Connected to public water supply		Connected to public sewer		With central heating				No central heating	
		Exclusive use		Shared use		Exclusive use		Shared use								All rooms		Some rooms			
		Number	Per cent	Number	Per cent	Number	Per cent	Number	Per cent	Number	Per cent	Number	Per cent	Number	Per cent	Number	Per cent	Number	Per cent	Number	Per cent
Carrickfergus																					
Households in all dwellings																					
All sizes	11,870	11,777	99.2	26	0.2	11,797	99.4	15	0.1	38	0.3	11,737	98.9	11,256	94.8	8,211	69.2	1,455	12.3	2,204	18.6
1-3 rooms	809	790	97.7	10	1.2	795	98.3	8	1.0	2	0.2	802	99.1	780	96.4	471	58.2	66	8.2	272	33.6
4 rooms	1,369	1,342	98.0	5	0.4	1,345	98.2	4	0.3	15	1.1	1,356	99.1	1,311	95.8	824	60.2	154	11.2	391	28.6
5 rooms	4,124	4,096	99.3	7	0.2	4,105	99.5	2	0.0	10	0.2	4,096	99.3	3,978	96.5	2,663	64.6	766	18.6	695	16.9
6 or more rooms	5,568	5,549	99.7	4	0.1	5,552	99.7	1	0.0	11	0.2	5,483	98.5	5,187	93.2	4,253	76.4	469	8.4	846	15.2
Households in unshared dwellings (permanent)																					
All sizes	11,762	11,689	99.4	10	0.1	11,702	99.5	6	0.1	38	0.3	11,636	98.9	11,160	94.9	8,157	69.4	1,444	12.3	2,161	18.4
1-3 rooms	741	735	99.2	-	-	738	99.6	-	-	2	0.3	738	99.6	718	96.9	434	58.6	62	8.4	245	33.1
4 rooms	1,346	1,321	98.1	4	0.3	1,323	98.3	4	0.3	15	1.1	1,335	99.2	1,291	95.9	813	60.4	152	11.3	381	28.3
5 rooms	4,113	4,087	99.4	5	0.1	4,095	99.6	1	0.0	10	0.2	4,086	99.3	3,968	96.5	2,659	64.6	762	18.5	692	16.8
6 or more rooms	5,562	5,546	99.7	1	0.0	5,546	99.7	1	0.0	11	0.2	5,477	98.5	5,183	93.2	4,251	76.4	468	8.4	843	15.2
Households in shared dwellings (permanent)																					
All sizes	13	-	-	13	100.0	4	30.8	9	69.2	-	-	12	92.3	13	100.0	4	30.8	-	-	9	69.2
1-3 rooms	10	-	-	10	100.0	2	20.0	8	80.0	-	-	9	90.0	10	100.0	4	40.0	-	-	6	60.0
4 rooms	1	-	-	1	100.0	1	100.0	-	-	-	-	1	100.0	1	100.0	-	-	-	-	1	100.0
5 rooms	1	-	-	1	100.0	-	-	1	100.0	-	-	1	100.0	1	100.0	-	-	-	-	1	100.0
6 or more rooms	1	-	-	1	100.0	1	100.0	-	-	-	-	1	100.0	1	100.0	-	-	-	-	1	100.0
Households in non-permanent dwellings																					
All sizes	11	7	63.6	-	-	7	63.6	-	-	-	-	5	45.5	1	9.1	4	36.4	1	9.1	6	54.5
1-3 rooms	5	2	40.0	-	-	2	40.0	-	-	-	-	2	40.0	-	-	1	20.0	-	-	4	80.0
4 rooms	2	1	50.0	-	-	1	50.0	-	-	-	-	-	-	-	-	1	50.0	-	-	1	50.0
5 rooms	1	1	100.0	-	-	1	100.0	-	-	-	-	-	-	-	-	1	100.0	-	-	-	-
6 or more rooms	3	3	100.0	-	-	3	100.0	-	-	-	-	3	100.0	1	33.3	1	33.3	1	33.3	1	33.3

Households	Total households	With fixed bath or shower				With inside flush toilet (WC)				With outside flush toilet (WC) only		Connected to public water supply		Connected to public sewer		With central heating				No central heating	
		Exclusive use		Shared use		Exclusive use		Shared use								All rooms		Some rooms			
		Number	Per cent	Number	Per cent	Number	Per cent	Number	Per cent	Number	Per cent	Number	Per cent	Number	Per cent	Number	Per cent	Number	Per cent	Number	Per cent
Castlereagh																					
Households in all dwellings																					
All sizes	22,910	22,832	99.7	27	0.1	22,867	99.8	13	0.1	16	0.1	22,887	99.9	21,932	95.7	18,571	81.1	2,627	11.5	1,712	7.5
1-3 rooms	1,642	1,627	99.1	9	0.5	1,636	99.6	1	0.1	2	0.1	1,638	99.8	1,607	97.9	1,103	67.2	318	19.4	221	13.5
4 rooms	2,777	2,754	99.2	2	0.1	2,759	99.4	2	0.1	9	0.3	2,773	99.9	2,687	96.8	2,012	72.5	458	16.5	307	11.1
5 rooms	7,250	7,233	99.8	7	0.1	7,244	99.9	1	0.0	3	0.0	7,247	100.0	7,055	97.3	5,853	80.7	834	11.5	563	7.8
6 or more rooms	11,241	11,218	99.8	9	0.1	11,228	99.9	9	0.1	2	0.0	11,229	99.9	10,583	94.1	9,603	85.4	1,017	9.0	621	5.5
Households in unshared dwellings (permanent)																					
All sizes	22,818	22,750	99.7	18	0.1	22,777	99.8	12	0.1	16	0.1	22,796	99.9	21,853	95.8	18,528	81.2	2,602	11.4	1,688	7.4
1-3 rooms	1,581	1,574	99.6	2	0.1	1,577	99.7	-	-	2	0.1	1,578	99.8	1,553	98.2	1,074	67.9	306	19.4	201	12.7
4 rooms	2,753	2,732	99.2	-	-	2,735	99.3	2	0.1	9	0.3	2,749	99.9	2,667	96.9	2,001	72.7	447	16.2	305	11.1
5 rooms	7,245	7,228	99.8	7	0.1	7,239	99.9	1	0.0	3	0.0	7,242	100.0	7,051	97.3	5,852	80.8	832	11.5	561	7.7
6 or more rooms	11,239	11,216	99.8	9	0.1	11,226	99.9	9	0.1	2	0.0	11,227	99.9	10,582	94.2	9,601	85.4	1,017	9.0	621	5.5
Households in shared dwellings (permanent)																					
All sizes	7	-	-	7	100.0	7	100.0	-	-	-	-	7	100.0	7	100.0	6	85.7	-	-	1	14.3
1-3 rooms	6	-	-	6	100.0	6	100.0	-	-	-	-	6	100.0	6	100.0	5	83.3	-	-	1	16.7
4 rooms	1	-	-	1	100.0	1	100.0	-	-	-	-	1	100.0	1	100.0	1	100.0	-	-	-	-
5 rooms	-	-	-	-	-	-	-	-	-	-	-	-	-	-	-	-	-	-	-	-	-
6 or more rooms	-	-	-	-	-	-	-	-	-	-	-	-	-	-	-	-	-	-	-	-	-
Households in non-permanent dwellings																					
All sizes	24	23	95.8	-	-	23	95.8	-	-	-	-	23	95.8	13	54.2	6	25.0	5	20.8	13	54.2
1-3 rooms	14	13	92.9	-	-	13	92.9	-	-	-	-	13	92.9	9	64.3	1	7.1	2	14.3	11	78.6
4 rooms	7	7	100.0	-	-	7	100.0	-	-	-	-	7	100.0	3	42.9	4	57.1	2	28.6	1	14.3
5 rooms	2	2	100.0	-	-	2	100.0	-	-	-	-	2	100.0	1	50.0	-	-	1	50.0	1	50.0
6 or more rooms	1	1	100.0	-	-	1	100.0	-	-	-	-	1	100.0	-	-	1	100.0	-	-	-	-

Table 12 Households by dwelling type, number of rooms and household amenities – **continued**

Households	Total households	With fixed bath or shower				With inside flush toilet (WC)				With outside flush toilet (WC) only		Connected to public water supply		Connected to public sewer		With central heating				No central heating	
		Exclusive use		Shared use		Exclusive use		Shared use								All rooms		Some rooms			
		Number	Per cent	Number	Per cent	Number	Per cent	Number	Per cent	Number	Per cent	Number	Per cent	Number	Per cent	Number	Per cent	Number	Per cent	Number	Per cent
Coleraine																					
Households in all dwellings																					
All sizes	17,870	17,625	98.6	71	0.4	17,704	99.1	33	0.2	42	0.2	17,604	98.5	14,959	83.7	12,598	70.5	1,904	10.7	3,368	18.8
1-3 rooms	1,239	1,150	92.8	38	3.1	1,175	94.8	21	1.7	9	0.7	1,202	97.0	1,141	92.1	788	63.6	111	9.0	340	27.4
4 rooms	2,074	2,026	97.7	8	0.4	2,046	98.6	-	-	7	0.3	2,034	98.1	1,827	88.1	1,229	59.3	219	10.6	626	30.2
5 rooms	6,019	5,965	99.1	12	0.2	5,979	99.3	6	0.1	13	0.2	5,968	99.2	5,382	89.4	4,134	68.7	708	11.8	1,177	19.6
6 or more rooms	8,538	8,484	99.4	13	0.2	8,504	99.6	6	0.1	13	0.2	8,400	98.4	6,609	77.4	6,447	75.5	866	10.1	1,225	14.3
Households in unshared dwellings (permanent)																					
All sizes	17,391	17,209	99.0	20	0.1	17,259	99.2	8	0.0	40	0.2	17,140	98.6	14,532	83.6	12,418	71.4	1,810	10.4	3,163	18.2
1-3 rooms	1,024	977	95.4	5	0.5	988	96.5	-	-	7	0.7	995	97.2	948	92.6	709	69.2	85	8.3	230	22.5
4 rooms	1,948	1,907	97.9	1	0.1	1,920	98.6	-	-	7	0.4	1,910	98.0	1,717	88.1	1,183	60.7	182	9.3	583	29.9
5 rooms	5,938	5,893	99.2	5	0.1	5,903	99.4	3	0.1	13	0.2	5,891	99.2	5,309	89.4	4,098	69.0	690	11.6	1,150	19.4
6 or more rooms	8,481	8,432	99.4	9	0.1	8,448	99.6	5	0.1	13	0.2	8,344	98.4	6,558	77.3	6,428	75.8	853	10.1	1,200	14.1
Households in shared dwellings (permanent)																					
All sizes	45	-	-	44	97.8	21	46.7	24	53.3	-	-	45	100.0	43	95.6	9	20.0	2	4.4	34	75.6
1-3 rooms	31	-	-	31	100.0	10	32.3	21	67.7	-	-	31	100.0	30	96.8	6	19.4	-	-	25	80.6
4 rooms	5	-	-	5	100.0	5	100.0	-	-	-	-	5	100.0	4	80.0	1	20.0	1	20.0	3	60.0
5 rooms	4	-	-	4	100.0	2	50.0	2	50.0	-	-	4	100.0	4	100.0	1	25.0	1	25.0	2	50.0
6 or more rooms	5	-	-	4	80.0	4	80.0	1	20.0	-	-	5	100.0	5	100.0	1	20.0	-	-	4	80.0
Households in non-permanent dwellings																					
All sizes	53	40	75.5	2	3.8	44	83.0	-	-	2	3.8	39	73.6	16	30.2	21	39.6	5	9.4	27	50.9
1-3 rooms	24	15	62.5	-	-	17	70.8	-	-	2	8.3	16	66.7	8	33.3	5	20.8	1	4.2	18	75.0
4 rooms	12	11	91.7	1	8.3	12	100.0	-	-	-	-	10	83.3	1	8.3	6	50.0	2	16.7	4	33.3
5 rooms	10	7	70.0	1	10.0	8	80.0	-	-	-	-	6	60.0	4	40.0	6	60.0	1	10.0	3	30.0
6 or more rooms	7	7	100.0	-	-	7	100.0	-	-	-	-	7	100.0	3	42.9	4	57.1	1	14.3	2	28.6

Table 12 Households by dwelling type, number of rooms and household amenities – **continued**

Households	Total households	With fixed bath or shower: Exclusive use Number	Exclusive use Per cent	Shared use Number	Shared use Per cent	With inside flush toilet (WC): Exclusive use Number	Exclusive use Per cent	Shared use Number	Shared use Per cent	With outside flush toilet (WC) only Number	Per cent	Connected to public water supply Number	Per cent	Connected to public sewer Number	Per cent	With central heating: All rooms Number	All rooms Per cent	Some rooms Number	Some rooms Per cent	No central heating Number	Per cent
Cookstown																					
Households in all dwellings																					
All sizes	9,222	8,962	97.2	16	0.2	9,029	97.9	5	0.1	50	0.5	9,061	98.3	5,200	56.4	6,045	65.5	948	10.3	2,229	24.2
1-3 rooms	516	423	82.0	6	1.2	443	85.9	2	0.4	11	2.1	466	90.3	287	55.6	224	43.4	40	7.8	252	48.8
4 rooms	1,259	1,181	93.8	2	0.2	1,209	96.0	-	-	13	1.0	1,229	97.6	862	68.5	587	46.6	125	9.9	547	43.4
5 rooms	2,986	2,939	98.4	5	0.2	2,953	98.9	2	0.1	13	0.4	2,960	99.1	1,979	66.3	1,828	61.2	368	12.3	790	26.5
6 or more rooms	4,461	4,419	99.1	3	0.1	4,424	99.2	1	0.0	13	0.3	4,406	98.8	2,072	46.4	3,406	76.4	415	9.3	640	14.3
Households in unshared dwellings (permanent)																					
All sizes	9,106	8,862	97.3	11	0.1	8,919	97.9	4	0.0	50	0.5	8,955	98.3	5,160	56.7	5,992	65.8	932	10.2	2,182	24.0
1-3 rooms	455	377	82.9	2	0.4	388	85.3	1	0.2	11	2.4	412	90.5	269	59.1	201	44.2	35	7.7	219	48.1
4 rooms	1,221	1,143	93.6	2	0.2	1,171	95.9	-	-	13	1.1	1,194	97.8	845	69.2	567	46.4	116	9.5	538	44.1
5 rooms	2,972	2,925	98.4	5	0.2	2,939	98.9	2	0.1	13	0.4	2,946	99.1	1,974	66.4	1,821	61.3	366	12.3	785	26.4
6 or more rooms	4,458	4,417	99.1	2	0.0	4,421	99.2	1	0.0	13	0.3	4,403	98.8	2,072	46.5	3,403	76.3	415	9.3	640	14.4
Households in shared dwellings (permanent)																					
All sizes	1	-	-	1	100.0	-	-	1	100.0	-	-	1	100.0	1	100.0	-	-	-	-	1	100.0
1-3 rooms	1	-	-	1	100.0	-	-	1	100.0	-	-	1	100.0	1	100.0	-	-	-	-	1	100.0
4 rooms	-	-	-	-	-	-	-	-	-	-	-	-	-	-	-	-	-	-	-	-	-
5 rooms	-	-	-	-	-	-	-	-	-	-	-	-	-	-	-	-	-	-	-	-	-
6 or more rooms	-	-	-	-	-	-	-	-	-	-	-	-	-	-	-	-	-	-	-	-	-
Households in non-permanent dwellings																					
All sizes	79	67	84.8	1	1.3	74	93.7	-	-	-	-	69	87.3	6	7.6	31	39.2	12	15.2	36	45.6
1-3 rooms	45	33	73.3	1	2.2	40	88.9	-	-	-	-	38	84.4	4	8.9	13	28.9	4	8.9	28	62.2
4 rooms	22	22	100.0	-	-	22	100.0	-	-	-	-	19	86.4	1	4.5	11	50.0	7	31.8	4	18.2
5 rooms	10	10	100.0	-	-	10	100.0	-	-	-	-	10	100.0	1	10.0	5	50.0	1	10.0	4	40.0
6 or more rooms	2	2	100.0	-	-	2	100.0	-	-	-	-	2	100.0	-	-	2	100.0	-	-	-	-

Households	Total households	With fixed bath or shower				With inside flush toilet (WC)				With outside flush toilet (WC) only		Connected to public water supply		Connected to public sewer		With central heating				No central heating	
		Exclusive use		Shared use		Exclusive use		Shared use								All rooms		Some rooms			
		Number	Per cent	Number	Per cent	Number	Per cent	Number	Per cent	Number	Per cent	Number	Per cent	Number	Per cent	Number	Per cent	Number	Per cent	Number	Per cent
Craigavon																					
Households in all dwellings																					
All sizes	24,915	24,542	98.5	34	0.1	24,621	98.8	20	0.1	147	0.6	24,790	99.5	21,448	86.1	19,519	78.3	2,479	9.9	2,917	11.7
1-3 rooms	1,574	1,501	95.4	12	0.8	1,517	96.4	8	0.5	14	0.9	1,547	98.3	1,429	90.8	1,188	75.5	116	7.4	270	17.2
4 rooms	2,828	2,724	96.3	6	0.2	2,740	96.9	1	0.0	47	1.7	2,806	99.2	2,545	90.0	2,045	72.3	305	10.8	478	16.9
5 rooms	9,318	9,195	98.7	6	0.1	9,226	99.0	2	0.0	57	0.6	9,288	99.7	8,553	91.8	7,019	75.3	1,082	11.6	1,217	13.1
6 or more rooms	11,195	11,122	99.3	10	0.1	11,138	99.5	9	0.1	29	0.3	11,149	99.6	8,921	79.7	9,267	82.8	976	8.7	952	8.5
Households in unshared dwellings (permanent)																					
All sizes	24,655	24,307	98.6	19	0.1	24,374	98.9	13	0.1	146	0.6	24,536	99.5	21,259	86.2	19,364	78.5	2,444	9.9	2,847	11.5
1-3 rooms	1,421	1,368	96.3	1	0.1	1,375	96.8	2	0.1	13	0.9	1,400	98.5	1,316	92.6	1,095	77.1	99	7.0	227	16.0
4 rooms	2,762	2,661	96.3	3	0.1	2,675	96.9	1	0.0	47	1.7	2,740	99.2	2,491	90.2	2,012	72.8	291	10.5	459	16.6
5 rooms	9,291	9,170	98.7	5	0.1	9,200	99.0	1	0.0	57	0.6	9,261	99.7	8,537	91.9	6,999	75.3	1,081	11.6	1,211	13.0
6 or more rooms	11,181	11,108	99.3	10	0.1	11,124	99.5	9	0.1	29	0.3	11,135	99.6	8,915	79.7	9,258	82.8	973	8.7	950	8.5
Households in shared dwellings (permanent)																					
All sizes	11	-	-	10	90.9	7	63.6	4	36.4	-	-	11	100.0	11	100.0	6	54.5	1	9.1	4	36.4
1-3 rooms	10	-	-	9	90.0	6	60.0	4	40.0	-	-	10	100.0	10	100.0	6	60.0	-	-	4	40.0
4 rooms	1	-	-	1	100.0	1	100.0	-	-	-	-	1	100.0	1	100.0	-	-	1	100.0	-	-
5 rooms	-	-	-	-	-	-	-	-	-	-	-	-	-	-	-	-	-	-	-	-	-
6 or more rooms	-	-	-	-	-	-	-	-	-	-	-	-	-	-	-	-	-	-	-	-	-
Households in non-permanent dwellings																					
All sizes	87	75	86.2	3	3.4	78	89.7	3	3.4	1	1.1	81	93.1	18	20.7	43	49.4	7	8.0	37	42.5
1-3 rooms	44	35	79.5	1	2.3	37	84.1	2	4.5	1	2.3	38	86.4	6	13.6	13	29.5	2	4.5	29	65.9
4 rooms	19	18	94.7	1	5.3	18	94.7	-	-	-	-	19	100.0	7	36.8	12	63.2	2	10.5	5	26.3
5 rooms	15	13	86.7	1	6.7	14	93.3	1	6.7	-	-	15	100.0	4	26.7	13	86.7	-	-	2	13.3
6 or more rooms	9	9	100.0	-	-	9	100.0	-	-	-	-	9	100.0	1	11.1	5	55.6	3	33.3	1	11.1

Table 12 Households by dwelling type, number of rooms and household amenities – **continued**

Households	Total households	With fixed bath or shower				With inside flush toilet (WC)				With outside flush toilet (WC) only		Connected to public water supply		Connected to public sewer		With central heating				No central heating	
		Exclusive use		Shared use		Exclusive use		Shared use								All rooms		Some rooms			
		Number	Per cent	Number	Per cent	Number	Per cent	Number	Per cent	Number	Per cent	Number	Per cent	Number	Per cent	Number	Per cent	Number	Per cent	Number	Per cent
Derry																					
Households in all dwellings																					
All sizes	28,015	27,688	98.8	74	0.3	27,803	99.2	31	0.1	104	0.4	27,884	99.5	25,924	92.5	22,736	81.2	1,731	6.2	3,548	12.7
1-3 rooms	2,196	2,101	95.7	25	1.1	2,126	96.8	8	0.4	22	1.0	2,149	97.9	2,055	93.6	1,655	75.4	142	6.5	399	18.2
4 rooms	3,603	3,510	97.4	10	0.3	3,543	98.3	3	0.1	39	1.1	3,587	99.6	3,406	94.5	2,650	73.5	216	6.0	737	20.5
5 rooms	11,541	11,455	99.3	18	0.2	11,489	99.5	10	0.1	29	0.3	11,517	99.8	10,945	94.8	9,513	82.4	660	5.7	1,368	11.9
6 or more rooms	10,675	10,622	99.5	21	0.2	10,645	99.7	10	0.1	14	0.1	10,631	99.6	9,518	89.2	8,918	83.5	713	6.7	1,044	9.8
Households in unshared dwellings (permanent)																					
All sizes	27,496	27,227	99.0	29	0.1	27,318	99.4	13	0.0	94	0.3	27,382	99.6	25,451	92.6	22,424	81.6	1,696	6.2	3,376	12.3
1-3 rooms	1,876	1,811	96.5	4	0.2	1,829	97.5	-	-	13	0.7	1,844	98.3	1,761	93.9	1,449	77.2	123	6.6	304	16.2
4 rooms	3,482	3,397	97.6	2	0.1	3,425	98.4	1	0.0	38	1.1	3,468	99.6	3,293	94.6	2,588	74.3	206	5.9	688	19.8
5 rooms	11,490	11,417	99.4	9	0.1	11,441	99.6	7	0.1	29	0.3	11,466	99.8	10,902	94.9	9,488	82.6	657	5.7	1,345	11.7
6 or more rooms	10,648	10,602	99.6	14	0.1	10,623	99.8	5	0.0	14	0.1	10,604	99.6	9,495	89.2	8,899	83.6	710	6.7	1,039	9.8
Households in shared dwellings (permanent)																					
All sizes	40	-	-	37	92.5	22	55.0	17	42.5	1	2.5	40	100.0	38	95.0	12	30.0	2	5.0	26	65.0
1-3 rooms	22	-	-	20	90.9	14	63.6	8	36.4	-	-	22	100.0	21	95.5	6	27.3	1	4.5	15	68.2
4 rooms	4	-	-	4	100.0	2	50.0	1	25.0	1	25.0	4	100.0	4	100.0	1	25.0	1	25.0	2	50.0
5 rooms	7	-	-	6	85.7	4	57.1	3	42.9	-	-	7	100.0	6	85.7	3	42.9	-	-	4	57.1
6 or more rooms	7	-	-	7	100.0	2	28.6	5	71.4	-	-	7	100.0	7	100.0	2	28.6	-	-	5	71.4
Households in non-permanent dwellings																					
All sizes	58	49	84.5	1	1.7	43	74.1	-	-	9	15.5	43	74.1	26	44.8	22	37.9	2	3.4	34	58.6
1-3 rooms	32	24	75.0	1	3.1	17	53.1	-	-	9	28.1	18	56.2	14	43.7	5	15.6	1	3.1	26	81.2
4 rooms	10	10	100.0	-	-	10	100.0	-	-	-	-	9	90.0	5	50.0	5	50.0	1	10.0	4	40.0
5 rooms	11	10	90.9	-	-	11	100.0	-	-	-	-	11	100.0	6	54.5	7	63.6	-	-	4	36.4
6 or more rooms	5	5	100.0	-	-	5	100.0	-	-	-	-	5	100.0	1	20.0	5	100.0	-	-	-	-

Table 12 Households by dwelling type, number of rooms and household amenities – **continued**

Households	Total households	With fixed bath or shower				With inside flush toilet (WC)				With outside flush toilet (WC) only		Connected to public water supply		Connected to public sewer		With central heating				No central heating	
		Exclusive use		Shared use		Exclusive use		Shared use								All rooms		Some rooms			
		Number	Per cent	Number	Per cent	Number	Per cent	Number	Per cent	Number	Per cent	Number	Per cent	Number	Per cent	Number	Per cent	Number	Per cent	Number	Per cent
Down																					
Households in all dwellings																					
All sizes	18,061	17,636	97.6	57	0.3	17,752	98.3	24	0.1	130	0.7	17,852	98.8	12,691	70.3	12,493	69.2	2,222	12.3	3,346	18.5
1-3 rooms	1,196	1,055	88.2	21	1.8	1,090	91.1	14	1.2	36	3.0	1,134	94.8	943	78.8	660	55.2	105	8.8	431	36.0
4 rooms	2,309	2,182	94.5	11	0.5	2,217	96.0	1	0.0	45	1.9	2,270	98.3	1,754	76.0	1,290	55.9	275	11.9	744	32.2
5 rooms	5,945	5,852	98.4	14	0.2	5,875	98.8	4	0.1	33	0.6	5,904	99.3	4,658	78.4	3,963	66.7	883	14.9	1,099	18.5
6 or more rooms	8,611	8,547	99.3	11	0.1	8,570	99.5	5	0.1	16	0.2	8,544	99.2	5,336	62.0	6,580	76.4	959	11.1	1,072	12.4
Households in unshared dwellings (permanent)																					
All sizes	17,704	17,336	97.9	28	0.2	17,426	98.4	10	0.1	125	0.7	17,514	98.9	12,438	70.3	12,328	69.6	2,196	12.4	3,180	18.0
1-3 rooms	998	894	89.6	4	0.4	914	91.6	2	0.2	32	3.2	949	95.1	791	79.3	574	57.5	95	9.5	329	33.0
4 rooms	2,229	2,113	94.8	3	0.1	2,140	96.0	-	-	44	2.0	2,194	98.4	1,703	76.4	1,246	55.9	264	11.8	719	32.3
5 rooms	5,890	5,804	98.5	12	0.2	5,826	98.9	3	0.1	33	0.6	5,851	99.3	4,627	78.6	3,939	66.9	881	15.0	1,070	18.2
6 or more rooms	8,587	8,525	99.3	9	0.1	8,546	99.5	5	0.1	16	0.2	8,520	99.2	5,317	61.9	6,569	76.5	956	11.1	1,062	12.4
Households in shared dwellings (permanent)																					
All sizes	24	-	-	23	95.8	14	58.3	10	41.7	-	-	24	100.0	23	95.8	7	29.2	2	8.3	15	62.5
1-3 rooms	15	-	-	14	93.3	6	40.0	9	60.0	-	-	15	100.0	15	100.0	5	33.3	1	6.7	9	60.0
4 rooms	6	-	-	6	100.0	5	83.3	1	16.7	-	-	6	100.0	6	100.0	2	33.3	1	16.7	3	50.0
5 rooms	1	-	-	1	100.0	1	100.0	-	-	-	-	1	100.0	1	100.0	-	-	-	-	1	100.0
6 or more rooms	2	-	-	2	100.0	2	100.0	-	-	-	-	2	100.0	1	50.0	-	-	-	-	2	100.0
Households in non-permanent dwellings																					
All sizes	131	101	77.1	4	3.1	111	84.7	3	2.3	5	3.8	113	86.3	35	26.7	60	45.8	5	3.8	66	50.4
1-3 rooms	65	46	70.8	1	1.5	53	81.5	2	3.1	4	6.2	53	81.5	24	36.9	19	29.2	1	1.5	45	69.2
4 rooms	32	27	84.4	2	6.2	30	93.7	-	-	1	3.1	28	87.5	4	12.5	20	62.5	3	9.4	9	28.1
5 rooms	28	22	78.6	1	3.6	22	78.6	1	3.6	-	-	26	92.9	5	17.9	16	57.1	1	3.6	11	39.3
6 or more rooms	6	6	100.0	-	-	6	100.0	-	-	-	-	6	100.0	2	33.3	5	83.3	-	-	1	16.7

Table 12 Households by dwelling type, number of rooms and household amenities – **continued**

Households	Total households	With fixed bath or shower				With inside flush toilet (WC)				With outside flush toilet (WC) only		Connected to public water supply		Connected to public sewer		With central heating				No central heating	
		Exclusive use		Shared use		Exclusive use		Shared use								All rooms		Some rooms			
		Number	Per cent	Number	Per cent	Number	Per cent	Number	Per cent	Number	Per cent	Number	Per cent	Number	Per cent	Number	Per cent	Number	Per cent	Number	Per cent
Dungannon																					
Households in all dwellings																					
All sizes	13,653	13,195	96.6	40	0.3	13,289	97.3	17	0.1	115	0.8	13,298	97.4	8,116	59.4	9,158	67.1	1,257	9.2	3,238	23.7
1-3 rooms	868	706	81.3	12	1.4	741	85.4	6	0.7	29	3.3	788	90.8	561	64.6	392	45.2	56	6.5	420	48.4
4 rooms	1,658	1,538	92.8	8	0.5	1,563	94.3	2	0.1	33	2.0	1,596	96.3	1,151	69.4	861	51.9	160	9.7	637	38.4
5 rooms	4,738	4,635	97.8	11	0.2	4,658	98.3	5	0.1	27	0.6	4,661	98.4	3,310	69.9	2,996	63.2	474	10.0	1,268	26.8
6 or more rooms	6,389	6,316	98.9	9	0.1	6,327	99.0	4	0.1	26	0.4	6,253	97.9	3,094	48.4	4,909	76.8	567	8.9	913	14.3
Households in unshared dwellings (permanent)																					
All sizes	13,453	13,035	96.9	26	0.2	13,105	97.4	14	0.1	111	0.8	13,122	97.5	8,041	59.8	9,071	67.4	1,234	9.2	3,148	23.4
1-3 rooms	779	644	82.7	6	0.8	663	85.1	3	0.4	26	3.3	710	91.1	525	67.4	369	47.4	50	6.4	360	46.2
4 rooms	1,610	1,495	92.9	3	0.2	1,516	94.2	2	0.1	33	2.0	1,554	96.5	1,129	70.1	836	51.9	152	9.4	622	38.6
5 rooms	4,692	4,596	98.0	9	0.2	4,616	98.4	5	0.1	26	0.6	4,620	98.5	3,297	70.3	2,971	63.3	467	10.0	1,254	26.7
6 or more rooms	6,372	6,300	98.9	8	0.1	6,310	99.0	4	0.1	26	0.4	6,238	97.9	3,090	48.5	4,895	76.8	565	8.9	912	14.3
Households in shared dwellings (permanent)																					
All sizes	7	-	-	7	100.0	4	57.1	2	28.6	1	14.3	7	100.0	6	85.7	-	-	2	28.6	5	71.4
1-3 rooms	3	-	-	3	100.0	1	33.3	2	66.7	-	-	3	100.0	3	100.0	-	-	-	-	3	100.0
4 rooms	3	-	-	3	100.0	3	100.0	-	-	-	-	3	100.0	3	100.0	-	-	2	66.7	1	33.3
5 rooms	1	-	-	1	100.0	-	-	-	-	1	100.0	1	100.0	-	-	-	-	-	-	1	100.0
6 or more rooms	-	-	-	-	-	-	-	-	-	-	-	-	-	-	-	-	-	-	-	-	-
Households in non-permanent dwellings																					
All sizes	145	115	79.3	5	3.4	133	91.7	-	-	3	2.1	121	83.4	28	19.3	61	42.1	12	8.3	72	49.7
1-3 rooms	70	48	68.6	2	2.9	62	88.6	-	-	3	4.3	59	84.3	18	25.7	17	24.3	3	4.3	50	71.4
4 rooms	29	27	93.1	2	6.9	28	96.6	-	-	-	-	23	79.3	3	10.3	14	48.3	4	13.8	11	37.9
5 rooms	32	26	81.2	1	3.1	29	90.6	-	-	-	-	27	84.4	5	15.6	19	59.4	3	9.4	10	31.2
6 or more rooms	14	14	100.0	-	-	14	100.0	-	-	-	-	12	85.7	2	14.3	11	78.6	2	14.3	1	7.1

Table 12 Households by dwelling type, number of rooms and household amenities – **continued**

Households	Total households	With fixed bath or shower: Exclusive use Number	Exclusive use Per cent	Shared use Number	Shared use Per cent	With inside flush toilet (WC): Exclusive use Number	Exclusive use Per cent	Shared use Number	Shared use Per cent	With outside flush toilet (WC) only Number	Per cent	Connected to public water supply Number	Per cent	Connected to public sewer Number	Per cent	With central heating: All rooms Number	All rooms Per cent	Some rooms Number	Some rooms Per cent	No central heating Number	Per cent
Fermanagh																					
Households in all dwellings																					
All sizes	16,901	15,986	94.6	50	0.3	16,124	95.4	42	0.2	148	0.9	16,269	96.3	9,153	54.2	11,139	65.9	1,812	10.7	3,950	23.4
1-3 rooms	1,154	778	67.4	18	1.6	825	71.5	15	1.3	33	2.9	915	79.3	586	50.8	472	40.9	90	7.8	592	51.3
4 rooms	2,073	1,891	91.2	1	0.0	1,918	92.5	2	0.1	42	2.0	1,985	95.8	1,401	67.6	1,101	53.1	243	11.7	729	35.2
5 rooms	5,405	5,239	96.9	16	0.3	5,272	97.5	12	0.2	39	0.7	5,297	98.0	3,546	65.6	3,491	64.6	690	12.8	1,224	22.6
6 or more rooms	8,269	8,078	97.7	15	0.2	8,109	98.1	13	0.2	34	0.4	8,072	97.6	3,620	43.8	6,075	73.5	789	9.5	1,405	17.0
Households in unshared dwellings (permanent)																					
All sizes	16,541	15,722	95.0	29	0.2	15,830	95.7	29	0.2	147	0.9	15,964	96.5	8,954	54.1	10,979	66.4	1,767	10.7	3,795	22.9
1-3 rooms	922	619	67.1	4	0.4	649	70.4	4	0.4	33	3.6	728	79.0	460	49.9	384	41.6	64	6.9	474	51.4
4 rooms	2,004	1,830	91.3	-	-	1,852	92.4	1	0.0	42	2.1	1,920	95.8	1,352	67.5	1,062	53.0	234	11.7	708	35.3
5 rooms	5,364	5,210	97.1	12	0.2	5,237	97.6	11	0.2	38	0.7	5,261	98.1	3,529	65.8	3,469	64.7	684	12.8	1,211	22.6
6 or more rooms	8,251	8,063	97.7	13	0.2	8,092	98.1	13	0.2	34	0.4	8,055	97.6	3,613	43.8	6,064	73.5	785	9.5	1,402	17.0
Households in shared dwellings (permanent)																					
All sizes	15	-	-	15	100.0	5	33.3	10	66.7	-	-	15	100.0	11	73.3	3	20.0	4	26.7	8	53.3
1-3 rooms	12	-	-	12	100.0	2	16.7	10	83.3	-	-	12	100.0	9	75.0	2	16.7	3	25.0	7	58.3
4 rooms	-	-	-	-	-	-	-	-	-	-	-	-	-	-	-	-	-	-	-	-	-
5 rooms	2	-	-	2	100.0	2	100.0	-	-	-	-	2	100.0	2	100.0	1	50.0	-	-	1	50.0
6 or more rooms	1	-	-	1	100.0	1	100.0	-	-	-	-	1	100.0	-	-	-	-	1	100.0	-	-
Households in non-permanent dwellings																					
All sizes	156	83	53.2	1	0.6	105	67.3	1	0.6	1	0.6	104	66.7	19	12.2	39	25.0	16	10.3	101	64.7
1-3 rooms	102	45	44.1	-	-	59	57.8	-	-	-	-	60	58.8	10	9.8	15	14.7	10	9.8	77	75.5
4 rooms	24	17	70.8	-	-	22	91.7	-	-	-	-	20	83.3	6	25.0	11	45.8	2	8.3	11	45.8
5 rooms	24	16	66.7	1	4.2	19	79.2	1	4.2	1	4.2	19	79.2	3	12.5	11	45.8	2	8.3	11	45.8
6 or more rooms	6	5	83.3	-	-	5	83.3	-	-	-	-	5	83.3	-	-	2	33.3	2	33.3	2	33.3

Table 12 Households by dwelling type, number of rooms and household amenities – **continued**

Households	Total households	With fixed bath or shower				With inside flush toilet (WC)				With outside flush toilet (WC) only		Connected to public water supply		Connected to public sewer		With central heating				No central heating	
		Exclusive use		Shared use		Exclusive use		Shared use								All rooms		Some rooms			
		Number	Per cent	Number	Per cent	Number	Per cent	Number	Per cent	Number	Per cent	Number	Per cent	Number	Per cent	Number	Per cent	Number	Per cent	Number	Per cent
Larne																					
Households in all dwellings																					
All sizes	10,409	10,152	97.5	17	0.2	10,204	98.0	3	0.0	112	1.1	9,933	95.4	8,433	81.0	6,500	62.4	1,037	10.0	2,872	27.6
1-3 rooms	651	599	92.0	8	1.2	618	94.9	-	-	18	2.8	623	95.7	576	88.5	358	55.0	52	8.0	241	37.0
4 rooms	1,459	1,367	93.7	4	0.3	1,385	94.9	1	0.1	43	2.9	1,418	97.2	1,287	88.2	773	53.0	125	8.6	561	38.5
5 rooms	3,062	2,999	97.9	2	0.1	3,012	98.4	-	-	26	0.8	2,971	97.0	2,681	87.6	1,907	62.3	312	10.2	843	27.5
6 or more rooms	5,237	5,187	99.0	3	0.1	5,189	99.1	2	0.0	25	0.5	4,921	94.0	3,889	74.3	3,462	66.1	548	10.5	1,227	23.4
Households in unshared dwellings (permanent)																					
All sizes	10,286	10,041	97.6	14	0.1	10,085	98.0	3	0.0	111	1.1	9,828	95.5	8,352	81.2	6,425	62.5	1,032	10.0	2,829	27.5
1-3 rooms	584	542	92.8	7	1.2	555	95.0	-	-	17	2.9	568	97.3	531	90.9	318	54.5	50	8.6	216	37.0
4 rooms	1,422	1,332	93.7	2	0.1	1,348	94.8	1	0.1	43	3.0	1,386	97.5	1,264	88.9	751	52.8	122	8.6	549	38.6
5 rooms	3,049	2,986	97.9	2	0.1	2,999	98.4	-	-	26	0.9	2,959	97.0	2,673	87.7	1,898	62.2	312	10.2	839	27.5
6 or more rooms	5,231	5,181	99.0	3	0.1	5,183	99.1	2	0.0	25	0.5	4,915	94.0	3,884	74.2	3,458	66.1	548	10.5	1,225	23.4
Households in shared dwellings (permanent)																					
All sizes	2	-	-	2	100.0	2	100.0	-	-	-	-	2	100.0	2	100.0	2	100.0	-	-	-	-
1-3 rooms	1	-	-	1	100.0	1	100.0	-	-	-	-	1	100.0	1	100.0	1	100.0	-	-	-	-
4 rooms	1	-	-	1	100.0	1	100.0	-	-	-	-	1	100.0	1	100.0	1	100.0	-	-	-	-
5 rooms	-	-	-	-	-	-	-	-	-	-	-	-	-	-	-	-	-	-	-	-	-
6 or more rooms	-	-	-	-	-	-	-	-	-	-	-	-	-	-	-	-	-	-	-	-	-
Households in non-permanent dwellings																					
All sizes	49	40	81.6	-	-	45	91.8	-	-	1	2.0	31	63.3	10	20.4	17	34.7	3	6.1	29	59.2
1-3 rooms	25	16	64.0	-	-	21	84.0	-	-	1	4.0	13	52.0	4	16.0	3	12.0	1	4.0	21	84.0
4 rooms	18	18	100.0	-	-	18	100.0	-	-	-	-	13	72.2	5	27.8	10	55.6	2	11.1	6	33.3
5 rooms	5	5	100.0	-	-	5	100.0	-	-	-	-	4	80.0	1	20.0	3	60.0	-	-	2	40.0
6 or more rooms	1	1	100.0	-	-	1	100.0	-	-	-	-	1	100.0	-	-	1	100.0	-	-	-	-

Table 12 Households by dwelling type, number of rooms and household amenities – **continued**

Households	Total households	With fixed bath or shower				With inside flush toilet (WC)				With outside flush toilet (WC) only		Connected to public water supply		Connected to public sewer		With central heating				No central heating	
		Exclusive use		Shared use		Exclusive use		Shared use								All rooms		Some rooms			
		Number	Per cent	Number	Per cent	Number	Per cent	Number	Per cent	Number	Per cent	Number	Per cent	Number	Per cent	Number	Per cent	Number	Per cent	Number	Per cent
Limavady																					
Households in all dwellings																					
All sizes	8,489	8,339	98.2	16	0.2	8,359	98.5	7	0.1	37	0.4	8,325	98.1	6,324	74.5	6,431	75.8	671	7.9	1,387	16.3
1-3 rooms	552	478	86.6	1	0.2	484	87.7	-	-	14	2.5	502	90.9	415	75.2	341	61.8	37	6.7	174	31.5
4 rooms	1,070	1,042	97.4	1	0.1	1,047	97.9	-	-	8	0.7	1,048	97.9	893	83.5	767	71.7	80	7.5	223	20.8
5 rooms	3,313	3,291	99.3	6	0.2	3,295	99.5	3	0.1	9	0.3	3,289	99.3	2,785	84.1	2,433	73.4	305	9.2	575	17.4
6 or more rooms	3,554	3,528	99.3	8	0.2	3,533	99.4	4	0.1	6	0.2	3,486	98.1	2,231	62.8	2,890	81.3	249	7.0	415	11.7
Households in unshared dwellings (permanent)																					
All sizes	8,412	8,283	98.5	14	0.2	8,298	98.6	7	0.1	34	0.4	8,263	98.2	6,289	74.8	6,402	76.1	662	7.9	1,348	16.0
1-3 rooms	505	450	89.1	-	-	452	89.5	-	-	11	2.2	468	92.7	395	78.2	328	65.0	31	6.1	146	28.9
4 rooms	1,057	1,030	97.4	1	0.1	1,035	97.9	-	-	8	0.8	1,037	98.1	888	84.0	759	71.8	80	7.6	218	20.6
5 rooms	3,300	3,279	99.4	5	0.2	3,282	99.5	3	0.1	9	0.3	3,276	99.3	2,777	84.2	2,427	73.5	303	9.2	570	17.3
6 or more rooms	3,550	3,524	99.3	8	0.2	3,529	99.4	4	0.1	6	0.2	3,482	98.1	2,229	62.8	2,888	81.4	248	7.0	414	11.7
Households in shared dwellings (permanent)																					
All sizes	1	-	-	1	100.0	1	100.0	-	-	-	-	1	100.0	1	100.0	-	-	-	-	1	100.0
1-3 rooms	-	-	-	-	-	-	-	-	-	-	-	-	-	-	-	-	-	-	-	-	-
4 rooms	-	-	-	-	-	-	-	-	-	-	-	-	-	-	-	-	-	-	-	-	-
5 rooms	1	-	-	1	100.0	1	100.0	-	-	-	-	1	100.0	1	100.0	-	-	-	-	1	100.0
6 or more rooms	-	-	-	-	-	-	-	-	-	-	-	-	-	-	-	-	-	-	-	-	-
Households in non-permanent dwellings																					
All sizes	43	24	55.8	-	-	27	62.8	-	-	3	7.0	28	65.1	7	16.3	14	32.6	4	9.3	25	58.1
1-3 rooms	28	10	35.7	-	-	13	46.4	-	-	3	10.7	15	53.6	5	17.9	6	21.4	2	7.1	20	71.4
4 rooms	7	6	85.7	-	-	6	85.7	-	-	-	-	5	71.4	1	14.3	4	57.1	-	-	3	42.9
5 rooms	6	6	100.0	-	-	6	100.0	-	-	-	-	6	100.0	1	16.7	3	50.0	1	16.7	2	33.3
6 or more rooms	2	2	100.0	-	-	2	100.0	-	-	-	-	2	100.0	-	-	1	50.0	1	50.0	-	-

Table 12 Households by dwelling type, number of rooms and household amenities – **continued**

Households	Total households	With fixed bath or shower: Exclusive use		With fixed bath or shower: Shared use		With inside flush toilet (WC): Exclusive use		With inside flush toilet (WC): Shared use		With outside flush toilet (WC) only		Connected to public water supply		Connected to public sewer		With central heating: All rooms		With central heating: Some rooms		No central heating	
		Number	Per cent	Number	Per cent	Number	Per cent	Number	Per cent	Number	Per cent	Number	Per cent	Number	Per cent	Number	Per cent	Number	Per cent	Number	Per cent
Lisburn																					
Households in all dwellings																					
All sizes	33,277	32,886	98.8	72	0.2	33,020	99.2	34	0.1	98	0.3	33,121	99.5	27,911	83.9	26,859	80.7	2,337	7.0	4,081	12.3
1-3 rooms	2,096	1,997	95.3	20	1.0	2,031	96.9	5	0.2	18	0.9	2,065	98.5	1,908	91.0	1,534	73.2	146	7.0	416	19.8
4 rooms	4,287	4,169	97.2	11	0.3	4,202	98.0	7	0.2	46	1.1	4,259	99.3	3,819	89.1	2,995	69.9	409	9.5	883	20.6
5 rooms	11,422	11,321	99.1	25	0.2	11,365	99.5	13	0.1	18	0.2	11,386	99.7	10,386	90.9	9,285	81.3	729	6.4	1,408	12.3
6 or more rooms	15,472	15,399	99.5	16	0.1	15,422	99.7	9	0.1	16	0.1	15,411	99.6	11,798	76.3	13,045	84.3	1,053	6.8	1,374	8.9
Households in unshared dwellings (permanent)																					
All sizes	32,976	32,635	99.0	38	0.1	32,744	99.3	19	0.1	96	0.3	32,831	99.6	27,729	84.1	26,683	80.9	2,299	7.0	3,994	12.1
1-3 rooms	1,969	1,900	96.5	3	0.2	1,918	97.4	-	-	16	0.8	1,946	98.8	1,830	92.9	1,464	74.4	135	6.9	370	18.8
4 rooms	4,194	4,081	97.3	7	0.2	4,112	98.0	5	0.1	46	1.1	4,167	99.4	3,760	89.7	2,937	70.0	393	9.4	864	20.6
5 rooms	11,365	11,273	99.2	17	0.1	11,311	99.5	10	0.1	18	0.2	11,329	99.7	10,353	91.1	9,254	81.4	719	6.3	1,392	12.2
6 or more rooms	15,448	15,381	99.6	11	0.1	15,403	99.7	4	0.0	16	0.1	15,389	99.6	11,786	76.3	13,028	84.3	1,052	6.8	1,368	8.9
Households in shared dwellings (permanent)																					
All sizes	19	-	-	19	100.0	8	42.1	11	57.9	-	-	19	100.0	18	94.7	14	73.7	1	5.3	4	21.1
1-3 rooms	10	-	-	10	100.0	7	70.0	3	30.0	-	-	10	100.0	9	90.0	5	50.0	1	10.0	4	40.0
4 rooms	2	-	-	2	100.0	1	50.0	1	50.0	-	-	2	100.0	2	100.0	2	100.0	-	-	-	-
5 rooms	2	-	-	2	100.0	-	-	2	100.0	-	-	2	100.0	2	100.0	2	100.0	-	-	-	-
6 or more rooms	5	-	-	5	100.0	-	-	5	100.0	-	-	5	100.0	5	100.0	5	100.0	-	-	-	-
Households in non-permanent dwellings																					
All sizes	135	114	84.4	5	3.7	125	92.6	-	-	2	1.5	126	93.3	20	14.8	77	57.0	12	8.9	46	34.1
1-3 rooms	52	36	69.2	3	5.8	43	82.7	-	-	2	3.8	45	86.5	6	11.5	18	34.6	5	9.6	29	55.8
4 rooms	42	40	95.2	1	2.4	41	97.6	-	-	-	-	41	97.6	8	19.0	33	78.6	5	11.9	4	9.5
5 rooms	27	25	92.6	1	3.7	27	100.0	-	-	-	-	27	100.0	3	11.1	17	63.0	2	7.4	8	29.6
6 or more rooms	14	13	92.9	-	-	14	100.0	-	-	-	-	13	92.9	3	21.4	9	64.3	-	-	5	35.7

Table 12 Households by dwelling type, number of rooms and household amenities – **continued**

Households	Total households	With fixed bath or shower				With inside flush toilet (WC)				With outside flush toilet (WC) only		Connected to public water supply		Connected to public sewer		With central heating				No central heating	
		Exclusive use		Shared use		Exclusive use		Shared use								All rooms		Some rooms			
		Number	Per cent	Number	Per cent	Number	Per cent	Number	Per cent	Number	Per cent	Number	Per cent	Number	Per cent	Number	Per cent	Number	Per cent	Number	Per cent
Magherafelt																					
Households in all dwellings																					
All sizes	10,398	10,036	96.5	25	0.2	10,084	97.0	17	0.2	104	1.0	10,026	96.4	5,771	55.5	6,632	63.8	1,096	10.5	2,670	25.7
1-3 rooms	628	484	77.1	5	0.8	497	79.1	3	0.5	29	4.6	526	83.8	321	51.1	267	42.5	54	8.6	307	48.9
4 rooms	1,212	1,109	91.5	3	0.2	1,126	92.9	3	0.2	38	3.1	1,151	95.0	758	62.5	607	50.1	135	11.1	470	38.8
5 rooms	3,597	3,535	98.3	8	0.2	3,547	98.6	5	0.1	20	0.6	3,549	98.7	2,505	69.6	2,067	57.5	441	12.3	1,089	30.3
6 or more rooms	4,961	4,908	98.9	9	0.2	4,914	99.1	6	0.1	17	0.3	4,800	96.8	2,187	44.1	3,691	74.4	466	9.4	804	16.2
Households in unshared dwellings (permanent)																					
All sizes	10,269	9,931	96.7	23	0.2	9,976	97.1	16	0.2	103	1.0	9,924	96.6	5,748	56.0	6,569	64.0	1,082	10.5	2,618	25.5
1-3 rooms	555	435	78.4	3	0.5	445	80.2	2	0.4	28	5.0	478	86.1	307	55.3	242	43.6	47	8.5	266	47.9
4 rooms	1,181	1,078	91.3	3	0.3	1,095	92.7	3	0.3	38	3.2	1,121	94.9	754	63.8	586	49.6	130	11.0	465	39.4
5 rooms	3,579	3,517	98.3	8	0.2	3,529	98.6	5	0.1	20	0.6	3,532	98.7	2,502	69.9	2,055	57.4	439	12.3	1,085	30.3
6 or more rooms	4,954	4,901	98.9	9	0.2	4,907	99.1	6	0.1	17	0.3	4,793	96.8	2,185	44.1	3,686	74.4	466	9.4	802	16.2
Households in shared dwellings (permanent)																					
All sizes	-	-	-	-	-	-	-	-	-	-	-	-	-	-	-	-	-	-	-	-	-
1-3 rooms	-	-	-	-	-	-	-	-	-	-	-	-	-	-	-	-	-	-	-	-	-
4 rooms	-	-	-	-	-	-	-	-	-	-	-	-	-	-	-	-	-	-	-	-	-
5 rooms	-	-	-	-	-	-	-	-	-	-	-	-	-	-	-	-	-	-	-	-	-
6 or more rooms	-	-	-	-	-	-	-	-	-	-	-	-	-	-	-	-	-	-	-	-	-
Households in non-permanent dwellings																					
All sizes	112	89	79.5	1	0.9	92	82.1	-	-	1	0.9	85	75.9	7	6.2	50	44.6	14	12.5	48	42.9
1-3 rooms	62	39	62.9	1	1.6	42	67.7	-	-	1	1.6	37	59.7	4	6.5	17	27.4	7	11.3	38	61.3
4 rooms	29	29	100.0	-	-	29	100.0	-	-	-	-	28	96.6	2	6.9	20	69.0	5	17.2	4	13.8
5 rooms	15	15	100.0	-	-	15	100.0	-	-	-	-	14	93.3	-	-	9	60.0	2	13.3	4	26.7
6 or more rooms	6	6	100.0	-	-	6	100.0	-	-	-	-	6	100.0	1	16.7	4	66.7	-	-	2	33.3

Table 12 Households by dwelling type, number of rooms and household amenities – **continued**

Households	Total households	With fixed bath or shower				With inside flush toilet (WC)				With outside flush toilet (WC) only		Connected to public water supply		Connected to public sewer		With central heating				No central heating	
		Exclusive use		Shared use		Exclusive use		Shared use								All rooms		Some rooms			
		Number	Per cent	Number	Per cent	Number	Per cent	Number	Per cent	Number	Per cent	Number	Per cent	Number	Per cent	Number	Per cent	Number	Per cent	Number	Per cent
Moyle																					
Households in all dwellings																					
All sizes	4,721	4,566	96.7	15	0.3	4,591	97.2	15	0.3	27	0.6	4,475	94.8	3,099	65.6	2,671	56.6	667	14.1	1,383	29.3
1-3 rooms	372	318	85.5	2	0.5	328	88.2	2	0.5	9	2.4	337	90.6	269	72.3	197	53.0	32	8.6	143	38.4
4 rooms	685	639	93.3	1	0.1	644	94.0	1	0.1	11	1.6	649	94.7	500	73.0	324	47.3	106	15.5	255	37.2
5 rooms	1,519	1,496	98.5	2	0.1	1,499	98.7	3	0.2	6	0.4	1,473	97.0	1,144	75.3	775	51.0	238	15.7	506	33.3
6 or more rooms	2,145	2,113	98.5	10	0.5	2,120	98.8	9	0.4	1	0.0	2,016	94.0	1,186	55.3	1,375	64.1	291	13.6	479	22.3
Households in unshared dwellings (permanent)																					
All sizes	4,662	4,520	97.0	11	0.2	4,540	97.4	11	0.2	26	0.6	4,420	94.8	3,062	65.7	2,644	56.7	656	14.1	1,362	29.2
1-3 rooms	348	301	86.5	1	0.3	309	88.8	1	0.3	8	2.3	316	90.8	255	73.3	188	54.0	29	8.3	131	37.6
4 rooms	662	619	93.5	-	-	622	94.0	-	-	11	1.7	627	94.7	485	73.3	310	46.8	101	15.3	251	37.9
5 rooms	1,515	1,492	98.5	2	0.1	1,495	98.7	3	0.2	6	0.4	1,469	97.0	1,142	75.4	773	51.0	238	15.7	504	33.3
6 or more rooms	2,137	2,108	98.6	8	0.4	2,114	98.9	7	0.3	1	0.0	2,008	94.0	1,180	55.2	1,373	64.2	288	13.5	476	22.3
Households in shared dwellings (permanent)																					
All sizes	5	-	-	4	80.0	1	20.0	4	80.0	-	-	5	100.0	2	40.0	-	-	3	60.0	2	40.0
1-3 rooms	1	-	-	1	100.0	-	-	1	100.0	-	-	1	100.0	-	-	-	-	1	100.0	-	-
4 rooms	1	-	-	1	100.0	-	-	1	100.0	-	-	1	100.0	-	-	-	-	1	100.0	-	-
5 rooms	-	-	-	-	-	-	-	-	-	-	-	-	-	-	-	-	-	-	-	-	-
6 or more rooms	3	-	-	2	66.7	1	33.3	2	66.7	-	-	3	100.0	2	66.7	-	-	1	33.3	2	66.7
Households in non-permanent dwellings																					
All sizes	25	17	68.0	-	-	21	84.0	-	-	1	4.0	21	84.0	9	36.0	11	44.0	2	8.0	12	48.0
1-3 rooms	11	5	45.5	-	-	7	63.6	-	-	1	9.1	8	72.7	4	36.4	3	27.3	-	-	8	72.7
4 rooms	10	8	80.0	-	-	10	100.0	-	-	-	-	9	90.0	4	40.0	6	60.0	2	20.0	2	20.0
5 rooms	3	3	100.0	-	-	3	100.0	-	-	-	-	3	100.0	1	33.3	1	33.3	-	-	2	66.7
6 or more rooms	1	1	100.0	-	-	1	100.0	-	-	-	-	1	100.0	-	-	1	100.0	-	-	-	-

Table 12 Households by dwelling type, number of rooms and household amenities – **continued**

Households	Total households	With fixed bath or shower				With inside flush toilet (WC)				With outside flush toilet (WC) only		Connected to public water supply		Connected to public sewer		With central heating				No central heating	
		Exclusive use		Shared use		Exclusive use		Shared use								All rooms		Some rooms			
		Number	Per cent	Number	Per cent	Number	Per cent	Number	Per cent	Number	Per cent	Number	Per cent	Number	Per cent	Number	Per cent	Number	Per cent	Number	Per cent
Newry and Mourne																					
Households in all dwellings																					
All sizes	24,418	23,808	97.5	61	0.2	23,916	97.9	28	0.1	181	0.7	24,023	98.4	17,397	71.2	17,106	70.1	2,315	9.5	4,997	20.5
1-3 rooms	1,932	1,651	85.5	25	1.3	1,686	87.3	15	0.8	75	3.9	1,774	91.8	1,433	74.2	1,068	55.3	172	8.9	692	35.8
4 rooms	3,038	2,886	95.0	8	0.3	2,916	96.0	2	0.1	44	1.4	2,974	97.9	2,265	74.6	1,720	56.6	321	10.6	997	32.8
5 rooms	8,646	8,546	98.8	10	0.1	8,565	99.1	7	0.1	36	0.4	8,568	99.1	6,848	79.2	5,885	68.1	912	10.5	1,849	21.4
6 or more rooms	10,802	10,725	99.3	18	0.2	10,749	99.5	4	0.0	26	0.2	10,707	99.1	6,851	63.4	8,433	78.1	910	8.4	1,459	13.5
Households in unshared dwellings (permanent)																					
All sizes	23,984	23,437	97.7	40	0.2	23,539	98.1	17	0.1	152	0.6	23,635	98.5	17,130	71.4	16,896	70.4	2,275	9.5	4,813	20.1
1-3 rooms	1,695	1,467	86.5	8	0.5	1,500	88.5	4	0.2	49	2.9	1,578	93.1	1,278	75.4	995	58.7	149	8.8	551	32.5
4 rooms	2,921	2,773	94.9	7	0.2	2,803	96.0	2	0.1	42	1.4	2,861	97.9	2,190	75.0	1,641	56.2	314	10.7	966	33.1
5 rooms	8,585	8,489	98.9	9	0.1	8,506	99.1	7	0.1	35	0.4	8,508	99.1	6,822	79.5	5,838	68.0	907	10.6	1,840	21.4
6 or more rooms	10,783	10,708	99.3	16	0.1	10,730	99.5	4	0.0	26	0.2	10,688	99.1	6,840	63.4	8,422	78.1	905	8.4	1,456	13.5
Households in shared dwellings (permanent)																					
All sizes	20	-	-	20	100.0	9	45.0	11	55.0	-	-	20	100.0	19	95.0	4	20.0	2	10.0	14	70.0
1-3 rooms	17	-	-	17	100.0	6	35.3	11	64.7	-	-	17	100.0	16	94.1	3	17.6	2	11.8	12	70.6
4 rooms	1	-	-	1	100.0	1	100.0	-	-	-	-	1	100.0	1	100.0	-	-	-	-	1	100.0
5 rooms	-	-	-	-	-	-	-	-	-	-	-	-	-	-	-	-	-	-	-	-	-
6 or more rooms	2	-	-	2	100.0	2	100.0	-	-	-	-	2	100.0	2	100.0	1	50.0	-	-	1	50.0
Households in non-permanent dwellings																					
All sizes	204	163	79.9	1	0.5	160	78.4	-	-	27	13.2	160	78.4	48	23.5	78	38.2	15	7.4	111	54.4
1-3 rooms	110	76	69.1	-	-	72	65.5	-	-	24	21.8	71	64.5	34	30.9	18	16.4	8	7.3	84	76.4
4 rooms	43	40	93.0	-	-	39	90.7	-	-	2	4.7	39	90.7	6	14.0	26	60.5	-	-	17	39.5
5 rooms	39	35	89.7	1	2.6	37	94.9	-	-	1	2.6	38	97.4	4	10.3	28	71.8	3	7.7	8	20.5
6 or more rooms	12	12	100.0	-	-	12	100.0	-	-	-	-	12	100.0	4	33.3	6	50.0	4	33.3	2	16.7

Table 12 Households by dwelling type, number of rooms and household amenities – **continued**

Households	Total households	With fixed bath or shower				With inside flush toilet (WC)				With outside flush toilet (WC) only		Connected to public water supply		Connected to public sewer		With central heating				No central heating	
		Exclusive use		Shared use		Exclusive use		Shared use								All rooms		Some rooms			
		Number	Per cent	Number	Per cent	Number	Per cent	Number	Per cent	Number	Per cent	Number	Per cent	Number	Per cent	Number	Per cent	Number	Per cent	Number	Per cent
Newtownabbey																					
Households in all dwellings																					
All sizes	26,491	26,315	99.3	38	0.1	26,372	99.6	16	0.1	65	0.2	26,381	99.6	24,753	93.4	20,634	77.9	2,409	9.1	3,448	13.0
1-3 rooms	1,776	1,735	97.7	11	0.6	1,742	98.1	9	0.5	9	0.5	1,757	98.9	1,708	96.2	1,292	72.7	143	8.1	341	19.2
4 rooms	3,243	3,183	98.1	7	0.2	3,195	98.5	3	0.1	32	1.0	3,233	99.7	3,099	95.6	2,147	66.2	350	10.8	746	23.0
5 rooms	9,271	9,224	99.5	11	0.1	9,246	99.7	2	0.0	19	0.2	9,251	99.8	8,916	96.2	7,093	76.5	1,026	11.1	1,152	12.4
6 or more rooms	12,201	12,173	99.8	9	0.1	12,189	99.9	2	0.0	5	0.0	12,140	99.5	11,030	90.4	10,102	82.8	890	7.3	1,209	9.9
Households in unshared dwellings (permanent)																					
All sizes	26,377	26,237	99.5	9	0.0	26,274	99.6	5	0.0	63	0.2	26,272	99.6	24,670	93.5	20,556	77.9	2,400	9.1	3,421	13.0
1-3 rooms	1,732	1,706	98.5	1	0.1	1,712	98.8	-	-	7	0.4	1,717	99.1	1,674	96.7	1,267	73.2	139	8.0	326	18.8
4 rooms	3,211	3,157	98.3	1	0.0	3,165	98.6	1	0.0	32	1.0	3,201	99.7	3,076	95.8	2,126	66.2	348	10.8	737	23.0
5 rooms	9,249	9,209	99.6	6	0.1	9,224	99.7	2	0.0	19	0.2	9,229	99.8	8,900	96.2	7,076	76.5	1,024	11.1	1,149	12.4
6 or more rooms	12,185	12,165	99.8	1	0.0	12,173	99.9	2	0.0	5	0.0	12,125	99.5	11,020	90.4	10,087	82.8	889	7.3	1,209	9.9
Households in shared dwellings (permanent)																					
All sizes	28	-	-	27	96.4	17	60.7	11	39.3	-	-	28	100.0	26	92.9	24	85.7	2	7.1	2	7.1
1-3 rooms	10	-	-	10	100.0	1	10.0	9	90.0	-	-	10	100.0	8	80.0	8	80.0	2	20.0	-	-
4 rooms	5	-	-	5	100.0	3	60.0	2	40.0	-	-	5	100.0	5	100.0	3	60.0	-	-	2	40.0
5 rooms	5	-	-	4	80.0	5	100.0	-	-	-	-	5	100.0	5	100.0	5	100.0	-	-	-	-
6 or more rooms	8	-	-	8	100.0	8	100.0	-	-	-	-	8	100.0	8	100.0	8	100.0	-	-	-	-
Households in non-permanent dwellings																					
All sizes	34	28	82.4	-	-	29	85.3	-	-	2	5.9	29	85.3	8	23.5	21	61.8	3	8.8	10	29.4
1-3 rooms	10	5	50.0	-	-	5	50.0	-	-	2	20.0	6	60.0	3	30.0	1	10.0	1	10.0	8	80.0
4 rooms	10	10	100.0	-	-	10	100.0	-	-	-	-	10	100.0	1	10.0	9	90.0	1	10.0	-	-
5 rooms	9	8	88.9	-	-	9	100.0	-	-	-	-	9	100.0	3	33.3	7	77.8	-	-	2	22.2
6 or more rooms	5	5	100.0	-	-	5	100.0	-	-	-	-	4	80.0	1	20.0	4	80.0	1	20.0	-	-

Table 12 Households by dwelling type, number of rooms and household amenities – **continued**

Households	Total households	With fixed bath or shower				With inside flush toilet (WC)				With outside flush toilet (WC) only		Connected to public water supply		Connected to public sewer		With central heating				No central heating	
		Exclusive use		Shared use		Exclusive use		Shared use								All rooms		Some rooms			
		Number	Per cent	Number	Per cent	Number	Per cent	Number	Per cent	Number	Per cent	Number	Per cent	Number	Per cent	Number	Per cent	Number	Per cent	Number	Per cent
North Down																					
Households in all dwellings																					
All sizes	26,619	26,392	99.1	133	0.5	26,466	99.4	83	0.3	64	0.2	26,602	99.9	25,928	97.4	20,802	78.1	2,766	10.4	3,051	11.5
1-3 rooms	1,925	1,812	94.1	101	5.2	1,848	96.0	69	3.6	6	0.3	1,921	99.8	1,896	98.5	1,253	65.1	220	11.4	452	23.5
4 rooms	2,981	2,936	98.5	6	0.2	2,949	98.9	3	0.1	27	0.9	2,978	99.9	2,903	97.4	1,941	65.1	411	13.8	629	21.1
5 rooms	7,738	7,716	99.7	9	0.1	7,726	99.8	4	0.1	8	0.1	7,737	100.0	7,611	98.4	6,041	78.1	843	10.9	854	11.0
6 or more rooms	13,975	13,928	99.7	17	0.1	13,943	99.8	7	0.1	23	0.2	13,966	99.9	13,518	96.7	11,567	82.8	1,292	9.2	1,116	8.0
Households in unshared dwellings (permanent)																					
All sizes	26,247	26,140	99.6	17	0.1	26,167	99.7	10	0.0	64	0.2	26,230	99.9	25,567	97.4	20,661	78.7	2,721	10.4	2,865	10.9
1-3 rooms	1,695	1,685	99.4	2	0.1	1,686	99.5	1	0.1	6	0.4	1,691	99.8	1,669	98.5	1,186	70.0	201	11.9	308	18.2
4 rooms	2,895	2,855	98.6	1	0.0	2,865	99.0	1	0.0	27	0.9	2,892	99.9	2,821	97.4	1,894	65.4	398	13.7	603	20.8
5 rooms	7,708	7,693	99.8	2	0.0	7,698	99.9	2	0.0	8	0.1	7,707	100.0	7,583	98.4	6,027	78.2	838	10.9	843	10.9
6 or more rooms	13,949	13,907	99.7	12	0.1	13,918	99.8	6	0.0	23	0.2	13,940	99.9	13,494	96.7	11,554	82.8	1,284	9.2	1,111	8.0
Households in shared dwellings (permanent)																					
All sizes	112	-	-	109	97.3	44	39.3	68	60.7	-	-	112	100.0	111	99.1	23	20.5	8	7.1	81	72.3
1-3 rooms	98	-	-	95	96.9	33	33.7	65	66.3	-	-	98	100.0	97	99.0	17	17.3	7	7.1	74	75.5
4 rooms	4	-	-	4	100.0	3	75.0	1	25.0	-	-	4	100.0	4	100.0	3	75.0	-	-	1	25.0
5 rooms	5	-	-	5	100.0	4	80.0	1	20.0	-	-	5	100.0	5	100.0	1	20.0	-	-	4	80.0
6 or more rooms	5	-	-	5	100.0	4	80.0	1	20.0	-	-	5	100.0	5	100.0	2	40.0	1	20.0	2	40.0
Households in non-permanent dwellings																					
All sizes	8	7	87.5	-	-	8	100.0	-	-	-	-	8	100.0	5	62.5	4	50.0	1	12.5	3	37.5
1-3 rooms	2	1	50.0	-	-	2	100.0	-	-	-	-	2	100.0	2	100.0	-	-	-	-	2	100.0
4 rooms	3	3	100.0	-	-	3	100.0	-	-	-	-	3	100.0	2	66.7	2	66.7	1	33.3	-	-
5 rooms	1	1	100.0	-	-	1	100.0	-	-	-	-	1	100.0	-	-	-	-	-	-	1	100.0
6 or more rooms	2	2	100.0	-	-	2	100.0	-	-	-	-	2	100.0	1	50.0	2	100.0	-	-	-	-

Table 12 Households by dwelling type, number of rooms and household amenities – **continued**

Households	Total households	With fixed bath or shower				With inside flush toilet (WC)				With outside flush toilet (WC) only		Connected to public water supply		Connected to public sewer		With central heating				No central heating	
		Exclusive use		Shared use		Exclusive use		Shared use								All rooms		Some rooms			
		Number	Per cent	Number	Per cent	Number	Per cent	Number	Per cent	Number	Per cent	Number	Per cent	Number	Per cent	Number	Per cent	Number	Per cent	Number	Per cent
Omagh																					
Households in all dwellings																					
All sizes	13,417	12,986	96.8	50	0.4	13,075	97.5	30	0.2	73	0.5	12,768	95.2	7,902	58.9	10,118	75.4	1,184	8.8	2,115	15.8
1-3 rooms	893	694	77.7	22	2.5	728	81.5	16	1.8	22	2.5	756	84.7	555	62.2	458	51.3	51	5.7	384	43.0
4 rooms	1,593	1,501	94.2	7	0.4	1,523	95.6	1	0.1	18	1.1	1,513	95.0	1,106	69.4	1,054	66.2	145	9.1	394	24.7
5 rooms	4,460	4,375	98.1	11	0.2	4,389	98.4	10	0.2	23	0.5	4,309	96.6	3,122	70.0	3,339	74.9	463	10.4	658	14.8
6 or more rooms	6,471	6,416	99.2	10	0.2	6,435	99.4	3	0.0	10	0.2	6,190	95.7	3,119	48.2	5,267	81.4	525	8.1	679	10.5
Households in unshared dwellings (permanent)																					
All sizes	13,145	12,792	97.3	20	0.2	12,859	97.8	11	0.1	60	0.5	12,553	95.5	7,754	59.0	9,977	75.9	1,162	8.8	2,006	15.3
1-3 rooms	724	577	79.7	-	-	600	82.9	-	-	19	2.6	621	85.8	454	62.7	382	52.8	45	6.2	297	41.0
4 rooms	1,548	1,461	94.4	4	0.3	1,479	95.5	1	0.1	17	1.1	1,476	95.3	1,087	70.2	1,022	66.0	141	9.1	385	24.9
5 rooms	4,414	4,348	98.5	8	0.2	4,357	98.7	7	0.2	14	0.3	4,278	96.9	3,102	70.3	3,317	75.1	452	10.2	645	14.6
6 or more rooms	6,459	6,406	99.2	8	0.1	6,423	99.4	3	0.0	10	0.2	6,178	95.6	3,111	48.2	5,256	81.4	524	8.1	679	10.5
Households in shared dwellings (permanent)																					
All sizes	24	-	-	24	100.0	7	29.2	17	70.8	-	-	24	100.0	23	95.8	2	8.3	-	-	22	91.7
1-3 rooms	20	-	-	20	100.0	4	20.0	16	80.0	-	-	20	100.0	20	100.0	1	5.0	-	-	19	95.0
4 rooms	2	-	-	2	100.0	2	100.0	-	-	-	-	2	100.0	2	100.0	1	50.0	-	-	1	50.0
5 rooms	2	-	-	2	100.0	1	50.0	1	50.0	-	-	2	100.0	1	50.0	-	-	-	-	2	100.0
6 or more rooms	-	-	-	-	-	-	-	-	-	-	-	-	-	-	-	-	-	-	-	-	-
Households in non-permanent dwellings																					
All sizes	138	89	64.5	2	1.4	100	72.5	1	0.7	13	9.4	82	59.4	20	14.5	58	42.0	21	15.2	59	42.8
1-3 rooms	75	43	57.3	2	2.7	50	66.7	-	-	3	4.0	42	56.0	8	10.7	20	26.7	6	8.0	49	65.3
4 rooms	25	24	96.0	-	-	24	96.0	-	-	1	4.0	17	68.0	1	4.0	18	72.0	4	16.0	3	12.0
5 rooms	32	16	50.0	-	-	20	62.5	1	3.1	9	28.1	17	53.1	8	25.0	14	43.7	11	34.4	7	21.9
6 or more rooms	6	6	100.0	-	-	6	100.0	-	-	-	-	6	100.0	3	50.0	6	100.0	-	-	-	-

Table 12 Households by dwelling type, number of rooms and household amenities – **continued**

Households	Total households	With fixed bath or shower: Exclusive use Number	Exclusive use Per cent	Shared use Number	Shared use Per cent	With inside flush toilet (WC): Exclusive use Number	Exclusive use Per cent	Shared use Number	Shared use Per cent	With outside flush toilet (WC) only Number	Per cent	Connected to public water supply Number	Per cent	Connected to public sewer Number	Per cent	With central heating: All rooms Number	All rooms Per cent	Some rooms Number	Some rooms Per cent	No central heating Number	Per cent
Strabane																					
Households in all dwellings																					
All sizes	10,750	10,319	96.0	41	0.4	10,423	97.0	9	0.1	76	0.7	10,171	94.6	7,110	66.1	7,017	65.3	1,016	9.5	2,717	25.3
1-3 rooms	758	552	72.8	13	1.7	598	78.9	2	0.3	26	3.4	619	81.7	473	62.4	309	40.8	60	7.9	389	51.3
4 rooms	1,470	1,368	93.1	10	0.7	1,389	94.5	-	-	19	1.3	1,393	94.8	1,045	71.1	815	55.4	141	9.6	514	35.0
5 rooms	4,143	4,067	98.2	10	0.2	4,088	98.7	5	0.1	23	0.6	4,043	97.6	3,206	77.4	2,678	64.6	417	10.1	1,048	25.3
6 or more rooms	4,379	4,332	98.9	8	0.2	4,348	99.3	2	0.0	8	0.2	4,116	94.0	2,386	54.5	3,215	73.4	398	9.1	766	17.5
Households in unshared dwellings (permanent)																					
All sizes	10,533	10,186	96.7	18	0.2	10,249	97.3	5	0.0	66	0.6	9,999	94.9	7,003	66.5	6,950	66.0	996	9.5	2,587	24.6
1-3 rooms	614	472	76.9	2	0.3	488	79.5	-	-	19	3.1	513	83.6	399	65.0	281	45.8	48	7.8	285	46.4
4 rooms	1,436	1,345	93.7	3	0.2	1,359	94.6	-	-	17	1.2	1,362	94.8	1,027	71.5	800	55.7	136	9.5	500	34.8
5 rooms	4,116	4,047	98.3	6	0.1	4,065	98.8	3	0.1	22	0.5	4,018	97.6	3,194	77.6	2,665	64.7	414	10.1	1,037	25.2
6 or more rooms	4,367	4,322	99.0	7	0.2	4,337	99.3	2	0.0	8	0.2	4,106	94.0	2,383	54.6	3,204	73.4	398	9.1	765	17.5
Households in shared dwellings (permanent)																					
All sizes	9	-	-	9	100.0	6	66.7	3	33.3	-	-	9	100.0	9	100.0	4	44.4	-	-	5	55.6
1-3 rooms	6	-	-	6	100.0	4	66.7	2	33.3	-	-	6	100.0	6	100.0	2	33.3	-	-	4	66.7
4 rooms	1	-	-	1	100.0	1	100.0	-	-	-	-	1	100.0	1	100.0	-	-	-	-	1	100.0
5 rooms	1	-	-	1	100.0	-	-	1	100.0	-	-	1	100.0	1	100.0	1	100.0	-	-	-	-
6 or more rooms	1	-	-	1	100.0	1	100.0	-	-	-	-	1	100.0	1	100.0	1	100.0	-	-	-	-
Households in non-permanent dwellings																					
All sizes	134	71	53.0	3	2.2	95	70.9	-	-	10	7.5	89	66.4	33	24.6	38	28.4	9	6.7	87	64.9
1-3 rooms	94	39	41.5	3	3.2	62	66.0	-	-	7	7.4	56	59.6	26	27.7	14	14.9	6	6.4	74	78.7
4 rooms	15	11	73.3	-	-	11	73.3	-	-	2	13.3	12	80.0	2	13.3	8	53.3	1	6.7	6	40.0
5 rooms	17	14	82.4	-	-	15	88.2	-	-	1	5.9	15	88.2	5	29.4	9	52.9	2	11.8	6	35.3
6 or more rooms	8	7	87.5	-	-	7	87.5	-	-	-	-	6	75.0	-	-	7	87.5	-	-	1	12.5

Table 13 Households by number of cars

Households	Total private households	Households with: No car – Households	No car – Persons	1 car – Households	1 car – Persons	2 cars – Households	2 cars – Persons	3 or more cars – Households	3 or more cars – Persons	Total cars
NORTHERN IRELAND										
All households	530,369	188,129	418,410	236,676	728,204	88,556	332,183	17,008	75,741	464,812
1-3 person households	343,373	151,110	243,486	148,025	299,873	40,014	100,026	4,224	11,379	240,725
4 person household	89,917	16,839	67,356	42,950	171,800	24,748	98,992	5,380	21,520	108,586
5 person household	52,411	9,842	49,210	24,844	124,220	13,940	69,700	3,785	18,925	64,079
6 or more person households	41,807	8,725	58,358	19,915	132,311	9,627	63,465	3,540	23,917	49,789
Other households *	2,861	1,613	-	942	-	227	-	79	-	1,633
Antrim										
All households	14,166	4,253	9,687	6,606	20,396	2,731	10,132	576	2,567	13,796
1-3 person households	8,925	3,391	5,629	4,137	8,535	1,266	3,192	131	352	7,062
4 person household	2,652	432	1,728	1,265	5,060	763	3,052	192	768	3,367
5 person household	1,481	232	1,160	664	3,320	444	2,220	141	705	1,975
6 or more person households	1,066	178	1,170	521	3,481	256	1,668	111	742	1,366
Other households *	42	20	-	19	-	2	-	1	-	26
Ards										
All households	22,832	6,470	13,234	10,237	28,670	5,091	18,001	1,034	4,274	23,521
1-3 person households	15,269	5,486	8,734	7,037	14,176	2,452	6,018	294	798	12,823
4 person household	4,429	527	2,108	1,902	7,608	1,610	6,440	390	1,560	6,292
5 person household	2,101	272	1,360	881	4,405	724	3,620	224	1,120	3,001
6 or more person households	966	159	1,032	382	2,481	301	1,923	124	796	1,356
Other households *	67	26	-	35	-	4	-	2	-	49
Armagh										
All households	15,720	3,911	8,324	7,896	25,968	3,242	13,117	671	3,208	16,393
1-3 person households	9,226	3,225	4,930	4,576	9,231	1,295	3,312	130	364	7,556
4 person household	2,700	278	1,112	1,416	5,664	815	3,260	191	764	3,619
5 person household	1,893	188	940	955	4,775	603	3,015	147	735	2,602
6 or more person households	1,869	201	1,342	940	6,298	528	3,530	200	1,345	2,596
Other households *	32	19	-	9	-	1	-	3	-	20
Ballymena										
All households	19,137	5,337	11,092	9,164	27,289	3,865	14,235	771	3,448	19,207
1-3 person households	12,506	4,499	7,158	5,998	12,265	1,819	4,624	190	521	10,206
4 person household	3,453	430	1,720	1,649	6,596	1,124	4,496	250	1,000	4,647
5 person household	1,865	220	1,100	879	4,395	589	2,945	177	885	2,588
6 or more person households	1,273	169	1,114	620	4,033	330	2,170	154	1,042	1,742
Other households *	40	19	-	18	-	3	-	-	-	24
Ballymoney										
All households	7,730	2,084	4,703	3,903	12,277	1,447	5,689	296	1,406	7,685
1-3 person households	4,791	1,669	2,699	2,440	5,093	614	1,589	68	182	3,872
4 person household	1,370	180	720	712	2,848	402	1,608	76	304	1,744
5 person household	832	137	685	398	1,990	233	1,165	64	320	1,056
6 or more person households	717	88	599	346	2,346	196	1,327	87	600	999
Other households *	20	10	-	7	-	2	-	1	-	14
Banbridge										
All households	10,984	2,829	5,748	5,146	15,656	2,508	9,607	501	2,330	11,665
1-3 person households	6,832	2,390	3,680	3,257	6,619	1,078	2,737	107	286	5,734
4 person household	2,012	211	844	938	3,752	719	2,876	144	576	2,808
5 person household	1,205	129	645	544	2,720	416	2,080	116	580	1,724
6 or more person households	911	91	579	392	2,565	294	1,914	134	888	1,382
Other households *	24	8	-	15	-	1	-	-	-	17

* Households where the persons present were not usually resident

Households	Total private households	Households with								Total cars
		No car		1 car		2 cars		3 or more cars		
		Households	Persons	Households	Persons	Households	Persons	Households	Persons	
Belfast										
All households	107,394	57,647	125,902	37,692	106,096	10,228	35,987	1,827	7,187	63,629
1-3 person households	77,817	46,548	75,888	25,536	50,283	5,123	12,551	610	1,601	37,612
4 person household	14,664	5,064	20,256	6,293	25,172	2,720	10,880	587	2,348	13,494
5 person household	7,997	2,867	14,335	3,338	16,690	1,430	7,150	362	1,810	7,284
6 or more person households	5,549	2,341	15,423	2,143	13,951	847	5,406	218	1,428	4,491
Other households *	1,367	827	-	382	-	108	-	50	-	748
Carrickfergus										
All households	11,870	3,806	7,949	5,531	15,523	2,189	7,539	344	1,439	10,941
1-3 person households	8,222	3,192	5,200	3,798	7,769	1,138	2,831	94	261	6,356
4 person household	2,205	330	1,320	1,094	4,376	657	2,628	124	496	2,780
5 person household	992	168	840	441	2,205	298	1,490	85	425	1,292
6 or more person households	408	88	589	186	1,173	93	590	41	257	495
Other households *	43	28	-	12	-	3	-	-	-	18
Castlereagh										
All households	22,910	6,521	12,219	10,961	28,645	4,599	15,484	829	3,296	22,646
1-3 person households	16,603	5,744	8,821	8,063	15,857	2,540	6,368	256	713	13,911
4 person household	4,046	454	1,816	1,859	7,436	1,367	5,468	366	1,464	5,691
5 person household	1,640	211	1,055	766	3,830	516	2,580	147	735	2,239
6 or more person households	554	82	527	242	1,522	170	1,068	60	384	762
Other households *	67	30	-	31	-	6	-	-	-	43
Coleraine										
All households	17,870	5,965	12,647	8,435	24,187	2,926	10,633	544	2,357	15,919
1-3 person households	11,820	4,726	7,785	5,597	11,069	1,349	3,345	148	393	8,739
4 person household	3,030	555	2,220	1,473	5,892	838	3,352	164	656	3,641
5 person household	1,627	280	1,400	800	4,000	432	2,160	115	575	2,009
6 or more person households	1,065	186	1,242	493	3,226	275	1,776	111	733	1,376
Other households *	328	218	-	72	-	32	-	6	-	154
Cookstown										
All households	9,222	2,425	5,283	4,653	16,352	1,746	7,215	398	2,009	9,339
1-3 person households	5,170	1,956	2,995	2,487	5,207	666	1,727	61	158	4,002
4 person household	1,607	208	832	854	3,416	446	1,784	99	396	2,043
5 person household	1,171	132	660	617	3,085	327	1,635	95	475	1,556
6 or more person households	1,259	120	796	691	4,644	306	2,069	142	980	1,729
Other households *	15	9	-	4	-	1	-	1	-	9
Craigavon										
All households	24,915	8,769	20,219	11,375	35,725	4,000	15,027	771	3,472	21,688
1-3 person households	15,803	6,930	11,319	6,916	14,402	1,778	4,489	179	491	11,009
4 person household	4,556	865	3,460	2,291	9,164	1,150	4,600	250	1,000	5,341
5 person household	2,538	484	2,420	1,219	6,095	648	3,240	187	935	3,076
6 or more person households	1,944	454	3,020	919	6,064	416	2,698	155	1,046	2,216
Other households *	74	36	-	30	-	8	-	-	-	46
Derry										
All households	28,015	12,709	36,054	11,827	42,832	2,937	12,190	542	2,619	19,327
1-3 person households	15,591	8,561	14,867	5,844	12,441	1,060	2,661	126	325	8,342
4 person household	4,903	1,559	6,236	2,458	9,832	750	3,000	136	544	4,366
5 person household	3,463	1,096	5,480	1,700	8,500	559	2,795	108	540	3,142
6 or more person households	3,912	1,387	9,471	1,796	12,059	561	3,734	168	1,210	3,422
Other households *	146	106	-	29	-	7	-	4	-	55

* Households where the persons present were not usually resident

Households	Total private households	Households with: No car		1 car		2 cars		3 or more cars		Total cars
		Households	Persons	Households	Persons	Households	Persons	Households	Persons	
Down										
All households	18,061	4,935	11,090	8,505	27,082	3,852	14,928	769	3,516	18,516
1-3 person households	10,847	3,953	6,271	5,091	10,278	1,623	4,031	180	486	8,877
4 person household	3,240	445	1,780	1,533	6,132	1,028	4,112	234	936	4,291
5 person household	2,031	249	1,245	930	4,650	681	3,405	171	855	2,805
6 or more person households	1,871	262	1,794	913	6,022	514	3,380	182	1,239	2,487
Other households *	72	26	-	38	-	6	-	2	-	56
Dungannon										
All households	13,653	3,703	8,202	6,805	23,521	2,589	10,661	556	2,678	13,651
1-3 person households	7,856	2,982	4,523	3,750	7,733	1,006	2,548	118	313	6,116
4 person household	2,207	286	1,144	1,173	4,692	617	2,468	131	524	2,800
5 person household	1,702	196	980	887	4,435	484	2,420	135	675	2,260
6 or more person households	1,859	226	1,555	980	6,661	482	3,225	171	1,166	2,457
Other households *	29	13	-	15	-	-	-	1	-	18
Fermanagh										
All households	16,901	4,765	10,079	8,433	28,027	3,088	12,556	615	2,906	16,454
1-3 person households	10,191	3,986	6,127	4,856	9,778	1,226	3,090	123	312	7,677
4 person household	2,712	324	1,296	1,441	5,764	758	3,032	189	756	3,524
5 person household	1,853	178	890	1,005	5,025	544	2,720	126	630	2,471
6 or more person households	2,092	258	1,766	1,104	7,460	553	3,714	177	1,208	2,741
Other households *	53	19	-	27	-	7	-	-	-	41
Larne										
All households	10,409	3,631	7,619	4,685	13,678	1,725	6,245	368	1,617	9,239
1-3 person households	7,071	3,022	4,830	3,114	6,359	846	2,119	89	243	5,073
4 person household	1,792	356	1,424	843	3,372	468	1,872	125	500	2,154
5 person household	984	168	840	457	2,285	271	1,355	88	440	1,263
6 or more person households	543	81	525	257	1,662	139	899	66	434	733
Other households *	19	4	-	14	-	1	-	-	-	16
Limavady										
All households	8,489	2,651	7,140	4,265	15,081	1,323	5,462	250	1,209	7,661
1-3 person households	4,711	1,892	3,223	2,281	4,945	493	1,235	45	125	3,402
4 person household	1,600	298	1,192	862	3,448	369	1,476	71	284	1,813
5 person household	1,021	214	1,070	536	2,680	209	1,045	62	310	1,140
6 or more person households	1,142	240	1,655	581	4,008	250	1,706	71	490	1,294
Other households *	15	7	-	5	-	2	-	1	-	12
Lisburn										
All households	33,277	10,195	23,473	14,704	43,088	6,974	24,644	1,404	5,904	32,864
1-3 person households	21,558	8,012	13,073	9,697	19,645	3,480	8,598	369	1,018	17,764
4 person household	6,336	1,054	4,216	2,698	10,792	2,040	8,160	544	2,176	8,410
5 person household	3,387	634	3,170	1,424	7,120	1,009	5,045	320	1,600	4,402
6 or more person households	1,934	464	3,014	858	5,531	441	2,841	171	1,110	2,253
Other households *	62	31	-	27	-	4	-	-	-	35
Magherafelt										
All households	10,398	2,713	6,289	5,193	18,535	1,988	8,643	504	2,644	10,681
1-3 person households	5,632	2,124	3,353	2,751	5,780	685	1,749	72	197	4,337
4 person household	1,757	259	1,036	893	3,572	493	1,972	112	448	2,215
5 person household	1,350	164	820	730	3,650	341	1,705	115	575	1,757
6 or more person households	1,644	157	1,080	814	5,533	468	3,217	205	1,424	2,365
Other households *	15	9	-	5	-	1	-	-	-	7

* Households where the persons present were not usually resident

Households	Total private households	Households with: No car – Households	No car – Persons	1 car – Households	1 car – Persons	2 cars – Households	2 cars – Persons	3 or more cars – Households	3 or more cars – Persons	Total cars
Moyle										
All households	4,721	1,627	3,688	2,297	7,514	657	2,680	140	692	4,031
1-3 person households	2,904	1,302	2,067	1,332	2,676	248	630	22	63	1,894
4 person household	760	147	588	402	1,608	176	704	35	140	859
5 person household	555	91	455	301	1,505	122	610	41	205	668
6 or more person households	493	85	578	255	1,725	111	736	42	284	603
Other households *	9	2	-	7	-	-	-	-	-	7
Newry and Mourne										
All households	24,418	7,770	18,429	11,902	42,260	3,923	16,570	823	4,177	22,217
1-3 person households	13,685	6,009	9,519	6,142	12,632	1,396	3,540	138	354	9,348
4 person household	3,992	702	2,808	2,161	8,644	950	3,800	179	716	4,598
5 person household	3,178	486	2,430	1,719	8,595	770	3,850	203	1,015	3,868
6 or more person households	3,501	549	3,672	1,848	12,389	802	5,380	302	2,092	4,358
Other households *	62	24	-	32	-	5	-	1	-	45
Newtownabbey										
All households	26,491	8,658	17,932	12,295	35,564	4,824	17,023	714	2,894	24,085
1-3 person households	18,032	7,294	11,870	8,159	16,954	2,377	6,024	202	551	13,519
4 person household	4,979	709	2,836	2,460	9,840	1,534	6,136	276	1,104	6,356
5 person household	2,380	396	1,980	1,168	5,840	658	3,290	158	790	2,958
6 or more person households	976	194	1,246	462	2,930	248	1,573	72	449	1,174
Other households *	124	65	-	46	-	7	-	6	-	78
North Down										
All households	26,619	6,962	12,621	12,384	32,444	6,285	21,837	988	3,875	27,918
1-3 person households	18,671	6,205	9,308	9,009	17,379	3,099	7,555	358	969	16,281
4 person household	4,861	458	1,832	2,085	8,340	1,975	7,900	343	1,372	7,064
5 person household	2,164	165	825	886	4,430	900	4,500	213	1,065	3,325
6 or more person households	839	103	656	362	2,295	300	1,882	74	469	1,184
Other households *	84	31	-	42	-	11	-	-	-	64
Omagh										
All households	13,417	3,845	8,419	6,744	23,884	2,368	9,985	460	2,381	12,860
1-3 person households	7,539	3,133	4,841	3,496	7,119	840	2,141	70	187	5,386
4 person household	2,302	309	1,236	1,271	5,084	619	2,476	103	412	2,818
5 person household	1,658	200	1,000	908	4,540	445	2,225	105	525	2,113
6 or more person households	1,891	191	1,342	1,056	7,141	462	3,143	182	1,257	2,526
Other households *	27	12	-	13	-	2	-	-	-	17
Strabane										
All households	10,750	3,948	10,368	5,038	17,910	1,451	6,093	313	1,636	8,879
1-3 person households	6,101	2,879	4,776	2,661	5,648	517	1,322	44	116	3,827
4 person household	1,752	399	1,596	924	3,696	360	1,440	69	276	1,851
5 person household	1,343	285	1,425	691	3,455	287	1,435	80	400	1,505
6 or more person households	1,529	371	2,571	754	5,111	284	1,896	120	844	1,682
Other households *	25	14	-	8	-	3	-	-	-	14

* Households where the persons present were not usually resident

Table 14 One and two person households containing persons of pensionable age by sex/condition combination

Local Government Districts	Total one and two person households containing persons of pensionable age	One person households containing persons of pensionable age: Male 65 and over	One person households containing persons of pensionable age: Female 60 and over	Two person households: Total	A male and a female: Married couple: Husband pensionable	Married couple: Wife pensionable	Married couple: Both pensionable	Other relationships: Male pensionable	Other relationships: Female pensionable	Other relationships: Both pensionable	Two males: One pensionable	Two males: Both pensionable	Two females: One pensionable	Two females: Both pensionable	Total persons of pensionable age in one and two person households: All	One pensionable	Both pensionable
NORTHERN IRELAND	**132,020**	**15,352**	**53,068**	**63,600**	**2,268**	**8,246**	**31,907**	**1,041**	**8,563**	**1,997**	**1,699**	**429**	**4,903**	**2,547**	**168,900**	**95,140**	**73,760**
Antrim	2,683	335	989	1,359	49	196	647	30	186	48	38	6	108	51	3,435	1,931	1,504
Ards	5,793	613	2,229	2,951	111	402	1,651	32	324	68	53	8	201	101	7,621	3,965	3,656
Armagh	3,745	489	1,446	1,810	74	181	826	33	309	69	57	18	166	77	4,735	2,755	1,980
Ballymena	4,641	551	1,711	2,379	72	290	1,177	44	309	104	64	17	183	119	6,058	3,224	2,834
Ballymoney	1,816	226	667	923	37	106	429	16	141	37	33	12	68	44	2,338	1,294	1,044
Banbridge	2,677	333	1,009	1,335	51	153	675	29	178	46	26	6	120	51	3,455	1,899	1,556
Belfast	31,996	3,758	13,948	14,290	357	1,893	7,181	258	1,923	403	367	61	1,196	651	40,292	23,700	16,592
Carrickfergus	2,739	279	1,100	1,360	61	242	741	18	117	25	18	5	91	42	3,552	1,926	1,626
Castlereagh	6,574	612	2,541	3,421	109	588	1,978	38	290	43	54	6	222	93	8,694	4,454	4,240
Coleraine	4,376	437	1,752	2,187	102	243	1,198	33	244	67	48	13	141	98	5,752	3,000	2,752
Cookstown	2,046	264	770	1,012	37	96	455	14	184	55	36	17	86	32	2,605	1,487	1,118
Craigavon	5,733	628	2,340	2,765	106	394	1,390	37	344	76	66	14	214	124	7,337	4,129	3,208
Derry	5,273	590	2,186	2,497	61	304	1,090	53	441	77	85	12	250	124	6,576	3,970	2,606
Down	4,196	499	1,636	2,061	84	223	986	43	319	74	64	12	161	95	5,363	3,029	2,334
Dungannon	3,222	441	1,229	1,552	67	174	668	36	292	77	46	24	118	50	4,041	2,403	1,638
Fermanagh	4,359	680	1,542	2,137	106	187	908	43	404	134	88	42	165	60	5,503	3,215	2,288
Larne	2,767	301	1,146	1,320	48	177	658	12	179	38	37	8	101	62	3,533	2,001	1,532
Limavady	1,585	202	599	784	31	82	340	15	148	28	41	13	56	30	1,996	1,174	822
Lisburn	7,284	736	2,959	3,589	141	529	1,912	53	389	84	71	7	260	143	9,430	5,138	4,292
Magherafelt	2,242	336	801	1,105	39	109	497	22	199	46	43	19	101	30	2,834	1,650	1,184
Moyle	1,281	198	482	601	25	67	264	11	92	32	25	8	53	24	1,609	953	656
Newry and Mourne	5,602	776	2,238	2,588	106	271	1,152	46	430	104	95	41	239	104	7,003	4,201	2,802
Newtownabbey	6,348	608	2,498	3,242	118	594	1,728	36	327	56	63	6	220	94	8,232	4,464	3,768
North Down	7,758	642	3,291	3,825	158	532	2,332	48	286	70	54	2	199	144	10,306	5,210	5,096
Omagh	2,901	464	1,097	1,340	71	108	540	22	285	78	68	29	88	51	3,599	2,203	1,396
Strabane	2,383	354	862	1,167	47	105	484	19	223	58	59	23	96	53	3,001	1,765	1,236

Table 15 Persons enumerated in each type of non-private establishment

Type of establishment and area in which situated	Total persons present			Residential classification								
				Managers and staff			Boarders/patients/inmates			Others		
	Persons	Males	Females	Persons	Males	Females	Persons	Males	Females	Persons	Males	Females
1. Hotels etc.												
Antrim	48	31	17	14	8	6	34	23	11	-	-	-
Ards	2	2	-	2	2	-	-	-	-	-	-	-
Armagh	36	35	1	3	2	1	33	33	-	-	-	-
Ballymena	43	17	26	16	9	7	27	8	19	-	-	-
Banbridge	6	4	2	3	2	1	3	2	1	-	-	-
Belfast	100	76	24	6	6	-	94	70	24	-	-	-
Carrickfergus	28	23	5	7	4	3	17	17	-	4	2	2
Castlereagh	29	26	3	1	-	1	28	26	2	-	-	-
Coleraine	93	45	48	8	6	2	83	39	44	2	-	2
Craigavon	5	2	3	-	-	-	5	2	3	-	-	-
Derry	20	12	8	2	-	2	18	12	6	-	-	-
Down	44	12	32	19	6	13	25	6	19	-	-	-
Dungannon	7	4	3	5	2	3	2	2	-	-	-	-
Fermanagh	26	20	6	8	6	2	16	14	2	2	-	2
Larne	38	27	11	3	-	3	35	27	8	-	-	-
Limavady	13	8	5	-	-	-	13	8	5	-	-	-
Lisburn	20	16	4	2	1	1	18	15	3	-	-	-
Moyle	9	5	4	1	1	-	8	4	4	-	-	-
Newry and Mourne	107	46	61	28	14	14	79	32	47	-	-	-
Newtownabbey	13	10	3	-	-	-	11	8	3	2	2	-
North Down	21	17	4	3	1	2	18	16	2	-	-	-
Omagh	9	6	3	4	1	3	5	5	-	-	-	-
Strabane	1	1	-	1	1	-	-	-	-	-	-	-
TOTAL	718	445	273	136	72	64	572	369	203	10	4	6
2. N.H.S. Hospitals and Statutory Homes (Psychiatric)												
Antrim	371	160	211	53	13	40	317	147	170	1	-	1
Belfast	119	28	91	1	1	-	118	27	91	-	-	-
Carrickfergus	24	9	15	-	-	-	24	9	15	-	-	-
Castlereagh	835	301	534	46	1	45	788	300	488	1	-	1
Coleraine	29	8	21	-	-	-	29	8	21	-	-	-
Derry	3	1	2	-	-	-	3	1	2	-	-	-
Down	5	-	5	-	-	-	5	-	5	-	-	-
Fermanagh	13	9	4	-	-	-	13	9	4	-	-	-
Lisburn	64	11	53	-	-	-	64	11	53	-	-	-
Magherafelt	9	5	4	-	-	-	9	5	4	-	-	-
Newry and Mourne	695	691	4	20	20	-	675	671	4	-	-	-
North Down	65	31	34	2	-	2	63	31	32	-	-	-
Omagh	419	212	207	16	4	12	403	208	195	-	-	-
TOTAL	2,651	1,466	1,185	138	39	99	2,511	1,427	1,084	2	-	2

Table 15 Persons enumerated in each type of non-private establishment – **continued**

Type of establishment and area in which situated	Total persons present			Residential classification								
				Managers and staff			Boarders/patients/inmates			Others		
	Persons	Males	Females	Persons	Males	Females	Persons	Males	Females	Persons	Males	Females
3. N.H.S. Hospitals and Statutory Homes (Others)												
Antrim	690	366	324	6	3	3	684	363	321	-	-	-
Ards	283	70	213	38	-	38	245	70	175	-	-	-
Armagh	594	299	295	2	1	1	591	297	294	1	1	-
Ballymena	386	141	245	31	8	23	348	133	215	7	-	7
Ballymoney	85	16	69	-	-	-	84	16	68	1	-	1
Banbridge	101	37	64	-	-	-	101	37	64	-	-	-
Belfast	2,607	1,016	1,591	440	72	368	2,129	934	1,195	38	10	28
Carrickfergus	7	7	-	6	6	-	1	1	-	-	-	-
Castlereagh	628	217	411	90	10	80	538	207	331	-	-	-
Coleraine	145	68	77	1	1	-	142	67	75	2	-	2
Craigavon	583	187	396	124	18	106	459	169	290	-	-	-
Derry	1,025	437	588	124	17	107	898	419	479	3	1	2
Down	547	239	308	23	5	18	524	234	290	-	-	-
Dungannon	251	100	151	10	7	3	241	93	148	-	-	-
Fermanagh	216	81	135	25	8	17	191	73	118	-	-	-
Larne	159	54	105	5	1	4	154	53	101	-	-	-
Limavady	60	21	39	8	-	8	52	21	31	-	-	-
Lisburn	329	110	219	28	-	28	301	110	191	-	-	-
Magherafelt	163	81	82	10	5	5	150	76	74	3	-	3
Moyle	29	13	16	-	-	-	29	13	16	-	-	-
Newry and Mourne	265	113	152	15	4	11	250	109	141	-	-	-
Newtownabbey	261	90	171	13	2	11	248	88	160	-	-	-
North Down	97	37	60	5	2	3	88	32	56	4	3	1
Omagh	204	68	136	7	3	4	197	65	132	-	-	-
Strabane	46	17	29	-	-	-	46	17	29	-	-	-
TOTAL	9,761	3,885	5,876	1,011	173	838	8,691	3,697	4,994	59	15	44
4. Non N.H.S. Hospitals and Statutory Homes (Psychiatric)												
Ards	14	3	11	2	1	1	12	2	10	-	-	-
Armagh	55	16	39	-	-	-	55	16	39	-	-	-
Ballymena	63	17	46	4	1	3	59	16	43	-	-	-
Ballymoney	14	4	10	2	-	2	12	4	8	-	-	-
Belfast	151	45	106	-	-	-	151	45	106	-	-	-
Carrickfergus	31	8	23	-	-	-	31	8	23	-	-	-
Castlereagh	53	4	49	-	-	-	53	4	49	-	-	-
Craigavon	75	16	59	-	-	-	75	16	59	-	-	-
Derry	30	7	23	-	-	-	30	7	23	-	-	-
Down	95	28	67	-	-	-	95	28	67	-	-	-
Larne	21	10	11	-	-	-	21	10	11	-	-	-
Lisburn	86	10	76	-	-	-	84	10	74	2	-	2
Moyle	40	13	27	-	-	-	40	13	27	-	-	-
Newry and Mourne	12	9	3	-	-	-	12	9	3	-	-	-
Newtownabbey	42	7	35	-	-	-	42	7	35	-	-	-
North Down	54	2	52	-	-	-	54	2	52	-	-	-
TOTAL	836	199	637	8	2	6	326	197	629	2	-	2

Table 15 Persons enumerated in each type of non-private establishment – **continued**

Type of establishment and area in which situated	Total persons present			Residential classification								
				Managers and staff			Boarders/patients/inmates			Others		
	Persons	Males	Females	Persons	Males	Females	Persons	Males	Females	Persons	Males	Females
5. Non N.H.S. Hospitals and Statutory Homes (Others)												
Antrim	49	29	20	-	-	-	49	29	20	-	-	-
Ards	16	7	9	-	-	-	16	7	9	-	-	-
Armagh	39	11	28	-	-	-	39	11	28	-	-	-
Ballymena	22	3	19	-	-	-	22	3	19	-	-	-
Ballymoney	6	1	5	1	-	1	5	1	4	-	-	-
Belfast	293	104	189	17	-	17	276	104	172	-	-	-
Carrickfergus	14	4	10	2	-	2	12	4	8	-	-	-
Coleraine	110	47	63	4	1	3	103	45	58	3	1	2
Craigavon	18	10	8	-	-	-	18	10	8	-	-	-
Derry	71	25	46	1	-	1	70	25	45	-	-	-
Down	64	21	43	2	1	1	62	20	42	-	-	-
Dungannon	103	34	69	1	-	1	102	34	68	-	-	-
Fermanagh	26	16	10	-	-	-	26	16	10	-	-	-
Larne	74	33	41	-	-	-	74	33	41	-	-	-
Lisburn	70	42	28	-	-	-	70	42	28	-	-	-
Magherafelt	69	33	36	2	-	2	67	33	34	-	-	-
Moyle	34	8	26	3	-	3	31	8	23	-	-	-
Newry and Mourne	273	145	128	19	8	11	254	137	117	-	-	-
Newtownabbey	108	47	61	-	-	-	108	47	61	-	-	-
North Down	118	44	74	4	2	2	114	42	72	-	-	-
Omagh	45	16	29	-	-	-	45	16	29	-	-	-
TOTAL	1,622	680	942	56	12	44	1,563	667	896	3	1	2
6. Homes for Old and Disabled												
Antrim	273	74	199	3	-	3	270	74	196	-	-	-
Ards	480	90	390	3	1	2	477	89	388	-	-	-
Armagh	297	92	205	-	-	-	297	92	205	-	-	-
Ballymena	228	53	175	5	1	4	223	52	171	-	-	-
Ballymoney	106	29	77	1	-	1	105	29	76	-	-	-
Banbridge	58	18	40	-	-	-	58	18	40	-	-	-
Belfast	2,181	489	1,692	50	2	48	2,119	480	1,639	12	7	5
Carrickfergus	221	41	180	2	-	2	219	41	178	-	-	-
Castlereagh	257	62	195	2	-	2	254	61	193	1	1	-
Coleraine	369	105	264	12	2	10	354	101	253	3	2	1
Cookstown	210	76	134	1	1	-	209	75	134	-	-	-
Craigavon	290	66	224	5	-	5	285	66	219	-	-	-
Derry	247	65	182	3	-	3	244	65	179	-	-	-
Down	564	157	407	4	1	3	560	156	404	-	-	-
Dungannon	131	32	99	1	-	1	130	32	98	-	-	-
Fermanagh	320	123	197	2	-	2	318	123	195	-	-	-
Larne	79	24	55	-	-	-	79	24	55	-	-	-
Limavady	96	33	63	-	-	-	96	33	63	-	-	-
Lisburn	287	66	221	1	-	1	286	66	220	-	-	-
Magherafelt	35	12	23	-	-	-	35	12	23	-	-	-
Moyle	135	39	96	-	-	-	135	39	96	-	-	-
Newry and Mourne	390	125	265	6	1	5	384	124	260	-	-	-
Newtownabbey	387	78	309	-	-	-	387	78	309	-	-	-
North Down	473	100	373	7	-	7	464	99	365	2	1	1
Omagh	146	55	91	1	-	1	145	55	90	-	-	-
Strabane	66	27	39	-	-	-	66	27	39	-	-	-
TOTAL	8,326	2,131	6,195	109	9	100	8,199	2,111	6,088	18	11	7

Table 15 Persons enumerated in each type of non-private establishment – **continued**

Type of establishment and area in which situated	Total persons present			Residential classification								
				Managers and staff			Boarders/patients/inmates			Others		
	Persons	Males	Females	Persons	Males	Females	Persons	Males	Females	Persons	Males	Females
7. Childrens' Homes												
Ards	14	7	7	2	-	2	12	7	5	-	-	-
Banbridge	5	4	1	-	-	-	5	4	1	-	-	-
Belfast	72	28	44	9	3	6	63	25	38	-	-	-
Craigavon	17	12	5	-	-	-	17	12	5	-	-	-
Down	13	3	10	2	-	2	9	3	6	2	-	2
Larne	14	6	8	-	-	-	14	6	8	-	-	-
Lisburn	30	20	10	-	-	-	30	20	10	-	-	-
North Down	21	12	9	-	-	-	21	12	9	-	-	-
Omagh	20	7	13	-	-	-	20	7	13	-	-	-
TOTAL	206	99	107	13	3	10	191	96	95	2	-	2
8. Educational Establishments												
Antrim	86	79	7	1	1	-	85	78	7	-	-	-
Armagh	87	38	49	9	8	1	78	30	48	-	-	-
Banbridge	5	4	1	1	-	1	4	4	-	-	-	-
Belfast	1,822	836	986	79	31	48	1,741	805	936	2	-	2
Coleraine	467	219	248	11	5	6	456	214	242	-	-	-
Derry	21	10	11	-	-	-	21	10	11	-	-	-
Dungannon	45	31	14	4	2	2	41	29	12	-	-	-
Fermanagh	31	21	10	2	1	1	29	20	9	-	-	-
Larne	51	49	2	8	6	2	43	43	-	-	-	-
Lisburn	31	19	12	2	1	1	29	18	11	-	-	-
Newry and Mourne	48	46	2	7	5	2	41	41	-	-	-	-
Newtownabbey	346	156	190	-	-	-	346	156	190	-	-	-
North Down	51	32	19	3	1	2	47	30	17	1	1	-
TOTAL	3,091	1,540	1,551	127	61	66	2,961	1,478	1,483	3	1	2
9. Places of Detention												
Belfast	343	343	-	-	-	-	343	343	-	-	-	-
Castlereagh	196	196	-	-	-	-	196	196	-	-	-	-
Coleraine	36	2	34	-	-	-	36	2	34	-	-	-
Craigavon	3	3	-	3	3	-	-	-	-	-	-	-
Dungannon	3	3	-	1	1	-	2	2	-	-	-	-
Fermanagh	5	5	-	4	4	-	1	1	-	-	-	-
Limavady	212	212	-	4	4	-	208	208	-	-	-	-
Lisburn	543	508	35	2	2	-	541	506	35	-	-	-
Moyle	19	11	8	2	-	2	17	11	6	-	-	-
North Down	65	48	17	-	-	-	65	48	17	-	-	-
TOTAL	1,425	1,331	94	16	14	2	1,409	1,317	92	-	-	-

Table 15 Persons enumerated in each type of non-private establishment – **continued**

Type of establishment and area in which situated	Total persons present			Residential classification: Managers and staff			Residential classification: Boarders/patients/inmates			Residential classification: Others		
	Persons	Males	Females	Persons	Males	Females	Persons	Males	Females	Persons	Males	Females
10. Defence Establishments including Naval Vessels and Service Hospitals												
Antrim	700	649	51	-	-	-	700	649	51	-	-	-
Armagh	353	333	20	-	-	-	353	333	20	-	-	-
Ballymena	110	108	2	-	-	-	110	108	2	-	-	-
Belfast	382	373	9	-	-	-	382	373	9	-	-	-
Castlereagh	2	2	-	-	-	-	2	2	-	-	-	-
Coleraine	4	4	-	-	-	-	4	4	-	-	-	-
Cookstown	108	106	2	-	-	-	108	106	2	-	-	-
Craigavon	2	2	-	-	-	-	2	2	-	-	-	-
Derry	642	571	71	-	-	-	642	571	71	-	-	-
Down	332	312	20	-	-	-	332	312	20	-	-	-
Dungannon	226	222	4	-	-	-	226	222	4	-	-	-
Fermanagh	577	571	6	-	-	-	577	571	6	-	-	-
Limavady	433	406	27	-	-	-	433	406	27	-	-	-
Lisburn	1,723	1,548	175	-	-	-	1,723	1,548	175	-	-	-
Magherafelt	2	2	-	-	-	-	2	2	-	-	-	-
North Down	100	99	1	-	-	-	100	99	1	-	-	-
Omagh	477	449	28	-	-	-	477	449	28	-	-	-
Strabane	3	3	-	-	-	-	3	3	-	-	-	-
TOTAL	6,176	5,760	416	-	-	-	6,176	5,760	416	-	-	-
11. Civilian Ships, Boats and Barges												
Belfast	97	94	3	-	-	-	97	94	3	-	-	-
Derry	17	17	-	-	-	-	17	17	-	-	-	-
Larne	5	4	1	-	-	-	5	4	1	-	-	-
TOTAL	119	115	4	-	-	-	119	115	4	-	-	-
12. Hostels and Lodging Houses												
Ballymena	6	3	3	2	-	2	4	3	1	-	-	-
Banbridge	24	15	9	-	-	-	24	15	9	-	-	-
Belfast	421	297	124	13	5	8	408	292	116	-	-	-
Carrickfergus	8	2	6	-	-	-	8	2	6	-	-	-
Castlereagh	17	10	7	1	-	1	16	10	6	-	-	-
Coleraine	58	39	19	-	-	-	58	39	19	-	-	-
Craigavon	20	17	3	-	-	-	20	17	3	-	-	-
Derry	207	77	130	-	-	-	206	76	130	1	1	-
Down	14	13	1	8	7	1	6	6	-	-	-	-
Dungannon	2	2	-	-	-	-	2	2	-	-	-	-
Fermanagh	6	4	2	-	-	-	6	4	2	-	-	-
Larne	14	2	12	1	1	-	12	1	11	1	-	1
Lisburn	13	7	6	1	-	1	12	7	5	-	-	-
Moyle	2	2	-	2	2	-	-	-	-	-	-	-
Newry and Mourne	18	15	3	1	-	1	17	15	2	-	-	-
North Down	58	36	22	6	2	4	46	33	13	6	1	5
Omagh	11	2	9	-	-	-	11	2	9	-	-	-
TOTAL	899	543	356	35	17	18	856	524	332	8	2	6

Table 15 Persons enumerated in each type of non-private establishment – **continued**

Type of establishment and area in which situated	Total persons present			Residential classification								
				Managers and staff			Boarders/patients/inmates			Others		
	Persons	Males	Females	Persons	Males	Females	Persons	Males	Females	Persons	Males	Females
13. Other Miscellaneous Communal Establishments												
Antrim	3	1	2	2	-	2	1	1	-	-	-	-
Ards	9	6	3	9	6	3	-	-	-	-	-	-
Armagh	48	13	35	21	2	19	27	11	16	-	-	-
Ballymena	55	37	18	6	5	1	49	32	17	-	-	-
Belfast	257	131	126	59	49	10	98	82	116	-	-	-
Castlereagh	5	5	-	-	-	-	5	5	-	-	-	-
Coleraine	64	20	44	-	-	-	64	20	44	-	-	-
Cookstown	30	18	12	2	2	-	28	16	12	-	-	-
Craigavon	65	16	49	5	-	5	60	16	44	-	-	-
Derry	116	18	98	5	3	2	11	15	96	-	-	-
Down	40	22	18	14	14	-	26	8	18	-	-	-
Dungannon	58	11	47	20	8	12	38	3	35	-	-	-
Fermanagh	33	13	20	4	4	-	29	9	20	-	-	-
Larne	7	-	7	5	-	5	2	-	2	-	-	-
Limavady	10	4	6	3	1	2	7	3	4	-	-	-
Lisburn	438	427	11	418	410	8	20	17	3	-	-	-
Magherafelt	13	-	13	-	-	-	13	-	13	-	-	-
Newry and Mourne	226	66	160	35	14	21	91	52	139	-	-	-
North Down	182	88	94	43	19	24	03	57	46	36	12	24
Omagh	73	30	43	5	3	2	64	24	40	4	3	1
Strabane	21	1	20	-	-	-	21	1	20	-	-	-
TOTAL	1,753	927	826	656	540	116	1,057	372	685	40	15	25
14. Campers and Vagrants	-	-	-	-	-	-	-	-	-	-	-	-
NORTHERN IRELAND TOTAL	**37,583**	**19,121**	**18,462**	**2,305**	**942**	**1,363**	**35,131**	**18,130**	**17,001**	**147**	**49**	**98**

Economic activity	Males	Females	Married females	
			Total	Part - time
NORTHERN IRELAND				
TOTAL POPULATION AGED 16 AND OVER	**559,171**	**608,767**	**344,768**	**64,013**
TOTAL ECONOMICALLY ACTIVE	**406,726**	**275,294**	**168,573**	**64,013**
Out of employment	77,326	29,744	13,006	-
In employment	329,400	245,550	155,567	64,013
On a Government employment or training scheme	8,649	4,596	1,197	-
Status				
Total self-employed	63,767	9,948	7,406	47
Self-employed without employees	41,752	5,079	3,594	27
Self-employed with employees	22,015	4,869	3,812	20
Total employees	256,984	231,006	146,964	63,966
Managers	32,028	12,801	8,050	1,041
extra large establishments	2,290	795	470	47
large establishments	15,065	4,862	3,003	255
small establishments	14,673	7,144	4,577	739
Foremen and supervisors	13,410	9,851	6,762	1,239
manual	7,468	1,556	1,148	253
non-manual	5,942	8,295	5,614	986
Professional employees	13,464	3,770	2,043	479
Other employees	198,082	204,584	130,109	61,207
TOTAL ECONOMICALLY INACTIVE	**152,445**	**333,473**	**176,195**	**-**
Looking after the home	3,786	162,665	123,206	-
Long-term sick/disabled	34,800	24,542	14,403	-
Retired	76,692	104,084	36,323	-
Students	35,246	39,283	565	-
Others economically inactive	1,921	2,899	1,698	-
Antrim				
TOTAL POPULATION AGED 16 AND OVER	**16,210**	**16,745**	**9,747**	**2,000**
TOTAL ECONOMICALLY ACTIVE	**12,255**	**8,232**	**5,272**	**2,000**
Out of employment	1,738	739	332	-
In employment	10,517	7,493	4,940	2,000
On a Government employment or training scheme	228	139	36	-
Status				
Total self-employed	1,930	276	209	1
Self-employed without employees	1,291	131	101	-
Self-employed with employees	639	145	108	1
Total employees	8,359	7,078	4,695	1,999
Managers	1,027	396	259	33
extra large establishments	49	32	23	2
large establishments	501	144	95	9
small establishments	477	220	141	22
Foremen and supervisors	442	325	225	35
manual	258	71	48	7
non-manual	184	254	177	28
Professional employees	306	72	45	13
Other employees	6,584	6,285	4,166	1,918
TOTAL ECONOMICALLY INACTIVE	**3,955**	**8,513**	**4,475**	**-**
Looking after the home	83	4,187	3,227	-
Long-term sick/disabled	1,203	852	361	-
Retired	1,673	2,299	819	-
Students	949	1,096	14	-
Others economically inactive	47	79	54	-

Economic activity	Males	Females	Married females	
			Total	Part - time
Ards				
TOTAL POPULATION AGED 16 AND OVER	**23,670**	**25,789**	**15,774**	**3,364**
TOTAL ECONOMICALLY ACTIVE	**17,867**	**12,288**	**8,138**	**3,364**
Out of employment	1,910	843	395	-
In employment	15,957	11,445	7,743	3,364
On a Government employment or training scheme	258	154	46	-
Status				
Total self-employed	3,387	622	488	4
Self-employed without employees	2,124	289	213	3
Self-employed with employees	1,263	333	275	1
Total employees	12,312	10,669	7,209	3,360
Managers	1,816	591	407	58
extra large establishments	170	42	22	3
large establishments	876	217	149	13
small establishments	770	332	236	42
Foremen and supervisors	709	502	361	60
manual	364	66	47	6
non-manual	345	436	314	54
Professional employees	541	137	89	20
Other employees	9,246	9,439	6,352	3,222
TOTAL ECONOMICALLY INACTIVE	**5,803**	**13,501**	**7,636**	**-**
Looking after the home	118	6,591	5,194	-
Long-term sick/disabled	1,111	837	546	-
Retired	3,312	4,600	1,787	-
Students	1,219	1,351	14	-
Others economically inactive	43	122	95	-
Armagh				
TOTAL POPULATION AGED 16 AND OVER	**18,306**	**19,055**	**10,899**	**2,004**
TOTAL ECONOMICALLY ACTIVE	**13,111**	**8,436**	**5,424**	**2,004**
Out of employment	2,454	859	438	-
In employment	10,657	7,577	4,986	2,004
On a Government employment or training scheme	247	135	44	-
Status				
Total self-employed	2,795	372	270	2
Self-employed without employees	1,902	196	134	-
Self-employed with employees	893	176	136	2
Total employees	7,615	7,070	4,672	2,002
Managers	811	327	219	29
extra large establishments	30	21	17	2
large establishments	370	139	94	9
small establishments	411	167	108	18
Foremen and supervisors	362	309	252	57
manual	205	52	44	18
non-manual	157	257	208	39
Professional employees	326	88	39	10
Other employees	6,116	6,346	4,162	1,906
TOTAL ECONOMICALLY INACTIVE	**5,195**	**10,619**	**5,475**	**-**
Looking after the home	119	4,906	3,940	-
Long-term sick/disabled	1,361	869	455	-
Retired	2,320	3,111	980	-
Students	1,317	1,584	12	-
Others economically inactive	78	149	88	-

Economic activity	Males	Females	Married females	
			Total	Part - time
Ballymena				
TOTAL POPULATION AGED 16 AND OVER	**20,792**	**22,201**	**12,978**	**2,497**
TOTAL ECONOMICALLY ACTIVE	**15,429**	**10,331**	**6,623**	**2,497**
Out of employment	1,969	858	347	-
In employment	13,460	9,473	6,276	2,497
On a Government employment or training scheme	293	169	34	-
Status				
Total self-employed	3,007	415	328	1
Self-employed without employees	2,057	194	150	1
Self-employed with employees	950	221	178	-
Total employees	10,160	8,889	5,914	2,496
Managers	1,138	442	292	33
extra large establishments	133	17	11	-
large establishments	500	169	119	7
small establishments	505	256	162	26
Foremen and supervisors	518	378	271	53
manual	344	61	44	13
non-manual	174	317	227	40
Professional employees	472	111	58	16
Other employees	8,032	7,958	5,293	2,394
TOTAL ECONOMICALLY INACTIVE	**5,363**	**11,870**	**6,355**	**-**
Looking after the home	99	5,911	4,521	-
Long-term sick/disabled	1,120	702	402	-
Retired	2,832	3,715	1,326	-
Students	1,254	1,413	12	-
Others economically inactive	58	129	94	-
Ballymoney				
TOTAL POPULATION AGED 16 AND OVER	**8,760**	**9,101**	**5,322**	**829**
TOTAL ECONOMICALLY ACTIVE	**6,433**	**3,945**	**2,447**	**829**
Out of employment	1,253	365	160	-
In employment	5,180	3,580	2,287	829
On a Government employment or training scheme	144	64	30	-
Status				
Total self-employed	1,543	177	137	-
Self-employed without employees	1,085	90	65	-
Self-employed with employees	458	87	72	-
Total employees	3,493	3,339	2,120	829
Managers	286	126	75	6
extra large establishments	11	7	5	-
large establishments	116	46	22	-
small establishments	159	73	48	6
Foremen and supervisors	174	124	96	13
manual	122	40	33	4
non-manual	52	84	63	9
Professional employees	126	38	18	3
Other employees	2,907	3,051	1,931	807
TOTAL ECONOMICALLY INACTIVE	**2,327**	**5,156**	**2,875**	**-**
Looking after the home	58	2,803	2,143	-
Long-term sick/disabled	601	312	173	-
Retired	1,192	1,417	503	-
Students	440	559	5	-
Others economically inactive	36	65	51	-

Economic activity	Males	Females	Married females: Total	Married females: Part - time
Banbridge				
TOTAL POPULATION AGED 16 AND OVER	**12,127**	**12,765**	**7,589**	**1,346**
TOTAL ECONOMICALLY ACTIVE	**9,024**	**5,958**	**3,847**	**1,346**
Out of employment	1,152	462	220	-
In employment	7,872	5,496	3,627	1,346
On a Government employment or training scheme	121	76	26	-
Status				
Total self-employed	2,150	256	192	-
Self-employed without employees	1,497	129	92	-
Self-employed with employees	653	127	100	-
Total employees	5,601	5,164	3,409	1,346
Managers	661	255	177	35
extra large establishments	34	16	12	4
large establishments	289	77	53	9
small establishments	338	162	112	22
Foremen and supervisors	319	242	174	24
manual	186	36	23	4
non-manual	133	206	151	20
Professional employees	247	59	42	8
Other employees	4,374	4,608	3,016	1,279
TOTAL ECONOMICALLY INACTIVE	**3,103**	**6,807**	**3,742**	**-**
Looking after the home	61	3,256	2,535	-
Long-term sick/disabled	748	519	340	-
Retired	1,626	2,131	798	-
Students	647	823	8	-
Others economically inactive	21	78	61	-
Belfast				
TOTAL POPULATION AGED 16 AND OVER	**97,363**	**116,359**	**58,357**	**11,561**
TOTAL ECONOMICALLY ACTIVE	**67,647**	**51,182**	**27,278**	**11,561**
Out of employment	16,909	7,176	2,863	-
In employment	50,738	44,006	24,415	11,561
On a Government employment or training scheme	1,687	926	190	-
Status				
Total self-employed	5,356	1,182	801	7
Self-employed without employees	3,098	643	409	5
Self-employed with employees	2,258	539	392	2
Total employees	43,695	41,898	23,424	11,554
Managers	5,350	2,671	1,322	178
extra large establishments	471	187	85	9
large establishments	2,386	1,044	494	42
small establishments	2,493	1,440	743	127
Foremen and supervisors	2,128	1,688	949	205
manual	1,112	211	153	50
non-manual	1,016	1,477	796	155
Professional employees	3,315	1,190	560	152
Other employees	32,902	36,349	20,593	11,019
TOTAL ECONOMICALLY INACTIVE	**29,716**	**65,177**	**31,079**	**-**
Looking after the home	773	28,562	19,483	-
Long-term sick/disabled	6,673	5,094	3,053	-
Retired	16,277	25,039	8,253	-
Students	5,690	6,011	144	-
Others economically inactive	303	471	146	-

Economic activity	Males	Females	Married females Total	Married females Part - time
Carrickfergus				
TOTAL POPULATION AGED 16 AND OVER	**11,873**	**12,980**	**7,953**	**1,600**
TOTAL ECONOMICALLY ACTIVE	**8,996**	**6,472**	**4,398**	**1,600**
Out of employment	1,185	536	264	-
In employment	7,811	5,936	4,134	1,600
On a Government employment or training scheme	199	90	25	-
Status				
Total self-employed	794	188	154	2
Self-employed without employees	495	88	70	1
Self-employed with employees	299	100	84	1
Total employees	6,818	5,658	3,955	1,598
Managers	886	397	299	29
extra large establishments	66	24	17	2
large establishments	457	165	121	10
small establishments	363	208	161	17
Foremen and supervisors	392	233	162	25
manual	220	35	27	3
non-manual	172	198	135	22
Professional employees	388	76	49	8
Other employees	5,152	4,952	3,445	1,536
TOTAL ECONOMICALLY INACTIVE	**2,877**	**6,508**	**3,555**	**-**
Looking after the home	70	3,257	2,449	-
Long-term sick/disabled	657	449	292	-
Retired	1,481	2,057	754	-
Students	635	661	22	-
Others economically inactive	34	84	38	-
Castlereagh				
TOTAL POPULATION AGED 16 AND OVER	**22,792**	**25,886**	**15,226**	**3,532**
TOTAL ECONOMICALLY ACTIVE	**16,439**	**13,295**	**8,478**	**3,532**
Out of employment	1,638	821	393	-
In employment	14,801	12,474	8,085	3,532
On a Government employment or training scheme	184	113	33	-
Status				
Total self-employed	1,701	349	268	2
Self-employed without employees	977	193	147	1
Self-employed with employees	724	156	121	1
Total employees	12,916	12,012	7,784	3,530
Managers	2,118	809	502	75
extra large establishments	202	79	43	3
large establishments	1,070	352	218	25
small establishments	846	378	241	47
Foremen and supervisors	738	590	382	59
manual	342	44	29	10
non-manual	396	546	353	49
Professional employees	862	232	120	23
Other employees	9,198	10,381	6,780	3,373
TOTAL ECONOMICALLY INACTIVE	**6,353**	**12,591**	**6,748**	**-**
Looking after the home	67	4,990	3,851	-
Long-term sick/disabled	1,128	914	574	-
Retired	3,852	5,355	2,237	-
Students	1,189	1,202	22	-
Others economically inactive	117	130	64	-

Economic activity	Males	Females	Married females	
			Total	Part - time
Coleraine				
TOTAL POPULATION AGED 16 AND OVER	**18,085**	**20,208**	**11,267**	**2,090**
TOTAL ECONOMICALLY ACTIVE	**12,999**	**9,067**	**5,581**	**2,090**
Out of employment	2,332	973	392	-
In employment	10,667	8,094	5,189	2,090
On a Government employment or training scheme	275	145	31	-
Status				
Total self-employed	2,335	494	363	2
Self-employed without employees	1,454	223	161	1
Self-employed with employees	881	271	202	1
Total employees	8,057	7,455	4,795	2,088
Managers	916	377	234	23
extra large establishments	41	16	10	3
large establishments	418	130	79	6
small establishments	457	231	145	14
Foremen and supervisors	449	309	215	36
manual	248	58	37	11
non-manual	201	251	178	25
Professional employees	520	127	63	18
Other employees	6,172	6,642	4,283	2,011
TOTAL ECONOMICALLY INACTIVE	**5,086**	**11,141**	**5,686**	**-**
Looking after the home	126	5,631	4,128	-
Long-term sick/disabled	922	585	309	-
Retired	2,679	3,354	1,161	-
Students	1,326	1,495	36	-
Others economically inactive	33	76	52	-
Cookstown				
TOTAL POPULATION AGED 16 AND OVER	**10,747**	**11,039**	**6,430**	**941**
TOTAL ECONOMICALLY ACTIVE	**7,678**	**4,473**	**2,682**	**941**
Out of employment	1,842	646	305	-
In employment	5,836	3,827	2,377	941
On a Government employment or training scheme	185	101	21	-
Status				
Total self-employed	1,887	224	163	1
Self-employed without employees	1,325	115	78	1
Self-employed with employees	562	109	85	-
Total employees	3,764	3,502	2,193	940
Managers	319	147	95	7
extra large establishments	3	4	3	1
large establishments	134	51	24	1
small establishments	182	92	68	5
Foremen and supervisors	149	129	92	14
manual	92	17	10	2
non-manual	57	112	82	12
Professional employees	119	28	17	4
Other employees	3,177	3,198	1,989	915
TOTAL ECONOMICALLY INACTIVE	**3,069**	**6,566**	**3,748**	**-**
Looking after the home	76	3,576	2,880	-
Long-term sick/disabled	875	499	310	-
Retired	1,374	1,606	502	-
Students	700	832	9	-
Others economically inactive	44	53	47	-

Table 16 Economically active persons by sex and status - **continued**

Economic activity	Males	Females	Married females Total	Married females Part - time
Craigavon				
TOTAL POPULATION AGED 16 AND OVER	**26,418**	**28,885**	**16,843**	**2,974**
TOTAL ECONOMICALLY ACTIVE	**19,747**	**13,827**	**8,767**	**2,974**
Out of employment	3,413	1,451	700	-
In employment	16,334	12,376	8,067	2,974
On a Government employment or training scheme	361	206	63	-
Status				
Total self-employed	2,783	388	315	3
Self-employed without employees	1,793	191	153	1
Self-employed with employees	990	197	162	2
Total employees	13,190	11,782	7,689	2,971
Managers	1,454	557	357	31
extra large establishments	82	43	20	2
large establishments	715	198	127	6
small establishments	657	316	210	23
Foremen and supervisors	792	519	359	47
manual	514	131	100	11
non-manual	278	388	259	36
Professional employees	511	123	75	12
Other employees	10,433	10,583	6,898	2,881
TOTAL ECONOMICALLY INACTIVE	**6,671**	**15,058**	**8,076**	**-**
Looking after the home	170	6,382	4,909	-
Long-term sick/disabled	1,706	1,701	1,197	-
Retired	3,141	5,096	1,906	-
Students	1,619	1,805	15	-
Others economically inactive	35	74	49	-
Derry				
TOTAL POPULATION AGED 16 AND OVER	**31,240**	**34,057**	**18,928**	**2,791**
TOTAL ECONOMICALLY ACTIVE	**22,959**	**14,950**	**8,460**	**2,791**
Out of employment	6,742	2,232	958	-
In employment	16,217	12,718	7,502	2,791
On a Government employment or training scheme	847	314	96	-
Status				
Total self-employed	2,142	326	253	1
Self-employed without employees	1,242	159	114	-
Self-employed with employees	900	167	139	1
Total employees	13,228	12,078	7,153	2,790
Managers	1,371	560	358	36
extra large establishments	81	32	17	-
large establishments	565	214	145	7
small establishments	725	314	196	29
Foremen and supervisors	681	562	398	46
manual	423	130	88	10
non-manual	258	432	310	36
Professional employees	571	176	86	26
Other employees	10,605	10,780	6,311	2,682
TOTAL ECONOMICALLY INACTIVE	**8,281**	**19,107**	**10,468**	**-**
Looking after the home	329	10,112	7,790	-
Long-term sick/disabled	2,309	1,948	1,070	-
Retired	3,132	4,502	1,497	-
Students	2,441	2,420	57	-
Others economically inactive	70	125	54	-

Economic activity	Males	Females	Married females	
			Total	Part - time
Down				
TOTAL POPULATION AGED 16 AND OVER	**20,543**	**21,471**	**12,379**	**2,399**
TOTAL ECONOMICALLY ACTIVE	**15,011**	**9,877**	**6,469**	**2,399**
Out of employment	2,261	864	364	-
In employment	12,750	9,013	6,105	2,399
On a Government employment or training scheme	278	131	32	-
Status				
Total self-employed	3,543	513	388	2
Self-employed without employees	2,401	247	174	2
Self-employed with employees	1,142	266	214	-
Total employees	8,929	8,369	5,685	2,397
Managers	1,099	416	286	32
extra large establishments	64	27	19	2
large establishments	528	163	120	11
small establishments	507	226	147	19
Foremen and supervisors	476	369	277	45
manual	244	52	46	12
non-manual	232	317	231	33
Professional employees	416	100	62	18
Other employees	6,938	7,484	5,060	2,302
TOTAL ECONOMICALLY INACTIVE	**5,532**	**11,594**	**5,910**	**-**
Looking after the home	97	5,545	4,263	-
Long-term sick/disabled	1,272	801	422	-
Retired	2,688	3,605	1,163	-
Students	1,425	1,563	13	-
Others economically inactive	50	80	49	-
Dungannon				
TOTAL POPULATION AGED 16 AND OVER	**15,814**	**16,359**	**9,383**	**1,529**
TOTAL ECONOMICALLY ACTIVE	**11,298**	**6,663**	**4,154**	**1,529**
Out of employment	2,757	810	360	-
In employment	8,541	5,853	3,794	1,529
On a Government employment or training scheme	209	144	49	-
Status				
Total self-employed	2,575	337	238	-
Self-employed without employees	1,768	179	112	-
Self-employed with employees	807	158	126	-
Total employees	5,757	5,372	3,507	1,529
Managers	531	232	138	18
extra large establishments	12	12	8	1
large establishments	247	86	50	3
small establishments	272	134	80	14
Foremen and supervisors	233	208	156	37
manual	144	28	24	7
non-manual	89	180	132	30
Professional employees	240	67	35	5
Other employees	4,753	4,865	3,178	1,469
TOTAL ECONOMICALLY INACTIVE	**4,516**	**9,696**	**5,229**	**-**
Looking after the home	161	4,937	3,936	-
Long-term sick/disabled	1,141	661	379	-
Retired	2,054	2,522	835	-
Students	1,131	1,490	14	-
Others economically inactive	29	86	65	-

Economic activity	Males	Females	Married females	
			Total	Part - time
Fermanagh				
TOTAL POPULATION AGED 16 AND OVER	**19,440**	**19,526**	**11,058**	**1,556**
TOTAL ECONOMICALLY ACTIVE	**13,637**	**7,748**	**4,743**	**1,556**
Out of employment	3,027	862	352	-
In employment	10,610	6,886	4,391	1,556
On a Government employment or training scheme	262	108	36	-
Status				
Total self-employed	3,316	444	303	2
Self-employed without employees	2,475	247	160	-
Self-employed with employees	841	197	143	2
Total employees	7,032	6,334	4,052	1,554
Managers	609	275	187	18
extra large establishments	6	12	8	2
large establishments	258	69	44	3
small establishments	345	194	135	13
Foremen and supervisors	355	214	153	28
manual	211	40	29	4
non-manual	144	174	124	24
Professional employees	253	60	26	5
Other employees	5,815	5,785	3,686	1,503
TOTAL ECONOMICALLY INACTIVE	**5,803**	**11,778**	**6,315**	**-**
Looking after the home	157	6,464	4,945	-
Long-term sick/disabled	1,188	607	282	-
Retired	3,046	3,004	996	-
Students	1,355	1,609	8	-
Others economically inactive	57	94	84	-
Larne				
TOTAL POPULATION AGED 16 AND OVER	**10,935**	**11,776**	**6,713**	**1,284**
TOTAL ECONOMICALLY ACTIVE	**8,059**	**5,261**	**3,303**	**1,284**
Out of employment	1,332	480	201	-
In employment	6,727	4,781	3,102	1,284
On a Government employment or training scheme	168	96	17	-
Status				
Total self-employed	1,173	226	179	3
Self-employed without employees	764	114	87	2
Self-employed with employees	409	112	92	1
Total employees	5,386	4,459	2,906	1,281
Managers	533	244	167	25
extra large establishments	51	11	8	1
large establishments	250	90	61	8
small establishments	232	143	98	16
Foremen and supervisors	325	171	122	13
manual	224	36	27	2
non-manual	101	135	95	11
Professional employees	240	50	30	6
Other employees	4,288	3,994	2,587	1,237
TOTAL ECONOMICALLY INACTIVE	**2,876**	**6,515**	**3,410**	**-**
Looking after the home	57	3,371	2,469	-
Long-term sick/disabled	601	336	181	-
Retired	1,562	2,050	708	-
Students	630	700	9	-
Others economically inactive	26	58	43	-

Table 16 Economically active persons by sex and status - **continued**

Economic activity	Males	Females	Married females	
			Total	Part - time
Limavady				
TOTAL POPULATION AGED 16 AND OVER	**10,528**	**10,287**	**6,092**	**870**
TOTAL ECONOMICALLY ACTIVE	**8,150**	**4,517**	**2,672**	**870**
Out of employment	2,013	554	237	-
In employment	6,137	3,963	2,435	870
On a Government employment or training scheme	252	75	23	-
Status				
Total self-employed	1,289	162	126	1
Self-employed without employees	864	73	55	-
Self-employed with employees	425	89	71	1
Total employees	4,596	3,726	2,286	869
Managers	316	132	92	7
extra large establishments	15	5	4	-
large establishments	163	54	37	-
small establishments	138	73	51	7
Foremen and supervisors	226	134	105	17
manual	136	40	32	2
non-manual	90	94	73	15
Professional employees	122	33	19	3
Other employees	3,932	3,427	2,070	842
TOTAL ECONOMICALLY INACTIVE	**2,378**	**5,770**	**3,420**	**-**
Looking after the home	80	3,514	2,821	-
Long-term sick/disabled	557	305	167	-
Retired	1,095	1,197	399	-
Students	631	720	6	-
Others economically inactive	15	34	27	-
Lisburn				
TOTAL POPULATION AGED 16 AND OVER	**35,196**	**37,886**	**22,916**	**4,809**
TOTAL ECONOMICALLY ACTIVE	**26,832**	**18,375**	**12,034**	**4,809**
Out of employment	3,717	1,737	829	-
In employment	23,115	16,638	11,205	4,809
On a Government employment or training scheme	402	251	52	-
Status				
Total self-employed	3,564	596	470	4
Self-employed without employees	2,196	305	239	3
Self-employed with employees	1,368	291	231	1
Total employees	19,149	15,791	10,683	4,805
Managers	3,120	1,092	730	102
extra large establishments	222	78	55	5
large establishments	1,610	456	292	28
small establishments	1,288	558	383	69
Foremen and supervisors	952	686	502	123
manual	448	71	57	18
non-manual	504	615	445	105
Professional employees	1,075	300	180	48
Other employees	14,002	13,713	9,271	4,532
TOTAL ECONOMICALLY INACTIVE	**8,364**	**19,511**	**10,882**	**-**
Looking after the home	180	9,922	7,727	-
Long-term sick/disabled	1,722	1,380	877	-
Retired	3,911	5,812	2,121	-
Students	2,087	2,185	26	-
Others economically inactive	464	212	131	-

Table 16 Economically active persons by sex and status - **continued**

Economic activity	Males	Females	Married females Total	Married females Part - time
Magherafelt				
TOTAL POPULATION AGED 16 AND OVER	**12,757**	**12,877**	**7,374**	**1,065**
TOTAL ECONOMICALLY ACTIVE	**9,141**	**5,572**	**3,334**	**1,065**
Out of employment	1,901	637	305	-
In employment	7,240	4,935	3,029	1,065
On a Government employment or training scheme	211	105	30	-
Status				
Total self-employed	2,203	254	174	1
Self-employed without employees	1,561	142	87	1
Self-employed with employees	642	112	87	-
Total employees	4,826	4,576	2,825	1,064
Managers	418	157	110	14
extra large establishments	8	6	5	-
large establishments	186	57	44	5
small establishments	224	94	61	9
Foremen and supervisors	220	153	112	24
manual	149	38	28	7
non-manual	71	115	84	17
Professional employees	162	52	23	4
Other employees	4,026	4,214	2,580	1,022
TOTAL ECONOMICALLY INACTIVE	**3,616**	**7,305**	**4,040**	**-**
Looking after the home	97	3,949	3,097	-
Long-term sick/disabled	1,001	527	324	-
Retired	1,621	1,688	571	-
Students	864	1,080	9	-
Others economically inactive	33	61	39	-
Moyle				
TOTAL POPULATION AGED 16 AND OVER	**5,312**	**5,492**	**2,962**	**446**
TOTAL ECONOMICALLY ACTIVE	**3,646**	**2,100**	**1,247**	**446**
Out of employment	930	303	136	-
In employment	2,716	1,797	1,111	446
On a Government employment or training scheme	118	53	20	-
Status				
Total self-employed	914	89	60	-
Self-employed without employees	664	49	32	-
Self-employed with employees	250	40	28	-
Total employees	1,684	1,655	1,031	446
Managers	148	64	43	4
extra large establishments	7	-	-	-
large establishments	58	25	13	1
small establishments	83	39	30	3
Foremen and supervisors	72	72	47	13
manual	50	12	7	1
non-manual	22	60	40	12
Professional employees	46	18	8	2
Other employees	1,418	1,501	933	427
TOTAL ECONOMICALLY INACTIVE	**1,666**	**3,392**	**1,715**	**-**
Looking after the home	38	1,745	1,303	-
Long-term sick/disabled	359	190	74	-
Retired	858	942	291	-
Students	359	430	6	-
Others economically inactive	52	85	41	-

Economic activity	Males	Females	Married females	
			Total	Part - time
Newry and Mourne				
TOTAL POPULATION AGED 16 AND OVER	**28,742**	**29,672**	**16,690**	**2,476**
TOTAL ECONOMICALLY ACTIVE	**20,806**	**11,960**	**6,846**	**2,476**
Out of employment	5,393	1,756	724	-
In employment	15,413	10,204	6,122	2,476
On a Government employment or training scheme	584	325	83	-
Status				
Total self-employed	4,268	519	354	1
Self-employed without employees	2,848	271	173	1
Self-employed with employees	1,420	248	181	-
Total employees	10,561	9,360	5,685	2,475
Managers	956	385	240	29
extra large establishments	15	8	5	-
large establishments	361	103	65	3
small establishments	580	274	170	26
Foremen and supervisors	451	327	207	42
manual	301	57	37	11
non-manual	150	270	170	31
Professional employees	382	117	63	9
Other employees	8,772	8,531	5,175	2,395
TOTAL ECONOMICALLY INACTIVE	**7,936**	**17,712**	**9,844**	**-**
Looking after the home	263	9,632	7,690	-
Long-term sick/disabled	2,071	1,313	704	-
Retired	3,559	4,337	1,355	-
Students	1,974	2,323	23	-
Others economically inactive	69	107	72	-
Newtownabbey				
TOTAL POPULATION AGED 16 AND OVER	**26,764**	**29,723**	**18,038**	**4,065**
TOTAL ECONOMICALLY ACTIVE	**20,263**	**15,188**	**10,133**	**4,065**
Out of employment	2,627	1,247	637	-
In employment	17,636	13,941	9,496	4,065
On a Government employment or training scheme	332	225	67	-
Status				
Total self-employed	2,007	385	311	1
Self-employed without employees	1,244	195	156	1
Self-employed with employees	763	190	155	-
Total employees	15,297	13,331	9,118	4,064
Managers	2,132	831	567	79
extra large establishments	203	40	27	1
large establishments	999	327	207	20
small establishments	930	464	333	58
Foremen and supervisors	901	616	438	78
manual	492	96	75	13
non-manual	409	520	363	65
Professional employees	794	171	115	18
Other employees	11,470	11,713	7,998	3,889
TOTAL ECONOMICALLY INACTIVE	**6,501**	**14,535**	**7,905**	**-**
Looking after the home	135	6,571	5,043	-
Long-term sick/disabled	1,370	1,179	776	-
Retired	3,408	5,018	1,970	-
Students	1,534	1,632	36	-
Others economically inactive	54	135	80	-

Economic activity	Males	Females	Married females	
			Total	Part - time
North Down				
TOTAL POPULATION AGED 16 AND OVER	**26,004**	**29,660**	**17,660**	**3,787**
TOTAL ECONOMICALLY ACTIVE	**18,771**	**13,785**	**9,316**	**3,787**
Out of employment	1,575	891	425	-
In employment	17,196	12,894	8,891	3,787
On a Government employment or training scheme	232	175	48	-
Status				
Total self-employed	2,648	701	542	3
Self-employed without employees	1,462	380	283	2
Self-employed with employees	1,186	321	259	1
Total employees	14,316	12,018	8,301	3,784
Managers	3,234	966	654	120
extra large establishments	274	55	32	3
large establishments	1,680	360	237	25
small establishments	1,280	551	385	92
Foremen and supervisors	844	607	424	95
manual	334	37	28	5
non-manual	510	570	396	90
Professional employees	1,066	243	165	39
Other employees	9,172	10,202	7,058	3,530
TOTAL ECONOMICALLY INACTIVE	**7,233**	**15,875**	**8,344**	**-**
Looking after the home	81	7,564	5,669	-
Long-term sick/disabled	1,003	732	476	-
Retired	4,247	5,502	2,096	-
Students	1,838	1,906	24	-
Others economically inactive	64	171	79	-
Omagh				
TOTAL POPULATION AGED 16 AND OVER	**16,113**	**16,073**	**8,953**	**1,238**
TOTAL ECONOMICALLY ACTIVE	**11,467**	**6,727**	**4,117**	**1,238**
Out of employment	2,509	854	338	-
In employment	8,958	5,873	3,779	1,238
On a Government employment or training scheme	257	120	27	-
Status				
Total self-employed	2,648	278	194	2
Self-employed without employees	1,890	146	87	-
Self-employed with employees	758	132	107	2
Total employees	6,053	5,475	3,558	1,236
Managers	513	226	158	14
extra large establishments	18	13	11	1
large establishments	252	87	64	4
small establishments	243	126	83	9
Foremen and supervisors	302	231	170	21
manual	174	48	37	8
non-manual	128	183	133	13
Professional employees	262	72	38	7
Other employees	4,976	4,946	3,192	1,194
TOTAL ECONOMICALLY INACTIVE	**4,646**	**9,346**	**4,836**	**-**
Looking after the home	160	4,891	3,782	-
Long-term sick/disabled	1,110	628	298	-
Retired	2,140	2,316	695	-
Students	1,178	1,430	10	-
Others economically inactive	58	81	51	-

Table 16 Economically active persons by sex and status – **continued**

Economic activity	Males	Females	Married females	
			Total	Part - time
Strabane				
TOTAL POPULATION AGED 16 AND OVER	**12,640**	**12,895**	**7,237**	**960**
TOTAL ECONOMICALLY ACTIVE	**9,061**	**5,065**	**2,810**	**960**
Out of employment	2,747	788	331	-
In employment	6,314	4,277	2,479	960
On a Government employment or training scheme	315	156	38	-
Status				
Total self-employed	1,809	175	126	1
Self-employed without employees	1,275	90	62	1
Self-employed with employees	534	85	64	-
Total employees	4,190	3,946	2,315	959
Managers	266	126	82	6
extra large establishments	22	8	3	-
large establishments	76	39	29	-
small establishments	168	79	50	6
Foremen and supervisors	200	153	113	29
manual	131	49	38	14
non-manual	69	104	75	15
Professional employees	102	30	18	2
Other employees	3,622	3,637	2,102	922
TOTAL ECONOMICALLY INACTIVE	**3,579**	**7,830**	**4,427**	**-**
Looking after the home	131	4,396	3,411	-
Long-term sick/disabled	991	602	361	-
Retired	1,612	1,809	600	-
Students	814	963	11	-
Others economically inactive	31	60	44	-

Table 17 Population with long-term illness by area, age and sex

Local Government Districts	Total		Age last birthday																			
			0 - 14		15 - 19		20 - 24		25 - 34		35 - 44		45 - 54		55 - 59		60 - 64		65 - 74		75 and over	
	Males	Females	Males	Females	Males	Females	Males	Females	Males	Females	Males	Females	Males	Females	Males	Females	Males	Females	Males	Females	Males	Females
NORTHERN IRELAND	**85,251**	**100,816**	**4,794**	**3,466**	**1,824**	**1,434**	**2,330**	**2,058**	**5,621**	**5,790**	**7,737**	**7,113**	**11,816**	**11,280**	**8,336**	**7,704**	**11,116**	**8,983**	**18,005**	**21,384**	**13,672**	**31,604**
Antrim	2,440	2,579	159	107	76	55	77	69	257	191	318	281	342	343	202	212	288	197	422	434	299	690
Ards	3,179	4,116	156	139	71	48	74	65	149	170	305	271	417	446	283	324	424	383	731	916	569	1,354
Armagh	2,933	3,129	147	98	72	56	73	75	228	195	262	255	439	328	297	229	365	268	585	646	465	979
Ballymena	2,863	3,309	161	100	55	34	79	63	168	149	242	222	389	380	267	242	365	294	615	681	522	1,144
Ballymoney	1,315	1,317	55	35	24	29	37	33	94	63	120	80	199	168	141	87	181	121	274	325	190	376
Banbridge	1,775	1,963	76	59	33	21	41	40	127	124	173	159	237	223	174	168	230	157	386	426	298	586
Belfast	16,971	22,859	893	646	274	210	398	401	1,014	1,111	1,340	1,296	2,282	2,382	1,694	1,743	2,410	2,190	3,848	5,079	2,818	7,801
Carrickfergus	1,641	2,001	79	65	34	26	30	31	96	114	147	123	229	226	173	193	249	193	362	423	242	607
Castlereagh	3,303	4,391	110	92	40	27	80	53	152	182	221	251	389	456	314	353	496	430	894	1,040	607	1,507
Coleraine	2,532	2,976	134	90	56	42	67	52	149	133	190	199	338	311	249	209	318	246	585	647	446	1,047
Cookstown	1,865	1,856	101	70	51	32	48	46	142	132	176	153	287	218	179	121	225	141	352	408	304	535
Craigavon	3,925	5,104	282	189	99	76	110	129	287	369	354	441	618	747	425	470	503	428	696	903	551	1,352
Derry	4,963	5,974	419	299	159	126	164	162	369	472	492	536	794	802	522	500	610	501	864	1,183	570	1,393
Down	3,089	3,524	178	113	64	51	95	100	191	204	275	232	446	364	300	233	381	262	627	715	532	1,250
Dungannon	2,605	2,604	145	113	54	48	81	50	201	166	241	191	342	285	264	199	326	231	529	568	422	753
Fermanagh	3,105	2,963	134	105	71	47	74	65	188	134	267	188	385	299	284	195	400	234	684	685	618	1,011
Larne	1,538	1,732	81	68	22	26	45	29	85	89	147	105	222	170	172	133	193	181	336	365	235	566
Limavady	1,407	1,430	122	79	44	41	44	38	119	98	154	106	195	181	108	94	160	120	256	301	205	372
Lisburn	4,483	5,563	303	224	102	81	125	103	317	332	438	436	635	673	422	451	586	502	885	1,112	670	1,649
Magherafelt	2,129	1,971	119	72	53	40	85	56	162	156	206	176	309	230	200	135	252	157	424	418	319	531
Moyle	842	907	33	28	16	10	17	6	43	43	90	50	132	93	82	61	104	73	182	216	143	327
Newry and Mourne	4,572	4,803	303	218	112	89	152	113	345	395	507	371	644	497	448	367	522	393	896	988	643	1,372
Newtownabbey	3,650	4,572	180	129	69	58	112	91	239	301	336	344	477	548	394	387	551	469	788	930	504	1,315
North Down	3,309	4,488	156	119	61	66	74	75	187	199	268	267	364	381	287	253	417	385	824	1,017	671	1,726
Omagh	2,629	2,605	137	108	56	57	79	59	169	131	263	199	361	265	242	186	315	219	524	570	483	811
Strabane	2,188	2,080	131	101	56	38	69	54	143	137	205	181	344	264	213	159	245	208	436	388	346	550

Table 18 Population economically active aged 16 - 64 by occupation, religion and sex

Standard Occupational Classification	Total population		Roman Catholic		Presbyterian		Church of Ireland		Methodist		Other denominations		None		Not stated	
Major groups	Males	Females	Males	Females	Males	Females	Males	Females	Males	Females	Males	Females	Males	Females	Males	Females
TOTAL ECONOMICALLY ACTIVE AGED 16-64	**399,416**	**272,625**	**141,127**	**94,758**	**87,621**	**62,564**	**72,625**	**50,916**	**14,731**	**11,468**	**32,900**	**22,303**	**20,669**	**11,161**	**29,743**	**19,455**
Managers and Administrators	59,367	19,384	16,399	5,759	17,065	4,870	10,428	3,602	2,476	826	5,740	1,658	3,308	1,184	3,951	1,485
Professional Occupations	26,881	22,560	8,979	8,906	5,977	5,244	3,999	3,269	1,051	822	2,611	1,696	2,372	1,274	1,892	1,349
Associate Professional and Technical Occupations	18,735	25,644	5,780	10,068	4,145	5,521	3,041	3,738	784	923	1,718	2,357	1,741	1,313	1,526	1,724
Clerical and Secretarial Occupations	24,155	64,755	7,129	19,152	5,826	17,193	4,645	12,115	1,230	3,398	2,059	5,541	1,463	2,638	1,803	4,718
Craft and Related Occupations	91,017	15,522	34,238	6,440	19,716	2,963	16,577	3,144	3,376	464	6,778	1,067	3,765	401	6,567	1,043
Personal and Protective Service Occupations	32,874	33,380	7,393	11,949	7,347	7,259	8,170	6,408	1,399	1,297	4,084	2,968	2,081	1,257	2,400	2,242
Sales Occupations	16,022	25,419	4,607	7,394	3,931	6,338	2,923	5,227	755	1,322	1,737	2,299	929	972	1,140	1,867
Plant and Machine Operatives	48,975	13,366	17,012	4,256	11,166	3,237	9,732	2,966	1,799	513	3,611	1,010	2,019	457	3,636	927
Other Occupations	31,983	30,670	12,659	9,929	6,539	7,058	6,179	7,059	983	1,386	2,206	2,466	1,172	831	2,245	1,941
On a Government employment or training scheme	8,639	4,589	4,411	2,095	1,298	734	1,297	774	218	154	509	321	343	190	563	321
Employed Inadequate information/ occupation not stated	4,774	2,559	1,799	1,031	886	449	809	416	139	81	403	193	245	99	493	290
Unemployed Inadequate information/ occupation not stated	865	279	433	144	100	44	136	39	19	7	61	12	38	13	78	20
No paid job within the last 10 years	35,129	14,498	20,288	7,635	3,625	1,654	4,689	2,159	502	275	1,383	715	1,193	532	3,449	1,528

Table 19 Population economically active aged 16 - 64 by religion and sex

Local Government Districts	Total population		Roman Catholic		Presbyterian		Church of Ireland		Methodist		Other denominations		None		Not stated	
	Males	Females	Males	Females	Males	Females	Males	Females	Males	Females	Males	Females	Males	Females	Males	Females
TOTAL ECONOMICALLY ACTIVE AGED 16 - 64	**399,416**	**272,625**	**141,127**	**94,758**	**87,621**	**62,564**	**72,625**	**50,916**	**14,731**	**11,468**	**32,900**	**22,303**	**20,669**	**11,161**	**29,743**	**19,455**
Antrim	12,058	8,177	3,343	2,392	3,779	2,648	1,728	1,256	244	157	1,165	634	699	356	1,100	734
Ards	17,534	12,165	1,830	1,250	6,785	4,724	3,171	2,410	853	677	1,911	1,312	1,380	742	1,604	1,050
Armagh	12,827	8,373	5,396	3,435	2,269	1,487	2,724	1,907	311	222	1,061	698	282	144	784	480
Ballymena	15,132	10,244	2,547	1,753	6,984	4,804	1,869	1,253	382	300	1,656	1,150	612	324	1,082	660
Ballymoney	6,284	3,904	1,836	1,052	2,461	1,582	822	506	28	24	570	395	182	87	385	258
Banbridge	8,834	5,892	2,229	1,500	2,574	1,738	1,749	1,191	161	132	1,066	728	329	161	726	442
Belfast	66,437	50,551	24,724	19,200	11,013	8,885	11,872	8,801	3,317	2,735	4,870	3,834	5,103	3,078	5,538	4,018
Carrickfergus	8,901	6,427	594	495	2,742	1,979	2,109	1,477	777	650	1,105	833	844	472	730	521
Castlereagh	16,168	13,157	1,404	1,473	4,543	3,734	3,784	3,103	1,344	1,131	2,195	1,800	1,429	775	1,469	1,141
Coleraine	12,776	8,994	2,635	1,920	3,976	2,874	3,283	2,352	186	149	1,073	754	689	352	934	593
Cookstown	7,508	4,435	3,722	2,120	1,246	765	1,364	833	86	60	555	367	121	64	414	226
Craigavon	19,384	13,741	7,462	5,241	2,043	1,529	4,926	3,578	979	743	1,885	1,418	683	324	1,406	908
Derry	22,695	14,844	14,972	10,051	2,682	1,859	2,125	1,433	214	158	933	405	528	211	1,241	727
Down	14,676	9,750	7,759	5,353	2,519	1,534	1,584	1,149	135	107	927	586	571	283	1,181	738
Dungannon	11,057	6,586	5,762	3,260	1,561	966	2,192	1,424	225	152	617	398	139	69	561	317
Fermanagh	13,254	7,653	6,937	3,803	387	255	3,752	2,308	670	406	621	423	263	124	624	334
Larne	7,925	5,213	1,679	1,160	3,003	1,986	1,068	751	269	199	735	476	444	212	727	429
Limavady	8,010	4,491	3,840	2,180	1,572	1,008	1,482	742	51	37	313	146	172	79	580	299
Lisburn	26,435	18,224	5,873	4,106	5,607	4,189	7,585	5,101	1,134	823	2,572	1,691	1,648	909	2,016	1,405
Magherafelt	8,960	5,529	5,015	3,033	1,444	978	1,125	714	36	20	730	442	116	44	494	298
Moyle	3,567	2,071	1,742	1,045	728	399	654	396	10	5	108	71	77	45	248	110
Newry and Mourne	20,428	11,844	14,101	8,475	2,353	1,378	961	586	89	50	1,171	424	325	137	1,428	794
Newtownabbey	19,963	15,052	2,328	2,014	6,398	4,921	4,003	2,994	1,645	1,405	2,152	1,562	1,594	871	1,843	1,285
North Down	18,481	13,621	1,505	1,317	5,866	4,576	4,076	3,092	1,234	942	1,949	1,325	2,125	1,164	1,726	1,205
Omagh	11,224	6,664	6,724	4,107	1,375	870	1,463	916	207	115	703	276	193	92	559	288
Strabane	8,898	5,023	5,168	3,023	1,711	896	1,154	643	144	69	257	155	121	42	343	195

Table 20 Term-time address of students and schoolchildren

Northern Ireland

Term-time address	Number of students/ schoolchildren	Age last birthday				
		Under 7	7 - 11	12 - 18	19 - 24	25 +
TOTAL	**381,874**	**78,612**	**129,415**	**145,561**	**26,325**	**1,961**
At home	**365,957**	**78,594**	**129,218**	**143,659**	**13,120**	**1,366**
Elsewhere in NI -	**7,932**	**14**	**108**	**1,117**	**6,433**	**260**
Antrim	160	-	-	80	78	2
Ards	23	-	1	10	11	1
Armagh	28	-	3	21	3	1
Ballymena	13	-	-	6	7	-
Ballymoney	2	-	-	1	1	-
Banbridge	12	-	1	4	5	2
Belfast	5,050	3	40	479	4,375	153
Carrickfergus	97	-	-	1	91	5
Castlereagh	55	1	4	14	34	2
Coleraine	1,068	3	8	166	848	43
Cookstown	102	-	-	37	63	2
Craigavon	46	1	5	12	24	4
Derry	339	2	8	37	273	19
Down	15	1	4	7	2	1
Dungannon	13	1	1	6	5	-
Fermanagh	40	-	1	31	8	-
Larne	29	-	1	25	2	1
Limavady	4	-	2	2	-	-
Lisburn	36	-	2	20	9	5
Magherafelt	8	1	-	1	6	-
Moyle	10	1	1	8	-	-
Newry and Mourne	38	-	-	31	7	-
Newtownabbey	652	-	11	69	558	14
North Down	68	-	14	38	14	2
Omagh	21	-	-	9	9	3
Strabane	3	-	1	2	-	-
England	**5,123**	**3**	**65**	**510**	**4,354**	**191**
Wales	**283**	**-**	**2**	**20**	**249**	**12**
Scotland	**1,783**	**-**	**11**	**164**	**1,552**	**56**
Isle of Man and Channel Islands	**11**	**1**	**1**	**1**	**8**	**-**
Republic of Ireland	**490**	**-**	**5**	**65**	**362**	**58**
Abroad	**295**	**-**	**5**	**25**	**247**	**18**

Table 21 Population aged 16 years and over: Persons by age, sex and highest level of academic qualification

Northern Ireland

Age	Total population		Level 1		Level 2		Level 3		Level 4		Level 5		Level 6		Level 7	
	Males	Females	Males	Females	Males	Females	Males	Females	Males	Females	Males	Females	Males	Females	Males	Females
TOTAL POPULATION AGED 16 AND OVER	**559,171**	**608,767**	**42,234**	**34,263**	**14,903**	**4,580**	**29,207**	**36,379**	**12,594**	**5,772**	**78,416**	**110,315**	**19,897**	**20,593**	**361,920**	**396,865**
16	12,849	12,226	2	2	10	7	55	48	43	40	2,357	2,771	229	186	10,153	9,172
17	13,220	12,422	4	5	35	30	237	227	182	144	6,930	7,671	548	378	5,284	3,967
18	13,576	12,697	10	13	55	32	1,049	1,271	369	263	6,262	7,139	687	446	5,144	3,533
19	13,488	12,480	35	42	118	75	2,972	3,597	601	451	3,689	4,187	826	613	5,247	3,515
20 - 24	63,896	62,224	3,348	4,086	2,016	1,063	9,229	11,088	2,618	2,004	14,234	18,954	6,766	6,589	25,685	18,440
25 - 29	60,474	61,765	6,203	6,733	2,551	948	3,860	5,488	2,161	1,113	12,821	19,081	5,624	6,049	27,254	22,353
30 - 34	55,772	57,689	6,360	6,119	2,464	820	3,133	4,159	1,772	639	10,031	15,926	3,211	3,439	28,801	26,587
35 - 39	49,778	49,533	6,273	5,302	2,115	520	2,671	3,144	1,411	347	6,654	10,388	779	1,058	29,875	28,774
40 - 44	48,608	49,302	5,666	3,764	1,865	335	1,838	2,053	1,113	242	4,889	7,516	342	631	32,895	34,761
45 - 49	44,512	45,408	4,147	2,461	1,228	224	1,373	1,554	742	166	3,536	5,276	270	411	33,216	35,316
50 - 54	37,534	39,037	2,858	1,708	868	179	1,021	1,222	565	104	2,508	3,957	239	293	29,475	31,574
55 - 59	34,198	36,871	2,260	1,250	609	119	651	918	411	90	1,786	2,740	152	203	28,329	31,551
60 - 64	31,978	37,349	1,821	940	452	92	469	626	309	65	1,132	2,026	95	118	27,700	33,482
65 - 69	29,233	35,722	1,328	650	292	50	323	454	182	41	793	1,379	58	84	26,257	33,064
70 and over	50,055	84,042	1,919	1,188	225	86	326	530	115	63	794	1,304	71	95	46,605	80,776

Table 22 Population aged 16 years and over: Economic activity by religion, sex and highest level of academic qualification

Economic activity	Total population aged 16+		Level 1		Level 2		Level 3		Level 4		Level 5		Level 6		Level 7	
	Males	Females	Males	Females	Males	Females	Males	Females	Males	Females	Males	Females	Males	Females	Males	Females
NORTHERN IRELAND																
TOTAL POPULATION AGED 16 AND OVER	**559,171**	**608,767**	**42,234**	**34,263**	**14,903**	**4,580**	**29,207**	**36,379**	**12,594**	**5,772**	**78,416**	**110,315**	**19,897**	**20,593**	**361,920**	**396,865**
TOTAL ECONOMICALLY ACTIVE	**406,726**	**275,294**	**36,432**	**26,767**	**13,400**	**3,507**	**18,999**	**21,243**	**11,023**	**4,248**	**64,037**	**73,223**	**18,936**	**14,047**	**243,899**	**132,259**
Out of employment	77,326	29,744	1,419	1,157	609	190	1,924	1,345	722	262	7,197	5,206	3,203	1,767	62,252	19,817
In employment	329,400	245,550	35,013	25,610	12,791	3,317	17,075	19,898	10,301	3,986	56,840	68,017	15,733	12,280	181,647	112,442
On a Government employment or training scheme	8,649	4,596	111	124	47	34	164	173	147	61	2,083	1,477	607	305	5,490	2,422
Status																
Total self-employed	63,767	9,948	4,896	1,217	1,282	144	2,193	664	1,211	112	7,896	2,099	1,974	356	44,315	5,356
Self-employed without employees	41,752	5,079	1,745	637	623	59	1,106	337	724	60	4,859	1,036	1,504	179	31,191	2,771
Self-employed with employees	22,015	4,869	3,151	580	659	85	1,087	327	487	52	3,037	1,063	470	177	13,124	2,585
Total employees	256,984	231,006	30,006	24,269	11,462	3,139	14,718	19,061	8,943	3,813	46,861	64,441	13,152	11,619	131,842	104,664
Managers	32,028	12,801	7,032	2,543	2,821	532	3,802	1,454	1,395	333	6,886	3,724	680	472	9,412	3,743
extra large establishments	2,290	795	756	194	353	56	227	103	129	21	382	245	14	9	429	167
large establishments	15,065	4,862	3,844	1,235	1,488	246	2,006	616	649	143	3,158	1,360	247	125	3,673	1,137
small establishments	14,673	7,144	2,432	1,114	980	230	1,569	735	617	169	3,346	2,119	419	338	5,310	2,439
Foremen and supervisors	13,410	9,851	674	561	622	182	977	1,129	556	261	2,811	3,545	438	370	7,332	3,803
manual	7,468	1,556	134	20	314	14	179	23	299	23	1,012	224	263	87	5,267	1,165
non-manual	5,942	8,295	540	541	308	168	798	1,106	257	238	1,799	3,321	175	283	2,065	2,638
Professional employees	13,464	3,770	9,334	3,055	1,522	148	543	162	460	33	684	178	47	9	874	185
Other employees	198,082	204,584	12,966	18,110	6,497	2,277	9,396	16,316	6,532	3,186	36,480	56,994	11,987	10,768	114,224	96,933
TOTAL ECONOMICALLY INACTIVE	**152,445**	**333,473**	**5,802**	**7,496**	**1,503**	**1,073**	**10,208**	**15,136**	**1,571**	**1,524**	**14,379**	**37,092**	**961**	**6,546**	**118,021**	**264,606**
Looking after the home	3,786	162,665	77	3,152	25	508	61	3,729	21	553	173	17,874	58	5,433	3,371	131,416
Long-term sick/disabled	34,800	24,542	488	358	208	46	404	419	211	72	1,318	1,884	366	476	31,805	21,287
Retired	76,692	104,084	3,385	2,132	629	144	754	1,093	328	109	1,777	2,977	129	161	69,690	97,468
Students	35,246	39,283	1,730	1,679	613	350	8,898	9,718	980	767	10,841	13,933	337	396	11,847	12,440
Others economically inactive	1,921	2,899	122	175	28	25	91	177	31	23	270	424	71	80	1,308	1,995

Table 22 Population aged 16 years and over: Economic activity by religion, sex and highest level of academic qualification – **continued**

Economic activity	Total population aged 16+		Level 1		Level 2		Level 3		Level 4		Level 5		Level 6		Level 7	
	Males	Females	Males	Females	Males	Females	Males	Females	Males	Females	Males	Females	Males	Females	Males	Females
ROMAN CATHOLIC																
TOTAL POPULATION AGED 16 AND OVER	**197,827**	**217,757**	**13,521**	**12,584**	**3,769**	**1,749**	**10,558**	**13,450**	**3,361**	**2,236**	**27,000**	**40,226**	**7,126**	**7,170**	**132,492**	**140,342**
TOTAL ECONOMICALLY ACTIVE	**143,234**	**95,490**	**11,882**	**10,166**	**3,344**	**1,346**	**6,167**	**7,439**	**2,801**	**1,561**	**21,031**	**25,609**	**6,687**	**4,673**	**91,322**	**44,696**
Out of employment	40,647	13,863	572	461	251	86	931	655	312	144	3,729	2,408	1,722	760	33,130	9,349
In employment	102,587	81,627	11,310	9,705	3,093	1,260	5,236	6,784	2,489	1,417	17,302	23,201	4,965	3,913	58,192	35,347
On a Government employment or training scheme	4,416	2,097	55	54	19	20	68	102	70	24	987	646	314	140	2,903	1,111
Status																
Total self-employed	22,541	2,918	1,705	367	334	35	635	165	340	37	2,675	586	778	97	16,074	1,631
Self-employed without employees	15,029	1,437	592	177	151	11	327	80	217	20	1,656	254	586	40	11,500	855
Self-employed with employees	7,512	1,481	1,113	190	183	24	308	85	123	17	1,019	332	192	57	4,574	776
Total employees	75,630	76,612	9,550	9,284	2,740	1,205	4,533	6,517	2,079	1,356	13,640	21,969	3,873	3,676	39,215	32,605
Managers	7,661	3,632	1,812	874	599	161	976	416	287	106	1,675	1,036	180	124	2,132	915
extra large establishments	431	237	144	70	53	19	61	34	16	5	89	67	1	1	67	41
large establishments	3,364	1,407	929	425	309	78	477	172	137	48	737	385	61	31	714	268
small establishments	3,866	1,988	739	379	237	64	438	210	134	53	849	584	118	92	1,351	606
Foremen and supervisors	3,904	3,391	199	165	151	64	321	363	120	89	878	1,341	148	130	2,087	1,239
manual	2,175	552	36	9	71	2	62	9	61	8	312	81	91	32	1,542	411
non-manual	1,729	2,839	163	156	80	62	259	354	59	81	566	1,260	57	98	545	828
Professional employees	3,304	1,294	2,428	1,103	308	44	156	49	72	9	155	38	13	1	172	50
Other employees	60,761	68,295	5,111	7,142	1,682	936	3,080	5,689	1,600	1,152	10,932	19,554	3,532	3,421	34,824	30,401
TOTAL ECONOMICALLY INACTIVE	**54,593**	**122,267**	**1,639**	**2,418**	**425**	**403**	**4,391**	**6,011**	**560**	**675**	**5,969**	**14,617**	**439**	**2,497**	**41,170**	**95,646**
Looking after the home	1,824	63,705	31	777	7	152	25	1,098	8	225	72	6,360	26	2,010	1,655	53,083
Long-term sick/disabled	14,605	9,973	174	115	55	17	163	185	48	32	556	782	169	208	13,440	8,634
Retired	21,580	29,511	610	678	69	38	198	336	33	25	410	782	37	49	20,223	27,603
Students	15,867	18,235	778	789	285	190	3,974	4,339	463	391	4,840	6,572	178	210	5,349	5,744
Others economically inactive	717	843	46	59	9	6	31	53	8	2	91	121	29	20	503	582

Table 22 Population aged 16 years and over: Economic activity by religion, sex and highest level of academic qualification – **continued**

Economic activity	Total population aged 16+		Level 1		Level 2		Level 3		Level 4		Level 5		Level 6		Level 7	
	Males	Females	Males	Females	Males	Females	Males	Females	Males	Females	Males	Females	Males	Females	Males	Females
PRESBYTERIAN																
TOTAL POPULATION AGED 16 AND OVER	**126,116**	**141,557**	**9,713**	**7,659**	**3,809**	**1,004**	**6,156**	**8,431**	**3,279**	**1,287**	**17,677**	**25,573**	**4,229**	**4,428**	**81,253**	**93,175**
TOTAL ECONOMICALLY ACTIVE	**89,795**	**63,333**	**8,130**	**5,779**	**3,445**	**774**	**4,040**	**5,016**	**2,902**	**965**	**14,649**	**17,366**	**4,056**	**3,132**	**52,573**	**30,301**
Out of employment	9,828	4,373	192	197	92	30	218	189	107	32	974	806	424	289	7,821	2,830
In employment	79,967	58,960	7,938	5,582	3,353	744	3,822	4,827	2,795	933	13,675	16,560	3,632	2,843	44,752	27,471
On a Government employment or training scheme	1,298	737	12	16	7	1	23	19	26	11	375	252	104	46	751	392
Status																
Total self-employed	16,827	2,555	1,084	274	345	31	531	162	359	22	2,054	571	472	89	11,982	1,406
Self-employed without employees	11,034	1,293	319	135	174	19	239	78	210	9	1,273	295	359	43	8,460	714
Self-employed with employees	5,793	1,262	765	139	171	12	292	84	149	13	781	276	113	46	3,522	692
Total employees	61,842	55,668	6,842	5,292	3,001	712	3,268	4,646	2,410	900	11,246	15,737	3,056	2,708	32,019	25,673
Managers	8,693	3,223	1,790	499	797	147	947	345	390	80	1,924	1,001	171	122	2,674	1,029
extra large establishments	681	198	216	39	119	16	59	15	39	3	102	78	9	3	137	44
large establishments	4,103	1,214	971	231	426	69	486	155	177	34	918	365	57	32	1,068	328
small establishments	3,909	1,811	603	229	252	62	402	175	174	43	904	558	105	87	1,469	657
Foremen and supervisors	3,284	2,360	147	123	163	45	202	263	154	60	637	843	116	90	1,865	936
manual	1,902	351	34	6	89	7	36	6	86	3	241	50	79	18	1,337	261
non-manual	1,382	2,009	113	117	74	38	166	257	68	57	396	793	37	72	528	675
Professional employees	3,391	860	2,347	669	416	45	118	48	135	4	165	51	11	2	199	41
Other employees	46,474	49,225	2,558	4,001	1,625	475	2,001	3,990	1,731	756	8,520	13,842	2,758	2,494	27,281	23,667
TOTAL ECONOMICALLY INACTIVE	**36,321**	**78,224**	**1,583**	**1,880**	**364**	**230**	**2,116**	**3,415**	**377**	**322**	**3,028**	**8,207**	**173**	**1,296**	**28,680**	**62,874**
Looking after the home	522	35,466	6	823	3	115	4	874	-	120	27	4,051	9	1,096	473	28,387
Long-term sick/disabled	6,809	4,690	95	73	43	6	67	74	59	14	252	362	70	70	6,223	4,091
Retired	21,864	29,578	1,162	643	209	48	251	329	115	28	584	971	42	50	19,501	27,509
Students	6,752	7,652	302	306	106	57	1,776	2,096	198	151	2,113	2,701	42	61	2,215	2,280
Others economically inactive	374	838	18	35	3	4	18	42	5	9	52	122	10	19	268	607

Table 22 Population aged 16 years and over: Economic activity by religion, sex and highest level of academic qualification – **continued**

Northern Ireland

Economic activity	Total population aged 16+		Level 1		Level 2		Level 3		Level 4		Level 5		Level 6		Level 7	
	Males	Females	Males	Females	Males	Females	Males	Females	Males	Females	Males	Females	Males	Females	Males	Females
CHURCH OF IRELAND																
TOTAL POPULATION AGED 16 AND OVER	**103,447**	**114,854**	**6,591**	**5,192**	**2,709**	**665**	**4,579**	**5,781**	**2,308**	**921**	**13,458**	**19,038**	**3,758**	**4,060**	**70,044**	**79,197**
TOTAL ECONOMICALLY ACTIVE	**74,064**	**51,527**	**5,435**	**3,906**	**2,415**	**504**	**3,146**	**3,430**	**2,054**	**694**	**11,207**	**12,893**	**3,612**	**2,826**	**46,195**	**27,274**
Out of employment	11,654	4,914	161	123	82	24	211	153	112	31	846	802	478	330	9,764	3,451
In employment	62,410	46,613	5,274	3,783	2,333	480	2,935	3,277	1,942	663	10,361	12,091	3,134	2,496	36,431	23,823
On a Government employment or training scheme	1,298	775	11	18	5	3	18	15	19	9	291	268	77	59	877	403
Status																
Total self-employed	9,710	1,758	740	197	208	27	350	128	183	19	1,180	367	282	68	6,767	952
Self-employed without employees	6,395	920	256	115	100	12	177	74	113	10	724	186	230	38	4,795	485
Self-employed with employees	3,315	838	484	82	108	15	173	54	70	9	456	181	52	30	1,972	467
Total employees	51,402	44,080	4,523	3,568	2,120	450	2,567	3,134	1,740	635	8,890	11,456	2,775	2,369	28,787	22,468
Managers	6,254	2,501	1,247	446	547	95	764	276	292	61	1,316	714	132	94	1,956	815
extra large establishments	478	133	149	22	66	11	46	21	28	5	79	34	3	3	107	37
large establishments	3,132	963	734	232	307	40	431	120	150	21	614	261	53	32	843	257
small establishments	2,644	1,405	364	192	174	44	287	135	114	35	623	419	76	59	1,006	521
Foremen and supervisors	2,718	1,797	112	84	113	27	163	190	109	48	535	558	73	70	1,613	820
manual	1,589	339	16	1	56	5	36	3	72	6	203	28	41	19	1,165	277
non-manual	1,129	1,458	96	83	57	22	127	187	37	42	332	530	32	51	448	543
Professional employees	2,252	539	1,478	435	283	19	92	25	113	7	119	28	7	2	160	23
Other employees	40,178	39,243	1,686	2,603	1,177	309	1,548	2,643	1,226	519	6,920	10,156	2,563	2,203	25,058	20,810
TOTAL ECONOMICALLY INACTIVE	**29,383**	**63,327**	**1,156**	**1,286**	**294**	**161**	**1,433**	**2,351**	**254**	**227**	**2,251**	**6,145**	**146**	**1,234**	**23,849**	**51,923**
Looking after the home	594	29,049	10	549	1	86	7	694	1	87	15	3,088	9	1,041	551	23,504
Long-term sick/disabled	6,633	4,828	74	53	42	7	52	53	37	10	187	308	53	87	6,188	4,310
Retired	16,793	23,440	852	446	160	25	156	235	74	25	423	698	31	32	15,097	21,979
Students	5,099	5,504	208	212	89	39	1,211	1,346	134	101	1,591	1,973	46	56	1,820	1,777
Others economically inactive	264	506	12	26	2	4	7	23	8	4	35	78	7	18	193	353

Table 22 Population aged 16 years and over: Economic activity by religion, sex and highest level of academic qualification – **continued**

Economic activity	Total population aged 16+		Level 1		Level 2		Level 3		Level 4		Level 5		Level 6		Level 7	
	Males	Females	Males	Females	Males	Females	Males	Females	Males	Females	Males	Females	Males	Females	Males	Females
METHODIST																
TOTAL POPULATION AGED 16 AND OVER	**21,307**	**25,537**	**1,569**	**1,200**	**745**	**176**	**1,190**	**1,407**	**631**	**219**	**3,128**	**4,488**	**835**	**887**	**13,209**	**17,160**
TOTAL ECONOMICALLY ACTIVE	**15,080**	**11,608**	**1,353**	**945**	**662**	**134**	**812**	**875**	**556**	**170**	**2,602**	**3,070**	**801**	**628**	**8,294**	**5,786**
Out of employment	1,586	799	27	31	17	6	42	48	18	8	166	163	78	54	1,238	489
In employment	13,494	10,809	1,326	914	645	128	770	827	538	162	2,436	2,907	723	574	7,056	5,297
On a Government employment or training scheme	219	154	1	5	1	4	10	4	-	2	71	50	26	11	110	78
Status																
Total self-employed	1,922	369	153	48	51	5	80	26	48	5	266	78	62	18	1,262	189
Self-employed without employees	1,217	188	60	25	23	2	41	13	25	3	158	41	45	6	865	98
Self-employed with employees	705	181	93	23	28	3	39	13	23	2	108	37	17	12	397	91
Total employees	11,353	10,286	1,172	861	593	119	680	797	490	155	2,099	2,779	635	545	5,684	5,030
Managers	1,678	582	320	106	156	18	192	69	86	13	341	171	48	23	535	182
extra large establishments	145	47	46	15	22	2	14	6	14	-	16	14	1	-	32	10
large establishments	809	199	178	49	94	7	104	31	40	4	165	55	14	5	214	48
small establishments	724	336	96	42	40	9	74	32	32	9	160	102	33	18	289	124
Foremen and supervisors	600	457	24	28	34	4	42	57	33	10	128	160	20	17	319	181
manual	328	65	6	-	19	-	4	2	13	-	42	10	13	3	231	50
non-manual	272	392	18	28	15	4	38	55	20	10	86	150	7	14	88	131
Professional employees	631	103	384	73	86	4	25	9	29	3	46	6	2	-	59	8
Other employees	8,444	9,144	444	654	317	93	421	662	342	129	1,584	2,442	565	505	4,771	4,659
TOTAL ECONOMICALLY INACTIVE	**6,227**	**13,929**	**216**	**255**	**83**	**42**	**378**	**532**	**75**	**49**	**526**	**1,418**	**34**	**259**	**4,915**	**11,374**
Looking after the home	87	5,916	4	116	1	24	2	155	-	16	2	714	1	229	77	4,662
Long-term sick/disabled	1,154	951	16	17	9	2	23	11	8	2	47	74	8	19	1,043	826
Retired	3,831	5,727	155	90	56	11	31	38	36	14	105	142	9	2	3,439	5,430
Students	1,110	1,233	40	31	17	5	318	321	30	17	366	475	12	6	327	378
Others economically inactive	45	102	1	1	-	-	4	7	1	-	6	13	4	3	29	78

Table 22 Population aged 16 years and over: Economic activity by religion, sex and highest level of academic qualification - **continued**

Economic activity	Total population aged 16+		Level 1		Level 2		Level 3		Level 4		Level 5		Level 6		Level 7	
	Males	Females	Males	Females	Males	Females	Males	Females	Males	Females	Males	Females	Males	Females	Males	Females
OTHER DENOMINATIONS																
TOTAL POPULATION AGED 16 AND OVER	**44,905**	**49,084**	**3,675**	**2,807**	**1,501**	**366**	**2,428**	**3,146**	**1,277**	**486**	**7,101**	**9,255**	**1,875**	**1,770**	**27,048**	**31,254**
TOTAL ECONOMICALLY ACTIVE	**33,635**	**22,530**	**3,215**	**2,027**	**1,369**	**259**	**1,683**	**1,884**	**1,120**	**375**	**6,078**	**6,157**	**1,803**	**1,211**	**18,367**	**10,617**
Out of employment	3,827	1,857	126	106	56	12	148	93	62	22	442	381	172	121	2,821	1,122
In employment	29,808	20,673	3,089	1,921	1,313	247	1,535	1,791	1,058	353	5,636	5,776	1,631	1,090	15,546	9,495
On a Government employment or training scheme	511	321	6	8	4	3	12	10	11	7	148	106	42	17	288	170
Status																
Total self-employed	5,928	1,043	370	107	144	19	240	73	127	11	812	246	197	36	4,038	551
Self-employed without employees	3,745	566	138	64	70	7	122	33	65	6	489	126	151	21	2,710	309
Self-employed with employees	2,183	477	232	43	74	12	118	40	62	5	323	120	46	15	1,328	242
Total employees	23,369	19,309	2,713	1,806	1,165	225	1,283	1,708	920	335	4,676	5,424	1,392	1,037	11,220	8,774
Managers	3,122	1,090	634	172	286	54	345	111	139	28	651	310	67	43	1,000	372
extra large establishments	182	77	65	21	27	3	17	10	11	2	26	19	-	1	36	21
large establishments	1,479	386	361	74	155	29	193	37	55	15	293	120	28	11	394	100
small establishments	1,461	627	208	77	104	22	135	64	73	11	332	171	39	31	570	251
Foremen and supervisors	1,054	772	64	49	57	11	60	99	48	26	215	265	28	31	582	291
manual	589	122	22	-	29	-	6	1	24	2	84	25	14	8	410	86
non-manual	465	650	42	49	28	11	54	98	24	24	131	240	14	23	172	205
Professional employees	1,590	361	1,001	255	155	14	81	14	48	6	116	34	9	4	180	34
Other employees	17,603	17,086	1,014	1,330	667	146	797	1,484	685	275	3,694	4,815	1,288	959	9,458	8,077
TOTAL ECONOMICALLY INACTIVE	**11,270**	**26,554**	**460**	**780**	**132**	**107**	**745**	**1,262**	**157**	**111**	**1,023**	**3,098**	**72**	**559**	**8,681**	**20,637**
Looking after the home	240	12,858	12	457	4	65	6	411	5	44	14	1,718	6	462	193	9,701
Long-term sick/disabled	2,338	1,954	40	34	21	4	43	43	28	7	112	159	28	44	2,066	1,663
Retired	5,939	8,572	229	128	56	8	42	78	41	7	104	201	4	15	5,463	8,135
Students	2,525	2,848	154	135	40	23	640	706	76	49	755	972	24	28	836	935
Others economically inactive	228	322	25	26	11	7	14	24	7	4	38	48	10	10	123	203

Table 22 Population aged 16 years and over: Economic activity by religion, sex and highest level of academic qualification – **continued**

Northern Ireland

Economic activity	Total population aged 16+		Level 1		Level 2		Level 3		Level 4		Level 5		Level 6		Level 7	
	Males	Females	Males	Females	Males	Females	Males	Females	Males	Females	Males	Females	Males	Females	Males	Females
NONE																
TOTAL POPULATION AGED 16 AND OVER	**25,828**	**19,139**	**4,210**	**2,589**	**1,136**	**284**	**2,302**	**1,859**	**830**	**243**	**4,564**	**4,470**	**770**	**711**	**12,016**	**8,983**
TOTAL ECONOMICALLY ACTIVE	**20,794**	**11,214**	**3,766**	**2,139**	**1,038**	**229**	**1,719**	**1,146**	**752**	**182**	**3,894**	**3,081**	**733**	**471**	**8,892**	**3,966**
Out of employment	3,376	1,337	226	151	58	18	229	111	61	13	524	298	135	73	2,143	673
In employment	17,418	9,877	3,540	1,988	980	211	1,490	1,035	691	169	3,370	2,783	598	398	6,749	3,293
On a Government employment or training scheme	343	191	20	12	7	-	22	10	7	5	92	66	16	12	179	86
Status																
Total self-employed	2,698	537	462	129	102	16	223	58	78	12	407	114	56	15	1,370	193
Self-employed without employees	1,633	295	220	71	57	8	136	31	46	9	245	61	37	11	892	104
Self-employed with employees	1,065	242	242	58	45	8	87	27	32	3	162	53	19	4	478	89
Total employees	14,377	9,149	3,058	1,847	871	195	1,245	967	606	152	2,871	2,603	526	371	5,200	3,014
Managers	2,353	841	728	253	208	27	319	133	95	20	497	214	39	26	467	168
extra large establishments	212	46	83	17	35	2	17	11	12	1	37	12	-	1	28	2
large establishments	1,102	328	399	124	81	11	171	53	47	9	205	75	20	4	179	52
small establishments	1,039	467	246	112	92	14	131	69	36	10	255	127	19	21	260	114
Foremen and supervisors	804	436	83	72	46	16	96	78	44	10	195	146	17	11	323	103
manual	324	46	12	3	22	-	14	2	18	1	54	12	6	2	198	26
non-manual	480	390	71	69	24	16	82	76	26	9	141	134	11	9	125	77
Professional employees	1,315	331	1,039	286	124	12	37	9	28	2	41	11	2	-	44	11
Other employees	9,905	7,541	1,208	1,236	493	140	793	747	439	120	2,138	2,232	468	334	4,366	2,732
TOTAL ECONOMICALLY INACTIVE	**5,034**	**7,925**	**444**	**450**	**98**	**55**	**583**	**713**	**78**	**61**	**670**	**1,389**	**37**	**240**	**3,124**	**5,017**
Looking after the home	179	4,398	12	226	4	24	10	246	3	33	14	726	5	210	131	2,933
Long-term sick/disabled	1,188	599	50	25	22	7	38	24	17	3	84	89	13	13	964	438
Retired	1,948	1,373	216	71	40	4	41	33	16	-	72	72	3	3	1,560	1,190
Students	1,599	1,443	156	112	29	18	482	395	41	23	478	479	9	11	404	405
Others economically inactive	120	112	10	16	3	2	12	15	1	2	22	23	7	3	65	51

Table 22 Population aged 16 years and over: Economic activity by religion, sex and highest level of academic qualification – **continued**

Economic activity	Total population aged 16+		Level 1		Level 2		Level 3		Level 4		Level 5		Level 6		Level 7	
	Males	Females	Males	Females	Males	Females	Males	Females	Males	Females	Males	Females	Males	Females	Males	Females
NOT STATED																
TOTAL POPULATION AGED 16 AND OVER	**39,741**	**40,839**	**2,955**	**2,232**	**1,234**	**336**	**1,994**	**2,305**	**908**	**380**	**5,488**	**7,265**	**1,304**	**1,567**	**25,858**	**26,754**
TOTAL ECONOMICALLY ACTIVE	**30,124**	**19,592**	**2,651**	**1,805**	**1,127**	**261**	**1,432**	**1,453**	**838**	**301**	**4,576**	**5,047**	**1,244**	**1,106**	**18,256**	**9,619**
Out of employment	6,408	2,601	115	88	53	14	145	96	50	12	516	348	194	140	5,335	1,903
In employment	23,716	16,991	2,536	1,717	1,074	247	1,287	1,357	788	289	4,060	4,699	1,050	966	12,921	7,716
On a Government employment or training scheme	564	321	6	11	4	3	11	13	14	3	119	89	28	20	382	182
Status																
Total self-employed	4,141	768	382	95	98	11	134	52	76	6	502	137	127	33	2,822	434
Self-employed without employees	2,699	380	160	50	48	-	64	28	48	3	314	73	96	20	1,969	206
Self-employed with employees	1,442	388	222	45	50	11	70	24	28	3	188	64	31	13	853	228
Total employees	19,011	15,902	2,148	1,611	972	233	1,142	1,292	698	280	3,439	4,473	895	913	9,717	7,100
Managers	2,267	932	501	193	228	30	259	104	106	25	482	278	43	40	648	262
extra large establishments	161	57	53	10	31	3	13	6	9	5	33	21	-	-	22	12
large establishments	1,076	365	272	100	116	12	144	48	43	12	226	99	14	10	261	84
small establishments	1,030	510	176	83	81	15	102	50	54	8	223	158	29	30	365	166
Foremen and supervisors	1,046	638	45	40	58	15	93	79	48	18	223	232	36	21	543	233
manual	561	81	8	1	28	-	21	-	25	3	76	18	19	5	384	54
non-manual	485	557	37	39	30	15	72	79	23	15	147	214	17	16	159	179
Professional employees	981	282	657	234	150	10	34	8	35	2	42	10	3	-	60	18
Other employees	14,717	14,050	945	1,144	536	178	756	1,101	509	235	2,692	3,953	813	852	8,466	6,587
TOTAL ECONOMICALLY INACTIVE	**9,617**	**21,247**	**304**	**427**	**107**	**75**	**562**	**852**	**70**	**79**	**912**	**2,218**	**60**	**461**	**7,602**	**17,135**
Looking after the home	340	11,273	2	204	5	42	7	251	4	28	29	1,217	2	385	291	9,146
Long-term sick/disabled	2,073	1,547	39	41	16	3	18	29	14	4	80	110	25	35	1,881	1,325
Retired	4,737	5,883	161	76	39	10	35	44	13	10	79	111	3	10	4,407	5,622
Students	2,294	2,368	92	94	47	18	497	515	38	35	698	761	26	24	896	921
Others economically inactive	173	176	10	12	-	2	5	13	1	2	26	19	4	7	127	121

Table 23 Population aged 3 years and over by knowledge of Irish language

Local Government Districts	Total	Can speak Irish	Can read Irish	Can write Irish	Can read and speak Irish	Can read and write Irish	Can speak and write Irish	Can speak, read and write Irish	Do not know Irish	Not stated
NORTHERN IRELAND	**1,502,385**	**45,338**	**5,887**	**1,340**	**6,593**	**2,802**	**1,031**	**79,012**	**1,320,657**	**39,725**
Antrim	42,429	881	129	21	103	49	28	1,561	38,747	910
Ards	62,044	393	105	28	59	29	17	776	59,594	1,043
Armagh	49,215	2,168	274	88	394	130	54	3,983	41,040	1,084
Ballymena	54,247	751	138	31	124	49	23	1,282	50,810	1,039
Ballymoney	23,072	497	52	9	51	25	16	574	21,318	530
Banbridge	31,928	490	102	19	74	48	8	1,033	29,352	802
Belfast	266,384	10,253	924	146	1,368	418	144	15,665	228,700	8,766
Carrickfergus	31,180	149	29	4	21	10	1	279	30,224	463
Castlereagh	58,280	402	106	15	79	30	7	833	55,700	1,108
Coleraine	48,169	618	98	23	105	50	21	992	45,190	1,072
Cookstown	29,378	1,492	161	53	205	98	47	2,597	24,093	632
Craigavon	71,195	1,906	238	59	299	125	50	3,720	62,676	2,122
Derry	89,950	4,672	619	114	694	327	94	8,479	71,679	3,272
Down	55,112	1,953	277	81	276	113	48	2,831	48,168	1,365
Dungannon	43,065	3,289	275	67	481	128	67	5,694	31,342	1,722
Fermanagh	51,465	1,659	345	67	289	151	46	3,580	43,899	1,429
Larne	28,147	313	54	12	41	16	8	582	26,704	417
Limavady	27,943	622	93	44	99	51	33	1,189	24,982	830
Lisburn	94,417	2,147	176	31	284	68	33	3,002	86,644	2,032
Magherafelt	34,371	1,923	183	74	210	91	44	3,261	27,522	1,063
Moyle	14,095	504	59	17	53	32	14	1,016	12,041	359
Newry and Mourne	78,565	4,354	696	163	697	362	141	8,450	60,876	2,826
Newtownabbey	70,825	566	92	13	103	52	9	1,171	67,266	1,553
North Down	69,129	424	111	26	84	37	4	764	66,724	955
Omagh	43,462	1,933	377	89	259	224	53	3,762	35,403	1,362
Strabane	34,318	979	174	46	141	89	21	1,936	29,963	969

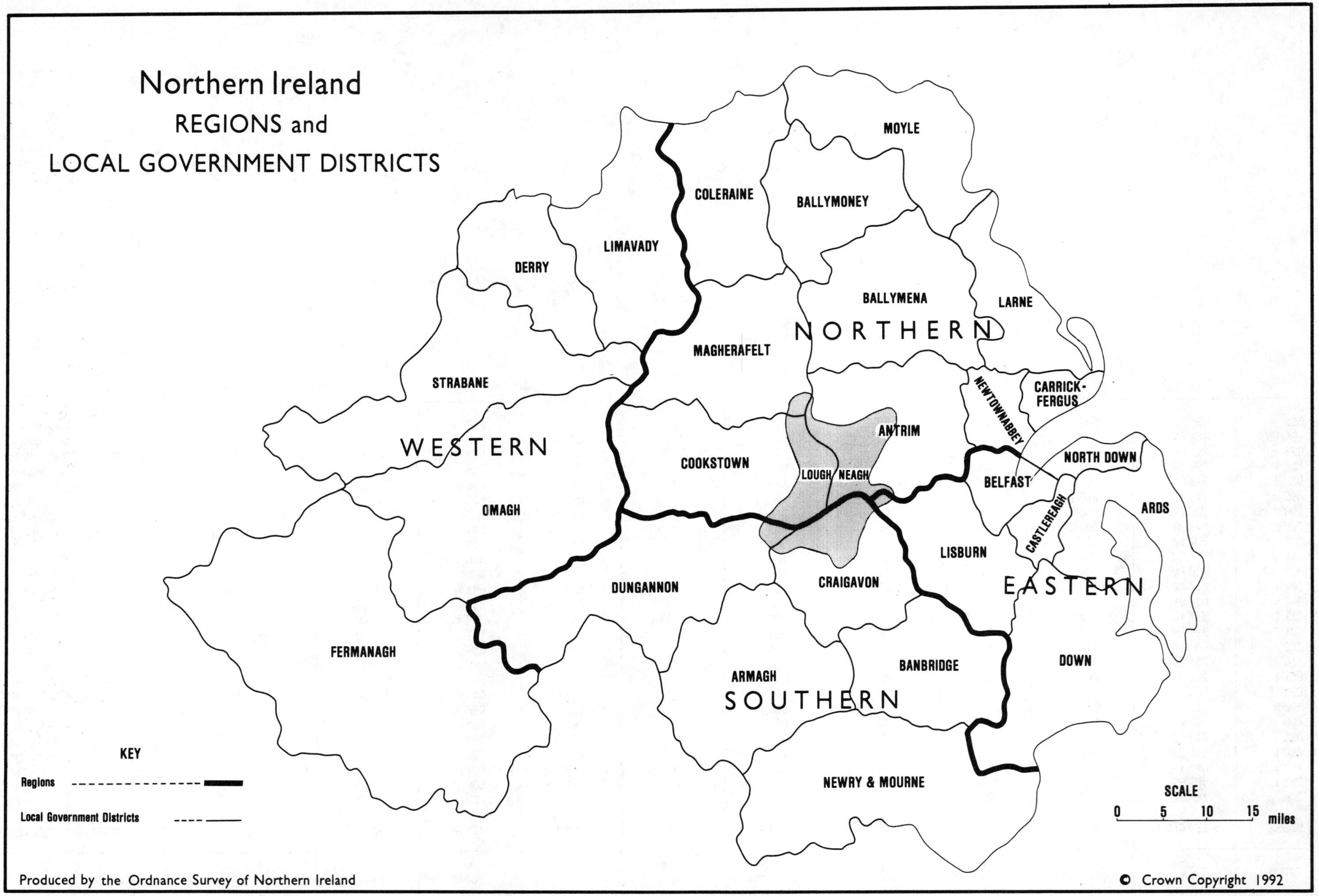

Northern Ireland
REGIONS and
LOCAL GOVERNMENT DISTRICTS
NORTHERN
WESTERN
SOUTHERN
EASTERN
MOYLE
COLERAINE
BALLYMONEY
LIMAVADY
DERRY
BALLYMENA
LARNE
MAGHERAFELT
STRABANE
NEWTOWNABBEY
CARRICK-FERGUS
ANTRIM
COOKSTOWN
LOUGH NEAGH
NORTH DOWN
BELFAST
OMAGH
ARDS
CASTLEREAGH
LISBURN
DUNGANNON
CRAIGAVON
FERMANAGH
ARMAGH
BANBRIDGE
DOWN
NEWRY & MOURNE
KEY
Regions
Local Government Districts
SCALE
0 5 10 15 miles
Produced by the Ordnance Survey of Northern Ireland
© Crown Copyright 1992

1991 Census
NORTHERN IRELAND
H Form for Private Households

To the Head or Joint Heads or members of the Household aged 16 or over

Please complete this form for all members of the household, including children, and have it ready for collection on Monday 22nd April. Your Census Enumerator will call to collect it then or soon afterwards and will help you with the form if you have any difficulties. The enclosed leaflet explains why the Census is necessary and how the information is used.

Completion of the form is compulsory under the Census Act (Northern Ireland)1969. If you refuse to complete it, or give false information, you may have to pay a fine of up to £400. There is no penalty for refusing to state religious denomination as this is a voluntary question.

Your answers will be treated in strict confidence and used only to produce statistics. No names and addresses will be put into the computer; only the postcode will be entered. The forms will be kept securely and treated as **confidential. No information about named individuals will be passed by the Census Office to any other Government Department or to any other authority or person.**

Anyone using or disclosing census information improperly will be liable to prosecution. For example, it would be improper for you to pass on to someone else information which you have been given in confidence by a visitor to enable you to complete the Census Form.

If any member of the household aged 16 or over does not wish you, or another member of the household, to see their information, please ask the Enumerator for an Individual Form with an envelope.

After completing the form, please sign the declaration on the last page.
Thank you for your co-operation.

R McMurray
Registrar General

Please read these instructions before filling in this form

A Household:

A household comprises either one person living alone or a group of people (not necessarily related) living at the same address with common housekeeping - that is, sharing at least one meal a day or sharing a living room or sitting room.

People staying temporarily with the household are included.

- ▶ If there is more than one household in this building, answer for your household only.
- ▶ First check **Panel A** and then answer questions **H1** on **this page** and **H2** to **H5** on the **back page.**
- ▶ When you have answered the household questions, answer the questions on the **inside pages** about each member of your household.
- ▶ If a member of the household is completing an Individual Form please enter their name and answer questions 5 and 6 on this form.
- ▶ Then complete **Panel B** and **Panel C** on the back page.
- ▶ *Answer each question by ticking the appropriate box or boxes where they are provided.* ☑
- ▶ *Please use ink or ballpoint pen.*

Enquiries to:-

Census Office
Department of Health and Social Services
Castle Buildings
Stormont
BELFAST BT4 3RA
Telephone Belfast 763939

FOR OFFICE USE ONLY

E.D. No.	1	Form No.	Grid Reference	Males	Females

District Council	Ward	Townland

Town or Village	BUA Code	Family Type
Street etc. with No. or name of house		
Postcode B T ☐ ☐ ■ ☐ ☐ ☐		
Name of head of household		

Panel A

To be completed by the Enumerator and amended, if necessary, by the person(s) signing this form.

Tick one box to show the type of accommodation which this household occupies.

A caravan or other mobile or temporary structure ☐ 1

A whole house or bungalow that is
- detached ☐ 2
- semi-detached ☐ 3
- terraced (include end of terrace) ☐ 4

The whole of a purpose built flat or maisonette
- in a commercial building (for example in an office building or hotel or over a shop) ☐ 5
- in a block of flats ☐ 6

Part of a converted or shared house, bungalow or flat
- separate entrance into the building ☐ 7
- shared entrance into the building ☐ 8

H 1 Accommodation

If box 7 or box 8 in Panel A is ticked, tick one box below to show the type of accommodation which your household occupies.

A one roomed flatlet
with private bath or shower, WC and kitchen facilities. ☐ 1

One room or bedsit, not self-contained
(to move from your room to bathroom, WC or kitchen facility you have to use a hall, landing or stairway open to other households). ☐ 2

A self-contained flat or accommodation with 2 or more rooms,
having bath or shower, WC and kitchen facilities all behind its own private door. ☐ 3

2 or more rooms, not self-contained
(to move between rooms or to bathroom, WC, or kitchen facilities you have to use a hall, landing or stairway open to other households). ☐ 4

Please turn to the back page and answer questions H2 to H5 ⟶

1-3 Name, sex and date of birth of people to be included

Important - please read the notes before answering the questions.

In answering the rest of the questions please include:

- every person who spends census night (21-22 April) in this household, **including anyone staying temporarily.**
- any other people who are usually members of the household but on census night are absent on holiday, at school or college, or for any other reason, even if you know they are being included on another census form elsewhere.
- anyone who arrives here on Monday 22nd April who was in Northern Ireland on Sunday 21st April and who has not been included as present on another census form.
- any baby born before 22 April, even if still in hospital. If not yet given a name write BABY and the surname.
- **Write the names in BLOCK CAPITALS starting with the head or a joint head of household.**

Person No. 1 — 21	Person No. 2 — 22
Name and surname	Name and surname
Sex: Male ☐ 1 / Female ☐ 2	Sex: Male ☐ 1 / Female ☐ 2
Date of birth: Day / Month / Year	Date of birth: Day / Month / Year

4 Marital status

On the 21st April what is the person's marital status?

If separated but not divorced, please tick 'Married (first marriage)' or 'Re-married' as appropriate.
Please tick one box.

Person No. 1	Person No. 2
Single (never married) ☐ 1	Single (never married) ☐ 1
Married (first marriage) ☐ 2	Married (first marriage) ☐ 2
Re-married ☐ 3	Re-married ☐ 3
Divorced (decree absolute) ☐ 4	Divorced (decree absolute) ☐ 4
Widowed ☐ 5	Widowed ☐ 5

5 Relationship in household

Tick the box which indicates the relationship of each person to the person in the first column.

A stepchild or adopted child should be included as the son or daughter of the step or adoptive parent.

Write in relationship of 'Other relative' - for example, father, daughter-in-law, niece, uncle, cousin. Write in position in household of an 'Unrelated' person - for example, boarder, housekeeper, friend, flatmate, foster child.

Person No. 2 — **Relationship to Person No.1**
- Husband or wife ☐ 1
- Living together as a couple ☐ 2
- Son or daughter ☐ 3
- Other relative ☐ 4 *please specify*
- Unrelated ☐ 5 *please specify*

6 Whereabouts on night of 21-22 April 1991

Please tick the appropriate box to indicate where the person was on the night of 21-22 April 1991.

Person No. 1	Person No. 2
At this address, out on night work or travelling to this address ☐ 1	At this address, out on night work or travelling to this address ☐ 1
Elsewhere in Northern Ireland ☐ 2	Elsewhere in Northern Ireland ☐ 2
Outside Northern Ireland ☐ 3	Outside Northern Ireland ☐ 3

7 All married, widowed, separated and divorced women

All married, widowed, separated and divorced women in the household.
a - enter in Box 1 the total number of children born alive to her.
b - enter in Box 2 how many of these children were born alive after 21st April 1990.

Person No. 1	Person No. 2
a Number of children ☐ 1	a Number of children ☐ 1
b Number of children ☐ 2	b Number of children ☐ 2

8 Usual address

If the person usually lives here please tick 'This address'. If not, tick 'Elsewhere' and write in the person's usual address.

For students and children away from home during term time, the home address should be taken as the usual address.

For any person who lives away from home for part of the week, the home address should be taken as the usual address.

Any person who is not a permanent member of the household should be asked what he or she considers to be his or her usual address.

Person No. 1	Person No. 2
This address ☐ 1	This address ☐ 1
Elsewhere ☐ 2	Elsewhere ☐ 2
If 'Elsewhere', please write the person's usual address and postcode below in BLOCK CAPITALS	If 'Elsewhere', please write the person's usual address and postcode below in BLOCK CAPITALS
Postcode	Postcode

9 Term time address of students and school children

If not a student or schoolchild, please tick first box.

For a student or schoolchild who lives here during term time, tick 'This address'.

If he or she does not live here during term time, tick 'Elsewhere' and write in the current or most recent term time address.

Person No. 1	Person No. 2
Not a student or schoolchild ☐ 1	Not a student or schoolchild ☐ 1
This address ☐ 2	This address ☐ 2
Elsewhere ☐ 3	Elsewhere ☐ 3
If 'Elsewhere', please write the term time address and postcode below in BLOCK CAPITALS	If 'Elsewhere', please write the term time address and postcode below in BLOCK CAPITALS
Postcode	Postcode

Person No. 3 (23)	Person No. 4 (24)	Person No. 5 (25)	Person No. 6 (26)
Name and surname	Name and surname	Name and surname	Name and surname
Sex: Male ☐ 1; Female ☐ 2	Sex: Male ☐ 1; Female ☐ 2	Sex: Male ☐ 1; Female ☐ 2	Sex: Male ☐ 1; Female ☐ 2
Date of birth: Day, Month, Year	Date of birth: Day, Month, Year	Date of birth: Day, Month, Year	Date of birth: Day, Month, Year
Single (never married) ☐ 1; Married (first marriage) ☐ 2; Re-married ☐ 3; Divorced (decree absolute) ☐ 4; Widowed ☐ 5	Single (never married) ☐ 1; Married (first marriage) ☐ 2; Re-married ☐ 3; Divorced (decree absolute) ☐ 4; Widowed ☐ 5	Single (never married) ☐ 1; Married (first marriage) ☐ 2; Re-married ☐ 3; Divorced (decree absolute) ☐ 4; Widowed ☐ 5	Single (never married) ☐ 1; Married (first marriage) ☐ 2; Re-married ☐ 3; Divorced (decree absolute) ☐ 4; Widowed ☐ 5
Relationship to Person No.1: Husband or wife ☐ 1; Living together as a couple ☐ 2; Son or daughter ☐ 3; Other relative ☐ 4 *please specify*; Unrelated ☐ 5 *please specify*	**Relationship to Person No.1**: Husband or wife ☐ 1; Living together as a couple ☐ 2; Son or daughter ☐ 3; Other relative ☐ 4 *please specify*; Unrelated ☐ 5 *please specify*	**Relationship to Person No.1**: Husband or wife ☐ 1; Living together as a couple ☐ 2; Son or daughter ☐ 3; Other relative ☐ 4 *please specify*; Unrelated ☐ 5 *please specify*	**Relationship to Person No.1**: Husband or wife ☐ 1; Living together as a couple ☐ 2; Son or daughter ☐ 3; Other relative ☐ 4 *please specify*; Unrelated ☐ 5 *please specify*
At this address, out on night work or travelling to this address ☐ 1; Elsewhere in Northern Ireland ☐ 2; Outside Northern Ireland ☐ 3	At this address, out on night work or travelling to this address ☐ 1; Elsewhere in Northern Ireland ☐ 2; Outside Northern Ireland ☐ 3	At this address, out on night work or travelling to this address ☐ 1; Elsewhere in Northern Ireland ☐ 2; Outside Northern Ireland ☐ 3	At this address, out on night work or travelling to this address ☐ 1; Elsewhere in Northern Ireland ☐ 2; Outside Northern Ireland ☐ 3
a Number of children ☐ 1; b Number of children ☐ 2	a Number of children ☐ 1; b Number of children ☐ 2	a Number of children ☐ 1; b Number of children ☐ 2	a Number of children ☐ 1; b Number of children ☐ 2
This address ☐ 1; Elsewhere ☐ 2. If 'Elsewhere', please write the person's usual address and postcode below in BLOCK CAPITALS. Postcode	This address ☐ 1; Elsewhere ☐ 2. If 'Elsewhere', please write the person's usual address and postcode below in BLOCK CAPITALS. Postcode	This address ☐ 1; Elsewhere ☐ 2. If 'Elsewhere', please write the person's usual address and postcode below in BLOCK CAPITALS. Postcode	This address ☐ 1; Elsewhere ☐ 2. If 'Elsewhere', please write the person's usual address and postcode below in BLOCK CAPITALS. Postcode
Not a student or schoolchild ☐ 1; This address ☐ 2; Elsewhere ☐ 3. If 'Elsewhere', please write the term time address and postcode below in BLOCK CAPITALS. Postcode	Not a student or schoolchild ☐ 1; This address ☐ 2; Elsewhere ☐ 3. If 'Elsewhere', please write the term time address and postcode below in BLOCK CAPITALS. Postcode	Not a student or schoolchild ☐ 1; This address ☐ 2; Elsewhere ☐ 3. If 'Elsewhere', please write the term time address and postcode below in BLOCK CAPITALS. Postcode	Not a student or schoolchild ☐ 1; This address ☐ 2; Elsewhere ☐ 3. If 'Elsewhere', please write the term time address and postcode below in BLOCK CAPITALS. Postcode

Please turn over →

1-3 Name, sex and date of birth of people to be included

Important - please read the notes before answering the questions.

In answering the rest of the questions please include:

- every person who spends census night (21-22 April) in this household, **including anyone staying temporarily.**
- any other people who are usually members of the household but on census night are absent on holiday, at school or college, or for any other reason, even if you know they are being included on another census form elsewhere.
- anyone who arrives here on Monday 22nd April who was in Northern Ireland on Sunday 21st April and who has not been included as present on another census form.
- any baby born before 22 April, even if still in hospital. If not yet given a name write BABY and the surname.
- **Write the names in BLOCK CAPITALS starting with the head or a joint head of household.**

Person No. 1 — 21	Person No. 2 — 22
Name and surname	Name and surname
Sex: Male ☐ 1 Female ☐ 2	Sex: Male ☐ 1 Female ☐ 2
Date of birth: Day Month Year	Date of birth: Day Month Year

10 Usual address one year ago

If the person's usual address one year ago (on the 21st April 1990) was the same as his or her current usual address (given in answer to question 8), please tick 'Same'. If not tick 'Different' and write in the usual address one year ago.

If everyone on the form has moved from the same address, please write the address in full for the first person and indicate with an arrow that this applies to the other people on the form.

For a child born since 21st April 1990, tick the 'Child under one' box.

Person No. 1 — 31	Person No. 2 — 32
Same as Question 8 ☐ 1	Same as Question 8 ☐ 1
Different ☐ 2	Different ☐ 2
Child under one ☐ 3	Child under one ☐ 3
If 'Different', please write the person's address and postcode on the 21st April 1990 below in BLOCK CAPITALS	If 'Different', please write the person's address and postcode on the 21st April 1990 below in BLOCK CAPITALS
Postcode	Postcode

11 Country of birth

Please tick the appropriate box.

Person No. 1	Person No. 2
Northern Ireland ☐ 1	Northern Ireland ☐ 1
England ☐ 2	England ☐ 2
Scotland ☐ 3	Scotland ☐ 3
Wales ☐ 4	Wales ☐ 4
Republic of Ireland ☐ 5	Republic of Ireland ☐ 5
Elsewhere ☐ 6	Elsewhere ☐ 6
If 'Elsewhere', please write in the present name of the country	If 'Elsewhere', please write in the present name of the country

12 Religion

Please state the Religion, Religious Denomination or Body to which the person belongs. The general term 'Protestant' should not be used alone and the denomination should be given as precisely as possible.

If none write NONE.

Person No. 1	Person No. 2
Religion	Religion

13 Long term illness

Does the person have any long term illness, health problem or handicap which limits his/her daily activities or the work he/she can do?

Include problems which are due to old age.

Person No. 1	Person No. 2
Yes, has a health problem which limits activities ☐ 1	Yes, has a health problem which limits activities ☐ 1
Has no such health problem ☐ 2	Has no such health problem ☐ 2

Person No. 3 — 23

Name and surname

Sex — Male ☐ 1 — Female ☐ 2

Date of birth — Day — Month — Year

33

Same as Question 8 ☐ 1
Different ☐ 2
Child under one ☐ 3

If 'Different', please write the person's address and postcode on the 21st April 1990 below in BLOCK CAPITALS

Postcode

Northern Ireland ☐ 1
England ☐ 2
Scotland ☐ 3
Wales ☐ 4
Republic of Ireland ☐ 5
Elsewhere ☐ 6

If 'Elsewhere', please write in the present name of the country

Religion

Yes, has a health problem which limits activities ☐ 1
Has no such health problem ☐ 2

Person No. 4 — 24

Name and surname

Sex — Male ☐ 1 — Female ☐ 2

Date of birth — Day — Month — Year

34

Same as Question 8 ☐ 1
Different ☐ 2
Child under one ☐ 3

If 'Different', please write the person's address and postcode on the 21st April 1990 below in BLOCK CAPITALS

Postcode

Northern Ireland ☐ 1
England ☐ 2
Scotland ☐ 3
Wales ☐ 4
Republic of Ireland ☐ 5
Elsewhere ☐ 6

If 'Elsewhere', please write in the present name of the country

Religion

Yes, has a health problem which limits activities ☐ 1
Has no such health problem ☐ 2

Person No. 5 — 25

Name and surname

Sex — Male ☐ 1 — Female ☐ 2

Date of birth — Day — Month — Year

35

Same as Question 8 ☐ 1
Different ☐ 2
Child under one ☐ 3

If 'Different', please write the person's address and postcode on the 21st April 1990 below in BLOCK CAPITALS

Postcode

Northern Ireland ☐ 1
England ☐ 2
Scotland ☐ 3
Wales ☐ 4
Republic of Ireland ☐ 5
Elsewhere ☐ 6

If 'Elsewhere', please write in the present name of the country

Religion

Yes, has a health problem which limits activities ☐ 1
Has no such health problem ☐ 2

Person No. 6 — 26

Name and surname

Sex — Male ☐ 1 — Female ☐ 2

Date of birth — Day — Month — Year

36

Same as Question 8 ☐ 1
Different ☐ 2
Child under one ☐ 3

If 'Different', please write the person's address and postcode on the 21st April 1990 below in BLOCK CAPITALS

Postcode

Northern Ireland ☐ 1
England ☐ 2
Scotland ☐ 3
Wales ☐ 4
Republic of Ireland ☐ 5
Elsewhere ☐ 6

If 'Elsewhere', please write in the present name of the country

Religion

Yes, has a health problem which limits activities ☐ 1
Has no such health problem ☐ 2

Please turn over →

1-3 Name, sex and date of birth of people to be included

Important - please read the notes before answering the questions.

In answering the rest of the questions please include:

- every person who spends census night (21-22 April) in this household, **including anyone staying temporarily.**
- any other people who are usually members of the household but on census night are absent on holiday, at school or college, or for any other reason, even if you know they are being included on another census form elsewhere.
- anyone who arrives here on Monday 22nd April who was in Northern Ireland on Sunday 21st April and who has not been included as present on another census form.
- any baby born before 22 April, even if still in hospital. If not yet given a name write BABY and the surname.
- **Write the names in BLOCK CAPITALS starting with the head or a joint head of household.**

Person No. 1 — 21	Person No. 2 — 22
Name and surname	Name and surname
Sex: Male ☐ 1 Female ☐ 2	Sex: Male ☐ 1 Female ☐ 2
Date of birth: Day Month Year	Date of birth: Day Month Year

This question is for all persons aged 3 or over (born before 22nd April 1988)

14 Irish language

Can the person speak, read or write Irish?

Please tick the appropriate box(es).

41	42
Can speak Irish ☐ 1	Can speak Irish ☐ 1
Can read Irish ☐ 2	Can read Irish ☐ 2
Can write Irish ☐ 4	Can write Irish ☐ 4
Does not know Irish ☐ 0	Does not know Irish ☐ 0

Answers to the remaining questions are not required for any person under 16 years of age (born after 21st April 1975)

15 Whether working, retired, looking after the home etc. last week

Which of the following things was the person doing **last week?**

Please read carefully right through the list. If the person did more than one of the things listed last week, **tick all the descriptions that apply.**

Casual or temporary work should be counted at boxes 1, 2, 3 or 4. Also tick boxes 1, 2, 3 or 4 if the person had a job last week but was off sick, on holiday, temporarily laid off or on strike. Working for an employer is **part time** if the hours worked, excluding any overtime and meal breaks, are usually 30 hours or less a week (box 2).

Unpaid work in a family business including a shop or farm.

Include for example ACE Scheme, Youth Training Programme and Job Training Programme.

Include any person wanting a job but prevented by holiday or temporary sickness from looking for one.

Do not count training given or paid for by an employer.

Include voluntary work and any other activity.

Person No. 1	Person No. 2
Was working for an employer full time (more than 30 hours a week) ☐ 1	Was working for an employer full time (more than 30 hours a week) ☐ 1
Was working for an employer part time (one hour or more a week) ☐ 2	Was working for an employer part time (one hour or more a week) ☐ 2
Was self-employed, employing other people ☐ 3	Was self-employed, employing other people ☐ 3
Was self-employed, not employing other people ☐ 4	Was self-employed, not employing other people ☐ 4
Unpaid work ☐ 5	Unpaid work ☐ 5
Was on a government employment or training scheme ☐ 6	Was on a government employment or training scheme ☐ 6
Was waiting to start a job he/she had already accepted ☐ 7	Was waiting to start a job he/she had already accepted ☐ 7
Was unemployed and looking for a job ☐ 8	Was unemployed and looking for a job ☐ 8
Was at school or in other full time education ☐ 9	Was at school or in other full time education ☐ 9
Was unable to work because of long term sickness or disability ☐ 10	Was unable to work because of long term sickness or disability ☐ 10
Was retired from paid work ☐ 11	Was retired from paid work ☐ 11
Was looking after the home or family ☐ 12	Was looking after the home or family ☐ 12
Other ☐ 13 *please specify*	Other ☐ 13 *please specify*

Person No. 3 — 23	Person No. 4 — 24	Person No. 5 — 25	Person No. 6 — 26
Name and surname	Name and surname	Name and surname	Name and surname
Sex: Male ☐1 Female ☐2	Sex: Male ☐1 Female ☐2	Sex: Male ☐1 Female ☐2	Sex: Male ☐1 Female ☐2
Date of birth: Day Month Year	Date of birth: Day Month Year	Date of birth: Day Month Year	Date of birth: Day Month Year

This question is for all persons aged 3 or over (born before 22nd April 1988)

43	44	45	46
Can speak Irish ☐ 1	Can speak Irish ☐ 1	Can speak Irish ☐ 1	Can speak Irish ☐ 1
Can read Irish ☐ 2	Can read Irish ☐ 2	Can read Irish ☐ 2	Can read Irish ☐ 2
Can write Irish ☐ 4	Can write Irish ☐ 4	Can write Irish ☐ 4	Can write Irish ☐ 4
Does not know Irish ☐ 0	Does not know Irish ☐ 0	Does not know Irish ☐ 0	Does not know Irish ☐ 0

Answers to the remaining questions are not required for any person under 16 years of age (born after 21st April 1975)

Person No. 3	Person No. 4	Person No. 5	Person No. 6
Was working for an employer full time (more than 30 hours a week) ☐ 1	Was working for an employer full time (more than 30 hours a week) ☐ 1	Was working for an employer full time (more than 30 hours a week) ☐ 1	Was working for an employer full time (more than 30 hours a week) ☐ 1
Was working for an employer part time (one hour or more a week) ☐ 2	Was working for an employer part time (one hour or more a week) ☐ 2	Was working for an employer part time (one hour or more a week) ☐ 2	Was working for an employer part time (one hour or more a week) ☐ 2
Was self-employed, employing other people ☐ 3	Was self-employed, employing other people ☐ 3	Was self-employed, employing other people ☐ 3	Was self-employed, employing other people ☐ 3
Was self-employed, not employing other people ☐ 4	Was self-employed, not employing other people ☐ 4	Was self-employed, not employing other people ☐ 4	Was self-employed, not employing other people ☐ 4
Unpaid work ☐ 5	Unpaid work ☐ 5	Unpaid work ☐ 5	Unpaid work ☐ 5
Was on a goverment employment or training scheme ☐ 6	Was on a goverment employment or training scheme ☐ 6	Was on a goverment employment or training scheme ☐ 6	Was on a goverment employment or training scheme ☐ 6
Was waiting to start a job he/she had already accepted ☐ 7	Was waiting to start a job he/she had already accepted ☐ 7	Was waiting to start a job he/she had already accepted ☐ 7	Was waiting to start a job he/she had already accepted ☐ 7
Was unemployed and looking for a job ☐ 8	Was unemployed and looking for a job ☐ 8	Was unemployed and looking for a job ☐ 8	Was unemployed and looking for a job ☐ 8
Was at school or in other full time education ☐ 9	Was at school or in other full time education ☐ 9	Was at school or in other full time education ☐ 9	Was at school or in other full time education ☐ 9
Was unable to work because of long term sickness or disability ☐ 10	Was unable to work because of long term sickness or disability ☐ 10	Was unable to work because of long term sickness or disability ☐ 10	Was unable to work because of long term sickness or disability ☐ 10
Was retired from paid work ☐ 11	Was retired from paid work ☐ 11	Was retired from paid work ☐ 11	Was retired from paid work ☐ 11
Was looking after the home or family ☐ 12	Was looking after the home or family ☐ 12	Was looking after the home or family ☐ 12	Was looking after the home or family ☐ 12
Other *please specify* ☐ 13	Other *please specify* ☐ 13	Other *please specify* ☐ 13	Other *please specify* ☐ 13

Please turn over →

1-3 **Name, sex and date of birth of people to be included**

Important - please read the notes before answering the questions.

In answering the rest of the questions please include:

- every person who spends census night (21-22 April) in this household, **including anyone staying temporarily.**
- any other people who are usually members of the household but on census night are absent on holiday, at school or college, or for any other reason, even if you know they are being included on another census form elsewhere.
- anyone who arrives here on Monday 22nd April who was in Northern Ireland on Sunday 21st April and who has not been included as present on another census form.
- any baby born before 22 April, even if still in hospital. If not yet given a name write BABY and the surname.
- **Write the names in BLOCK CAPITALS starting with the head or a joint head of household.**

Person No. 1 (21)	Person No. 2 (22)
Name and surname	Name and surname
Sex: Male ☐ 1, Female ☐ 2	Sex: Male ☐ 1, Female ☐ 2
Date of birth: Day, Month, Year	Date of birth: Day, Month, Year

Please read A below, tick the box that applies and follow the instruction by the box ticked. This will tell you which questions to answer for each person.

A Did the person have a paid job last week or do unpaid work in a family business, including a shop or farm (any of the boxes 1, 2, 3, 4 or 5 ticked at question 15)?

Person No. 1 (51)	Person No. 2 (52)
YES ☐ Answer questions 16, 17, 18, 19 and 20 about the **main** job last week, then go to question 21	YES ☐ Answer questions 16, 17, 18, 19 and 20 about the **main** job last week, then go to question 21
NO ☐ Answer B	NO ☐ Answer B

B Has the person had a paid job within the last 10 years?

Person No. 1	Person No. 2
YES ☐ Answer questions 16, 17 and 18 about the most recent job, then go on to question 21	YES ☐ Answer questions 16, 17 and 18 about the most recent job, then go on to question 21
NO ☐ Go on to question 21	NO ☐ Go on to question 21

16 **Hours worked a week**

How many hours a week does or did the person usually work in his or her main job?

Do not count overtime or meal breaks.

Person No. 1	Person No. 2
Number of hours worked a week	Number of hours worked a week

17 **Occupation**

Please give the full title of the person's present or last job and describe the main things he /she does or did in the job.

At a, give the full title by which the job is known , for example: 'packing machinist'; 'poultry processor'; 'jig and tool fitter'; 'supervisor of typists'; 'accounts clerk'; rather than general titles like 'machinist'; 'process worker'; 'supervisor' or 'clerk'. Give rank or grade if the person has one.

At b, write down the main things the person actually does or did in the job. If possible ask him/her to say what these things are and write them down.

Armed Forces - enter 'commissioned officer' or 'other rank' as appropriate at **a**, and leave **b** blank.

Civil Servants - give grade at **a**, and at **b** state discipline or specialism, for example: 'electrical engineer'; 'accountant'; 'chemist'; 'administrator'.

Other Public Officials - give rank or grade at **a** and description of duties at **b**.

Person No. 1	Person No. 2
a Full job title	**a** Full job title
b Main things done in job	**b** Main things done in job

18 **Name and business of employer (if self-employed give the name and nature of person's business)**

At a, please give the name of the employer. Give the trading name if one is used. Do not use abbreviations.

At b, describe clearly what the employer (or the person if self-employed) makes or does (or did).

Armed Forces - write 'Armed Forces' at **a** and leave **b** blank. For a member of the Armed Forces of a country other than the UK - add the name of the country.

Civil Servants - give name of Department at **a** and write 'Government Department' at **b**.

Other Public Officials - give name of employing authority at **a** and department in which employed at **b**.

Person No. 1	Person No. 2
a Name of employer	**a** Name of employer
b Description of employer's business	**b** Description of employer's business

Please turn over →

Person No. 3 — 23	Person No. 4 — 24	Person No. 5 — 25	Person No. 6 — 26
Name and surname	Name and surname	Name and surname	Name and surname
Sex: Male ☐1 Female ☐2	Sex: Male ☐1 Female ☐2	Sex: Male ☐1 Female ☐2	Sex: Male ☐1 Female ☐2
Date of birth: Day Month Year	Date of birth: Day Month Year	Date of birth: Day Month Year	Date of birth: Day Month Year

Please read A below, tick the box that applies and follow the instruction by the box ticked. This will tell you which questions to answer for each person.

53	54	55	56
YES ☐ Answer questions 16, 17, 18, 19 and 20 about the **main** job last week, then go to question 21	YES ☐ Answer questions 16, 17, 18, 19 and 20 about the **main** job last week, then go to question 21	YES ☐ Answer questions 16, 17, 18, 19 and 20 about the **main** job last week, then go to question 21	YES ☐ Answer questions 16, 17, 18, 19 and 20 about the **main** job last week, then go to question 21
NO ☐ Answer B	NO ☐ Answer B	NO ☐ Answer B	NO ☐ Answer B
YES ☐ Answer questions 16, 17 and 18 about the most recent job, then go on to question 21	YES ☐ Answer questions 16, 17 and 18 about the most recent job, then go on to question 21	YES ☐ Answer questions 16, 17 and 18 about the most recent job, then go on to question 21	YES ☐ Answer questions 16, 17 and 18 about the most recent job, then go on to question 21
NO ☐ Go on to question 21	NO ☐ Go on to question 21	NO ☐ Go on to question 21	NO ☐ Go on to question 21
Number of hours worked a week	Number of hours worked a week	Number of hours worked a week	Number of hours worked a week
a Full job title	a Full job title	a Full job title	a Full job title
b Main things done in job	b Main things done in job	b Main things done in job	b Main things done in job
a Name of employer	a Name of employer	a Name of employer	a Name of employer
b Description of employer's business	b Description of employer's business	b Description of employer's business	b Description of employer's business

Please turn over →

1-3 Name, sex and date of birth of people to be included

Important - please read the notes before answering the questions.

In answering the rest of the questions please include:

- every person who spends census night (21-22 April) in this household, **including anyone staying temporarily.**
- any other people who are usually members of the household but on census night are absent on holiday, at school or college, or for any other reason, even if you know they are being included on another census form elsewhere.
- anyone who arrives here on Monday 22nd April who was in Northern Ireland on Sunday 21st April and who has not been included as present on another census form.
- any baby born before 22 April, even if still in hospital. If not yet given a name write BABY and the surname.
- **Write the names in BLOCK CAPITALS starting with the head or a joint head of household.**

19 Address of place of work

Please give the full address of the person's place of work.

For a person employed on a site for a long period give the address of the site.

For a person not working regularly at one place who reports daily to a depot or other fixed address, give that address.

For a person not reporting daily to a fixed address, tick box 1.

For a person working mainly at home, tick box 2.

Armed Forces - leave blank.

20 Daily journey to work

Please tick the appropriate box to show how the longest part, by distance, of the person's daily journey to work is normally made.

For a person using different means of transport on different days, show the means most often used.

Car or van includes three-wheeled cars and motor caravans.

21 Academic, professional and vocational qualifications

A. Please tick the appropriate boxes if the person has obtained any of the qualifications listed aside.

B. Has the person obtained professional or vocational qualifications such as nursing or teaching qualifications?
If yes, please state qualifications held.

Person No. 1 21	Person No. 2 22
Name and surname	**Name and surname**
Sex Male ☐ 1 Female ☐ 2	**Sex** Male ☐ 1 Female ☐ 2
Date of birth Day Month Year	**Date of birth** Day Month Year
Please write full address and postcode of workplace below in BLOCK CAPITALS 61	Please write full address and postcode of workplace below in BLOCK CAPITALS 62
Postcode	Postcode
No fixed place ☐ 1	No fixed place ☐ 1
Mainly at home ☐ 2	Mainly at home ☐ 2
Train ☐ 1	Train ☐ 1
Public service bus ☐ 2	Public service bus ☐ 2
Employer's bus ☐ 3	Employer's bus ☐ 3
Motor cycle, moped, scooter ☐ 4	Motor cycle, moped, scooter ☐ 4
Car or van-pool, sharing driving ☐ 5	Car or van-pool, sharing driving ☐ 5
Driving a car or van ☐ 6	Driving a car or van ☐ 6
Passenger in a car or van ☐ 7	Passenger in a car or van ☐ 7
Pedal cycle ☐ 8	Pedal cycle ☐ 8
On foot ☐ 9	On foot ☐ 9
Other ☐ 10	Other ☐ 10
please specify	*please specify*
Works mainly at home ☐ 11	Works mainly at home ☐ 11
Degree level or higher ☐ 1	Degree level or higher ☐ 1
BTEC (Higher), BEC (Higher), TEC (Higher), HNC, HND ☐ 2	BTEC (Higher), BEC (Higher), TEC (Higher), HNC, HND ☐ 2
GCE 'A' Level, Advanced Senior Certificate ☐ 3	GCE 'A' Level, Advanced Senior Certificate ☐ 3
BTEC (National), TEC (National), BEC (National), ONC, OND ☐ 4	BTEC (National), TEC (National), BEC (National), ONC, OND ☐ 4
GCSE, GCE 'O' Level (including CSE Grade 1), Senior Certificate, BTEC (General), BEC (General) ☐ 5	GCSE, GCE 'O' Level (including CSE Grade 1), Senior Certificate, BTEC (General), BEC (General) ☐ 5
CSE (other than Grade 1) ☐ 6	CSE (other than Grade 1) ☐ 6
No formal qualifications as above ☐ 7	No formal qualifications as above ☐ 7

Person No. 3 — 23

Name and surname

Sex — Male 1 — Female 2

Date of birth — Day / Month / Year

63 — Please write full address and postcode of workplace below in BLOCK CAPITALS

Postcode

No fixed place 1
Mainly at home 2

Train 1
Public service bus 2
Employer's bus 3
Motor cycle, moped, scooter 4
Car or van-pool, sharing driving 5
Driving a car or van 6
Passenger in a car or van 7
Pedal cycle 8
On foot 9
Other 10

please specify

Works mainly at home 11

Degree level or higher 1
BTEC (Higher), BEC (Higher), TEC (Higher), HNC, HND 2
GCE 'A' Level, Advanced Senior Certificate 3
BTEC (National), TEC (National), BEC (National), ONC, OND 4
GCSE, GCE 'O' Level (including CSE Grade 1), Senior Certificate, BTEC (General), BEC (General) 5
CSE (other than Grade 1) 6
No formal qualifications as above 7

Person No. 4 — 24

Name and surname

Sex — Male 1 — Female 2

Date of birth — Day / Month / Year

64 — Please write full address and postcode of workplace below in BLOCK CAPITALS

Postcode

No fixed place 1
Mainly at home 2

Train 1
Public service bus 2
Employer's bus 3
Motor cycle, moped, scooter 4
Car or van-pool, sharing driving 5
Driving a car or van 6
Passenger in a car or van 7
Pedal cycle 8
On foot 9
Other 10

please specify

Works mainly at home 11

Degree level or higher 1
BTEC (Higher), BEC (Higher), TEC (Higher), HNC, HND 2
GCE 'A' Level, Advanced Senior Certificate 3
BTEC (National), TEC (National), BEC (National), ONC, OND 4
GCSE, GCE 'O' Level (including CSE Grade 1), Senior Certificate, BTEC (General), BEC (General) 5
CSE (other than Grade 1) 6
No formal qualifications as above 7

Person No. 5 — 25

Name and surname

Sex — Male 1 — Female 2

Date of birth — Day / Month / Year

65 — Please write full address and postcode of workplace below in BLOCK CAPITALS

Postcode

No fixed place 1
Mainly at home 2

Train 1
Public service bus 2
Employer's bus 3
Motor cycle, moped, scooter 4
Car or van-pool, sharing driving 5
Driving a car or van 6
Passenger in a car or van 7
Pedal cycle 8
On foot 9
Other 10

please specify

Works mainly at home 11

Degree level or higher 1
BTEC (Higher), BEC (Higher), TEC (Higher), HNC, HND 2
GCE 'A' Level, Advanced Senior Certificate 3
BTEC (National), TEC (National), BEC (National), ONC, OND 4
GCSE, GCE 'O' Level (including CSE Grade 1), Senior Certificate, BTEC (General), BEC (General) 5
CSE (other than Grade 1) 6
No formal qualifications as above 7

Person No. 6 — 26

Name and surname

Sex — Male 1 — Female 2

Date of birth — Day / Month / Year

66 — Please write full address and postcode of workplace below in BLOCK CAPITALS

Postcode

No fixed place 1
Mainly at home 2

Train 1
Public service bus 2
Employer's bus 3
Motor cycle, moped, scooter 4
Car or van-pool, sharing driving 5
Driving a car or van 6
Passenger in a car or van 7
Pedal cycle 8
On foot 9
Other 10

please specify

Works mainly at home 11

Degree level or higher 1
BTEC (Higher), BEC (Higher), TEC (Higher), HNC, HND 2
GCE 'A' Level, Advanced Senior Certificate 3
BTEC (National), TEC (National), BEC (National), ONC, OND 4
GCSE, GCE 'O' Level (including CSE Grade 1), Senior Certificate, BTEC (General), BEC (General) 5
CSE (other than Grade 1) 6
No formal qualifications as above 7

Please turn over and complete panels B and C→

Please answer questions H2-H5 about your household's accommodation

H 2 Rooms

7

Please count the number of rooms your household has for its own use.

Do not count: small kitchens under 2 metres (6 feet 6 inches) wide
bathrooms
toilets

Do count: living room
bedrooms
kitchens at least 2 metres (6 feet 6 inches) wide
all other rooms in your accommodation

Total number of rooms is ☐

H 3 Tenure

Please tick the box which best describes how you and your household occupy your accommodation.

As an owner occupier:

- through mortgage or loan ☐ 1
- owning the property outright ☐ 2

By renting, rent free or by lease:

- from a public authority (for example NI Housing Executive) ☐ 3
- from a housing association or charitable trust ☐ 4
- unfurnished from a private landlord, company or other organisation ☐ 5
- furnished from a private landlord, company or other organisation ☐ 6

In some other way: Please give details below ☐ 7

H 4 Amenities

Does your household - that is you and any people who usually live here with you - **have the use of:**

- A fixed bath or shower permanently connected to a water supply and waste pipe?
  - **Yes** - for use only by this household ☐ 1
  - **Yes** - for use also by another household ☐ 2
  - **No** - no bath or shower available ☐ 3

- A flush toilet (WC) with entrance **inside** the building?
  - **Yes** - for use only by this household ☐ 0
  - **Yes** - for use also by another household ☐ 1
  - **No** - flush toilet with outside entrance only ☐ 2
  - **No** - no flush toilet indoors or outdoors ☐ 3

- Central heating in living rooms and bedrooms (including night storage heaters, warm air or under-floor heating) whether actually used or not?
  - **Yes** - all living rooms and bedrooms centrally heated ☐ 1
  - **Yes** - some (not all) living rooms and bedrooms centrally heated ☐ 2
  - **No** - no living rooms or bedrooms centrally heated ☐ 3

- Water supply?
  - Public supply piped into the house ☐ 1
  - Public supply at a standpipe ☐ 2
  - Other ☐ 3

- Domestic sewage disposal?
  - Public Sewer ☐ 1
  - Septic tank/cesspit for use only by this household ☐ 2
  - Septic tank/cesspit for use also by another household ☐ 3
  - Dry closet/chemical toilet ☐ 4

H 5 Cars and vans

Please tick the appropriate box to indicate the number of cars and vans normally available for use by you or members of your household (other than visitors).

Include any car or van provided by employers if normally available for use by you or members of your household, but **exclude** vans used only for carrying goods.

- None ☐ 0
- One ☐ 1
- Two ☐ 2
- Three or more ☐ 3

Please turn to the first inside page

Panel B

Was there anyone else (such as a visitor) here on the night of 21-22 April whom you have not included because there was no room on the form? No ☐ Yes ☐

If yes ticked, please ask the Enumerator for another form.

Have you left anyone out because you were not sure whether they should be included on the form? No ☐ Yes ☐

If yes ticked, please give their names and the reason why you were not sure about including them.

Name
Reason

Name
Reason

Name
Reason

Panel C

Before you sign the form will you please check:

- that all questions which should have been answered have been answered for every member of your household
- that you have included everyone who spent the night of 21-22 April in your household
- that you have included everyone who usually lives here but was away from home on the night of 21-22 April
- that no visitors, boarders or newly born children, even if still in hospital, have been missed

It would help the Enumerator to be able to telephone you if there is a query on, or an omission from, your form.

If you have no objection, please write your telephone number here.

Telephone number ☐

Declaration

This form is correctly completed to the best of my knowledge and belief.

Signature(s)

Date **April 1991**

Printed in the United Kingdom for HMSO
Dd. 303784. C22. 10/92 Gp. 14672